God's Internationalists

GOD'S INTERNATIONALISTS

World Vision and the Age of Evangelical Humanitarianism

David P. King

PENN

UNIVERSITY OF PENNSYLVANIA PRESS

PHILADELPHIA

HANEY FOUNDATION SERIES

A volume in the Haney Foundation Series,

established in 1961 with the generous support of Dr. John Louis Haney

Published by
University of Pennsylvania Press
Philadelphia, Pennsylvania 19104-4112
www.upenn.edu/pennpress

Printed in the United States of America on acid-free paper

10 9 8 7 6 5 4 3 2 1

Library of Congress Cataloging-in-Publication Data

Names: King, David P., author.
Title: God's internationalists : World Vision and the age of evangelical
    humanitarianism / David P. King.
Other titles: Haney Foundation series.
Description: 1st edition. | Philadelphia : University of Pennsylvania Press, [2019] |
    Series: Haney Foundation series | Includes bibliographical references and index.
Identifiers: LCCN 2018051861| ISBN 9780812250961 (hardcover : alk. paper) | ISBN
    0812250966 (hardcover : alk. paper)
Subjects: LCSH: World Vision International—History. | Church charities—Developing
    countries—History. | Evangelicalism—United States—History. | Humanitarianism—
    Religious aspects—Christianity. | Non-governmental organizations—Developing
    countries—History. | Pierce, Bob, 1914–1978.
Classification: LCC BV2360.W885 K56 2019 | DDC 267/.13—dc23
LC record available at https://lccn.loc.gov/2018051861

For Lauren

CONTENTS

Introduction

AFTER ANOTHER LONG DAY of encountering poverty and death in war-torn Korea, American evangelist Bob Pierce scrawled a prayer in the flyleaf of his Bible: "Let my heart be broken . . . with the things that break the heart of God." With this simple yet expansive mission, Pierce established a small agency to raise funds for missionaries and orphans. He came to attain celebrity at home by publicizing suffering abroad—pioneering child sponsorship and producing films to bring images of the world to American Christians. Pierce founded his new fledgling agency in 1950, and World Vision struggled to keep up with his pace in raising aid for the poor and the spiritually lost around the globe.

Today World Vision still returns to Pierce's original prayer, yet it operates in remarkable contrast to its ragtag beginnings. World Vision International (WVI) is now the largest Christian humanitarian organization in the world. It maintains offices in nearly one hundred countries with 42,000 employees and an annual budget over two billion dollars. It stands three times larger than its nearest evangelical competitor and ranks among the ten largest international nongovernmental organizations (NGOs) of any kind worldwide.[1] Gone are the days of evangelistic crusades and orphanages. Today World Vision is an efficient international nongovernmental organization (INGO) undertaking emergency relief, large-scale community development, and advocacy work. Its leaders are no longer pastors and evangelists. It now recruits professionally trained development specialists and Ivy League–educated marketing directors. While founder Bob Pierce was an evangelist with street smarts, Rich Stearns, the organization's recently retired and longest-serving president, came to World Vision U.S. (WVUS) with an MBA from the University of Pennsylvania's Wharton School of Business and previous experience as CEO of several Fortune 500 companies. The new WVUS president, Edgar

Sandoval Sr., moved up from his role as WVUS chief operating officer to follow in Stearns's footsteps with decades of for-profit and nonprofit experience. If Pierce functioned largely within an evangelical subculture, now World Vision's leaders are widely respected NGO insiders who share the organization's mission not only in megachurches but also in the boardrooms of corporate donors, in front of the United Nations, and on Capitol Hill.

World Vision moved from Christian missions to corporate culture; from donations collected in local churches to multimillion-dollar grants from the federal government. How can we account for that change? As it grew, World Vision began to work with new partners, appeal to broader audiences, and transform its operations. On-the-ground experience in humanitarian hotspots around the world led World Vision to see beyond traditional Western political or theological dichotomies (right or left; conservative or liberal). Interactions with a growing global Christianity and partnerships across religious traditions allowed it to rearticulate its religious identity outside the strictly American evangelical subculture in which it had first taken root. Expanding beyond the traditional mission offerings of local churches to interact with ecumenical and secular development NGOs, it pursued government grants and adopted professional fund-raising techniques through direct mail, television, and the internet.

These transitions led World Vision to reinterpret its identity as more an agency of Christian humanitarianism than missionary evangelization, more mainstream than religiously sectarian, and at times more professional than pious in the sense that American evangelicalism has often understood the term. World Vision remained decidedly Christian, but among its peers, it often earned the reputation as an elite INGO managed efficiently by professional experts fluent in the language of both marketing and international development.

Even as the United States was becoming a global superpower, so was American evangelicalism. The story of World Vision is the story of that transformation, and it offers a lens through which to explore the global outlook of American evangelicals. Cold War politics fanned the initial flames of the burgeoning international engagement of post–World War II evangelicals. As they sought to reclaim their role in society, they also sought to win the world for Christ and America, spreading the gospel alongside democracy and capitalism. At the same time, their reengagement both at home and abroad gave many the opportunity to see the world and their role in it differently as they redefined their approaches to missions and faith-based humanitarianism by establishing new nongovernmental organizations, receiving federal funding, and adopting professional relief and development principles. This same global engagement that forced evangelicals to reframe their work abroad also forced them to reframe their own identities at home as they reflected upon what it meant to be American and evangelical in an increasingly global world.

This is a story historians have largely overlooked. We have seen evangelicals through evangelists like Billy Graham, businesses like Chick-fil-A, or political coalitions such as those born out of the Religious Right.[2] Yet following World War II, it was often the evangelical mission agencies that mushroomed in size and market share. The faithful invested twelve dollars toward foreign missions and international aid for every one dollar they spent on political organizations. Alongside this renewed global expansion came a gradual shift in emphases away from evangelism and church planting toward relief and development.[3]

Calling evangelicals the "new internationalists," *New York Times* editorialist Nicholas Kristof has popularized the deepening of an evangelical social conscience.[4] While potentially news to readers of the *New York Times*, this commitment to global social engagement was not lost on many American evangelicals. Harking back to William Wilberforce's efforts to end the British slave trade, American temperance crusaders, and YMCA field-workers, or more recent foreign missionaries building schools, orphanages, and hospitals, evangelicals argued they had served at the forefront of international engagement for generations.

Yet the nature of evangelical engagement began to take new forms. In the first half of the twentieth century, an optimistic Protestant consensus and shared global outlook shattered into multiple constituencies. Protestant mainline denominations developed new global humanitarian institutions while also wielding the soft power that came from rubbing shoulders with political and economic elites. Fundamentalists began to separate themselves from the engine of institutions driving the Protestant mainline, but they did not bury their heads in the sand. Instead they built new global networks—popular and effective with their own audiences but often outside the halls of power in which mainline Protestants had operated. Conservative Protestants continued to debate humanitarianism, foreign policy, and global engagement, but these debates were often ignored or unappreciated among foreign policy makers, the aid industry, politicians, and mainstream media.

In the wake of World War II, America's leading evangelist, Billy Graham, served as adviser to U.S. presidents, and many new evangelicals followed in his footsteps, reemerging from a self-imposed separatism with a renewed interest in influencing popular culture and the political mainstream. But even as evangelicals began to seek out such influence, they were routinely discouraged. Few wielded equal political influence behind closed doors at policy gatherings in places such as Washington, D.C, Geneva, or Davos, Switzerland. American evangelicals themselves did not always agree on the proper role of humanitarianism or political action. Nor did they all agree how best to engage the government in shaping policy, receiving federal funding, and working across faith lines. Many of the established aid agencies (religious and secular) denied evangelicals a seat at the table, questioning their methods, motives, and expertise as naive and underdeveloped.

Times changed. Evangelical agencies grew in influence as the broader field of global development came to appreciate their size, experience, and expertise. (In addition to World Vision, evangelical agencies make up four of the top ten largest INGOs. Forty-five percent of all religious NGOs are evangelical, by far the largest percentage of any religious tradition.)[5] Having once been forced to argue for social ministry as appropriate activity among fellow evangelicals, agencies like World Vision now carried the torch for others eager to join with the likes of U2 front man Bono, Microsoft founder and humanitarian Bill Gates, and the United Nations in pursuit of a more just and humane civil society. Together this complex set of allies combats AIDS, sex trafficking, and global poverty.

To understand the dramatic growth in evangelical global social engagement, this book chronicles how evangelicals changed in the ways they saw themselves and their world in the period following World War II. By focusing on the particular prominence of World Vision and its global encounters, this book places the recent history of American evangelicalism in transnational perspective and offers a new lens through which to explore the role that a particular kind of American faith played in politics, popular culture, and especially the field of international relief and development. Attending to the complex interactions of a global evangelicalism stands to reframe many scholars' traditional interpretations of

American evangelicalism, while narrating evangelicals' own broadening view of themselves.

Religious Humanitarianism and the Rise of International Relief and Development

While evangelicalism may serve as the central lens, World Vision's story cannot be told apart from the rapid rise of Western humanitarianism in the twentieth century. American investment in the humanitarian industry helped to shape U.S. foreign policy. In the wake of two world wars, humanitarian agencies helped influence American responses to the demise of colonialism in Africa and Asia as well as the practice of state-craft throughout the Cold War. At the same time, these agencies shaped the global imaginations of Americans themselves. Newspapers, radio, and television brought information into Americans' living rooms, but humanitarian fund-raising appeals confronted countless Americans with images and personal stories from the front lines of war, refugee camps, and famine—giving them a picture of an often unfamiliar world as well as a way to respond personally.[6]

Much of the popular growth and institutionalization of American humanitarianism was due to the rapid expansion of *religious* humanitarian agencies. With a sense of American exceptionalism and global optimism, a "three faiths consortium" of mainline Protestant, Catholic, and Jewish philanthropies dominated federal aid funding after World War II, with agencies like Catholic Relief Services (1943), Church World Service (1946), Lutheran World Relief (1945), and the American-Jewish Joint Distribution Committee (1914) leading the way. Despite the fact that a list of the largest agencies and recipients of federal aid rarely changed before the Vietnam War, a plethora of new religious agencies continued to emerge. These new agencies would lead to increased diversity, a variety of approaches, and competition for resources.

The prominence of religious agencies within humanitarianism has not yet generated much scholarly exploration. In the past, most research into religious humanitarianism has been relegated to a history of missions. There is an extensive literature on missionaries, and it has continued to mature in recent years as scholars have broadened their approaches to consider how overseas actors have not only shaped but are also shaped by the new cultures they encounter.[7] This book is not missionary history, yet it traces how traditional missions made a substantial transition to religious humanitarianism through shifts in practice, methodology, and theology. On balance, the size and influence of these humanitarian NGOs in shaping foreign policy, public opinion, and popular culture now far exceeds that of missionaries.

If overlooked among the recent scholarship of humanitarianism, the influence of religion on American political and social history has more recently attracted a great deal of attention.[8] Heeding the call of historians such as Andrew Preston to bridge "the gap between the sacred and secular in the history of foreign relations," historians have responded by exploring the significant religious rhetoric of subjects such as President Woodrow Wilson's early internationalism or the complexity underneath the "Christian America versus atheistic communism" language of the early Cold War.[9] This is a welcome turn, but the majority of work still focuses on leading politicians or corporate titans. Such work misses the significant role of a third sector that exists alongside government and business.

This book examines the rise of religious humanitarianism to demonstrate that the third sector did not operate out of the way and on its own, but rather most often served as the context in an increasingly global civil society where governments, international bodies, corporations, nonprofits, and religious communities intersected to make sense of their engagement with global issues. Underneath the formal speeches and government bureaucracies are networks of agencies shaping institutional practices, public rhetoric, and on-the-ground activities as well as the global imaginaries of American citizens.

In the studies of humanitarianism that do exist, scholars have often painted particular organizations' religious identities with broad brushstrokes, ignoring the diversity of religious experience and discounting the role religion often played.[10] In taking the religious identity of religious humanitarianism seriously, this book seeks to keep several questions in mind for readers. How has an organization's religious identity affected its practice of humanitarianism? How has that religious identity evolved over time? How has the diversity of religious identities created divisions, alliances, and compromises between organizations, governments, and funders?

How do particular religious identities provide various lenses through which many Americans see and interact with the world?

For most Americans, discussions of religious NGOs have been dominated by coverage of the federal funding for domestic faith-based initiatives initiated under President Bill Clinton, expanded under President George W. Bush, and continued under Barack Obama and Donald Trump. Yet the debates over faith-based initiatives have rarely applied to the funding for large-scale international development. Indeed, most religious aid agencies that operate overseas have benefited from government funding for decades and are accountable to multiple professional and humanitarian standards as a part of a shared field of relief and development. This book introduces new actors and new questions in the study of America's global humanitarian engagement by attending to the different debates within international religious agencies.

Defining Evangelicalism Through International Humanitarianism

Outside the "three faiths consortium" of mainline Protestants, Catholics, and Jews whose humanitarian agencies initially dominated foreign aid funding, evangelical agencies such as World Vision initially toiled on the edges. Evangelicals started small, both out of necessity (they lacked access to federal funding) and out of principle (in order to maintain their mission and evangelical identity). World Vision founder Bob Pierce prided himself on relying strictly on small gifts from individuals who heard about his work at revival meetings, through direct mail, over the radio, or by watching his films in church basements. Like other evangelical mission agencies, World Vision had to make sense of its religious identity as it grew, shifted operations, and adopted new funding streams. Over time, six of the seven largest evangelical mission agencies developed primarily into relief and development organizations. And while such history has been, in general, understudied, the story of World Vision does not simply detail the rise of evangelical international aid agencies; it also explores how an increasingly global outlook helped to shape American evangelicals' own identity.[11]

World Vision's use of the label "evangelical" is a complicated story. The organization is deeply rooted in the culture of American evangelicals and clearly saw as part of its mission shaping the global outlook of this influential strand of American Christianity. But that international mission was often wrapped up in the struggle over evangelical identity in America.

Pollsters have often defined individuals as "evangelical" if those persons identify themselves with the term, claim a "born-again" experience, hold to a certain set of beliefs, or belong to a specific denomination. Journalists use "evangelical" as shorthand for theological and cultural conservatives or a political voting bloc.[12] Historians have also struggled with defining evangelicals. Some refer to distinctive theological beliefs, such as historian David Bebbington's well known quadrilateral: commitment to the authority of the Bible, the necessity of conversion, the atoning work of Christ, and the active application of the gospel through evangelism and service.[13] Such broad theological commonalities demonstrate the potential diversity among evangelicals, from black Baptists to Missouri Synod Lutherans, Mennonites to faith-healing Pentecostals, conservative Presbyterians to charismatic televangelists. Yet theological unity—to the extent that it marks the movement—often masks real sociological and cultural differences. Many of the members of these groups may not even identify themselves or one another as evangelicals even if characteristic traits, temperament, or common vernaculars bind them together in myriad ways.

Because of the difficulty of definition, I often use the term "evangelical" as it has been employed by historical actors to describe themselves. (Of course, these actors have used the term to describe themselves and others in multiple ways throughout history.) In focusing particularly on the evolution of American evangelicalism after 1945, this book turns to the particular self-designated evangelical movement that emerged from the separatist fundamentalist subculture in the 1940s. As the historian George Marsden has explained, this transdenominational network of leaders, institutions, and publications emerged through shared norms of behavior, history, and culture that enabled them to function as an informal denomination. If that transdenominational network serves as the starting point, the book then explores how such an evangelical movement grew to spill well beyond those initial boundary lines. Over the past fifty-plus years, World Vision has remained a central character in what historian Steven P. Miller has called "the age of evangelicalism" that has come to operate outside any particular subculture to shape American culture broadly, both high and low.[14]

Yet, exploring American evangelicals' global engagement in the second half of the twentieth century again requires the acknowledgment that this is not a new phenomenon. Historian Mark Noll has claimed, "At its core, [evangelicalism] is a faith with a global vision."[15] That global vision has almost always served as a leading factor defining evangelicalism at home and abroad. The mutual alliances and multiple contestations of American evangelicals, their nation, and their world demonstrate that the movement has always thought of itself as a global one that must be understood transnationally, for that is how the evangelical movement saw itself.

In the English-speaking world, the earliest evangelicals emerged from an early eighteenth-century transatlantic revivalism. Figures such as American theologian Jonathan Edwards, British revivalist George Whitefield, and the itinerant founder of Methodism John Wesley were well known throughout England and America as their ideas spread through their writings and travel. As evangelicalism in the Anglo-American world took off, foreign missions would soon follow. British Baptist William Carey left his trade as a cobbler to set sail for India in 1792. Before he left he articulated a mandate for missions that came to serve as an essential hallmark of evangelical identity. That spark may have been the Great Commission, but missions always meant more than proclamation. The Great Commandment also followed. Western missionaries brought education, health care, and work for women's rights with them under a rubric of modernization even as they also debated the proper lines between spreading Christ and culture.[16] While they may have disagreed on what all to include, early evangelicals envisioned their global mission work as a comprehensive gospel.

American evangelicals were not far behind. By the 1820s, evangelical Protestantism had become the dominant expression of American Christianity. Throughout much of the nineteenth century, a loose evangelical movement formed around a common penchant for revival and reform. Camp meetings and voluntary societies propelled this impulse at home as evangelicals sought to reshape American society not only through conversion but also through a benevolent empire led by movements for literacy, better health, temperance, and (most controversially) abolition. The voluntary associations that evangelicals founded gave them maximum flexibility to move past theological or institutional boundaries to rally around common causes while also providing far more social support than a young U.S. government could or would offer. These reform efforts sought to convert a culture. American evangelicals did not always work in concert with a U.S. political narrative, but notions of America's "chosenness" worked well in these efforts at home. They also worked well as motivation to export these values abroad.

In the latter half of the nineteenth century, thousands of men and women carried confidence in a benevolent empire overseas. What American missionaries originally inherited from British evangelicals they quickly spun off as essentially American. If the United States had marks of a chosen nation, homegrown evangelicals were keen on exporting the moral virtues of the new country. Nineteenth-century missionaries were often the American public's eyes and ears embedded around the world in ways the U.S. government and military had never dreamed. The popular consumption of their reports from the field in letters and religious periodicals shaped Americans' global imaginaries as much as it defined evangelicalism.[17] They basked in their distaste of empire and how it set them apart from European competitors even as they benefited from safe travel, military support, and commerce available through British colonies. American evangelicals abroad demonstrated that the United States was different from other nations, even if they did promote an informal, moral empire. In the late nineteenth century, the best and brightest joined the mission cause heading out under the banner of the Student Volunteer Movement or YMCA to reshape the world with the technology, culture, and virtues that the West deemed universally beneficial. Evangelical missions often merged with America's international outlook as each influenced the other.

By 1925, the fundamentalist-modernist controversy had fractured the Protestant evangelical consensus. If most American Protestants resonated with the evangelical label in the nineteenth century, now both sides of a new theological divide forfeited the term. Most often historians have recounted this feud in the context of denominations and theological education. Certainly, these institutions were a major part of the story, but as significant were divisions in American foreign missions. By the 1920s, much of the broadscale optimism was gone, and so was the uniting vision of a comprehensive gospel. American global missions evolved for many reasons, but a significant one was a theological divide that split those who appealed to the primacy of evangelism and those who focused on social and cultural change. Yet, this divide did more than separate conservatives and liberals; it disencumbered a broad-based and united evangelical mission enterprise and its primary role in shaping Americans' global outlooks. These views drastically began to change in the twentieth century with the end of colonialism and increased U.S. international engagement, and while American Christians continued to play a significant role, it was a different one. Not only was the way in which American Christians engaged the world fervently debated, but various approaches often served to define them.

By the 1940s, a coalition of "neo-evangelicals" reclaimed the term cast aside by all parties a generation before. Symbolized by the National Association of Evangelicals and their slogan "Cooperation Without Compromise," these new U.S.-based evangelicals defined themselves against fundamentalists by seeking to reengage mainstream culture, restore a Christian America, and regain the social standing of traditional Christianity as they understood it. But they also preserved a boundary between themselves and the ecumenical Protestants, for many years the so-called mainline, who symbolized for them the dangers of deviation from orthodoxy and the elevation of political over spiritual aims. In contrast to ecumenical missions, for example, neo-evangelicals embraced evangelism, not social action, as their sole end. World Vision emerged out of this context.

This initial coalition, however, remained short-lived as evangelicals continually redrew their boundary lines. By the 1970s, evangelicalism lost much of its definitional precision as it outgrew its function as a united movement, fracturing instead into a number of smaller interest groups. In the late 1960s and 1970s, "young evangelicals" revolted against the newly established evangelical leaders, and an "evangelical left" emerged under leaders like Ron Sider and Jim Wallis, who challenged evangelicals to accept responsibility for social issues, theological dialogue, and political awareness. Beginning in the 1980s, the Religious Right attempted to build a conservative coalition in opposition to liberals and secularists. The past decades have led to further fragmentation and internal diversity.

While evangelicals rarely agreed upon a single vision for their movement, they invested the term "evangelicalism" with various meanings through defining, maintaining, and transgressing a number of definitional boundaries. Boundary disputes led to internal squabbles as to who counted as an evangelical, but they also led evangelicals to define themselves in contrast to others across the theological spectrum, from fundamentalists and the Protestant mainline to Catholics and secularists.

Throughout the movement's history and definitely as a renewed form of evangelicalism emerged in the second of the twentieth century, these boundary disputes often turned on global issues.[18] In overseas mission efforts, evangelicals debated the relationship between evangelism and social action and questioned whether cooperation with nonevangelicals or government agencies watered down one's religious identity. In politics, they most often championed an ardent Cold War anticommunism and U.S. interventionist efforts in underdeveloped nations, even as they debated the impact of economic and cultural globalization. As evangelicals took an active interest in U.S efforts to shape the world during the "American century," their support helped to influence public engagement abroad and to rework their status at home as the nation's mainstream faith even while demonstrating evangelicalism's own internal diversity.

If globalization played a significant role in postwar evangelical history, then no organization illustrates the impact of such global engagement more than World Vision. As it sought to expose Americans to global need, it shaped the view evangelicals had of the world even as its own global encounters reshaped the organization itself. World Vision leaders positioned themselves at the forefront of these shifting global dynamics as institutional insiders, serving alongside the likes of evangelist Billy Graham, Campus Crusade founder Bill Bright, and *Christianity Today* editor Carl F. H. Henry. Their words and actions shaped how the evangelical establishment debated the relationship of evangelism and social action, ecumenical engagement, and American foreign policy.

Yet, World Vision's success was even more evident at the popular level. As the organization evolved in its own identity as evangelical, American, and missionary/humanitarian, the popular reception of its message exposed a wide range of American Christians to spiritual and physical needs abroad. It also offered many a way to participate in a new brand of religious humanitarianism at home.

Most scholars have examined American evangelicalism through politics, theology, social status, or culture. Some highlight the embourgeoisement of evangelicals through their increasing education, wealth, or popular appeal.

Others focus on the maintenance of a subculture and the continued conservative-liberal divide, with its widely publicized political and theological wrangling. These approaches are clarifying but insufficient because they miss the effect of global forces on a significant number of American organizations.[19] In contrast to much of the scholarship on American evangelicalism, the dichotomy between evangelical left and right was never so clear on the ground, and it was often an increased global awareness that produced a type of evangelicalism unable or unwilling to fit neatly into either camp. Through its own exposure to diverse global evangelical and humanitarian communities, World Vision redefined its identity outside the narrow American evangelical subculture in which it had first taken root. Intensely aware of the divisions in American Christianity, it promoted a new stream of evangelical humanitarianism that appealed to a broad theological and political spectrum. It succeeded precisely because its new global perspective transcended American categories that grew less attractive to countless Americans who still considered themselves evangelical, or at least comfortable within a general born-again spirituality. At the same time, World Vision also appealed to an increasingly broad theological and political spectrum.

The Nature of Religious Identity

World Vision's transformation is not simply another story of a small, narrow organization encountering modernity and subordinating its religious identity to secular methods in order to flourish. As a number of mission agencies have moved toward international relief and development, it is tempting to define this evolution through a narrative of secularization, but that would be too simplistic. While there were a number of religious organizations that dropped evangelism or disentangled any religious underpinning to their work, most cases were more complicated.

Applying a modified "neo-institutional approach" taken from the field of organization studies makes it possible to identify how organizations function within a field of institutions. In many ways, international relief and development is a perfect example of such an institutional field. As organizations began to expand, gain access to governmental funding, professionalize, and compete with one another for resources and programs, they began to look alike. Because the field of international relief and development has become highly professionalized (and many would argue secularized), many scholars claim that an organization's religious identity does not matter. Religious or not, as a multibillion-dollar humanitarian agency, World Vision would be expected to act just like any other leading relief and development organization.[20]

The reality, however, is that an organization functions within not only one field but rather multiple fields—often simultaneously. For example, World Vision has operated within an American evangelical subculture, a collection of missionary agencies, a global evangelicalism, large-scale fundraising nonprofit organizations, and a secular development INGO network. Understanding World Vision fully requires investigating the multiple contexts and networks in which it operates and the various audiences to which it articulates its identity. Therefore, debates between evangelicals and ecumenical Christians on the relationship of evangelism and social action, secular and religious approaches to mission and development, and the acceptability or distaste of child-sponsorship marketing are not superfluous side issues but rather conversations and contentions full of meaning for the organization itself and its many constituencies.

If World Vision's growth does not follow a secularization narrative, neither does it fit within another commonly told story of American evangelicalism's politicization or polarization. World Vision grew from a small evangelical missionary support organization to a massive relief and development agency shaped by evangelical missiology and ecumenical theology as well as mainstream media, technology, and professional management in partnership with secular INGOs, as well as in cooperation with the global church. World Vision's religious identity evolved as a result of popularizing, professionalizing, and internationalizing forces in a period of increased global connections. The religious identity of a faith-based organization is not distinct and isolated but often intertwined with the structural shifts the organization undergoes over time, the tensions it encounters from both internal and external pressures, and the practices and production of its humanitarian work.

Religious identity is rarely static. Throughout the history of World Vision, it was precisely the rearticulation of its religious identity that contributed in surprising ways to the evolving self-definition of the organization. The question then is not *whether* World Vision as a development organization is Christian, but *how* it is Christian. The religious identity of faith-based philanthropies and the religious motivations of their various donor constituencies are only two of many forces that define these agencies. How does religion *function* in religiously motivated relief and development? Attending to the evolution and interplay of World Vision's practices, theology, rhetoric, and organizational structure helps demonstrate that institutions are never simply hierarchies or bureaucracies, but they also embody cultural logics—assumptions or ideas that motivate people. This approach pays attention not only to organizational structure but also to cultural and religious change, and this is often a two-way exchange. Sometimes religious practices and theology help produce structural change. At other times, structural changes alter religious identity.

The Role of International Religious Humanitarianism

The relevance of religion in international humanitarianism is abundantly clear and can be found daily in various media. Evangelicals unite to fight against religious persecution in the Middle East, end sex trafficking in Southeast Asia, send funds to drill wells for clean water in Zimbabwe, and educate girls in rural Afghanistan. During the 2014 Ebola epidemic in West Africa, Dr. Kent Brantley of the conservative evangelical agency Samaritan's Purse became a hero for his sacrifice working on the front lines. Having contracted and survived Ebola, he then served as a critic against what he saw as an inadequate U.S. government response and an advocate for increased public and private support. Editorials in *Slate* and the *New York Times* debated the implications that it was missionary doctors rather than World Health Organization officials who were on the ground treating this terrifying outbreak. In March 2015, Nicholas Kristof's column highlighted another missionary in rural Angola to demonstrate that international humanitarianism as much as opposition to abortion or same-sex marriage characterized evangelicalism.[21]

Leaders in the relief and development sector have also come to realize that they can no longer overlook the role religion plays in their work. In the recent past, scholars and professionals within the field of relief and development often viewed religion in one of two ways. Some continued to perpetuate the unhelpful dichotomization of religious and secular organizations, segregating the two into separate spheres with little common practice or purpose. This separation led development scholars to overlook religion's role and refuse religious agencies a seat at the table. Others saw leading religious agencies as part of a shared relief and development sector, but they understood the sector as a shared culture that was highly rationalized, production-oriented, and professionalized. This view embodied a presumed secularization. Religious organizations may claim a religious motivation, but it was insignificant to the shared language and structures of secular development.[22]

In recent years, a third perspective has come to appreciate the role of religion within development. Development studies saw religious agencies as fruitful dialogue partners in articulating notions of the common good.[23] They also realized that religion served as an asset and key cultural factor in local communities. The limitation, however, was that too often this perspective simply used religion as an instrumental addition to its current agenda. Without fully engaging it, development idealized religion as a static set of beliefs. It encouraged "good religion" that benefited established development outcomes like the Millennium Development Goals, targets to eradicate global poverty initially agreed upon in 2000 by leaders of 189 countries, while it sought to keep "bad religion" that stifled development at bay. The relief and development sector rediscovered religion, but too often its perspectives led to the segregation, ignorance, or instrumentalization of religion in faith-based humanitarianism. In taking a broader perspective to engage the multiple fields in which faith-based humanitarianism operates, World Vision's story demonstrates how religious identity matters and is a key component in political, professional, and popular debates.

In addition, this study exhibits a growing trend to focus American religious history transnationally.[24] Without overlooking the global encounters that occur when religious Americans engage others outside their own home contexts, it is also important to note that global encounters are not limited to immigration, mission trips, international development projects, and foreign policy directives. Transnational religious histories should be concerned not only with the debates over American empire and its policy and practices overseas, but also with the cultural imaginaries of American citizens. Whether it be a Christian America crusading against a godless communism, stories of religious persecution in the Middle East, or images of malnourished African children, how did evangelicals' views of the world come to shape their self-understandings?[25] How did World Vision's own evolving understanding of its identity impact the global engagement that it then shared with its donors at home?

World Vision has continued to experience exponential growth. In the past fifteen years, its income has nearly doubled. Why? At one level, World Vision expanded as it continued to move beyond its American and evangelical origins through its embrace of professional development over conventional missions, international governance over American unilateralism, and ecumenical inclusiveness over religious separatism. At another level, World Vision grew as global issues caught the attention of American evangelicals. The organization returned to the local church not so much with a new message as a hope that evangelicals were entering a period in which organizations like World Vision and the culture that it represented could form a new evangelical mainstream.

It would be wrong to say that World Vision has completely transcended the culture wars of the last several decades. Over the past few years, in the United States it has sometimes found itself at the center of debates over sexuality, hiring coreligionists, and federal funding to religious agencies. While globally the organization is quite diverse, its American donor base still identifies overwhelmingly as evangelical or born-again. Yet, World Vision succeeded precisely as its new global perspective transcended traditional Western dichotomies that grew less attractive to countless American Christians. Intensely aware of the divisions in American Christianity, it worked to expand globally among Catholic, mainline, and secular organizations while later coming to hire nonevangelical and even non-Christian staff. As Western Christians debated the priority of saving souls or saving bodies, World Vision championed both: speaking out for justice and social reform without dismissing the need for individual conversion. Whether through sponsoring a child, traveling on a Vision trip overseas, or advocating for increased funding to fight AIDS in Africa, World Vision supporters took part in a new stream of religious humanitarianism that saw its Christian responsibility as both a quiet sharing of faith and an intense passion to alleviate the suffering of those whom the Christian scriptures described as "the least of these."

A single snapshot cannot capture the current World Vision. The organization conjures up contradictory images. Some see relief workers after a massive earthquake. Others see child sponsorship and Christian education. Some see development experts testifying before the United Nations. Others picture short-term mission trips and a contemporary Christian music concert. Some see a culture warrior fighting secular forces and defending its religious rights. Others think of its efforts to build a broad-based coalition to work across traditional boundaries to reduce global poverty and preventable diseases. All of these images convey a small piece of the truth. World Vision is a diverse, complicated, global organization, and no one generalization encompasses it. For that reason, its history makes for a perfect study of how American evangelicals have come to understand their own development at home precisely through interpretations of their work in the world.

CHAPTER 1

Bob Pierce Becomes
Evangelicals' Global Ambassador

WHILE TODAY WORLD VISION is the largest Christian relief and development agency in the world, its current success bears little relation to its simple origins. World Vision emerged out of the passion of one man, Bob Pierce, a young, traveling evangelist with big dreams. Riding a wave of post–World War II growth, Pierce hitched his wagon to the new Youth for Christ (YFC) movement that packaged revivalism with a renewed evangelical penchant for popular culture, civic faith, and a burgeoning global outreach. Yet even as Pierce poured himself into Youth for Christ's work, he found himself overshadowed by bigger upstarts like Billy Graham. In early 1947, when YFC founder Torrey Johnson backed out of a commitment to preach in China, Pierce jumped at the chance to fill in and hopped the first plane headed for the Far East. With only enough money to make it to the Philippines, Pierce lay stranded while praying that friends would wire him the rest. When a Christian Filipino businessman put in his hands to the penny the exact amount he needed to buy the ticket to China, he took it as a sign that he was following God's will, boarded the plane, and arrived in Shanghai hours before he was scheduled to lead a major revival.[1]

Pierce had never experienced a foreign culture, and he was overwhelmed as he took it all in. If he had typically spoken to crowds of several hundred at churches back home in the United States, now he found himself in Shanghai preaching to a full amphitheater of five thousand Chinese nationals. He was enraptured by the sights, sounds, and smells of a new culture, even as he was heart-stricken by the disease and poverty he encountered. He was also smitten with the newfound prestige he experienced as an informal American ambassador. Days after preaching his first open-air revival where thousands made decisions for Christ, he found himself face-to-face with Madame Chiang, wife of the Chinese Nationalist leader Chiang Kai-shek, chief American political ally, and Western media darling in the couple's early fight against communism. With no experience meeting dignitaries, Pierce threw his hotel towel over his shoulders to wipe away the summer sweat as he sat across from Madame Chiang, presenting China's Christian leaders with a Bible on behalf of "the young people of America."[2]

Pierce had left for China seeking adventure but returned with a calling. The numbers that came to hear him preach, the poverty he experienced firsthand, and the high political stakes in the midst of a Chinese civil war led Pierce to see that the real need was overseas. From China, Pierce wrote to his wife, "These people are so needy, so hungry for the Gospel that even a nobody like me can, under God, do so much that I doubt if I'll ever be willing to just 'go through the motions' of evangelizing in America again."[3] With his eyes now opened, he returned to the United States, challenging fellow Christians to take notice of the world's physical and spiritual suffering. Discovering his own role in playing politics abroad, he would return to preach in the Chiangs' personal chapel multiple times and recounted to his U.S. audiences each head of state he met and counseled. Never one to settle down and stay in one place, Pierce would label himself a missionary ambassador, a man in the gap, bringing the stories of international need to American Christians and shuttling back overseas to deliver the resources he raised to the missionaries, indigenous Christian leaders, and orphans who desperately needed them. He established World Vision in 1950 as a simple conduit for the money he raised at home and then distributed overseas.

With Pierce's first trip to China, he joined a new generation of young American evangelicals after World War II intent on saving the world. They embarked with a sense of adventure, optimism about America's place in the world, a passion for world missions, and an interest in international affairs. While the rapid growth of postwar evangelicalism has most often been explained through lenses of theology, politics, and popular culture, American evangelicals' increasing encounter with the world changed the movement as much as any other single factor. The world beyond U.S. boundaries broadened evangelicals' worldview, altered their self-definitions, subtly changed their relationship to their own country, and formed anew their attitudes toward mainstream culture. The result was a new evangelical global humanitarianism. Bob Pierce and World Vision represent, as clearly as any other person or movement, this evangelical transformation.

Bob Pierce

To understand World Vision's history, one must understand Pierce. To understand Pierce, one must also understand the American fundamentalist subculture that shaped his understanding of the world at home and abroad. Robert Willard Pierce was born to Fred and Flora Belle Pierce in Fort Dodge, Iowa, on October 8, 1914, the youngest of seven children.[4] Fred Pierce was a carpenter who soon moved the family to Greeley, Colorado, in search of work and then moved them again to Southern California in 1924. Settling outside of Los Angeles in Redondo Beach, Fred Pierce found a steady job at a Safeway grocery store. The Pierce family joined close to a million and a half other Midwesterners migrating to California during the 1920s. The population of Los Angeles itself increased twenty-five-fold between 1890 and 1930.[5]

These new migrants flocked to faith communities that offered a familiar gospel packaged in new forms. In 1915, the Midwestern fundamentalist Reuben Torrey established BIOLA (Bible Institute of Los Angeles) and the Church of the Open Door, modeling them after revivalist Dwight L. Moody, his Moody Bible Institute, and Moody Church in Chicago. In 1923, Sister Aimee Semple McPherson, the most celebrated woman preacher of the era, consecrated her Angelus Temple to complement her radio station and growing national reputation. In 1937, Charles Fuller's *Old Fashioned Revival Hour* produced its first nationwide broadcast and a few years later, the show was attracting over twenty million listeners weekly. These religious celebrities taught "old-time religion" to displaced people in search of both stability and new adventure. It preached well. Local churches also benefited as almost 80 percent of their members came from people who had lived there less than a decade.[6] The Pierce family fit right in as they revived their Midwestern Wesleyanism by joining the local Grace Church of the Nazarene.

A young Bob Pierce immersed himself in his Nazarene congregation, made a "personal decision" for Christ at the age of eleven, and fell under the influence of the local pastor, Earle Mack. The congregation became the comforting family Pierce needed. By age twelve, Pierce began taking odd jobs to support the family with the sudden death of his father. Yet alongside these responsibilities, Pierce made time to ride the "Gospel Car," the church's converted bus that traveled through town on Saturdays to save the lost. Most weeks young Pierce stumped for the Lord on a soapbox, preaching to passersby.[7]

Pierce felt drawn to the pulpit but not to education for it.[8] With his pastor's urging, however, he completed high school and enrolled in the local Pasadena Nazarene College. What he lacked in intellect, he made up in charisma. His classmates knew him as a fun-loving prankster, and that was enough for them to elect him as the student body president. That same year, in 1936, he met Lorraine Johnson, daughter of traveling evangelist Floyd Johnson, and fell in love.

By the time Floyd Johnson came to Los Angeles, he was well known. Fundamentalist institutions and revival circuits were nationwide networks. Johnson was converted under Christian and Missionary Alliance (CMA) revivalist Paul Rader, the fiery but folksy preacher at Chicago's Moody Church and later founder of the "Steel Tent," Chicago Gospel Tabernacle. In 1925, Rader became the first fundamentalist on the Chicago airwaves and pioneered the medium by broadcasting not only sermons but also musical montages and entertaining variety shows. Johnson went to work for Rader, producing his own popular gospel music radio show broadcast live from the Wrigley Building. Soon Johnson went out on his own, and Pierce's local Nazarenes invited him to Southern California.

When Johnson finished his stint in Los Angeles, he returned home to Chicago but allowed his daughter Lorraine to stay, enroll at Pasadena Nazarene College, and be courted by the young Bob Pierce. In the depths of the Depression, finances were tight, and soon Lorraine's father had to call her home. Smitten, Pierce soon dropped out of school and hitchhiked to Chicago to see her. Realizing that long distance was not working, they spontaneously decided to get married at the Methodist parsonage next door.[9]

Lorraine Johnson had dreamed of marrying a preacher, but as Pierce returned to Los Angeles later that year, he put his call to preach on hold. He had no money, no job, and no degree. Unless he finished college, the Nazarenes would not license him. In the middle of the Great Depression, dejected, he moved from job to job, working to earn enough money to bring his bride from Chicago to Southern California. After a year of drifting and admittedly "unchristian living," he renewed his call to preach at a local camp meeting, put his faith in the Lord to provide financially, and sent for Lorraine. After committing himself to trusting in God's provision, he found a Baptist church willing to ordain him without the Nazarene's education requirement and started preaching. He accepted any invitation to lead revivals and recount his return to the straight and narrow.[10]

The reunited newlyweds traveled up and down the West Coast with Pierce preaching in any small church that would have him. Pierce's plain-spoken rhetoric and youthful appearance appealed to congregations, but it did not bring much money. The Pierces relied on the hospitality of host churches for lodging and goodwill offerings for income. For more than a year and a half, he averaged five dollars a week, but Pierce did not measure success by finances. While clearing only four hundred dollars in eighteen months, he counted 260 conversions.[11] At age twenty-three, Pierce was beginning to build a regional reputation. Churches promoted Pierce's preaching as "the flaming truths of salvation, in burning words from the anointed lips of youth."[12] He loved the limelight and the sense of adventure—itinerating from place to place and relying on faith in God for support.

Yet if Pierce was fueled by such a peripatetic pace, his young wife struggled to adapt. Life on the road with limited means was even harder once her father returned to Southern California. While the Pierces traveled the local revivalist circuit, Floyd Johnson had returned to Los Angeles at the invitation of Aimee Semple McPherson for an extended thirteen-month engagement. When he completed his commitment at Angelus Temple in 1938, Johnson decided to stay and build his own church, the Los Angeles Evangelistic Center. The church grew, and with his wife wanting to stay closer to home, Pierce gave up a life on the road to become his father-in-law's associate pastor. With the congregation meeting every Wednesday and Friday and three times on Sunday, Pierce stayed busy establishing the youth program, singing in the radio quartet, writing for the church newspaper, and preaching each Monday on the radio.

Despite the church's success, Pierce resented his father-in-law for squelching his ambition and his wife for being too tied to her father. By 1941, a headstrong Pierce left the security of the congregation and resumed the revival meeting circuit. When few invitations came his way, he tried to enlist in World War II as a chaplain, but the army turned him down because of poor vision. The trying circumstances led to a second crisis of faith. He abruptly abandoned revivals, his faith, and his family. He drifted from job to job as a carpenter and a dockworker, living in ways that he would later recall as unbecoming of a preacher. He sank into depression and even sued his wife for divorce. Lorraine Pierce wanted a stable Christian home; her husband proved too restless to be tied down. Not until they met at the lawyer's office did she persuade him to withdraw the divorce papers. He returned home, but family life would no longer be the same. He refused to step foot in church, dropping his wife off on Sunday and waiting in the car until the service ended.

After a year and a half, Pierce finally slipped into the back pew of his father-in-law's church one Sunday to listen to Paul Rood, president of the World Christian Fundamentals Association. At the end of the sermon, he went to the altar, fell prostrate on the ground, confessed his sins, and asked for forgiveness. The church welcomed him back "home," and his father-in-law soon welcomed him back to the church staff.[13]

For the next two years, Pierce poured himself into the work of the Los Angeles Evangelistic Center and worked to repair his marriage, but he remained restless. To battle the monotony of local church ministry, he borrowed a camera and tried his hand at producing Christian films. Like many other fundamentalists he had no reservations about using the media of popular culture on behalf of the gospel. To counter Hollywood secularity, he would produce Christian alternatives. In his first two films, Pierce first interviewed thirty of the world's best loved hymn writers and then focused on successful Christian businessmen. His experience with film would later serve as his avenue to introduce American evangelicals to the world.

In 1944, a black gospel group, the Eureka Jubilee Singers, came to the Los Angeles Evangelistic Center on tour.[14] Drawn by Pierce's style and energy, they offered to accompany him on his own three-month evangelistic tour. While the Jubilee Singers were well known, Pierce was not, but the deal struck made Pierce responsible for paying all expenses, his own travel and publicity as well as the singers. Yet, the offer promised an escape from his father-in-law's authority and the monotony he associated with local church ministry. "All I knew for sure was that I was called to be an evangelist and win souls," Pierce recalled. "And I knew that no one else would hire me to do it." Lacking both capital and assurance of success, he set out again in 1944 to make his way as an evangelist.[15]

Pierce's restlessness, pride, and pugnacious personality fit a certain evangelist profile. While the social status of evangelists had declined since the heyday of Dwight L. Moody's crusades, the calling retained a special

cachet in the fundamentalist imagination. Their oratorical flair could garner them celebrity status. They also embodied a muscular Christianity that
often portrayed their work as more masculine than that of local church
ministry. According to John R. Rice, editor of the fundamentalist organ
Sword of the Lord, "One can be a modernist and be a pastor. . . . But one
cannot be a modernist and be a real evangelist." Rice believed that "a pastor
content to 'teach' his congregation was a 'backslider at ease in Zion, luke-
warm, not willing to pay the awful price that it takes to be a real soul-
winner.'"[16] Evangelists also modeled a sacrificial faith. In contrast to a sala-
ried local pastor, they lived by faith, depending on goodwill offerings to
make ends meet and sacrificing comforts of home and time with family for
a life on the road. While most were content to laud evangelists rather than
take on such a life, Pierce found the ideals of celebrity, muscular faith, and
adventure intoxicating. Even if cost him his family and a comfortable life,
Pierce was willing to pay the price.

Yet even as images of tent meetings on the sawdust trail persisted, other
fundamentalists were eager to adapt to changing times. The death of Billy
Sunday in 1935 felt more like the passing of the baton to a new generation
of evangelists moving outside local churches and temporary tabernacles
into large city auditoriums. With new music, shorter sermons, and celebrity
guests, these youthful revivalists adapted their message to a new culture as
they strove to become the best show in town.

Pierce found himself between these two generations. Without forgoing
the lifestyle of the former, he adopted the new approach of the younger
evangelists. Early in 1944 he followed the typical revival circuit, preaching
to local churches like Powder Horn Baptist in Minneapolis, where 350 people filled the church. Never satisfied with the status quo, the following week
he decided to make a splash. He borrowed the money for an advertisement
in the newspaper and booked the Civic Auditorium. The next week he was
preaching to four thousand. The gamble paid off, and other young evangelists took notice. As his invitations increased, Pierce felt he had turned a
corner and joined a growing cadre of youthful evangelists setting out to
win America for Christ.[17]

Youth for Christ

By the end of World War II, youth revivalism had burst on the scene
through the emerging Youth for Christ (YFC) movement, and Pierce

yearned to get in on the ground floor. Just a dream a few years earlier, by Memorial Day weekend 1945, Youth for Christ filled Chicago's Soldier Field with seventy thousand young people. Just three weeks after victory in Europe (May 8, 1945, V-E Day), effusive patriotism, preaching, celebrities, and pomp and circumstance were on full display. Five hundred uniformed nurses marched in all white uniforms to create a living white cross before the platform. World War II soldiers gave their testimony and were honored as a five-thousand-member choir and a three-hundred-member band led the music. The Olympic mile champion Gil Dodds ran two laps around the stadium and then gave his Christian testimony. Missionary representatives from China, India, Africa, and Russia processed in native dress to add images of missionary pageant. YFC succeeded as it adopted popular culture, civic faith, and a potentially global outreach.[18]

Committed to this popular approach, youth revivalism had begun to spread throughout the country in the early 1940s. As one of the earliest new youth revivalists, Jack Wyrtzen, a former New York City nightlife musician who "found religion," took his swing band to warm up the crowd before his evangelistic sermons and soon began to fill Carnegie Hall. By 1944, twenty thousand people were coming to his "Victory Rallies" in Madison Square Garden.[19] Wyrtzen's success soon inspired similar youth rallies around the country. From Minneapolis to Los Angeles, North Carolina to Texas, these events attracted thousands each Saturday night.[20]

By 1944, the youth revival movement reached Chicago. With schools like Wheaton College (in Wheaton, Illinois, a suburb of Chicago), congregations like Moody Church, and a host of religious radio and newspaper outlets, the city served as a nationwide hub for conservative Christianity, and that soon translated into the new Youth for Christ movement as well. As Chicago's weekly revivals filled to capacity each Saturday night and garnered media publicity, they began to hear requests from across the nation, asking for organizational advice. Soon the disparate revivals coalesced into a loose organization called Youth for Christ. Torrey Johnson, pastor of the large Midwest Bible Church in Chicago, served as the movement's first president. A preacher and radio personality, he had a good eye for new talent. Earlier in 1944, he had invited Billy Graham, a recent Wheaton graduate and pastor of the small Village Church, to host a radio show, *Songs in the Night*, on his station. A year later after the success of the Soldier Field gathering, Johnson hired Graham as the first full-time YFC staffer.[21]

Pierce also longed to be in on the ground floor of this dynamic movement. While he had caught the eye of local Youth for Christ leaders after the initial success of his evangelistic meetings, Torrey Johnson also recalled Pierce coming to him broken in spirit when interest at his revivals began to flag. Pierce pleaded for an opportunity in the new organization. Their face-to-face meeting resulted in Johnson sending Pierce out with the humble task of peddling the organization's magazine back home in Southern California, but Pierce took it as an opportunity to keep preaching. By the fall of 1944, Seattle was looking for a director for its local YFC chapter, and organizers chose Pierce. He stayed fourteen months, making the Pacific Northwest one of the strongest regions of the movement. Pierce had earned his stripes, and by 1945 he served as one of eleven regional vice presidents to the first YFC convention that confidently set out an agenda to coordinate spiritual revival across America. Back preaching around the country, Pierce had found a home, however peripatetic, in YFC.[22]

YFC's growth personified the emergence of a neo-evangelicalism, but few used the new term as a descriptor in the 1940s. In 1942, a number of evangelicals came together to form the National Association of Evangelicals (NAE). Using the slogan "Cooperation Without Compromise," NAE founders shared a conservative theology and believed they served as an alternative to the ecumenical movement, which symbolized for them the dangers of deviation from orthodoxy and the elevation of the political over the spiritual. At the same time, they disliked the separatist stance that characterized much of fundamentalism.[23] By 1947, the NAE included a broadening constituency of thirty denominations representing 1.3 million church members as well as an additional three million associated with the mainline, but its members were too diverse, independent, and entrepreneurial for the organization to serve as a singular voice for evangelicalism.[24] The majority of conservative Christians agreed on core theological tenets and used "evangelical" and "fundamentalist" interchangeably well into the 1950s.[25] A defining characteristic of this new ethos that evangelicals claimed as distinctive was their renewed optimism that sought to extend beyond a single subculture in order to restore a Christian America and evangelize the world.[26]

As one of dozens of organizations formed out of a renewed optimism to reach America and the world, YFC may have taken off the fastest through the late 1940s with an estimated weekly attendance of one million people across the country and thousands more listening over radio. If the NAE framed theology, formed mission strategy, and issued resolutions, YFC offered a pragmatic pietism that embraced the language of the day and the styles of contemporary culture. The organization sought to conquer America for Christ with the "old-fashioned truth for up-to-date youth."[27]

They succeeded as they packaged their message through the perfect mix of popular entertainment and efficient organization. YFC promoted "a new effervescence of evangelical entrepreneurialism."[28] Its evangelists mimicked the styles of contemporary entertainers. One reporter called Torrey Johnson "the religious counterpart to Frank Sinatra." Gone were sweat-drenched outdated suits. These young preachers sported wide ties and white buck shoes and spoke "the language of the bobby-soxers." Tight harmony quartets or swing-style bands played an updated gospel music, often using the talents of Christian musicians who had once been disc jockeys or dance hall performers.[29] The rallies traded on celebrity, soliciting aid from sports stars, war heroes, and movie actors, who often dropped in to offer their testimonies. Publicity was slick and voluminous. Radio spots, handbills, and press releases advertised the Saturday night meetings. Promoters depicted the meetings as a "dream date" for Christian young people and entertainment for soldiers with a weekend pass. Always an early adopter, Pierce was glad to try any gimmick he felt would draw a crowd. Before his sermons, he often selected the soldier farthest from home and brought him on stage to call his family and broadcast the surprised conversation for the full stadium to hear.[30]

While gimmicks and entertainment popularized the rallies, they prospered mainly through efficient organization. In contrast to local churches, the rallies formed a coalition that included evangelists, local pastors, Christian businessmen, and local government leaders. The evangelists could "sell the rallies," but they needed community support. While particular theological distinctives often limited institutional cooperation, for citywide revivals, churches were willing to work together. The rallies remained largely interdenominational, gathering Baptists, Presbyterians, Methodists, and even Pentecostals together.[31] Local officials cut through red tape to offer city facilities. Christian businessmen provided capital.[32] Modeling themselves after the Chicago rallies, the meetings followed a common pattern. Evangelical theologian Carl Henry described a typical rally: "The pattern stays pretty much the same: a radio broadcast with audience participations, programs timed to the minute (individuals testifying in the Chicagoland Youth for Christ are given 45 seconds each, and it must be written and checked beforehand), short sermon keyed to youth, music thoroughly rehearsed and technically perfect, and the entire program centered on salvation."[33] Each program ended by inviting youth to commit their lives to Christ or to "surrender" themselves to Christian service. But YFC had no patience for long-winded preachers; the meetings ended in a timely fashion. Rallies ran professionally, a well-oiled and efficient operation.[34]

The Youth for Christ movement, entertaining and efficient, also succeeded as it resonated with Americans' heightened civic faith in the wake of World War II. Fundamentalists had always maintained a dual citizenship. When a separatist ideal predominated in the early twentieth century, fundamentalists lamented America's alleged demise from a distance. Once they reengaged a broader public, they reclaimed their duty to restore a Christian America. While these newer evangelicals clung to their doctrines, they packaged traditional values in ways that exploited civil religion. Youth for Christ rallies honored the nation by hanging American flags, welcoming soldiers as war heroes, and honoring the war dead. One caption under the report of a YFC rally read, "Young Americans are finding that patriotism and the gospel go well together."[35]

Beyond a public patriotism, their vision of a Christian America also led them to confront a perceived demise of morality. Yet, these were not simply fundamentalists preaching against all forms of fun. If many mainline Protestants still hoped to reform social structures, these new evangelicals insisted that only personal commitment to Christ could change society. Many of the evangelists or celebrities had been Christians only for a short time. They testified to their past path of immorality, and they claimed that good Christian living was far better.[36]

The time was right for Americans to listen to such a message. The general public also worried about the rise of ducktail haircuts, divorce rates, and juvenile delinquency. Americans were eager for messages of traditional morality, religious faith, and civic virtues because they felt it was essential to protect hearts and minds from outside subversive and un-American impulses. From local mayors and state governors to FBI director J. Edgar Hoover and President Harry Truman, politicians supported the youth rallies as a public good. Businessmen were happy to contribute and serve on the local YFC board in their community. Newspaper magnate William Randolph Hearst saw clean-cut evangelists like Bob Pierce or Billy Graham as poster children for a new Americanism he sought to promote. At the onset of the Cold War, Hearst and other leaders were clear that winning hearts and minds at home was necessary to win the war abroad, and he continually publicized YFC in all of his twenty-two papers.[37] Not since the 1925 Scopes trial had fundamentalists received such national coverage, but this time much of the coverage was positive.

In seeking America's spiritual revival, these new evangelicals also looked beyond American shores. Torrey Johnson told *Time* magazine in 1946 that his organization's goal was the "spiritual revitalization of America and the complete evangelization of the world in our generation."[38] At the beginning of the twentieth century, American missionaries had grown popular and powerful. U.S. presidents spoke at missionary conferences while mission leaders served as foreign diplomats.[39] The mission movement united across theological lines to "conquer" the world spiritually and socially. The 1910 Edinburgh Conference embodied this enthusiasm "for the immediate conquest of the world" and coined the phrase the "evangelization of the world in this generation." The height of imperialism, missionary leaders called for non-Western countries to embrace Christian conversion and civilization.[40]

After World War I, the appeal of Edinburgh's watchword began to falter as many within the dominant mainline denominations adopted a broader internationalist language, and following Woodrow Wilson's Fourteen Points, the League of Nations, and calls for the right to self-determination for all peoples, they spoke more of world unity than of world conquest.[41] While missions continued to grow slowly in the 1920s and 1930s, these new directions shattered the united missionary enterprise.[42] Yet, in contrast to the mainline, fundamentalists never relinquished this motto of global missions. They simply toiled out of the public eye.

With a rekindling of public interest in Pax Americana and the decisive role of the United States in World War II, broad calls for missionary service reappeared. Youth for Christ sponsored hundreds of "world vision" rallies promoting the work of international missionaries.[43] If tens of thousands gave their lives to Christ at YFC evangelistic rallies, thousands more dedicated their lives to missionary service, exploding the ranks of Bible colleges and traditional mission agencies while also spinning off dozens of new specialized mission agencies like World Vision.

As World War II engulfed the lives of everyday Americans, they also became more aware of their connection with the wider world. Images from *National Geographic*, *Time*, *Life*, and *Harper's* brought the other side of the world into their homes. Weekly newsreels played in their theaters before the John Wayne double feature. Their sons and husbands returned from

Europe, Asia, and North Africa with stories to tell as well. More aware of the world, Americans were also more willing to do something about it. With the menacing threats of totalitarianism and communism growing, all Americans could unite to see themselves as custodians of the free world. Echoing such sentiments, Youth for Christ evangelists reminded their audience that America was God's chosen nation. Harking back to Puritan jeremiads, Torrey Johnson questioned the nation's readiness: "If we have another lost generation . . . America is sunk. We are headed either for a definite turning to God or the greatest calamity ever to strike the human race."[44] Only revival and morality at home could lead to global revival and ensured political stability abroad.

New missionary recruits enlisted through YFC's "world vision" rallies out of a sense of responsibility to evangelize and fortify America's role in the world. Like Pierce, many were also seeking adventure, and YFC marketed the missionary experience as such. For many returning servicemen, missionary service gave them a chance to rekindle that sense of sacrifice and adventure now with a religious call. YFC did not highlight the meek missionary teaching Bible stories on flannelgraph. They pointed to pilots, Bible translators working among unknown tribes, and chaplains behind the walls of the Iron Curtain. Torrey Johnson declared that "young people want something that challenges the heroic. They want something that demands sacrifice . . . that is worth living and dying for."[45]

Christian conversion was the antidote to global suffering, communism, and materialism. Avoiding partisan politics but engaging in full-fledged public patriotism, the evangelists staged revivals that promoted the Christian gospel as the heart of America's international relations. A number of generals and heads of state agreed. General Douglas MacArthur invited Youth for Christ to postwar Japan to "provide the surest foundation for the firm establishment of democracy." Johnson replied, "Who knows but what we've got an army of occupation for the purpose of establishing Youth for Christ." Youth for Christ became both a mission society and a model of American triumphalism.[46]

Skeptics predicted the demise of YFC with waning public patriotism after the end of World War II, but its international focus gave it a second life. Some U.S. soldiers, "saved" at YFC rallies in America before deployment and now stationed overseas, organized YFC chapters wherever they landed. Missionaries and national Christians, hearing of YFC's success in America, invited the evangelists to lead revivals. With the world hungry for all things American, many of these young U.S evangelists embarked on their first trips abroad to spread a Christian message and American-style values in every school, auditorium, and governmental palace opened to them. America was the liberator, and YFC evangelists proclaimed both political and Christian freedom.[47]

As invitations poured in, YFC established itself as an international agency—Youth for Christ International (YFCI)—in 1947 and co-opted militaristic metaphors as evangelists served as "Christian commandos" setting up "beachheads" for further "infiltration" of the gospel. Torrey Johnson would partner two or three evangelists, labeled "invasion teams," to deploy on three- to six-month evangelistic tours around the world.[48] The most popular voices—preachers like Billy Graham and Johnson—toured England, Scotland, and France, while others headed to Eastern Europe or North Africa, South America, the Caribbean, India, Japan, the Philippines, and China. In a twelve-month period from 1947 to 1948, YFCI sent out ten international teams. Before embarking, few had firsthand experience overseas. Their international rallies copied the revivals at home, but no matter how much was lost in translation, the evangelistic sermons, upbeat music, Christian celebrities, and massive promotion, coupled with America's global cachet, heightened international curiosity.

At times, these young evangelists overplayed their newfound self-importance and their global naïveté backfired with cultural insensitivities and political overstepping, but more often they met enormous audiences they interpreted to those back home as hungry for their message. The reaction was intoxicating, and they felt the time was ripe for "greater conquests for Christ"—they would change the world now or never.[49] As Western Christians, they could battle communism, false religions, and poverty with the Christian gospel. Much to the satisfaction of their supporters back home who lived vicariously through their evangelistic exploits, YFC revivalists took a largely American gospel to the world.

Bob Pierce Becomes a Global Ambassador

At first, Bob Pierce had little interest in world missions. As a newly minted YFC vice president, he raised $10,000 for his colleague Dave Morken to evangelize throughout Asia, but Pierce was content that his call was here at home. Yet, by the summer of 1947, he was headed to Shanghai. By Pierce's account, Torrey Johnson had grown homesick after his most recent European tour with Billy Graham. Instead of heading to China, he flew to Los Angeles to enlist Pierce to take his place. Knowing his YFC work required constant travel, Pierce had moved his wife and infant daughter back to Los Angles from Portland to be near family the year before. His wife's health was suffering. The family described it as a mental breakdown and exhaustion that confined her to the house and even bed many days. If Pierce had broken free of home responsibilities to follow a greater calling, his family suffered. In that context, Torrey Johnson personally sat next to Lorraine Pierce's bed and asked her to "release" her husband to the Lord's call in China. With little choice, she eventually relented, and Pierce was on a plane headed east two weeks later.[50]

YFC's shoestring budget could not offer Pierce much financial support. A June YFC rally at the Hollywood Bowl led by Billy Graham pulled in $300 for Pierce. Graham brought Pierce to the platform and presented him with the Bible that he would later personally present to Chiang Kai-shek and his wife on behalf of the young people of America. A picture of the presentation appeared in next morning's *Los Angeles Times*, but Pierce probably missed it.[51] With assurances from Christian businessmen that they would take care of his family, Pierce used the previous night's receipts to book passage as far as the funds would take him—Hawaii. After arriving there, he made friends with local YFC supporters, preaching and praying for additional funds to come. He had already cashed in his own savings and hoped God would provide the rest. From Hawaii to the Philippines, to Hong Kong and then China, Pierce quickly became enamored with the same sense of adventure and celebrity that drew him to the life of an evangelist. As cameramen met him coming off the plane in each location, Pierce remarked his surprise at being treated as a Western celebrity as he preached to packed auditoriums and met with leading politicians.[52]

When Johnson tapped Pierce for China, Asia was second fiddle to Europe in the minds of YFC. Asia, however, had long dominated the missionary imagination. Throughout the early twentieth century, Protestant churches had directed special attention to Asia. In 1919, they made up over 70 percent of the missionary force in the three largest "mission fields" of China, India, and Japan.[53] Yet by the 1930s, new nationalisms, modernization, and maturing indigenous Christian communities began to question missionary motives. China fell into civil war beginning in 1927; India rebelled against British colonial rule in 1920; and Japan went to war with China in 1937. The new situation devastated Protestant missions.[54]

During and after World War II, however, Asian nations once again became prizes to be won, especially as the Cold War absorbed the attention of America and the Soviet Union. The China lobby in America, led by powerful men like Henry R. Luce, publisher of *Time* and *Life*, publicized the Nationalists' fight against the Communists and lauded the Christian faith of Nationalist Generalissimo Chiang Kai-shek and Madame Chiang.[55] The Chiangs knew how to speak to their Western supporters and welcomed Christian missionaries to China to build schools and hospitals.[56] The secular media like the *New York Times* and *Reader's Digest*, along with the religious press, from the liberal *Christian Century* to the conservative *Moody Monthly*, all reported on Christian progress in China.[57]

Without knowing it, Pierce had stumbled into one of the most vital and volatile regions of the postwar world. With no knowledge of Chinese culture and language, he began his evangelistic meetings just as he had in America's heartland. As his interpreter translated his message into Chinese, the crowds and the conversions amazed him. For four months, Pierce averaged two services a day. Some days he held as many as seven. Massive crowds usually filled the largest auditorium in town. At the end of the trip, Pierce had recorded 17,852 decisions in the flyleaf of his Bible.[58] In the midst of civil war, Pierce preached in and out of war zones, discovering a Christian mission equal to the challenge of a godly and masculine evangelist jumping from plane to plane without knowing what the next day held. Relieved of cares for wife and family, Pierce had found an even greater outlet to fuel his need for adventure and sacrifice.

Pierce quickly became enthralled with his first experience on the other side of the world. In describing a train trip, street life, or a ride in a rickshaw to friends back home, he found China to be a fascinating mix of ancient and modern, exotic and familiar:

Old and new, everywhere. Coolies shoulder their ageless burdens, while trucks beep for them to get out the way. Farm boys work their foot-operated water lifts while, overhead, a DC-3 flashes its silver wings in the sun. Take away the plane. Take away the truck. Take away the train. And you have the China that Marco Polo found six centuries ago. Old and new. Which is better? The new has brought

. . . Well, what has it brought? War. Greed. New modes of sin. Good things too, but also these. Is it worth the price? China makes you think about things like that.[59]

On one hand, Pierce depicted China as an Eastern "other" with superstitions that had no place in the advanced and modernized West. On the other, he described a modernizing China not so distant from what Americans knew. As his confidence grew in his ability to interpret the country to audiences back home, he would present a China with more nuance than most expected or imagined.

He praised the Chinese openness to the gospel and their culture, but his encounters with poverty deeply troubled him. He often felt guilty simply "making speeches" in the face of such physical suffering, and between evangelistic meetings, he often went to observe missionaries who worked with the poorest of the poor.[60] In Kunming, he met American missionary Beth Albert, who ran a home for lepers through the China Inland Mission. Pierce and his traveling companion Ken Anderson described her in their reports through *Youth for Christ* magazine: "Work among lepers is a thing of joy. Beth Albert is no weird ascetic. . . . Beth Albert is a normal, enthusiastic American girl. . . . Beth Albert loves the lepers because she has found the will of God for her life."[61] Pierce's letters back home soon began to share his regret in being unable to do more to respond to the physical needs he encountered even as he continued to celebrate his evangelistic success.

One particular encounter with poverty provided the founding myth for World Vision that Pierce retold thousands of times.[62] In Amoy, China, Dutch Reformed missionary Tena Hoelkeboer invited Pierce to preach to her school of four hundred girls. In retelling the story, Pierce admitted his naïveté: "I hadn't brains enough, or insight, to know that there was a cultural difference between Youth for Christ in America and the Chinese way up in the interior of China, so I was preaching the same stuff. I never thought through the differences in their cultural background or how incomprehensible my Western Judeo-Christian ideas and concepts would be to this five-thousand-year-old culture. . . . I told these kids, 'Go home and tell your folks you're going to be a Christian.' "[63] When one of Hoelkeboer's students, White Jade, informed her father that she had converted to Christianity, he beat her and threw her out of the house. Hoelkeboer, distressed at the prospect of taking on yet another orphan, demanded of Pierce, "What are you going to do about it?" Pierce gave Hoelkeboer five

Figure 1. Bob Pierce's earliest exposure to physical need and encounters with orphans. Here he visits Korean children at a World Vision–sponsored orphanage in the late 1950s. © World Vision, Inc. 2011. All rights reserved. Reprinted by permission.

dollars, all the money he had left, and promised to send more each month on his return to the States.[64] After his return, he recounted the story to American audiences, asking them how anyone could ignore "the half of Asia that goes to bed hungry and without knowing Christ."[65]

Pierce's first trip to China lasted four months, but that was long enough for him to discover that international evangelism was now his calling and "God's time was now" for China. With his flair for the dramatic, Pierce wrote, "If I had the choice of laboring in any generation since Christ walked on earth, I would rather stand as a harvester in the midst of the present field of China than to have been Martin Luther, [Charles] Finney, Moody or Sunday in their fields at their ripest. In 18 weeks, God gave us over 17,000 decisions."[66] His daughter Marilee Pierce Dunker declared that Pierce "went to China a young man in search of adventure, but came home a man with a mission."[67] In short, the world changed him, and he began to think of himself as a "man in the gap," American evangelicals' global ambassador and advocate for the poor.

Pierce returned to America in October 1947 to share what God was doing in China. "I had gone there to preach the gospel, true enough," he admitted to *Youth for Christ* magazine's editor Ken Anderson, "but I had also gone there to capture the need of the people and to bring that need back to America."[68] Audiences responded by packing churches and civic auditoriums to hear about God's work in a foreign land gripped by spiritual and political crises. While his evangelistic success attracted most attention, Pierce brought both spiritual and physical needs to the attention of American evangelicals through his images and stories. He assumed that when American Christians heard of the suffering, and he confronted them with Tena Hoelkeboer's question—"What are you going to do about it?"—then they would not ignore the need.

Many did respond. In nine months at home, he raised over $67,000 for Youth for Christ work overseas. While Pierce could have kept exposing American evangelicals to China through his stories for another nine months, he was eager to return to China; Youth for Christ was eager to send him. In 1948, YFC hosted its first International Conference in Beatenberg, Switzerland, which gathered 320 delegates from thirty countries to plan world evangelization. There YFC officially named him an international evangelist and missionary at large, and the following month, he returned to China with the editor of *Youth for Christ* magazine, Ken Anderson. YFC leaders knew Pierce had attracted attention in America, and they hoped to capitalize on his second trip with increased publicity for the organization.[69]

After identifying the cities as the battlefields in the spiritual war for China, Pierce concentrated his efforts on this trip in urban areas. Once more he generated enthusiasm with capacity crowds at every event. Better prepared for the poverty he would encounter, he brought funds from America and gave them to the missionaries who worked among the poor. Pierce no longer conceived of his work as simply evangelistic. He gathered more images and stories of social conditions to share with his audience in the West. He praised the missionaries he encountered, making sure that his audience back home knew that they both preached the gospel and ministered to China's overwhelming physical needs.

He was not prepared, however, for the growing danger. Pierce learned of pastors and missionaries captured or killed by the Communists. Preaching within miles of the front lines, he lauded the sacrifices of Nationalist soldiers and portrayed refugees streaming from Communist territory, many recounting stories of torture and abuse on account of their faith: "Hourly the shadow of communism moves down upon the great area of China. Most of the North is already gone. Student centers are still open, but these, too, may momentarily be closed. Today is still the day of harvest. Tomorrow may see missionaries forced to vacate the entire country. Then the door of our opportunity will be closed. Maybe it will be closed forever."[70] When Pierce returned to the States this time, he had little patience for Western ambivalence. Time was of the essence, as he told audiences they might never have another chance to infiltrate Asia with the gospel.

Pierce's Emerging Message to American Evangelicals

In 1949, evangelical Zondervan press published *This Way to the Harvest*, Ken Anderson and Bob Pierce's account of their most recent trip. It sold through its first edition of 10,000 copies in under five months. Pierce had borrowed a camera and film for this trip to China and hoped his images would give his American audience insight into what Asia was "really like." A chance encounter with local Los Angeles film producer Dick Ross, an early pioneer in the Christian film industry, led Pierce to enlist Ross' help to splice his firsthand footage together in an unused Sunday school room to create his first public film, the thirty-eight-minute *China Challenge*. For decades, missionaries had offered glimpses of their work by dressing in native garb and showing slides. Pierce offered much more. In the opening scene, he turned to the viewer at the outset: "one picture is worth a thousand words. . . . You'll permit the camera to show you the physical and spiritual needs of a land which words alone could never describe."[71]

The seeming realism of his film captivated evangelicals. As travelogue, the camera depicted "the sights and sounds of the Orient"—street vendors, children playing, Buddhist temples, and Christian churches. For social commentary, Pierce showed starving children, families living in garbage dumps, and leper colonies with no medical treatment. *China Challenge* also attested to evangelistic success. Clips of Pierce preaching to thousands alternated with scenes of Chinese coming forward to receive Christ. The film highlighted the work of missionaries as experts and sacrificial heroes. Pierce challenged Americans to take part in the adventure, and he continued to share his firsthand stories as he stumped across America, raising both awareness and funds for his work overseas. YFC would hire additional liaisons to show Pierce's film and offer an evangelistic message when he was traveling elsewhere. With countless retellings, his message coalesced into a new evangelical humanitarianism that admonished American evangelicals that now was their time to act for the sake of the gospel and the world.[72]

Pierce wanted evangelicals to experience the East vicariously. He portrayed the sights, sounds, and smells by describing the cuisine, street life, religious practices, and family structures. He wanted his audiences to appreciate the Chinese and began to see that the East could speak to the West. He affirmed Americans' work abroad most often through heaping praise on missionaries, whom he described as red-blooded, adventurous Westerners living out a call from God. He also noted the benefits of the American military and Western industrial and economic modernization, but he challenged his fellow Americans to consider whether westernization was an unqualified good. Beyond East and West, however, Pierce strived to emphasize the common faith Chinese Christians shared with his evangelical audiences: "Even in pagan communities, China is a land of hospitality," Pierce recalled, "and when a Chinese becomes a Christian, his congeniality becomes even more pronounced." Pierce felt such images of fellow Chinese Christians humanized his missionary mandate.[73]

He also integrated the call for evangelization with a plea for aid to the poor. Pierce appealed to evangelicals' social conscience with stories and graphic images of suffering overseas. The same year Pierce embarked on his first trip to China, Carl Henry, the preeminent evangelical theologian of his generation published his manifesto *The Uneasy Conscience of Modern Fundamentalism*. Henry worried that the new revivalism of organizations like YFC left little room for any social ethic. Henry wanted neo-evangelicals to be intellectually respectable, socially responsible, and culturally involved. He feared that as fundamentalists revolted "against the Social Gospel" for abandoning belief in biblical supernaturalism and individual salvation, they had led a "revolt against the Christian social imperative."[74] Henry believed that by ignoring a social ethic, they would forfeit their right to be heard as agents of the gospel. It would be a safe bet that Pierce had not read Henry's *Uneasy Conscience* before he encountered poverty in China, and if he did, he would have had little time or talent to draft a theological response. Pierce succeeded precisely because he tied evangelism and social concern together with insider evangelical language that completely avoided the language of a liberal social gospel that conservatives despised. And he did it through shocking images and firsthand accounts of suffering overseas that compelled those at home to respond.

On top of saving souls, feeding the hungry, and clothing lepers, Pierce was also dragging evangelicals along to see that their time on the world's stage was now. For instance, he narrated China's war as the front line of a battle between Christianity and communism that would determine the fate of the gospel in Asia. When much of the mainstream press began to question Chiang Kai-shek's commitment to democracy and his chances to win the civil war, Pierce, like other evangelicals, continued to celebrate his Christianity as the deciding factor. He praised the suffering Chinese Christians and the missionaries who had endured even martyrdom for their faith, but he was realistic that the evangelical opportunity could quickly close. Near the end of his second trip, Pierce cabled that they were "winning a thousand souls a day while barely staying ahead of advancing communists who were mutilating the bodies of Christians."[75] Pierce sought to chastise the complacency of American Christians whose faith merely led them to be upstanding citizens. He modeled the adventure and sacrifice of a true missionary evangelist, preaching and serving as if his life depended upon it. In China, Pierce felt he was on the front lines of God's activity in the world. In America he challenged evangelicals to take action on behalf of the poor, diseased, and spiritually lost by asking them, "What are you going to do about it?"

Pierce Establishes World Vision

In 1949, as Pierce was screening his *China Challenge* film and challenging American evangelicals to respond, China "fell" to Mao Tse-tung's Communists and closed its door to Western missionaries. The same year, Billy Graham's well-publicized Los Angeles crusade led him to become the face of evangelical revivalism in the United States. Pierce had shared Graham's same dream, but now he settled on becoming the "Billy Graham of Asia."[76] With China closed, he was stuck in America directing the local Los Angeles chapter of Youth for Christ. While he was back home with his family, his heart was elsewhere. After his experience abroad, local work felt too small and insignificant. Deep bouts of depression returned as he itched to return to Asia. In June 1949, a missionary couple he had befriended in China found themselves forced off the mainland and relocated to Korea. They invited Pierce to lead revivals in their new community, and he jumped at the chance.[77]

Yet his first Korean trip faltered before it even began. His wife, Lorraine, now pregnant with their second child, did not share the urgency Pierce felt for this new trip, and Pierce stubbornly intended to go to Asia via Paris where he had left his camera to be repaired. When he arrived in Paris, promised financial support fell through, the camera was still broken, and Pierce developed a major infection. Stranded with little money and with isolation sending him spiraling into depression, he felt his faith again slipping away. Letters to his family stopped as he drifted around Paris for months. Word filtered home that he had given up and decided he was not coming home. Finally, intervention from a few friends and a cable from his father-in-law explaining that anxiety over his whereabouts had put his pregnant wife on bed rest brought him home to Los Angeles, dejected and broken.[78]

While slowly returning from the depths of his depression, Pierce reclaimed his calling even if life at home with Lorraine and now two kids would never be easy. What he craved was adventure—being evangelicals' global ambassador to Asia. By the first of 1950, he had convinced YFC to send him out again. After raising the funds, he left for Korea in March 1950 for the "Save the Nation Evangelistic Crusade" and again found large crowds flocking to hear his evangelistic messages. In Korea, he found the same abject poverty that had initially confronted him in China. He was excited to connect with missionaries eager both to spread the gospel and to feed the poor, but he again confronted an imminent communist threat just across the border in the Soviet Union. Pierce left Korea in June at the invitation of Chiang Kai-shek to preach at his private chapel in Formosa (Taiwan). He learned that same weekend that the North had invaded and war had begun. The Korean pastors he had met with the week before were captured and held as prisoners of war for the next two and a half years. Now recounting his harrowing escape to American audiences back home alongside his evangelistic success and firsthand experience with the dire need to support missionaries and Korean leaders with food and medicine, he fretted that the war would close Korea just like China the year before.[79] This time, however, he was determined to return.

By October, he was off again, but he first took time to establish an organization to administer the funds he raised in the United States to distribute to missionaries and Koreans in need. Taking the name from YFC's "world vision rallies," Pierce chartered the organization as World Vision Inc., "an evangelical interdenominational missionary service organization meeting emergency world needs through established evangelical missions."[80] Pierce's World Vision harnessed the newfound enthusiasm of YFC's international teams and their reengagement with global politics and evangelical missions, while exporting its unique American revivalist style. Pierce hired Frank Phillips, an old friend from YFC days in Portland, to manage the operations of the new agency at home part-time with the help of a single secretary to handle the correspondence. He did not yet know what to expect from his new upstart missionary agency, but he knew that he needed the freedom to roam the world, preach the gospel, meet needs where he found them, and report back to fellow evangelicals back home as he saw fit.

CHAPTER 2

Opening Americans' Eyes to a New World

IN SEPTEMBER 1950, less than four months after the start of the Korean War, Pierce signed the paperwork to formalize his new nonprofit, World Vision Inc., and boarded the last civilian flight to Seoul. The Kilbournes, the Presbyterian missionary couple who had organized his original trip earlier that year, met him at the airport. Denominational boards had encouraged Western missionaries to evacuate as Communists marched on the capital city, and Pierce's friends were taking the same plane out on which he had arrived. Just months earlier as YFC's "missionary at large," Pierce had preached to thousands as a part of the "Save the Nation Evangelistic Crusade." When Pierce personally first met South Korean president Syngman Rhee, the Korean Christian statesman had confided in him, "Youth for Christ's type of evangelism will help hold back the flood of atheism which is flowing through the Far East."[1] The two agreed that Christian revival was the antidote to Communist aggression. Now six months later, Rhee was thrust into war for his country's survival, and almost all of Pierce's original contacts had either been captured or fled. With his missionary friends gone, he also had no place to stay.

Not sure of his next step, Pierce flagged down a young black U.S. soldier in an army jeep. With all his film equipment and luggage tags from Los Angeles, the soldier assumed he was a Hollywood cameraman. Pierce did not correct him, and, like so often happened, he found himself in the right place at the right time. By the next day he was sleeping in a hotel commandeered for American military officers with a jeep and a driver at the ready to take him around the country to document through film the physical destruction and human need the war was leaving behind.[2]

For the next three months, he traveled the country, filming, preaching, and meeting immediate humanitarian needs. Having encountered countless needs on his first trip, this time Pierce did not want to be caught empty-handed, and so he raised over $10,000 from American Christians to take with him on his return. In Korea, he distributed the cash whenever he discovered a need—at one point supporting families of evangelical missionaries he met who had refused to evacuate, at another time, buying food for dozens of starving Korean families. He personally paid for the transportation of six hundred pastors and their families to flee the North to avoid capture and torture by the Communists. At the invitation of U.S. and South Korean senior officers, he preached to large gatherings of soldiers, counseled them individually as they drove him around the country, and promised to pass along messages to friends and family back home. After committing to return as soon as he could with more resources, he flew back to America with fresh images of Korea's Christians, missionaries, American soldiers, and Communist aggressors to share at churches and YFC rallies and then ask for their sacrificial financial support.[3]

The needs were immense, but World Vision operated on a shoestring. Pierce advertised that every dollar he raised went entirely to "Oriental missions." With a barebones staff of three, World Vision initially had little purpose but to account for the funds Pierce raised and to funnel them to fulfill the promises he was making overseas. In the first year, World Vision raised $41,245.52. By 1951, it had disbursed $77,129.89. Most of the funds flowed to individual missionaries and Korean pastors to support hospitals, orphanages, and evangelism. Pierce took pride in World Vision's efficiency. He suggested that other mission agencies wasted valuable time in debates about priorities, while he raised and disbursed funds swiftly and efficiently.[4]

By 1951, Pierce regularly haunted the front lines of Korea, averaging over three trips and more than nine months a year in Korea throughout the war. With civilian travel grounded, he had to find another way in. By happenstance, he met a priest who had gained access as a Catholic war correspondent. When Pierce asked who represented Protestants, the priest responded, "Nobody." A few weeks later on his return to the United States, he stopped by Washington, D.C., filed the paperwork at the Pentagon, and was appointed a United Nations war correspondent as a reporter for the Evangelical Press Association. His newfound status gave him access to hop in the jump seat of military planes in and out of the country. As he filed stories for countless evangelical magazines, he brought the war—and the mission—to American Christians.[5]

Pierce came to envision himself as evangelicals' global ambassador, and his reporting of Korea's physical and spiritual needs allowed him to work out his own developing missionary message. He drew his share of converts by preaching to American and Korean soldiers as well as 160,000 captured North Korean and Chinese prisoners of war. But he also worried about the material needs of the country. He listed the atrocities: hundreds of Christians martyred, more than 1.5 million homeless, 12,000 villages flattened. With the outbreak of war, Pierce viewed Korea as the center of God's activity in the world. He blithely mixed the spiritual and the political. "Korea," he said, "is not only crucial in world affairs. It may well be the key to unlock again all of the Orient for the Gospel."[6]

Over the decade, World Vision grew alongside Pierce's own message of global evangelical humanitarianism. By the mid-1950s, Pierce reflected, "World Vision is more than a mere name or a title. It is an idea . . . an ideal . . . a concept of missions on a world-wide scale." He claimed that World Vision challenged Americans to see the world "through the eyes of need . . . physically . . . socially . . . spiritually."[7] To lead with anything other than evangelism already demonstrated a noticeable shift for Pierce that did not go unnoticed by fellow evangelicals debating the relationship between material and spiritual need, but he urged his audiences to greater global awareness through compelling stories that almost always included both. Pierce would still use the terms "fundamentalist," "evangelical," and even "Christian" interchangeably to describe himself. While he often mocked the theological feuds that served to define who was "in" or "out," Pierce was not naive to the boundary-defining significance of such debates and their role in establishing World Vision's identity and his own support base. Yet, too often he felt these feuds simply took time away from the immediate need. Who could question the sacrifice of missionaries and Korean Christians in the midst of war against atheistic communists or refuse to meet emergency humanitarian needs in the name of the gospel?

Pierce's evangelical humanitarianism remained a work in progress as he processed what he experienced on the ground in Korea to Americans back home, but he packaged his "new world outlook" in a familiar American idiom. World Vision's work followed the Cold War's hot spots: China, Korea, and then Vietnam. Pierce's Cold War ideology understood communism as a "godless religion" and the mission field as a battleground against it. In this crisis, Asia occupied the central stage. He believed the war with communism would determine the fate of both freedom and the gospel in Asia. His rhetoric employed metaphors of sacrifice, urgency, and opportunity. He worried that nationalism, secularism, liberalism, and resurgent traditional religions threatened to close the door to Western democracy and missions. At the same time, he recounted Christian conversions in the thousands and celebrated the desire of many Asians for freedom and Christianity. He showcased missionaries, orphans, and widows who encouraged Americans to undertake compassionate charity. World Vision grew as Pierce's message highlighted the world's needs in a vernacular that resonated with popular audiences and reflected the preexisting assumptions of an increasingly public American evangelicalism.

World Vision's Initial Message

With the outbreak of war in Korea, Americans sought news about the Communist advances and craved any information about the country many called the Hermit Kingdom; Pierce obliged. Returning home from his second visit to Korea with 15,000 feet of film, Pierce was determined to follow up on the success of his initial *China Challenge* with another film, this time from the front lines of the Korean War. As news of his intentions spread, Hollywood came calling. Warner Brothers offered to buy the footage at any price. Nobody else had full color footage of the war, local culture, and the developing humanitarian crisis. But Pierce refused to sell. He believed producing his own film would maintain his Christian focus, make him a household name, and serve as the key to his ongoing fund-raising support.[8] The resulting film, *38th Parallel*, was released just a few months later. Footage depicted the horrors of war and desperate humanitarian need alongside the vibrancy of Korean culture and the resiliency of the Korean people in the midst of Christian revival and political turmoil.[9] World Vision representatives would show the film in churches and community halls thousands of times across the country even as Pierce would continue to average at least one new film a year throughout the 1950s. On top of his movies, Pierce served as a go-to source for quotes in the religious and popular press. He produced his own national radio show, and he published his own national magazine. He flooded American Christians with stories and images and, in so doing, became a cultural broker between America and Asia as he recalibrated a new evangelical internationalism. In its early days, World Vision helped evangelicals reclaim their voice in domestic politics, international affairs, and foreign missions in the midst of a renewed popular belief in American exceptionalism and global engagement.

Pierce's friends in Youth for Christ claimed that "these are critical days of opportunity for evangelicals, a race against time, an all-out battle with the gathering forces of the anti-Christ across the world."[10] Shaking off their earlier separatism, they often saw themselves in the late 1940s as Christian America's new vanguard. In the 1950s, an increasingly public evangelicalism rode the coattails of patriotism, triumphalism, and Cold War anticommunism as evangelicals directed their attention overseas.

Ever since the 1940s some evangelicals had begun to attach the prefix "neo" to the labels that described them. As neo-evangelicals, they wanted to distinguish themselves from fundamentalism on the right and liberalism on the left, but few outsiders comprehended the distinctions. By the end of the 1950s, however, a new evangelicalism had succeeded in distinguishing itself. In 1957, Billy Graham drew record crowds and unprecedented publicity for his New York City Crusade, marking both evangelical popularity and division. Union Theological Seminary professor Reinhold Niebuhr spoke for a wing within mainline Protestantism by rebuking Graham in the pages of *Life* magazine for elevating individual conversion over social suffering.[11] From the other side, fundamentalists chided Graham for working alongside mainline churches and inviting the likes of Martin Luther King Jr. to join him on the platform. Ardent fundamentalists such as John R. Rice and Bob Jones saw the New York City Crusade as the final straw; they would no longer associate with Graham.

Just a year earlier, Billy Graham and others founded the periodical *Christianity Today* as the mouthpiece of a new evangelicalism. It soon eclipsed the mainline *Christian Century* in circulation among pastors and laypersons. Popular outlets like *Time* magazine would now identify evangelicalism as a growing third stream in American Protestantism.[12] Evangelicals, however, would go further—they saw themselves as the new mainstream. They took pride in their growing public influence, claiming leaders at the highest levels of business and politics. Graham himself had become a fixture within the Eisenhower White House. To the halls of power, they even made a demographic argument, claiming they best represented the popular perspective of the majority of American Christians.[13]

Politics: Christian America Versus Atheistic Communism

Pierce was less interested in evangelicals simply becoming the new main-stream. For him, the stakes were much higher. He insisted that the gospel and democracy would rise or fall in accord with the energies exerted by American Christians. Overseas, he claimed that "the Holy Spirit made it necessary for North Koreans to test their vicious attack below the 38th parallel," so that God could get the attention of American Christians. As early as 1951, Pierce recounted his travels to Korea, Japan, and Formosa, and acknowledged, "If Christian Americans fail these strategic points today, then all Asia may be lost to the witness of Christ tomorrow." Pierce could or would not parse religion and politics as separate spheres. Pax Americana and Christian proclamation went hand in hand in a high-stakes spiritual and political battle.[14]

Pierce's message not only attracted the imagination of these new evan-gelicals; it also resonated with the preoccupations of popular culture. In the 1950s, religious congregations reported record numbers of attenders at the same time sociologist William Herberg popularized a common Judeo-Christian faith bound by a shared "American way of life." A shared faith served as a key asset in rallying Americans against a common enemy, a monolithic godless communism.[15]

The popular media also made hay by combining religion and patriotism at almost every turn. Henry R. Luce had grown up in China as the son of Presbyterian missionaries. Now as a media magnate and publisher of *Time* and *Life*, Luce did not mince words. Historian Robert Ellwood paraphrases the thesis of Luce's 1941 book *The American Century* by claiming that America had a "special mission to preserve its own virtue, and moreover to present it to the rest of the world as the more excellent way, while defending earth from evil forces bent on destroying such righteousness."[16] By the 1950s, Luce was filling his magazines with encomiums to America and reli-gious virtue: "Christianity," he wrote, "itself is the living and revolutionary force which alone can halt communism."[17]

As publisher of *Reader's Digest*, the highest circulation general interest magazine in the United States by the mid-1950s, DeWitt Wallace purported to speak for Middle America when also lauding faith and anticommunism. In mapping an imagined global geography of American influence and com-munist aggression, *Reader's Digest* packaged the Cold War in human inter-est stories and travelogues designed for unsophisticated readers.[18] World

Vision's own early mission magazine modeled itself after these outlets even as reports of Pierce's own travels found their way into the pages of the popular press as well.

Beyond preachers and the popular press, politicians also used religion to great benefit for the purpose of Cold War containment. President Harry Truman had begun to unite Americans behind a religious cause: "God has created us and brought us to our present position of power and strength for some great purpose."[19] Conservatives and liberals alike joined Truman in mixing political and religious rhetoric. Conservative William F. Buckley Jr. claimed that "the duel between Christianity and atheism is the most important in the world," while liberal Democrat and Unitarian Adlai Stevenson referred to communism as the "anti-Christ" that "stalks our world."[20] Politicians across the spectrum rallied Americans around faith, freedom, and prosperity while railing against communists' dogmatic atheism.

The rhetoric of Truman's successor, President Dwight D. Eisenhower, followed suit: "What is our battle against communism if it is not a fight between anti-God and belief in the Almighty?"[21] For Eisenhower's secretary of state, John Foster Dulles, who acquiesced to political service while serving as a prominent lay leader within the ecumenical Federal Council of Churches, the fault line was not political but spiritual. Even before he entered Eisenhower's administration, he claimed America's "spiritual renewal" as a necessity to win the Cold War, and he argued that only the churches could rectify the nation's current spiritual apathy and "materialistic mood."[22]

Eisenhower's administration both institutionalized and further popularized what his predecessors had begun to preach. Upon becoming president, Eisenhower was baptized as a Presbyterian and highlighted his church attendance while in office. His administration initiated the Presidential Prayer Breakfasts. Congress added "under God" to the Pledge of Allegiance and "In God We Trust" to all U.S. currency. The pervasive spiritual language of the Eisenhower era promoted both individual and civil religion.[23]

In couching nationalism and anticommunism in religious language, politicians hoped to unite diverse traditions against America's enemy abroad, atheistic communism. Some politicians, however, could not resist the temptation to use religious language as a club to squelch dissenters at home. Wisconsin senator Joseph McCarthy preferred apocalyptic accents: "Today we are engaged in a final, all-out battle between communistic atheism and Christianity. The modern champions of communism have selected this as the time. And ladies and gentlemen, the chips are down— they are truly down."[24] Like McCarthy, FBI director J. Edgar Hoover feared that communists had infiltrated the home front. Hoover flooded the popular media with a torrent of anticommunist exhortations. "It [communism] is a moral foe of Christianity," he claimed. "Either it will survive or Christianity will triumph because in this land of ours the two cannot live side by side." Hoover admonished parents that they had a patriotic duty to bring their kids to Sunday school and church to inoculate them against communism in order to produce good Americans.[25]

For the most part, religious communities followed their politicians' lead in embracing faith as central to winning the Cold War. By the early 1950s, all the large religious denominations established anticommunist educational programs. While an occasional World Council of Churches (WCC) subcommittee may have voiced an objection to the direction of American foreign policy, the majority of mainline Protestants in the pews ignored such reports. Instead, they watched popular Protestant theologian Reinhold Niebuhr on *The Mike Wallace Interview*, read Luce's anticommunist editorials in *Time* and *Life*, or listened to patriotic sermons in their local Methodist or Presbyterian churches.

Catholics were even more outspoken in their support of this civic faith than mainline Protestants. As they continued to seek credibility and cultural influence on the national stage, anticommunism bolstered Catholics' American identity. Pope Pius XII drew attention to the millions of Catholics trapped behind the Iron Curtain, suffering for their faith at the hands of satanic regimes. National Catholic celebrities like Fulton Sheen and Cardinal Francis Spellman became anticommunist icons. In 1948, Spellman declared, "It is not alone in defense of my faith that I condemn atheistic Communism, but as an American in defense of my country. We stand at a crossroads of civilization, a civilization threatened with the crucifixion of Communism." America was exceptional, God's nation. It was every citizen's duty to defend it against Soviet godlessness.[26]

It was Pierce's fellow evangelicals, however, who may have had the most to gain from hitching their wagon to the Cold War cause. Eager to discard their past separatism, they became ardent cold warriors. As historian William Inboden noted, "what they lack in institutional and intellectual credibility, they tried to compensate for with organization and energy."[27] In the early 1950s, no one spoke louder than Billy Graham, and he never lowered his voice when he spoke about communism: "Western culture and its fruits had its foundation in the Bible, the Word of God, and in the revivals of the Seventeenth and Eighteenth Centuries. Communism, on the other hand, has decided against God, against Christ, against the Bible, and against all religion. Communism is not only an economic interpretation of life— Communism is a religion that is inspired, directed, and motivated by the Devil himself who has declared war against Almighty God."[28] Evangelicals like Graham thrived on the dichotomies that such language promoted and the new connections to power that a full embrace of such dichotomies invited.

Yet, a fervent anticommunism was more than a strategic evangelical power grab. It was rooted in a deeply theological vision. More than a few evangelicals viewed the Cold War through the filter of end-time prophecy. Apocalyptic scenarios found biblical allusions to atomic war, Soviet aggression, and world government. More typical, however, was a general premillennial eschatology that accented the need for evangelistic urgency before Christ's imminent return. The Reverend Dr. Donald Grey Barnhouse, radio preacher, religious journalist, and World Vision board member, embodied this perspective. As historian Paul S. Boyer would paraphrase Barnhouse's editorials in his monthly magazine, *Eternity*, current civilization resembled "a truck careening downhill with no brakes." Evangelicals could prevent the collision if they erected the right barriers.[29]

Evangelicals celebrated America's Christian heritage but were also not above lamenting its sins and faithlessness. Since the rise of the youth revivals in the 1940s, new evangelicals believed revival at home was essential to end materialism, secularism, liberalism, and juvenile delinquency. Now they expanded such admonitions to the dangers of communism. In 1954, Graham preached that communism was an "anti-Christian religion competing with Christianity for American souls." He would go on to say, "The greatest and most effective weapon against Communism today is to be a born again Christian." Individual rebirth was not essential to overcome eternal damnation; it served as the key to a renewed Christian America and the antidote to communist infiltration.[30]

Evangelicals also hoped for revival abroad. The Cold War was a battle for souls. With China already closed to the gospel, evangelicals feared that Korea and the rest of Asia were not far behind. As a fervent Cold War crusader, Bob Pierce epitomized the melding of evangelical mission and American intervention abroad. With titles such as *The Red Plague*, his films often described the "battle for souls" against communism, "a godless religion spawned in hell."[31] The Cold War pitted two great opposing missionary forces, and Pierce fretted that communism was winning: "The Communists are further ahead of us in evangelizing the world than they are in science. All over the world the Russians are outpreaching us, outsacrificing us, outworking us, outplanning us, outpropagandizing us and outdying us in order to attain their own ends."[32]

He shocked his audiences by claiming that communism had gained more converts in roughly thirty years than Christianity had gained in two thousand; communist success would mean an end to Christian mission.[33] In his 1953 film *This Gathering Storm,* threatening clouds on the horizon served as metaphors for communism, materialism, and the militancy of false religions. His conclusion was unequivocal: "One must make a choice between democracy and communism; God and the devil." Pierce mastered the use of images and anecdotes to force his audiences to take action.[34] Pierce wanted Christians to fight back with the gospel of Jesus Christ, acts of mercy, and the aid of Christian civilizations like the United States.

For many neo-evangelicals like Pierce, calls for revival abroad went hand in hand with the need for political action. A few decades earlier, the Reverend Abraham Vereide had organized what would become known as the Fellowship or International Christian Leadership (ICL) to lead former Christian business and civic leaders back to faith. Vereide's "Idea," as he called it, was one part muscular Christianity and another part American exceptionalism. Like Frank Buchman and the earlier Moral Re-Armament movement, Vereide sought to cultivate the spiritual and moral stamina necessary to defend Western civilization and counter the communists. By the 1950s, the organization was attracting business and political elite to meet in small groups throughout the country. Politicians such as Lieutenant General William K. Harrison, Kansas senator Frank Carlson, and Texas governor Price Daniels served as outspoken proponents. It was Senator Carlson who convinced President Eisenhower to establish the Presidential Prayer Breakfast, and in addressing that breakfast in 1955, Carlson coined the ICL's watchword, "a worldwide spiritual offensive." Walter Judd, former missionary to China and ranking Republican member of the House Committee on Foreign Affairs, hoped that the ICL might serve as the potential spiritual counterpart to the United Nations that he predicted would ultimately turn out to be more effective.[35]

The ICL may have had even greater impact abroad than at home as small groups of Christian leaders formed throughout the world, many of whom traveled to Washington, D.C., each year for the Presidential Prayer Breakfast. Because of his connections overseas, Pierce became a reliable ICL ally, and, in turn, Pierce relished the prestige his international access afforded him. By the mid-1950s, ICL leaders Lieutenant General Harrison, Senator Carlson, and Governor Daniels served on the World Vision board while Pierce served as an official ICL field representative. He spoke on behalf of the organization in Asia as he met with Chiang Kai-shek, Syngman Rhee, and Indian prime minister Jawaharlal Nehru as well as throughout Europe when meeting with ICL honorary president Queen Wilhelmina of the Netherlands and the outgoing French prime minister Pierre Eugène Jean Pflimlin.[36] While Pierce would not give up his own calling as missionary ambassador, he shared ICL's notion that defeating communism necessitated a return to Christian faith in America and its expansion throughout the world.[37]

Evangelicals could use their newfound political engagement as a wedge to set themselves apart from mainline Protestants in making their case that they best represented the religious mainstream. After the Korean War and McCarthy's Red Scare, a handful of mainline institutions qualified their past overwhelming Cold War support. The World Council of Churches invited religious leaders from communist countries to attend its meetings. Some ecumenical leaders reconsidered their past refusal to recognize Communist China. Evangelicals seized the opportunity by accusing them of going soft on communism. They encouraged government investigations of ecumenical institutions and even insinuated that communists and socialists were pulling the strings of mainline puppets. If evangelicals positioned themselves as reliable Americans, they depicted the mainline as out of touch.[38]

Having found a popular issue that resonated with most Americans, evangelicals simply doubled down. Graham's emergence as America's leading evangelical only bolstered his active political engagement and ardent anticommunism. The NAE almost annually approved resolutions citing the evils of godless communism and promoted its pamphlet series "Christian Answers to Communism" to all its constituent churches.[39] They funded all types of anticommunist education. In 1956, the ICL underwrote the adaptation of a Pentagon filmstrip, *Militant Liberty*, to train Americans "in the principles which underlie a Christian society in contrast to the Communist

Figure 2. As an ICL field representative, Pierce often gained audiences with world leaders. Here Bob Pierce (left) and Billy Graham (right) stand beside Indian prime minister Jawaharlal Nehru in February 1956. © World Vision, Inc. 2011. All rights reserved. Reprinted by permission.

threat which challenges the free way of life."[40] In 1958, Australian physician and Baptist pastor Fred Schwarz began to travel across the country to lead popular week-long Christian Anti-Communism Crusades on the dangers of communism.[41]

By the end of the 1950s, however, having solidified their reputation as patriots, these new evangelicals found themselves forced to deal with a different issue: distancing themselves from an increasingly militant anticommunism of the Far Right. Fundamentalists such as Carl McIntire and Billy James Hargis stayed in the headlines with their anticommunist accusations, but the Christian Far Right soon felt closer to the new John Birch Society than Billy Graham's crusades or ICL's prayer breakfasts. Continuing McCarthy's witch hunts, McIntire and the Birchers even accused President Eisenhower of communist sympathies for inviting mainline Protestants to the White House. The new evangelicals feared communism, as did most Americans, but most saw the tactics of the Far Right as uncouth and conspiratorial. They would rather reestablish a Christian America without losing a sense of decorum and respect for America's institutions.[42]

Even so, evangelicals worried that the West was not up to a spiritual battle with the communists. Religious membership may have been at an all-time high, but *Christianity Today* editor Carl Henry suggested that American spirituality was superficial.[43] Pierce was even often more critical than his peers of American shortcomings. Lethargic Americans, he said, could one day face suffering and dislocation: "Will God allow Christian America to be ground under by the godless Russian hordes?" And communists were not the only threat: "Would it be worthwhile for us to suffer, for all our churches to be turned into mosques?" Danger lurked just outside American doorsteps.[44]

At the same time that Pierce challenged Americans to gird their loins against a superficial faith at home, he challenged those fighting communists abroad to leave the worst of Western culture behind. While America helped rebuild Japan after World War II, Pierce lamented that the result was not new churches but temples dedicated to commerce with a preponderance of neon signs and juke joints. The same was true in Korea, where Pierce railed that the front lines had plenty of beer and movies but no churches. With close interaction with the military throughout Asia, Pierce praised the brave soldiers who represented the best of Christian and American ideals but excoriated those who fathered children in Korea and Vietnam and then left them to return home. Many of these children became the orphans for whom World Vision took responsibility.

Perhaps precisely because of his candor, the evangelical press gave Pierce credit for doing "more to prevent the spread of communism than any other person."[45] Serving as an ICL ambassador, cultivating foreign leaders, and courting the military, Pierce helped politicize apolitical evangelicals. At home, World Vision helped fund anticommunist education such as Schwarz's Christian Anti-Communist Crusades while overwhelming American audiences with Pierce's own images of the destructive effects of communism and the heroism of Christians who persevered. Abroad, he was one of the first American evangelicals to travel behind the Iron Curtain, and he brought home reports of empty churches, persecuted Christians, and the antireligious education of Russia's youth. Americans needed, he said, to understand communism's materialist and secular ideology and see it for what it was, the enemy of both democracy and Christianity. Even with the horrors he experienced firsthand, he remained confident that, with God's help, the dominoes would fall not for communism but for Christ.[46]

An Eastward Turn: Asia

Along with evangelicals' embrace of a public theology and ardent anticommunism, World Vision's growth also coincided with a cultural moment when Americans turned their attention eastward. With the postwar rebuilding of Japan, Mao Tse-tung's revolution in China, nationalism in India, and war in Korea, Asia was a formidable challenge that drew interest not only in Washington but also in local evangelical churches. As the "Billy Graham of Asia," Pierce was perfectly placed to meet this newfound interest in Asia by regaling audiences at home with images and firsthand accounts of daily life: the bright colors of the market, the smell of kimchi, or the human-drawn rickshaws. Yet he also showed them poverty, physical deformities, and squalor.

Pierce's images were orientalist. He made Asians seem exotic, and he demonized aspects of their "heathen" cultures as symbols of their "otherness." His 1953 film, *This Gathering Storm*, advertised the chance to view "rare scenes of Hindu worship . . . millions bathing in the Ganges . . . strange temple rites." The 1958 *Cry in the Night* offered a Balinese cockfight, a cremation ceremony, and a never before filmed ritual dance of "demon possession." At times, Pierce depicted Asians as gullible, naive masses whose false religions, poverty, and traditionalism meant that they stood little chance of resisting the lures of communism, materialism, and fatalism.[47]

At other times, though, Pierce portrayed Eastern commonalities with the West, highlighting shared democratic and Christian beliefs.[48] This message, too, found resonance in the politics and popular culture of the 1950s. In 1955, Eisenhower launched his People to People program to increase understanding between Americans and Asians. The popular novels and essays of James Michener gave him a reputation among many Americans as an Asian expert. Rodgers and Hammerstein's hit musicals *South Pacific* and *The King and I* romanticized Asian culture, depicting Asians not as a "yellow peril" but as childlike innocents. American filmmakers said to Asians, in effect, that the country was "getting to know you."[49] And the movies drew American applause.

Figure 3. This Gathering Storm, advertised on the back cover of *Youth for Christ* magazine, September 1953. © World Vision, Inc. 2011. All rights reserved. Reprinted by permission of Youth for Christ.

Asian leaders also became objects of admiration. The American press lauded them as sage and wise. Despite their "typically Asian" dictatorial and childlike qualities, the best ones were committed to Christianity and democracy. Michener noted that "Christianity persists as a major influence on the minds of the leaders of Asia. . . . They acknowledge with astonishing frequency that they owe much of their education, their attitude toward law and toward the world at large to this same alien religion."[50] No one shone in America more than the Chinese Nationalist Chiang Kai-shek, both before and after the 1949 revolution. Heralded as an "Old Testament general," he epitomized the success of the evangelistic mission. The *Christian Century* and *Time* reprinted his conversion testimony and reminded readers of his incessant Bible reading. Madame Chiang may have even eclipsed her husband's influence as she toured the United States to great acclaim among popular audiences, politicians, and church leaders. The United States offered similar treatment to South Korea's Christian president Syngman Rhee, Catholic Filipino leader Ramon Magsaysay, and South Vietnam's Catholic president Ngo Dinh Diem.[51]

Pierce capitalized on the popularity of this new generation of Asian leaders by constantly advertising his friendship with Chiang Kai-shek and his wife and reminding Americans that he had been one of the few Western evangelists to preach in their personal chapel. Even after many in the West soured on Chiang's autocratic rule after 1949, Pierce urged evangelicals to support him because he invited both democratic and missionary work in his exiled regime in Formosa.[52] Pierce also defended embattled South Korean president Syngman Rhee. He echoed Rhee's American biographers who proclaimed him "a great Messiah sent by Providence to save the Korean people" and reminded audiences of Rhee's Christian conversion by missionaries.[53] He testified to the sincerity of his faith by recounting his own personal prayers with the South Korean president. His personal friendships with Asia's leading Christian leaders assured World Vision supporters not only that the Cold War was a spiritual battle but also that Pierce was *the* credible authority on Christianity's advance in Asia.

Pierce sometimes told Americans that Asians were just like them. They merely sought freedom and a better life. He admired them for their hard work and their fight against communism. Pierce recounted a typical conversation he had after preaching in a Korean school: "We want you to preach your Christ, because even though most of us on the faculty are not Christians, we know that only Christianity offers a challenge strong enough and stirring enough to turn these young people from Communism." He reported that even unchurched Koreans respected the ties between Christianity and democracy and yearned for American freedoms.[54]

Though he labeled non-Christian religions as "heathen" and "backwards," he lauded the exemplary faith of Korea's Christians. Where was Christianity most alive? Pierce pointed to the small and often persecuted churches of Asia. He marveled at the size of the crowds and the number of conversions at his crusades. Thousands of Christians, he reported, traveled for hours to gather for predawn prayer meetings, and many ended up becoming martyrs for their faith.

As he exposed American Christians to their brothers and sisters in Christ across the world, he challenged his fellow evangelicals to follow in their footsteps. In serving as Billy Graham's guide throughout Asia for an international Billy Graham Evangelistic Association (BGEA) crusade, Pierce recounted convincing his friend of the vibrancy of the global church. Graham reported that through his first trips outside the West, he had seen glimpses of the apostolic church: "My travels in Asia and Africa have enabled me to meet so many Christians whose spiritual commitment, sensitiveness, and discipline are greater than anything I find at home (and) I shall not be surprised if more and more of them come to Europe and North America as 'missionaries.' "[55] The prospect of reverse missions to re-evangelize the West commended Christian work abroad while criticizing complacency at home. It also kept the future of Asia seared into the minds of many Americans.

The Revival of Evangelical Missions and a New Social Message

Film producer Dick Ross noted that "nobody in his generation had the impact on behalf of mission on the domestic audience as Bob Pierce."[56] As the United States reasserted itself as a global power and Americans turned their attention eastward, they debated the future of "Red" China, watched Korean War news serials, and fretted over communist influence in India, Indonesia, and Vietnam. At the same time, they supported a rising tide of missionaries and mission agencies that sought to evangelize the world. The rise of World Vision exemplified Americans' postwar passion for missions as Pierce embodied a new generation of religious entrepreneurs eager to

Figure 4. Billy Graham shares a Bible story with Korean children at a World Vision–sponsored orphanage. Bob Pierce served as a key liaison during Graham's first evangelistic tour of Asia, 1952. (Pierce, in bowtie, is in the middle of the crowd listening to Graham's message.) © World Vision, Inc. 2011. All rights reserved. Reprinted by permission.

reestablish evangelicals as the custodians of a Christian America and a revived internationalism.

A united missionary impulse had dissolved several decades earlier. By the 1920s, theological debates between fundamentalists and modernists had spilled over into denominational mission boards that saw a decline in finances and new candidates as they refocused attention away from evangelistic zeal toward social action and a shared world Christianity. Their missiology evolved as a response to the social sciences, nationalism, indigenization principles, and internationalism. As a result, many conservatives withdrew from the denominational mission boards and started their own independent mission agencies. Yet, even with these losses and their intentionally smaller Western footprint, the mainline boards maintained ten times more missionaries than the conservative independent agencies between 1920 and 1950.[57]

A number of new conservative mission agencies had started as independent "faith missions" in the late nineteenth century. Living "by faith," these missionaries relied only on God's provision for their financial support and did not assume a salary like the missionaries appointed by denominational boards. They also were willing to commission those who did not meet the standards of mainline denominational boards, such as single women or those without seminary training. The only requirement was often conservative doctrinal agreement.

The number of faith missions expanded as fundamentalists increasingly abandoned denominational boards. During this expansion, many of these agencies evolved from a "generalized, self-sufficient missionary society model" into specialized agencies. While "evangelism" still dominated, new ministries included Wycliffe Bible Translators, which focused on linguistics, the Far East Gospel Broadcasting Company, which pursued radio evangelism, and the Mission Aviation Fellowship, which flew missionaries into remote locations. Toiling outside the limelight of mainstream popular culture, these organizations combined optimism and technology to meet the challenge of worldwide evangelization while garnering prestige within independent fundamentalist networks.[58]

The end of World War II catapulted record numbers of new missionaries, under the traditional mainline mission boards as well as fundamentalist and newer evangelical missionary agencies, into the mission field with ample finances and confidence in American exceptionalism. General Douglas MacArthur challenged American churches to send ten thousand missionaries to Asia, and the churches surpassed his goal. By the end of the 1940s, however, the mainline had now fallen behind the new evangelicals. Former U.S. soldiers returned to study in Bible colleges on the GI Bill, joined mission societies, and returned overseas. If the number of mainline missionaries once far outpaced evangelicals, by 1955 conservative missionaries constituted the majority.[59]

As conservative missions expanded, they also sought to move from the margins to the mainstream of American culture, and their new missionary institutions often looked quite different from their predecessors. Dozens of religious entrepreneurs built specialized mission organizations like Youth for Christ, the Navigators, the Billy Graham Evangelistic Association, and World Vision. Evangelicals still clung to an optimism that could accomplish the "evangelization of the world in this generation," even if they consciously also aligned themselves with a 1950s popular civic faith and against what they considered a liberal mainline. Mainline missiology valued ecumenism and indigenization, but evangelicals largely ignored these aims. They remained high on optimism even if short on mission theory. Christians could reclaim America for Christ and accept the global responsibility that an American exceptionalism implied, but as the new majority, conservative missionaries saw evangelism as their priority.[60]

As a missionary service organization, World Vision grew as it sought to promote the expansion of an evangelical missionary enterprise. The organization's message amalgamated the popular rhetoric of American exceptionalism, Cold War ideology, orientalism, and missionary service into a familiar evangelical idiom. Yet, Pierce also pushed many evangelicals beyond their comfort zone with explicit humanitarian needs. Although theologian Carl Henry tried in 1947 to prick the "uneasy conscience" of evangelicals and told them to get to work in the world, most of them preferred conservative patriotism and popular revivalism. Setting themselves against the mainline, evangelicals would be "spiritual" not "social gospelers." They would stand on the Rock of Ages—and not move from there. In contrast to public theologians like Henry, however, Pierce built his organization on prayer and pragmatism. He had little patience for theologians who debated the explicit relationship between evangelism and social action. Pierce acknowledged both were essential and pointed to World Vision's simultaneous first purchases for its 1950s work in India as an example: a medical clinic and a tent for evangelistic crusades.[61]

In other words, Pierce avoided the dichotomy between evangelism and social action that had ripped apart the Protestant missionary enterprise. Without doubt, the gospel came first for him. He wanted conversions. But he wanted more: "We must meet people's physical needs so that we can meet their real (spiritual) needs."[62] He believed that conversion even led to material benefits, helping to alleviate poverty and ward off communism. Because he put conversion first, Americans evangelicals listened to his call for social amelioration. That was no small achievement.

Pierce motivated his audiences by highlighting individual needs over structural issues. He showed images of victims who suffered through no fault of their own: lepers, orphans, and widows. "If you believe God is interested in your aches and pains, don't you think the leper's sores touch His heart with compassion? Don't you think He hears the cry of starving children?"[63] In the America that he knew, too much talk about the "structural" causes of poverty had a "Red" tinge. Pierce called for Christian charity, not for structural justice.

Yet even if his depictions were through a particular lens, Pierce exposed American evangelicals to a world to which they might not have otherwise paid much attention. He shocked them with graphic images of destitute orphans overseas juxtaposed with well-fed, middle-class American children. He also contrasted pictures of orphans before and after World Vision's support: the malnourished Korean orphan in one photo appeared in a later photo as a healthy and happy child, flourishing in a World Vision orphanage.[64] He was also not shy in chastising Americans, blinded and unwilling to acknowledge what was happening beyond their comfortable pews, for their inaction. Yet his criticism was matched by an abiding trust that once American Christians saw the severity of humanitarian needs through a personal face, they would act. Pierce might not have convinced many evangelicals to become missionaries, but in casting his dramatic images and fresh approach alongside an increasingly popular American exceptionalism, he convinced a lot of them to open their pocketbooks.

A Rhetoric of Sacrifice

If Pierce dismissed heady theology, he specialized in emotion. Through his emotional appeals he perfected a rhetoric of sacrifice that served as the glue binding a fervent religious anticommunism, focus on Asia, and missionary zeal to his new evangelical humanitarian message. As a missionary ambassador bringing this message to the attention of comfortable American evangelicals, Pierce himself embodied the sacrifice he preached. "You cannot choose whether or not you will suffer," Pierce proclaimed. "The only thing you can choose is what you will suffer for." During World War II, Americans had bought war bonds, joined the Women's Army Corps (WAC), and planted victory gardens. At war's end, they commemorated the sacrifice of soldiers who gave their lives for a righteous cause. Now they applied the rhetoric of sacrifice and righteousness to the Cold War and the Korean conflict. Pierce capitalized on the language of shared sacrifice in claiming that World Vision's purpose was "to burden America with the physical and spiritual needs of foreign missions, resulting in an unprecedented increase in praying, giving and going to the mission field."[65]

The exemplars of sacrifice were persecuted Christians in Asian churches, and Pierce used "the suffering of the masses in Korea" as "a symbol of all lands under oppression." He praised their dedication, and when he introduced the Asian Christian leaders whom he placed before American audiences, he highlighted their sacrifice: "ready to give up everything, who will live on half enough food, to sleep in the dust and dirt, who face disease and death and persecution, and be cast out of their homes to preach."[66] He claimed that 80 percent of Korean Christian leaders died as martyrs at the hands of the communists during the Korean War. He told stories about the torture and death of Korean pastors and even depicted such atrocities in his films. Like the New Testament church, Pierce depicted Korean Christianity as "born in martyrdom and refined in the furnace of affliction."[67] Pierce reasoned that God had allowed this suffering to rouse a complacent Western Christianity and to challenge Americans to respond in kind. Typical was the response of Billy Graham, who, after Pierce led him on a tour of World Vision's work in Korea, mentioned feeling overwhelmed by the suffering of Asian Christians. "I came to the Orient a boy," Graham said, "I'm going home a man."[68]

Alongside Korean Christians, the other prime exemplars of sacrifice for Pierce were missionaries. They ministered to people, with truth and tangible goods, in impossible settings. Often remaining in war-torn countries after other expatriates had fled, they stretched their limited resources to care for the sick or take in orphans. Through their testimonies, Pierce tried to recruit even more missionaries. High on adventure and sacrifice, he attempted to coax American evangelicals away from comfort and safety in order to save the world. His only requirement remained a penchant for suffering.[69]

Of course, Pierce viewed his own life as a symbol of the sacrifice he preached. He claimed that he "made an agreement with God that I'll take care of His helpless little lambs overseas if He'll take care of mine at home." The months abroad meant Pierce often missed family events or holidays at home. The burden of travel as well as the horrors of war and disease sometimes left him irritable with family and coworkers. His health suffered too. World Vision's board suggested he take time away for mental and physical recuperation. He would often be forced to take extended medical leaves to

Figure 5. Bob Pierce in prayer during Korean travels in the 1950s. © World Vision, Inc. 2011. All rights reserved. Reprinted by permission.

regain sufficient strength for the work into which he poured himself, but he continued to live at the same pace, praying only that he might "burn out for God."[70]

As a missionary ambassador, Pierce saw himself literally as the bridge between American evangelicals and suffering Asians. One World Vision appeal letter asked supporters "to consider Bob Pierce as your emissary representing you as a good Samaritan giving help to beaten, down-trodden, naked, homeless humanity."[71] While certainly extending beyond mere metaphor, sacrifice served as an essential part of World Vision's emerging message, and Pierce played the leading role. He predicted his own death at the hands of the communists, preaching, "You cannot choose whether or not you will die—all you can choose is what you will die for." Few would follow Pierce's lead, but he along with his beloved missionaries and faithful Asian Christians could be sacrificial ambassadors for the safety and security of American Christians.[72]

In 1950, World Vision began as a new kind of evangelical mission. As the go-between for American Christians and a world in need, Pierce, with his shocking images and personal stories, opened the eyes of American evangelicals to meet the spiritual and physical needs of Asia's masses. He talked like a preacher, a missionary, a patriot, a businessman, a soldier, and a Cold War politician, flowing seamlessly from one to the other. Pierce's folksy message sidestepped theological debates, sometimes criticizing fellow evangelicals through their own vernacular even as he remained firmly ensconced within the American evangelical subculture himself. While it cost him tremendously, Pierce's message and personal sacrifice enabled World Vision's initial success. As he developed his own unique message of global humanitarianism that sometimes challenged his American audiences, he spoke as a leading proponent of evangelicals' efforts to reenter mainstream culture, domestic politics, and international affairs at the vanguard of a renewed popular belief in American exceptionalism. Yet, Pierce was a different kind of evangelical; World Vision would offer a different kind of evangelical message.

CHAPTER 3

A Growing Organization and
the Evolving Identity of American Evangelicalism

PIERCE OFFERED AMERICAN EVANGELICALS a new humanitarian message that resonated with their renewed interest in shaping values both at home and abroad. At the same time, his message prodded many American evangelicals beyond their comfort zones. Through World Vision, Pierce demonstrated a new way of doing missions. To make it happen, he built a new type of organization.

Just like Pierce himself, World Vision did not always fit easily alongside its evangelical peers. It often struggled to find its place as an organization even as Pierce emerged as one of the most recognizable evangelical celebrities of the 1950s. Yet Pierce's willingness to beg, borrow, and steal from others and his insistence to forge ahead despite resistance led to World Vision's continued growth. Innovations in programming abroad and new models of marketing and fund-raising at home would come to define the monumental success of World Vision. Dozens of faith-based relief agencies and hundreds of new evangelical parachurch agencies would follow suit. It was this parachurch model that would largely come to define American evangelicalism over the ensuing decades.

Pierce established World Vision in 1950 to account for the emergency funds he raised at the outbreak of war, $40,000 in the first year. By the end of the 1950s, World Vision was spending a million dollars annually, supporting 13,215 orphans throughout Asia, and operating an additional 250 projects in twenty-five total countries.[1] It was producing a national monthly mission magazine, a weekly radio show, and award-winning docudramas screened around the world. What started merely as an organization to hold funds that Pierce raised and quickly distributed to missionaries he encountered now had to develop processes and procedures as it grew in size and sophistication. Throughout the 1950s, the organization struggled to keep pace with its eccentric founder even as it fought to find its way among its evangelical, missionary, and humanitarian peers.

Pierce despised institutionalism and felt that strategic planning denied the Spirit's work. "Those were days when things happened fast," recalled board member Carlton Booth. "Bob turned everything into an emergency. Things had to happen *now*, and you could never tell Bob why they couldn't happen that way."[2] The organization often lacked clear financial accountability and funds received rarely matched the amounts that Pierce committed or proposed to spend.

Yet, Pierce's evangelical connections and popularity lent him authority as an international expert. Through the 1950s, Americans relied on several "religious" figures to interpret Asia. Mainline Protestants had Pulitzer Prize–winning author Pearl Buck. Her best seller *The Good Earth* gave Americans a window into China, and she continued to serve as a spokesperson to the West on behalf of contemporary Asian issues.[3] Catholics had humanitarian doctor Tom Dooley whose fervent anticommunism and daring service in Southeast Asia drew the attention of popular audiences to the developing war in Vietnam.[4]

Evangelicals came to rely on Bob Pierce. They trusted his expertise as an intrepid globetrotter on the front lines. He used his cachet to challenge evangelical presuppositions, even about missions. Pierce disliked the division between social action and evangelism. He disdained missiological debates he deemed overly theological, and he came to question the overreliance on the Western missionary at the expense of training indigenous pastors. He also disliked an evangelical separatism that refused to work with nonevangelicals on the mission field. He observed that theological divisions at home made little sense overseas. Finally, even as he supported a fervent anticommunism, he sometimes challenged the lack of self-reflection and sacrifice among his fellow American Christians at home.

Pierce occasionally challenged fellow evangelicals to redefine themselves and their views of America and the world, yet he still largely reflected evangelicals' general international outlook. American evangelicalism itself was changing in the 1950s, and often World Vision led the way. While Pierce did not always receive an invitation from the institutional gatekeepers to sit among the evangelical brass at conferences in Wheaton or Washington, he was a trusted guide for the tens of thousands listening to his electrifying stories of global mission through the radio, soaking in scenes from abroad via his films, or sending in a dollar after opening a letter signed by Pierce asking for his supporters to meet an immediate need. A majority of evangelicals looked to him for guidance. He was, after all, one of them.

Pierce had little patience for the status quo, anywhere and anytime. In fact, he thrived on constant change. With little strategic direction, he would take on additional commitments and programs wherever he felt he could make a difference, and World Vision's managers were often left to piece together how to resource Pierce's constant expansion. In the 1950s, the field of service was Korea, and World Vision continued to spend most of its money there, but as the war ended and Americans' attention drifted, Pierce also looked to other parts of Asia.

He had always supported work in other countries. At Madame Chiang Kai-shek's request, Pierce provided a copy of the Gospel of John to all of her husband's soldiers in Formosa. From his earliest trips to China, he had supported the work of the Canadian Presbyterian missionary Lillian Dickson among Formosa's mountain tribes, and he expanded World Vision's presence in Japan, India, the Philippines, and Vietnam. World Vision's expansion gave it a reputation as an Asian organization, so much so that in 1956 Billy Graham asked Pierce to accompany him on his crusade tour of Asia because no other evangelical had better connections on the continent.[5]

Yet even through rapid expansion, World Vision's identity as a missionary service organization remained central. Pierce repeatedly refused to establish his own institutions; rather he would fund the emergency needs of missionaries already on the ground: a month's food, supplies for a destitute leper colony, or a jeep for moving between villages. At other times, he would build an orphanage, leprosarium, or medical clinic only to hand over the keys and administration to missionaries and local Christians. Pierce's incessant search for the next need certainly gave him no patience for serving as administrator or landlord, and it often made World Vision a bit unpredictable. Such a haphazard approach, however, often allowed Pierce to be the first on the scene to respond to an emergency while being institutionally light. Relying on his rapport with missionaries and their willingness to take on administration of World Vision's initial work allowed him to dabble in new programs in new places as well as return home to champion missionaries as forgotten heroes and raise funds on their behalf.

One of those roles that Pierce, the former Youth for Christ ambassador, could not relinquish was international evangelist. As his reputation grew, Pierce began to headline large World Vision crusades. In 1956, he reported over five thousand conversions in Manila in the Philippines. In 1957, he counted over seventy thousand Koreans attending his Seoul crusade. In 1959, World Vision promoted its largest crusade in Osaka, Japan. Pierce came at the invitation of the local churches, but the crusades resembled his early YFC rallies. Focusing on Pierce's celebrity, the papers reported that "a great man of God" had come to the city. Ralph Carmichael, a noted composer of contemporary Christian music, accompanied Pierce on the trip to lead a three-hundred-voice Japanese choir and the city's symphony orchestra in his original compositions. The three-week crusade was the longest in Japanese history. It drew over 96,000 people to the city's largest auditorium and recorded 7,457 decisions for Christ. Tens of thousands more listened and watched on Japanese radio and television.[6]

World Vision did not limit its activities in Japan to crusade evangelism. Each day, staff also met with university students, businessmen, and civic leaders to instill in them moral and spiritual values, often with an American coloration. Asians were open to the gospel; Pierce proclaimed it while also trying to intertwine Christian faith with democratic ideals. With international press coverage and local support, the crusades went a long way toward establishing World Vision's name throughout Asia and rivaling what America's leading evangelist, Billy Graham, was setting out to accomplish internationally.

Yet if Pierce's crusades promoted an American-style evangelism, he also encouraged "indigenous" or "national" Christian pastors. In 1953, Pierce established World Vision pastor conferences to bring together local pastors for education, mutual encouragement, and fellowship. Akin to World Vision's origin story, where missionary Tena Hoelkeboer thrust an orphan into Pierce's arms and asked him what he was going to do about the needs of this single child, Pierce also traced this new ministry's origin to a single story: the widow of a martyred Korean pastor. Pressing her wedding ring into Pierce's hand, she asked that the proceeds from the sale of her only valuable possession be used to support Korean Christian leaders. That same year, 1953, Pierce brought together more than three hundred pastors. By 1954, he gathered more than two thousand, claiming that it was the largest gathering of clergy ever assembled in the Orient.[7]

Pierce had always promoted indigenous pastors alongside missionaries as heroes who sacrificed for the gospel, and so he expanded the conferences throughout Asia. By the end of the decade, World Vision had replicated the model in Africa and Latin America, staging five to six conferences a year, gathering around four thousand pastors for a week of training. American evangelical personalities such as prominent pastor and past NAE president Paul Rees, *Christianity Today* editor Carl Henry, and ICL insider Richard (Dick) Halverson anchored the programs as instructors. Over time, Pierce also recruited Asian Christian leaders to join the teaching team. K. C. Han, pastor of Korea's largest church, joined Mar Thoma bishop Alexander Mar Theophilus and Indian evangelist Rochunga Pudaite as frequent speakers on Pierce's tours. They offered the basics of pastoral ministry: the art of preaching, Bible study, and theological foundations. They also provided spiritual renewal and Christian fellowship while challenging the pastors to return to their communities with a revived energy for evangelism.[8]

World Vision's support of pastors' conferences, however, went beyond encouraging the local forgotten pastor. Pierce came to see these indigenous pastors as the key to Christianity's future outside the West to counter what he saw as a rise of heathenism, communism, and nationalism that he feared would soon "engulf the world."[9] Pierce also feared the further expulsion of Western missionaries throughout Asia that he had already witnessed in China, and so he encouraged fellow Americans to see it as their duty to train indigenous pastors for the day when the "welcome mat is pulled from beneath the white man."[10]

Indigenous leaders were necessary for another reason. "No matter how appealing the foreign message may be, and no matter how attractive the personality, it is still something packaged in America," Pierce acknowledged. "The day has passed when an American can command respect simply because he is an American. . . . The day of the white man and his work is coming to a close." As a result, Pierce's mantra became "if Asia is to be won for Christ, it must be won by Asians."[11]

According to Pierce, the pastors' conferences could also build "true ecumenicity." Before committing to a pastors' conference, World Vision required a joint invitation and commitment from all local churches. Pierce contrasted his conferences to the ecumenicity illustrated by the institutional ecumenical movement that seemed to bring a few select leaders together for highbrow debates. World Vision claimed that it engendered "practical ecumenicity—that many of the ecumenicists have not been able to create by articles and lengthy discourses on the subject." In funding the training of local pastors, World Vision also brought the power of the purse. As an interdenominational agency offering financial support, World Vision broke down denominational isolation and moved beyond theological and liturgical differences to create a greater diversity than almost any other Christian organization. In acknowledging World Vision's commitment to both indigenous missions and pragmatic ecumenicity, the best-known missionary in Afghanistan, J. Christy Wilson, endorsed World Vision as "practically the only interdenominational and independent group which works in full cooperation with the established missions on the field *and* the indigenous churches."[12]

Alongside his main task of supporting missionaries and emergency relief, Pierce's investment into evangelistic crusades and indigenous pastors' conferences shaped his young organization. But Pierce soon found an even more compelling cause to spur growth, a cause that would come to define World Vision as it soon became known as one of the largest child-sponsorship agencies. War orphans had become a major problem in Korea. Both sides—northern communists and South Korean soldiers would destroy entire villages, leaving only the children as survivors to fend for themselves. In addition, American soldiers fathered children with Korean women and often abandoned them when returning home. As mixed-raced children unaccepted within Korean culture, they were often abandoned by their Korean families as well. By 1954, there were over 170,000 orphans in Korea alone, only 50,000 of whom could be housed in existing orphanages.[13]

After staring into the faces of too many of these innocent children, Pierce quickly determined to make orphan care the backbone of World Vision's early ministry. "I never intended to be in the orphanage business," Pierce declared, but "taking care of orphans" was "the little job God has given me to do."[14] At first, he funneled resources through an array of denominational and missionary agencies with already established orphanage ministries. Funding whoever he could find already doing the work fit Pierce's pragmatic ecumenicity. In any given year during the 1950s, World Vision would send funds to the independent Oriental Missionary Society (OMS) and Australian Presbyterian Mission as well as denominations such as the Southern Presbyterians, Methodists, Southern Baptists, and Assemblies of God. When the pressing need could not be met by funding existing orphanages, Pierce would raise funds to build his own and then turn them over to missionaries or Korean Christians to administer.

The ministry to orphans led to dramatic expansion of budgets and fund-raising success as Pierce introduced the concept of child sponsorship to his American audiences. In 1953, Pierce recruited Erwin and Florence Raetz to head World Vision's orphan program in Korea. Pierce had met the Raetzes in China where they served with the China Children's Fund (CCF). While historians can point to individual child-sponsorship programs as early as 1920 in response to war-torn Europe and in the 1930s to meet the needs of U.S. children in Appalachia, CCF popularized the child-sponsorship program so much that it was often given credit for originating the concept.[15] Presbyterian minister J. Calvitt Clarke founded China's Children Fund in 1938, but he soon changed CCF's name to the Christian Children's Fund as it was forced to leave China under the new Communist government in 1949. With child sponsorship central, CCF grew throughout Asia and beyond to become the seventh largest among all private voluntary organizations (PVOs) by 1960 with an annual budget over $4.5 million.[16]

CCF remained a Christian organization even if some donors and staffers came to believe their mission was not "religious" enough. The Raetzes fit the latter category. After successfully developing the child-sponsorship model for CCF, the Raetzes left the organization once CCF administrators began to allow Buddhists to be placed in charge of their Christian orphanages. The Raetzes felt that CCF overlooked evangelism in focusing on the social ministries of feeding and clothing. Pierce saw this as an opportunity and reminded the Raetzes that evangelism remained central for World Vision, and he persuaded the couple to replicate what they had done for CCF in China for World Vision in Korea.[17]

A year later in 1954, World Vision unveiled its child-sponsorship program. Prospective donors could select a child from several dozen pictures included in a direct mail appeal, a World Vision advertisement in a religious periodical, or at an event where Pierce would speak or screen his newest film. World Vision would then forward funds to the Christian institutions caring for the children, and fixed percentages went for food, clothing, education, and religious teaching. In just two years, the funds devoted to orphanages mushroomed from $57,000 to $452,538. The number of sponsored orphans grew from 2,216 in 1954 to 13,215 by the end of the decade as orphan care grew from 44 percent to 79 percent of World Vision's Korean work.[18]

Child sponsorship quickly became the backbone of World Vision's financial success. The image of the innocent child helped World Vision

Figure 6. Advertisement for World Vision's Korean child sponsorship program, World Vision pamphlet, circa mid-1950s. © World Vision, Inc. 2011. All rights reserved. Reprinted by permission.

bypass divisive theological debates over the social structures of poverty while also avoiding donors' paralysis that can come from overwhelming statistics. Pierce presented an individual orphan, often the victim of war, with whom donors could develop a relationship. Sponsors exchanged photos and letters with their "foster" child as well as sending clothes, candy, and Bibles.

In the process, child sponsorship raised World Vision's profile by bringing it to the attention of both churches and other agencies. These funds soon also provided a new stream of income that differentiated it from many of its peer mission and relief agencies of similar size. Those agencies often depended primarily on either government or denominational funds; World Vision instead appealed to the public for support through relatively small but regular gifts. If new programs led to new fund-raising methods, it also positioned World Vision to grow in sustained ways that few other mission agencies were able to follow.

World Vision grew as Pierce personalized the overwhelming humanitarian need abroad in the language through which American evangelicals felt

comfortable; he also promoted the message by embracing all forms of popular media underutilized by his peer and predecessor religious institutions.
Pierce was an evangelist abroad and a trailblazer in publicity at home.

His films probably remained his most popular innovation. To a community that often had refused even to attend Hollywood movies, the documentaries both taught and entertained. Conservative Christians always
came to embrace new media and technology; they had already come to
dominate the radio waves. Pierce's films found a welcome audience among
evangelicals eager to do the same with moving pictures. While in 1939 only
one hundred U.S. churches owned film projectors, by 1954, the number
reached sixty thousand.[19]

Pierce was not the first to produce religious films, and other leading
parachurch agencies like the Billy Graham Evangelistic Association and
Campus Crusade soon followed suit, but no one produced as many and
relied on them as heavily as Pierce. He screened them at churches, mission conferences, and civic auditoriums, sometimes attracting audiences
of five to six thousand. Churches remained on waiting lists of six to eight
months for a scheduled showing. Realizing early on that he had reached
his own technical filmmaking limitations, Pierce hired the young filmmaker Dick Ross, who had left the burgeoning Christian film industry at
Moody to work back in Hollywood. Ross cut Pierce's original 1949 film
China Challenge, which fellow evangelicals boasted remained "one of the
most widely viewed and discussed 16 mm sound motion pictures ever
filmed." Even before he had officially founded World Vision, Pierce
formed Great Commission Films, guaranteeing Ross's first year's salary
to produce these new mission films full time. During the 1950s, World
Vision averaged more than one film a year, relying predominantly on
Pierce's firsthand footage from overseas but also experimenting with studio actors and original film scores.[20] Pierce spent large sums of money
and used cutting-edge technology in hopes of keeping up with Hollywood. The same year Hollywood produced a movie in "wide-screen Cin-
erama," World Vision followed suit, advertising that "it made the viewer
part of the scene."[21] Many future staffers for World Vision and leading
evangelical agencies began their careers as summer employees tasked to
travel the country, book screenings, set up the films, and collect offerings
for World Vision's work. Over a typical ten-month period in 1956–57,
World Vision reported that 58,914 people viewed at least one if its traveling films in screenings around the country.[22]

Figure 7. Pierce addressing an audience in a recording of *Bob Pierce Reports*, World Vision's national radio program. © World Vision, Inc. 2011. All rights reserved. Reprinted by permission.

If his films were the first innovation that put World Vision on the map, Pierce sought to diversify his media footprint in his efforts to make himself and World Vision a household name. He initiated a coast-to-coast radio broadcast in 1956. Evangelicals had flourished through radio, but *Bob Pierce Reports* was unique in that it adopted the variety show format with a specific focus on missions. Each week, Pierce recounted his international travels, juxtaposing the songs of the World Vision Quartet with short sermons, breaking news updates, and on-site interviews with missionaries and indigenous pastors around the world. At its peak, World Vision broadcast *Bob Pierce Reports* on 140 stations. Each show gave listeners the opportunity to become a child sponsor or support the "mission of the month." World Vision would send thank-you gifts such as records, books, or handicrafts to those who supported their ministry, and they systematically tracked which giveaways served as the highest incentive for donors to respond.

In 1957, World Vision began publishing the monthly *World Vision* magazine, which soon overtook and dwarfed the size of rival missions magazines. Having hired Larry Ward, the first managing director of *Christianity Today*, away from what had quickly become the flagship evangelical publication, Pierce tasked his new staff to use the new magazine to interpret the global headlines through a lens of Christian mission while also raising money.[23] It was a mix of serious theological reflection, missionary stories to be used in local churches, and, of course, haunting images of those in need. The magazine won national awards for its reporting, but perhaps more important for Pierce, it moved donors emotionally. The magazine would quickly double World Vision's income.

Pierce's new methods became models for others. After Pierce boasted to Billy Graham that he should also invest in film, Graham engaged Pierce's Great Commission Films to produce his first few pictures. Along with Great Commission Films' producer Dick Ross, Graham would give credit to Pierce for convincing him of the power of the medium, but Graham's budgets and popularity would soon lead him to produce movies on a scale impossible for a young World Vision. Yet it did not keep Pierce from a healthy sense of competition. While he would often hire away the best and brightest from other evangelical agencies with his powers of persuasion, Pierce could take great offense when he found himself on the other end. With Pierce hospitalized from exhaustion in Europe, Graham hired away Dick Ross, the mastermind behind World Vision's film production. In 1956, just a few years after Pierce had introduced Graham to filmmaking, Great Commission Films merged into Graham's own new film company, World Wide Pictures. Pierce felt betrayed by both Ross and Graham, and while World Vision's film production continued, later films no longer set World Vision apart in the same way.[24]

Pierce may have continued to hold a grudge, but he did get over his sense of betrayal enough to continue working with Graham. Few in the evangelical world had the luxury of ignoring Graham's soaring popularity. Boasting about the success of *World Vision* magazine, Pierce now convinced Graham that he needed his own organization organ beyond his constant coverage in the popular press. The result was Graham's *Decision* magazine, which drew thousands of supporters and additional funds to Graham's ministry.[25]

Pierce never shied away from drumming up attention for himself and World Vision's work. In 1955, wealthy Oregon farmer Harry Holt approached World Vision after watching one of Pierce's Korean films. Holt had already sponsored a number of orphans but wanted to do more, to adopt them and bring them to the United States. While World Vision communicated that it preferred for Korean orphans be cared for in Korea, the organization made allowances for the multiracial children fathered by American GIs. News of these impending international adoptions drew the widest media coverage World Vision had received up to that point, as Pierce and Holt had to lobby to change federal law to allow for the adoptions. Then as the plane with the first orphans arrived, Pierce was there smiling for the snapping flashbulbs as he carried each orphan off the plane in his arms. On a subsequent trip, Pierce delivered a Korean orphan to adoptive parents and Hollywood celebrities Roy Rogers and Dale Evans. Media outlets from the *New York Times* to *Life* magazine covered the event. Both Holt and Pierce carried outsized personalities, and working together proved difficult. In fact, Holt despised Pierce's publicity seeking, and he would soon start his own organization, Holt International, which remains one of the largest international adoption agencies in the United States.[26] Yet Pierce argued that the publicity aided World Vision by introducing the organization to mass audiences beyond the evangelicals who had typically supported his work to that point.[27]

Pierce's penchant for publicity went hand in hand with World Vision's innovative fund-raising practices. Like other mission organizations, World Vision placed advertisements in evangelical magazines, but it avoided traditional ad copy and instead displayed pictures of specific orphans whom donors could sponsor. It developed an extensive mailing list to which Pierce mailed personal appeals. Unlike most other agencies, World Vision did not depend on denominational or even local church partnerships. Pierce spoke directly to the donor.

Even as World Vision continued to become increasingly sophisticated in its fund-raising and marketing, Pierce modeled for the organization his tried-and-true technique of raising an offering by "passing the plate again." Like the faith missionaries he often supported, Pierce also subscribed to what he called the "God room" principle: God alone could provide the resources, and Pierce committed funding in his overseas travels that World Vision did not yet have. Only then would he pray in hopes the funding would follow.[28]

Pierce often did find his prayers answered when the funding came, but it rarely came through big gifts. While the evangelical world had few Rockefellers and Carnegies, it did have wealthy supporters like Herbert Taylor and Howard Pew to bankroll new ventures.[29] Initially, these donors were not interested in World Vision. Pierce's organization relied on small gifts, and he celebrated such an approach: "I would rather have eighty thousand people praying for us and giving us a dollar apiece, than one man giving us eighty thousand dollars."[30] His aim, after all, was to spread World Vision's mission to a broad constituency. He wanted it to support global missions in a way that offered a model of compassionate charity.

World Vision and International Humanitarianism

Even as Pierce adopted new methods at home and abroad, he insisted that World Vision remain true to its original purpose as a "missionary service organization meeting emergency needs in crisis areas of the world through existing evangelical agencies." By 1958, it came to articulate that specific purpose through five objectives: (1) Christian social welfare; (2) emergency aid; (3) evangelistic outreach; (4) Christian leadership development; (5) missionary challenge. World Vision's work in evangelism, pastors' conferences, and missions education were significant parts of its mission, but the first two (social welfare and emergency aid) were where World Vision came to spend the bulk of its time and money as it earned a reputation for its rapid response to humanitarian crises through its religious networks.

By exposing its largely evangelical constituency to physical need without belittling evangelism, World Vision carved out a unique identity. Pierce retained his close link to evangelical missions even while initially keeping his distance from other religious humanitarian agencies. Evangelical mission agencies proliferated in numbers and budgets throughout the 1950s, but they remained outside the circle of political and cultural power. In contrast, the "three faiths consortium" of mainline Protestants, Catholics, and Jews had ties with the U.S. government, which often aided and structured international humanitarian efforts. As Franklin Roosevelt enshrined "freedom from want" into his Four Freedoms, new international institutions such as the United Nations, International Monetary Fund, and World Bank sought to alleviate global poverty. Roosevelt established the American Council of Voluntary Agencies for Foreign Service (ACVAFS) to coordinate the relief work of American private voluntary agencies. In his 1949 inauguration address, President Harry Truman elevated PVOs by establishing his Point Four Program. Infused with a postwar renewal of belief in American exceptionalism and the need to contain communism, Truman claimed that a modernized West could relieve the world's suffering through international relief and development.[31]

A host of religious philanthropies, honed by their voluntary work during World War II, offered themselves as agencies to realize Truman's vision.[32] Catholic Relief Services (founded in 1943), Church World Service (1946), Lutheran World Relief (1945), CARE (1945), and the American Jewish Joint Distribution Committee (1914) captured the public imagination in the 1940s and attained wide recognition during the Cold War, especially through their work in Korea and Vietnam.[33] By 1947, 75 percent of private philanthropy overseas flowed through these Protestant, Catholic, and Jewish agencies. In the early 1950s, religious (rather than secular) agencies also received a majority of the federal aid for international humanitarianism.

In 1953, the International Cooperation Administration succeeded the ACVAFS to coordinate distribution efforts. While these agencies emerged as a perpetual alphabet soup, they served as the forerunners of the current United States Agency for International Development (USAID) established in 1961. With the U.S. government's passage of the Food for Peace legislation (Pub.L. 480, the Agricultural Trade Development and Assistance Act of 1954), officially registered relief organizations were allowed to apply for U.S. surplus goods as well as reimbursements for shipping costs as they transported government-donated food, surplus goods, and equipment overseas. Approval as a registered agency was not easy. Among religious agencies, the approved list covered a mix of mainline Protestants, Roman Catholics, and Jews, but it soon became an exclusive club. While not forgoing their religious identities, these increasingly large-scale agencies came to fall in line with American foreign policy and the budding language of relief and development, often highlighting humanitarian assistance over more traditional "religious work."[34]

Many of the largest religious humanitarian agencies served as arms of denominational or ecumenical bodies such as Catholic Relief Services or the National Council of Churches' Church World Service. A few independent agencies also registered with the government, such as the aforementioned Christian Children's Fund (CCF). Yet, this new fraternity of registered humanitarian agencies included few evangelicals among denominational or independent agencies.[35] One exception was World Relief. In 1944, the National Association of Evangelicals established the War Relief Commission to transport food and clothing to displaced Europeans; they renamed it World Relief in 1950, hoping to offer both material and spiritual goods. The agency registered to receive government aid in 1956 and grew modestly in size but worried about the risk of minimizing evangelism. World Relief funded humanitarian projects: hospitals, orphanages, and widow homes. It also shipped surplus food and clothing overseas. In each shipment, however, recipients would always find Bibles and religious tracts.[36] Its limited size and evangelistic proclivities left World Relief on the periphery of humanitarianism's inner circle.

If World Relief was kept at arm's length by the mainstream humanitarian establishment, this was even truer of World Vision, which they outright dismissed for its small size and sectarian evangelical theology. Such critiques rarely bothered Pierce. As an evangelical organization, he declared that World Vision operated in a different context. Fraternizing too closely with ecumenical mainline Protestants, much less Catholics, Jews, or secularists, was anathema. It also bordered upon promoting social welfare at the expense of evangelism. In addition to retaining elements of fundamentalist separatism, Pierce found the relief agencies far too programmatic. He met emergencies through his face-to-face encounters, entrusting missionary friends with World Vision's funds. He had no patience for the reporting, red tape, and coordination necessary for government partnerships. Bureaucracy quenched the Spirit.

Though global in scope, most of the new evangelical agencies fell outside the growing relief and development sector. World Relief looked like an evangelical alternative to the mainline agencies like Church World Service, but World Vision was even more distinct. Neither traditional mission agency nor humanitarian organization, World Vision was innovative, with a unique organization and a message attuned to American evangelicals' global imaginaries. In size, budget, and popular appeal, it soon far outpaced World Relief.[37]

World Vision and Evangelical Missions

While the circle of official religious humanitarian agencies tightened with no room for World Vision, by the mid-1950s, World Vision had begun to diversify its work overseas. It still primarily served as a first responder to emergencies on the mission field through funding orphans and missionaries, but Pierce also built an identity as an expert on global religious issues and his reputation as the missionary ambassador for American evangelicals.

Yet the gatekeepers within evangelical missions too remained skeptical about Pierce and his new organization. Many missionaries abroad adored Pierce because he supported them financially with salary, supplies, and meals.[38] The mission executives back home, however, were more hesitant, not quite sure what to make of his go-it-alone mentality. Pierce's haphazard approach of skipping from one emergency to another often struck the established agencies as a critique of their bureaucracies. Others took offense at Pierce's fund-raising model. They grew wary of his highly charged messages to the people in the pews, worrying that tactics such as child sponsorship played on emotions for short-term ends and shifted the allegiances of their own supporters.

Within the network of conservative missions in the United States, the Interdenominational Foreign Mission Association (IFMA) and the Evangelical Foreign Missionary Association (EFMA) served as the umbrellas for most agencies. Established in 1917, the IFMA began as an early association of independent faith mission societies. In 1945, the NAE chartered the EFMA to unite a broader group of evangelical agencies. Unlike the IFMA, it accepted both independent faith missions and denominational organizations. As a subsidiary of the NAE, the EFMA resisted the more explicit fundamentalism and separatism of the IFMA and modeled the general neo-evangelical adaptation to mainstream culture and reengagement with American civic and political life.

When World Vision applied for membership to both organizations, the IFMA flatly refused.[39] The EFMA finally allowed it to join in 1955. Even after joining, World Vision did not enjoy immediate acceptance as a peer. For some, it continued to be Pierce's fund-raising practices and lack of organizational structure that raised concerns. Others grew envious of the public attention and rapid growth that World Vision experienced. Still others resisted Pierce's pragmatism that dismissed the theological hair-splitting with which networks of conservative mission agencies often engaged. Many claimed he ignored boundaries that marked evangelical identity, such as requiring a commitment to evangelism as the first priority over relief work. They also felt Pierce was not careful enough to discriminate with whom he partnered. Occasionally he supported the work of missionaries from ecumenical World Council denominations. He even accepted an invitation from Princeton Theological Seminary president John McKay, himself a missionary kid from China, to share his experiences in Korea with Princeton seminarians.[40] Despite his stellar evangelical credentials and popular support, the

EFMA rarely invited Pierce and World Vision to sit at its head table. Instead, it used the organization. Pierce funded EFMA retreats and global mission tours, introduced mission leaders to foreign dignitaries, and supported missionaries in the field. Yet when the EFMA established an annual Mission Executives Retreat for leaders to debate pressing issues for global missions, Pierce was not initially invited.[41]

While Pierce never forgot such slights, he also had little interest in sitting around a boardroom table debating missiology. The mission executives around those tables, however, understood that despite their organizations' numerical growth, they had to rethink how they were making their case. They had largely entered the 1950s defining themselves in contrast to what they saw as a liberal ecumenical movement, but they learned that simple opposition to modernism, church union, and communism, while promoting a singular focus of world evangelization no longer sufficed. They had to reconsider both theory and practice.[42]

As many Asian countries stagnated in poverty, the evangelical agencies began to see the need for relief work, but they feared becoming aid workers rather than evangelists. At their inaugural 1953 Mission Executives Retreat, one EFMA leader remarked that "the world will look on us with distrust if we ignore this need, [for it is] hard to see a people and give them spiritual food without meeting the physical needs in measure." Another executive responded, "On every mission field poverty abounds, especially this is true in the Orient. It would be very easy to be pulled off center and soon be in relief work and not in evangelization." They saw the poverty, but they still debated whether they should be the ones to alleviate it.[43]

In addition, they realized that communism was refusing to go away quietly. While they continued to speak of "godless" communism and "Christian" America, by mid-decade these evangelical leaders stopped dismissing communism so quickly as merely "from the devil." Instead, they read Marx and Lenin in order to refute communist ideology and methodology. They treated it as another false religion but not merely "the other." Instead, just as they had done with other Eastern faiths, they took its ideas seriously in order to become better apologists for their own Western, democratic, and Christian faith.[44]

Even more puzzling at first to American evangelical leaders had been the critiques of Western imperialism by new nationalists who had little interest in communism. Now, however, evangelical agencies began to realize how far they lagged behind the ecumenical movement in creating national church councils and developing indigenous leaders. So they too began to talk of turning to indigenous preachers and missionaries. Yet, while they preferred indigenization in theory, they struggled to implement it in practice. Pleas for American missionaries to minister to unreached masses brought numerical and financial results. Sacrificing American exceptionalism and missionary idealism presented a risk that could redefine their entire recruiting and funding enterprise.[45]

World events tempered American triumphalism. Communism and new nationalisms hampered evangelical efforts. Evangelical mission agencies feared the impending merger of the International Missionary Council (IMC), one of the oldest and largest associations of mission-sending societies, with what they saw as a liberal World Council of Churches, which had forfeited missions in order to embrace social issues. Would such a merger undermine any commitment to evangelism and end mission as they had known it? They still wanted to evangelize the world in this generation, but they were less self-assured.[46]

Pierce continued to ignore ideological debates in favor of action. He chastised agencies that refused to support missionaries' relief efforts; he supplied the funds himself. He had no interest in reading Marx or Lenin, and he continued his anticommunist rhetoric by appealing to audiences through images of flattened villages, martyred pastors, and impoverished orphans. Nonetheless, through establishing pastors' conferences, funding local evangelists, and handing over control of programs to local staff, he incorporated indigenizing principles while other agencies merely theorized about them. At the same time, he continued his willingness to partner with almost anyone. He funded the missionary work of fundamentalist Carl McIntire's International Council of Christian Churches even as he also funded mainline Presbyterians and Methodists. To the chagrin of evangelical critics, he spoke before the Korean and Japanese National Christian Councils, subsidiaries of the World Council of Churches. When attacked, he reminded evangelicals at home each time that most of the missionaries he knew held an evangelistic faith unencumbered by American theological divisions. While Pierce continued to challenge traditional evangelical boundaries, mission executives continued to frown on the ways in which Pierce's actions demonstrated little respect for theological reflection.[47]

Pierce was fine, however, to dismiss the bureaucrats in favor of reaching the people in the pews. As a self-proclaimed missionary ambassador, Pierce used his radio show each week to celebrate missionaries from coast to coast.

Each month, *World Vision* magazine reached over 100,000 readers. Like *Life* or *Look*, the magazine was replete with color images and "facts from the field," describing the culture, geography, and needs of one or another mission. With correspondents throughout the world, the magazine provided international news from a missionary perspective. It gave churches practical suggestions for promoting missions and book reviews telling them what to read. Children could cut out paper dolls of international children in native dress. World Vision equipped its expanding popular audience with a missions-laden global outlook.

Each month, moreover, the magazine ran ads for people seeking a place to serve. Pierce lamented that many denominational missions and even faith missions excluded people without theological training or professional experience. "A nice, godly cultured seminary graduate would never in the world be worth a snap of a finger," Pierce preached. "I don't want a missionary who is ordained but one who knows how to work with the army." Thousands of jobs would go unfilled if they had to wait for educated missionaries to do them. Anyone could be a missionary; anyone could serve; Pierce would find them a place.[48]

If Pierce felt that his missionaries were often the forgotten heroes, he also turned some of them into iconic figures. His promotion of Lillian Dickson's work among "headhunting tribes in Formosa" brought her Mustard Seed organization to the attention of the U.S. and foreign governments. His stories of Gladys Aylward, British faith missionary to China, led Hollywood to turn her biography, *The Small Woman* by Alan Burgess (1957), into the acclaimed 1958 film *The Inn of the Sixth Happiness*. Soon after the film's success, World Vision sponsored Aylward on international speaking tours.[49]

Pierce embraced a gospel of masculinity and often painted his missionary friends as adventurous, red-blooded Americans. Flying in and out of danger and preaching on the front lines, he demonstrated the adventure available to someone in the mission field. While World Vision mainly supported women, Pierce wanted to see men in the field. He scolded them in one radio message: "I wonder what you're doing, Mister? Are you working as a great big brace grocery clerk or running a great big garage or a lathe, or are you piloting a huge desk in a great insurance company, while some frail woman does the job that God would have had you do in the face of rape and murder and piracy and slaughter and riot and hate and hell and Communism at the ends of the earth? It's something to think about, because somewhere there's something wrong when about four out of five on the mission field are women."[50] Female missionaries often faced great loneliness, Pierce said, as their missionary calling often cost them the chance to marry and have a family and the comforts of home. Pierce heralded these women because they took on the masculine roles forsaken by men. He resented what he called "the all-too-prevalent male response to the missionary call: 'Here am I, Lord—send my sister!'" Pierce did everything he could to reverse the trend.[51]

His special ire found expression when he thought about Americans who remained indifferent to suffering. He really believed at first that if only his fellow evangelicals could be confronted with conditions overseas, they could not refuse a call to action, but their lack of response continued to disappoint. He intensified his message of sacrifice: global Christians and missionaries were suffering while Americans sought wealth and comfort. Why did Americans not do more to help people with far less? The institutional mission agencies presented options for service and support; Pierce employed rhetoric of guilt and sacrifice.[52]

Pierce did initially appreciate what he saw as a synthesis of missions and American foreign policy that linked American triumphalism, anticommunism, and the Christian gospel. By the end of the decade, however, Pierce increasingly criticized American immorality and self-indulgence at home and worried that it hurt missions overseas. Still an outsider in the world of governmental and voluntary humanitarian organizations, he also began to differentiate between American foreign policy and Christian priorities.

In 1958, William J. Lederer and Eugene Burdick published *The Ugly American*, a novel that brought American foreign policy to readers of popular books. Serialized in the *Saturday Evening Post*, it topped the best-seller list for seventy-eight weeks and sold four million copies.[53] The book warned about communism but excoriated the incompetence and laziness of State Department officials and aid workers. Pierce publicly affirmed the book's analysis, recounting his own encounters with defense contractors, aid officials, and ambassadors who lived comfortably while refusing to learn local languages and customs. Pierce contrasted "ugly Americans" with "America's best ambassadors," sacrificial missionaries who served as "highly effective combatants in the fight against communism." He admitted that earlier missionaries had failed because they forced American values on Asians while communists adopted the local customs. But he said that missionaries had learned their lesson; the diplomats had not. Missionaries were politically valuable: they built trust as well as schools, orphanages, clinics, and churches, and they exemplified democracy. These were the best of both Christian and American ideals. Pierce still sometimes conflated Christianity with democracy and the defeat of communism, wondering if it were not the forgotten missionaries and indigenous pastors who best demonstrated both Christian and democratic ideals.[54]

World Vision and Evangelical Institutions

If Pierce operated both in and out of established evangelical missionary networks, he faced similar challenges among American evangelicals' expanding networks of parachurch agencies. The charismatic founders of these new agencies often shared ideological and personal connections. A generation of leaders emerged from YFC in the 1950s to start their own organizations and Pierce maintained personal relationships with most of them. He shared regular Bible study with Dawson Trotman of the Navigators and Dick Hillis of Orient Crusades. He opened doors for young Campus Crusade founder Bill Bright. He served as Billy Graham's tour guide in Asia. Graham, in turn, often introduced Pierce and World Vision at his own crusades.

As these evangelical entrepreneurs and their new institutions rose to prominence, World Vision grew alongside them. In 1956, World Vision moved its offices from Portland, Oregon, to the Los Angeles suburb of Eagle Rock, California. With Pierce away from home much of the year, the move to Southern California enabled his wife and kids to be closer to extended family in his absence; it also moved World Vision into the hub of prospering parachurch organizations making their home in the thriving Sunbelt region. World Vision shared office space with the Navigators, connected with Fuller Theological Seminary in nearby Pasadena and the Bible Institute of Los Angeles (BIOLA), and then hired their graduates.

Pierce knew the emerging generation of evangelical leaders and they knew him. At first, members of the old guard kept their distance, not quite sure what to make of the upstart Pierce. Yet over the decade, Pierce convinced several to bring their wisdom to his young organization. In 1958, Dr. Paul Rees joined World Vision's staff as vice president at large to coordinate its growing pastors' conference work. As longtime pastor of the First Covenant Church in Minneapolis and past president of the NAE, Rees brought World Vision an intellectual respectability to balance Pierce's uncouth brashness. The same was true of theologian Carl Henry who had initially found Pierce's lack of theological education and refinement distasteful. By the end of the decade, however, Henry had agreed to teach at pastors' conferences and to write scripts for World Vision's films. Pierce's overseas networks and popular support were too valuable for these elder statesmen to ignore.

By the end of the 1950s, World Vision was in the club of evangelical insiders. The organization's board looked like a who's who of evangelical leaders. Billy Graham served as board chairman alongside Henrietta Mears, a Presbyterian noted for her Bible teaching in Hollywood, EFMA chairman Clyde Taylor, Fuller professor Carlton Booth, Wheaton College president Raymond Edman, *Eternity* magazine editor Donald Barnhouse, and Richard Halverson, pastor of the Fourth Presbyterian Church in Bethesda, Maryland, and later chaplain of the U.S. Senate.[55]

While Pierce had clearly become a leading evangelical influencer, he could also be his own worst enemy. Nobody questioned his commitment to world evangelization and humanitarianism, but both friends and enemies acknowledged his divisiveness. Genteel theologians like Harold Ockenga and Carl Henry sometimes blanched at his populist style. Billy Graham charitably called him a "complex personality."[56] He was quick to speak, prone to anger, blunt, and bull-headed even as he was generous, loyal, and tender-hearted. He held a grudge and stewed over perceived slights longer than most, but he would often give those in need the shirt off his back. In the small circle of the evangelical elite, he was a wild card. He remained both inside and outside, ally and critic, leader and gadfly. Some appreciated his lack of polish, others tiptoed around him as a fanatic.

Nevertheless, alongside Pierce's popular rhetoric and maverick identity, the picture of the world he offered American evangelicals resonated with their global outlook. In 1958, Pierce produced the film *Cry in the Night*. It took top honors as the year's best evangelical mission film, and while it had a bigger budget and better quality than his earlier films, it still peered into an orientalist and exotic Asia, using images of forgotten Hindu temples, "pagan" dances with demon possession, forbidding jungles, and masses of humanity. He focused his camera on the poor and juxtaposed these images with testimonies of missionaries, local pastors, and his preaching. The old message about communism still permeated the script. The movie ended with the same appeal: now or never. And his message still struck a chord with audiences.[57]

Yet through his insistence on ignoring traditional evangelical boundaries and increasing World Vision's focus on humanitarian relief, Pierce both intentionally and unwittingly began to shift World Vision's work even as his message also led to subtle shifts among evangelicals and their global vision. By the end of the decade, evangelicals in the pages of *Christianity Today* and on the floor of NAE conventions began to reconsider the relationship of humanitarianism and evangelism. Did a singular preoccupation with evangelism undercut the responsibility to relieve the hungry and the thirsty? World Vision was able to serve "the least of these" without losing an evangelical identity. Why could other American evangelicals not do the same? The debate over the question would continue for decades.[58]

In its first decade, World Vision had no well-designed plan. In fact, Pierce felt that strategic planning denied the Spirit's work. The organization also lacked financial accountability. Its funds rarely matched the amounts that Pierce committed or proposed to spend. In 1958, Dr. Frank Phillips, who had served World Vision as its executive director since its founding in 1950 for almost no salary, abruptly resigned after being accused of the improper use of funds. The incident appeared to be overblown, but Phillips tragically died of a heart attack less than three days later. As the steady administrator back home, Phillips had tried to serve as the counterbalance to Pierce's extravagant vision, and his loss almost toppled the organization. World Vision was growing, but it was still quite fragile and taking no time to establish a solid foundation. Pierce would reply to such concerns by asking how could they possibly slow down when there were so many immediate needs to meet all over the world.[59]

Pierce was always eager to chase the next big thing and continue to grow even if it meant sacrificing successful enterprises from the past. By 1958, the hallmark of the ministry was orphan care, with World Vision supporting over 12,488 orphans in four countries. Child sponsorship brought in most of the money, and the organization often had to "borrow" funds designated for orphans to cover other expenses. Yet child sponsorship had become a managerial nightmare. World Vision had no orphanages; it turned them over to missionaries and Korean Christians. But then it had no way to supervise the staffs. When several of the orphanages got in trouble with the South Korean government for misappropriation of funds, Pierce worried about his organization's reputation. He lamented that World Vision had entered the "orphanage business" and had to get bogged down in administrative nightmares. He let his board know that he was ready to jettison his marquee ministry and hand it over to the denominations. He would return to his original vision of evangelizing the world and doling out money when emergencies came into view.[60]

He had similar problems with missionaries. In the early days, Pierce met missionaries and gave them the funds they needed right then and there and often promised to send more for a particular need. By the end of the decade, World Vision listed over eighty missionaries in its annual budget. Pierce worried that eighty was too many; their dependence on World Vision restricted his ability to meet emergencies and fund new ministries.[61]

World Vision embraced innovation and new opportunities even if that often led to scattershot programs all over Asia. By 1960, missionaries began inviting Pierce to come work in Africa. The United States in its foreign policy and global investment had also begun to rediscover Africa with the overthrow of European colonial empires and the birth of new nations. Pierce traveled throughout the region, but he remained hesitant to bring World Vision into the African countries. For once in his life, Pierce declined the new challenge. He realized that his organization lacked the resources and personnel to take advantage of the changes on that continent. He also clung to his first love—the people of Asia. He felt that the organization was not quite ready to embody a truly "world" vision.

If the organization he built still remained fragile, Pierce was too. Despite his authoritarian and charismatic personality, Pierce remained an unhealthy man with constant bouts of depression, exhaustion, and fits of anger. He remained estranged from his wife and daughters for the majority of the year only to reunite with them as if everything was normal if he happened to make it home for the holidays. His enemies spread accusations of affairs and substance abuse, while his general instability was an open secret among fellow evangelical leaders. But all of this remained out of the public eye as Pierce embodied the image of a suffering servant, the missionary ambassador mediating between American Christians and immeasurable needs around the world.[62]

In 1959, South Korean president Syngman Rhee presented Pierce with one of the country's highest honors, the Medal for Public Welfare Service, in "recognition of his exceptionally praiseworthy service to the Republic of Korea." He elicited similar praise in other Asian nations as a champion of democracy, Christian missions, and the meeting of humanitarian needs.[63] This reputation earned him a place within American evangelical and mission networks. In 1960, popular press McGraw-Hill even published an account of Pierce's travels, *Let My Heart Be Broken*, which became a best seller and exposed World Vision to nonevangelical audiences. Again, this was a World Vision marketing coup: give respected journalist Richard Gehman an advance for expenses and full access in return for a book that would spread World Vision's reputation beyond evangelical circles. By the book's end, Gehman, once a religious skeptic, is recounting his own religious conversion of sorts and a clear conversion to the legitimacy of World Vision's good work. By the end of the decade, politicians, the mainstream press, and Americans in general viewed Pierce and World Vision as experts on Asian affairs.[64]

As his reputation grew, however, Pierce remained true to his initial vision: help missionaries, aid the poor, and preach the gospel. He adopted a language of American internationalism while exposing audiences at home to an unfamiliar, suffering, overcrowded, disease-ridden, hungry, but often faith-filled world. He spoke in an evangelical vernacular but added new accents that made more than a few people uncomfortable. World Vision was becoming a prominent mission agency even if it often still lived on the edge as both evangelical insider and outsider. Pierce took pride in guiding World Vision in unpredictable directions wherever he felt the Spirit leading even if he too remained unsure where this new path might take him. At the end of its first decade one of the only things Pierce was completely sure of was that he was happiest leapfrogging throughout Asia, jumping out of planes, and being the first on the ground when new needs presented themselves.

CHAPTER 4

Between Missions and Humanitarianism in a Decade of Upheaval

AS WORLD VISION ENTERED the 1960s, child sponsorship and orphan care continued to dominate fund-raising and operations even as Pierce remained committed to individual missionaries, local pastors' conferences, and large-scale evangelistic crusades. At the same time, Pierce consistently pushed for aggressive expansion. World Vision entered the 1960s with an annual budget near $2 million; it would balloon to $9 million by the end of the decade. Its operational programs more than doubled (from 165 to 388) as did the number of sponsored children in its care (from 13,215 to 32,600). Pierce also tripled the number of countries where World Vision worked from three to nine. Of chief importance was the new Cold War hot spot, Vietnam. Pierce poured himself into the country, predicting it would be World Vision's next Korea.[1]

Unprecedented expansion brought its own challenges that the hard-charging Pierce rarely stopped to consider. Bigger budgets required greater accountability, and bigger programs demanded greater specialization. Alongside other prospering parachurch agencies, World Vision began to question how the need to professionalize might affect their founder's style of charismatic and autocratic leadership as well as his insistence on meeting immediate needs wherever the Spirit led him.

World Vision's growing pains, however, stretched beyond its need for greater capacity, expertise, and strategic planning. It also continued to search for its voice as a self-identified evangelical missionary service organization amid the new contexts of the 1960s. At home, American evangelicals were debating how to respond to issues such as civil rights, a growing counterculture, and a perceived secularism at home. Abroad, they questioned how best to maintain a fervent anticommunism, support for Vietnam, and championing of foreign missions. Beyond an American evangelical subculture, World Vision also sought to balance its commitment to both humanitarian aid and soul saving, even as the missionary enterprise itself was under criticism. Around the world, new nations overthrowing their colonial rulers challenged Western authority. At home, alternative service opportunities such as the Peace Corps recruited young people to a new vision of foreign aid. The federal government and other international bodies became even more dependent on voluntary agencies to take the lead in global relief and development as Americans' popular imaginations morphed from missions to humanitarianism.

Pierce had established World Vision to expand the global imagination of evangelicals at home. With his fresh approach, he maintained an evangelical identity, a missionary motivation, and an American exceptionalism. But the crises of the 1960s, both at home and abroad, challenged World Vision's original identity. At the same time, American evangelicals' self-professed establishment was debating how to hold the movement together and expand its public presence without watering down its theological distinctives. As many parachurch agencies grew and popular personalities emerged, elder statesmen such as Carl Henry wondered if a singular American evangelical vision had become a casualty of its own success. As staunch supporters of Cold War anticommunism, evangelicals debated what roles their patriotism might play in the work of statecraft abroad amid an increasingly skeptical public. Finally, evangelicals questioned how to maintain a primary commitment to evangelistic missions as they faced criticism from mainliners at home and the global church abroad. Some evangelicals began to take these critiques to heart, sparking debates among themselves over the relationship of missions and social action. Most mission agencies chose to press ahead with their work even without clarity on how best to respond to the clear shift to humanitarianism in public policy and popular opinion.

World Vision's challenges often mirrored these larger debates among American evangelicals themselves. At other times, the organization found itself ahead of the pack, sometimes a step behind, or often caught in between two sides in conflict. For that reason, World Vision serves as a lens on many of the debates shaping American Christians' global imaginations in the 1960s. In its second decade, World Vision sought to balance multiple languages and identities: charismatic and bureaucratic, missionary and humanitarian, evangelical and ecumenical, as well as American and international. Debates both inside and outside of World Vision would take their toll on the organization and Pierce himself. Its growth over the decade made it clear that Pierce's simple mission "to meet emergency needs through existing evangelical agencies" would never be so simple. Yet World Vision could not go back. It was forced to change as contexts changed around it.

American Evangelicals' Efforts to Define Themselves at Home and Abroad

In the 1950s, evangelicals transformed themselves from "embattled outposts to flourishing enterprises."[2] By the 1960s, they looked to solidify their success. Who counted as evangelical may have still been up for debate as the group remained diverse in social class, style, temperament, and theology, but as evangelical spokesmen like Billy Graham, Bill Bright, and Bob Pierce emerged, they promoted a shared rhetorical unity. *Christianity Today* crowned itself as the movement's mouthpiece by demarcating and advancing an evangelical agenda. By 1960, in four short years of publication, its circulation numbers outdistanced its mainline rival, the *Christian Century*.[3] *Christianity Today* cited its own polls to prove that more Protestant ministers were conservative than liberal, yet evangelicals were no longer satisfied with superior numbers.[4] They sought culture-shaping power and prestige. NAE founder Harold Ockenga presented evangelicals with an overall strategy for "resurgent evangelical leadership," while *Christianity Today*'s own strategic plan, "An Evangelical Protestant Strategy for the Late 1960s," bolstered theological conferences, promoted global missions, and lobbied for political policies.[5] Evangelical rhetoric was changing as its new leaders saw themselves less as outsiders and more as mainstream Americans with a voice in the public square.

These "establishment" evangelicals legitimized their public voice by affirming middle-American values they saw as increasingly under attack.[6] Abroad, this meant continuing to embrace an American exceptionalism and Cold War anticommunism with religious fervor. If such rhetoric was near universal a decade earlier, many politicians and mainline Protestants had tired of framing the Cold War as spiritual warfare. George Kennan, former U.S. ambassador to the Soviet Union, responded that although Christian values permeated the American conflict with Soviet power, Americans could not conclude that everything they wanted reflected the purpose of God and everything the Russians wanted reflected the purpose of the devil.[7] Evangelicals, however, relished the dichotomy. Billy Graham continued to preach that there was "no such thing as a compromise with atheistic Communism."[8] Upstarts such as Australian Fred Schwarz and his Christian Anti-Communist Crusade (CACC) also gained broad evangelical backing. While introduced to America by Carl McIntire and the Christian Far Right in the 1950s, Schwarz also received financial and promotional support from organizations like World Vision, and his annual revenues quadrupled between 1960 and 1961 to $1.2 million. Part evangelistic crusade, part pop-science lecture, and part anticommunist polemic, his weeklong sessions could pack twelve thousand people into the Hollywood Bowl with several million more watching on television. He replicated these crusades around the country, recruiting local leaders, national politicians, and conservative celebrities like Ronald Reagan, John Wayne, and Pat Boone to headline rallies.[9]

With the Bay of Pigs and the Cuban Missile Crisis bringing the communist threat closer to American shores, the NAE resolved to urge "all Christian Americans" to join in "an aggressive and unrelenting campaign against this enemy of righteousness and freedom."[10] Their spiritual offensive meant also fighting on a second front against what they saw as increasing secularism at home. FBI director J. Edgar Hoover became a frequent *Christianity Today* contributor to admonish American families that passing on traditional faith and morals was their best weapon to fight communism.[11] Evangelicals began to speak out against what they saw as a growing rejection of a Christian worldview. When the Supreme Court outlawed compulsory prayer in 1962 and Bible readings in public schools a year later, evangelicals felt their fears were warranted.[12] They lamented slipping ethical standards as well as declining respect for authority. They saw the 1960s as a decade of "riots, revolt, and revolution."[13] Not only the political New Left but even the Civil Rights Movement was subject to criticism. *Christianity Today* supported civil rights legislation, but it never even mentioned Martin Luther King Jr. by name in its pages until 1964. In 1966, *Christianity Today* referred to King's methods as "a sign of the lawlessness of our times."[14] Evangelicals had wanted to save the world. Now they believed that they must also save America, and they increasingly fretted about the approaches others were taking to the task.[15]

To save the world and restore their own country, American evangelicals often portrayed their efforts in direct contrast to those of the ecumenical movement. If evangelicals stood firm for the gospel, they accused ecumenism of promoting unity at the expense of theological conviction.[16] Yet, evangelicals' bigger frustration was an ecumenical penchant for social and political action. Evangelicals debated social issues but sought to keep spiritual and secular domains separated. From their perspective, the church lacked a biblical mandate for political meddling or social engineering, and it also lacked competence in such matters.[17] While Bob Pierce was willing to go further than most evangelicals of his day in taking on international issues such as poverty, his own response to debates over the Civil Rights Act of 1964 typified evangelicals' focus on individual action: "I believe in equal opportunity for those who are willing to take equal responsibility."[18] Evangelicals encouraged the votes of individual Christian citizens over public statements; they also promoted the need for converting individuals over changing social structures.

With growing confidence, American evangelicals also used their expanding voice to champion their missionary dominance both in numbers and popular support, yet they highlighted foreign missions as another arena where their commitments were under attack.[19] Evangelicals accused the ecumenical movement of giving up on evangelism and redefining mission as humanitarianism or interreligious dialogue. "Jesus commanded us to go into all the world and preach the Gospel to every creature," quipped one evangelical critic. "He did not command us to go into the world and organize a peace corps or civil disobedience demonstration."[20]

Yet, like their ecumenical counterparts, they too recognized the Western missionary enterprise was changing in the midst of increasing globalization. Countless evangelical mission conferences, including several convened by World Vision, debated the future of "Missions in a Revolutionary Age."[21] Some viewed it positively: "The notion of one world has so captured us that in spiritual things we have finally eliminated the false tags of 'home' and 'foreign,' 'we' and 'they.'"[22] Others noted disadvantages. As new nations threw off colonial powers, many closed their doors to Christian missionaries. Billy Graham's associate Sherwood Wirt lamented that "the missionary, we are told, is now regarded as a symbol of religious and cultural superiority, and as a part of a sinister political scheme for reestablishing Western supremacy in erstwhile colonial areas."[23] Western church leaders published popular books entitled *The Unpopular Missionary* and *Missionary, Go Home!*[24]

In the 1950s, the "younger" churches of Africa and Asia shaped American evangelicals' own views of the world, but they also still depended on missionaries. By the 1960s, new nations more forcefully repudiated Western superiority, and the "younger" churches also began to speak with their own voice. If missionaries were to remain, they would have to work alongside or under indigenous leaders, sometimes in hostile political environments. When the Congolese overthrew the ruling Belgians in 1960 and 1961, thousands of Protestant and Catholic missionaries fled or were expelled. In November 1964, the Congolese captured more than 250 whites and ultimately killed sixty hostages. The "Stanleyville massacre" dramatized the anger felt by some in new postcolonial nations. Such episodes created immense distress among evangelical advocates for missions at home.[25]

One enduring image of the massacre was the execution of American missionary Paul Carlson. He appeared as a martyr on the covers of *Time* and *Life* magazines, yet the cover stories overlooked the complexities of his missionary identity. While "evangelical" in theology, Carlson had an elite education, earning degrees in anthropology from Stanford and medicine from George Washington. He volunteered as a medical missionary after giving up a lucrative private practice in California. Serving under the conservative Evangelical Covenant Church (ECC), he both practiced medicine and evangelized among the Congolese. Theological distinctions may have baffled the popular press, but the journalists eulogized Carlson, claiming that he "symbolized all the white men—and there are many—who want nothing from Africa but a chance to help." *Life* managing editor George P. Hunt called Carlson "a heroic man of God who lived for the African—only to be killed by his hand." Carlson's death demonstrated that the West generally often idealized missionaries as heroes helping make sense of the dark, savage, and exotic other.[26]

American evangelicals were well aware that even as they defined themselves as fervent cold warriors, champions of traditional values at home, and defenders of evangelistic missions abroad, they too must evolve in the midst of revolutionary global change. They diligently patrolled their own theological boundaries, but when among themselves, they debated issues such as the future of the missionary enterprise. Most agreed they needed a new breed of missionary that brought both humility and specialized skills. They needed fewer Western evangelists and more doctors, businessmen, teachers, and farmers earning the right to be heard in a postcolonial world.

After a decade of work in Asia, World Vision veteran staffers presumed they came with the credibility to address these issues. For instance, World Vision vice president and former NAE president Paul Rees questioned the popular press's depiction of Carlson as a white savior. While he too lauded Carlson as a martyr, he dismissed the naive stereotypes of the valiant white missionary conveniently appropriated by the American public.[27] Through his own hard-earned education leading dozens of indigenous pastors' conferences around the world, Rees modeled the complexities of American evangelicals' approach to international engagement. As these debates unfolded, World Vision often served as the lightning rod at the center of American evangelicals' global imagination.

If World Vision's methods were sometimes unconventional and tested the patience of the evangelical establishment, Pierce's public message resonated squarely with evangelical popular audiences. Into the 1960s, Pierce continued to see the world as a spiritual and political battlefield in need of Western missionaries. He assured supporters that evangelism permeated World Vision's ministry, whether through chapel services at Korean orphanages or New Testaments included with relief goods. His theology sometimes lacked the subtlety that the evangelical establishment preferred, but he made sense to the people in the pews, and they trusted him with their money to save the world.

Pierce propelled World Vision into its second decade by taking out a full-page ad in *Christianity Today* to announce his 1961 Tokyo Crusade, the largest in Japanese history.[28] World Vision's board worried that tight resources made it an imprudent financial undertaking, but Pierce's response to the "Spirit's leading" always trumped rationality. He secured a ten-thousand-seat auditorium and the rights to broadcast on radio and television. He enlisted an eight-hundred-voice choir and a one-hundred-piece orchestra. Along with his own team of seasoned evangelists, he recruited upstarts such as young Campus Crusade founder Bill Bright and more than fifty other athletes, entertainers, and business executives to join the crusade team.[29]

Pierce knew a project this grand would garner attention, but the level of criticism he experienced surprised him. He should not have been surprised, however, because, as often happened, debates over World Vision's work encapsulated the evangelical arguments of the day. Alongside ongoing attacks from the communists, Pierce also faced criticism from Japanese Christians, the larger global church, and his own fellow evangelical missionaries.

Pierce argued that Christian conversion helped inoculate global citizens against communism, and so he registered pushback from the communist propaganda machine as a badge of honor. Radio Moscow labeled World Vision "a false religious organization of American business circles." Communists accused World Vision, underneath its "showy choir and preaching," of being a front for the "strengthening of Japan's dependence upon the United States. . . . The American Crusaders intend to bury the spirit of the Japanese people with money and to paralyze the Japanese desire for independence."[30] Stirred to action, some local Japanese urged the city to revoke World Vision's license for use of the municipal auditorium, and for several weeks Pierce's newfound critics purchased crusade tickets only to tear them up to ensure empty seats.

Pierce was more surprised to face opposition from local Japanese Christians as some made him a pawn in their own debates over missionary methods and ecumenical cooperation. While Pierce had secured an invitation from the largest bodies of Japanese Christians, a few national pastors voiced distaste for mass evangelism and World Vision's attempt to make "instant Christians." Some insisted that evangelism was a job for Japanese Christians without American interference. Others balked at the cost and lavishness of the production.[31]

Opposition extended beyond the Japanese response to debates within the larger global church. The same year as the crusade, the World Council of Churches (WCC) merged with the International Missionary Council (IMC). The ecumenical movement saw this as positive for the global church removing paternalistic labels of "sending" (Western) versus "receiving" (non-Western) churches. Missionaries would serve alongside or under the national church as "fraternal workers." Evangelicals understood in a time flush with new nationalistic spirit and a burgeoning anticolonialism that they must offer the younger churches increased respect and cooperation, but they refused to label missionaries as "fraternal workers." They feared the winnowing of Western missionary enterprises would lead not to greater partnership but to the extinguishing of evangelism.[32]

With these competing interests, evangelicals supported indigenization in theory but often struggled to implement it on the ground.[33] Pierce's crusade served as a case in point. When World Vision announced that Japan's National Christian Council president Rev. Ken Muto would be a member of its crusade planning committee, conservative missionaries revolted, questioning the orthodoxy of Japan's Christian Council and accusing Muto of being a pro-Shinto nationalist. Conservative Western missionaries, most often Pierce's biggest fans, now felt that World Vision had insulted them by not asking them to lead. Pierce replied that World Vision came at the invitation of the Japanese churches and not the mission organizations.[34]

Back home, leaders with American evangelicals' missionary establishment worried that Pierce was being duped by the ecumenical movement. Evangelicals knew Pierce as an independent spirit, but they feared that while he was "orthodox in doctrine," he proved "undiscerning in practice." With their motto "Cooperation Without Compromise" firmly in mind, the NAE's Evangelical Foreign Mission Agency (EFMA) sent Pierce a letter commending his evangelistic crusades but questioning their inclusiveness. They lauded his work with national churches but advised him that turning over control must be gradual, so that local believers could faithfully bear the "spiritual authority and evangelization of their own lands." They cautioned him that "ecumenical leaders seem to be deliberately cultivating a strategy of working with evangelicals in an effort to infiltrate our ranks and swallow us up." Pierce responded to their "words of caution" with a graceful reply and a commitment to appear more prominently at evangelical events.[35] Addressing the 1962 NAE Convention, he tried to calm their fears: "We want all the world to know that you are our people. We belong to you, and you belong to us. I'm an evangelical. I'm no longer afraid to be called a fundamentalist. I'm sick and tired of things that are not clear and certain."[36]

Despite Pierce's occasional kowtowing to remain in the good graces of the powers that be, criticism from fellow evangelicals continued. Many attacked World Vision for being too cozy with the World Council of Churches. Paul Rees, the most respected evangelical intellectual within World Vision, refuted the attacks and reminded critics that the organization had no formal affiliation with the WCC and agreed with the criticisms against ecumenism repeatedly appearing within *Christianity Today*. Yet Rees went further to articulate World Vision's position: "Out of years of overseas contacts and associations, [World Vision] is convinced that it is impossible to draw a rigid line of truth and error, evangelicalism and non-evangelicalism, by the over-simple device of asking, is your church affiliated with the World Council of Churches?" Rees and others within World Vision were tiring of defending themselves on all fronts—particularly among fellow evangelicals.[37]

Despite all the criticism, by the end of the monthlong crusade, World Vision claimed victory with over 237,000 in attendance and 8,940 conversions.[38] The secular and religious press gave the crusade broad coverage.[39] *Christianity Today* editor Carl Henry lauded Pierce for attempting to win an entire country for Christ.[40] The crusade raised World Vision's stature and highlighted its pro-American, anticommunist, and evangelistic identity among popular audiences. Yet the expense and criticisms almost broke the organization. World Vision would move on; it was Pierce's last major crusade.

Marketing, Management, and Mission

Attempts to portray and police an American evangelicalism that shared a single purpose and common rhetoric, however, masked the essential entrepreneurial forms of many prominent organizations like World Vision. With the ability to tailor messages directly to religious consumers in a diverse marketplace, the parachurch model allowed almost anyone to bypass older structures and appeal directly to the people.[41] World Vision's success turned less on the approval of the EFMA and NAE and more on its innovative marketing to grassroots evangelicals. Pierce's radio program, films, and mission magazine continued to propel World Vision's growth in the 1960s, and he kept his outlets fresh by moving his radio show outside the studio to broadcast "on location" around the world, adding the narration of a reputable CBS anchor to his films, and changing his magazine from a promotional house organ to an academically credible mission journal funded with subscriptions and advertising. By 1964, with a monthly circulation of 200,000, it rivaled *Christianity Today*.[42]

In every form, the essence of World Vision's marketing was to bring those in need around the world more intimately into the lives of American Christians. To keep up with the innovations in secular media, Pierce began sending glossy pictorials modeled after similar gifts from *Life* and *National Geographic* as thank-yous to sponsors, bringing World Vision's work to countless coffee tables. To entice donors to sponsor a child, World Vision offered a handmade craft, a prayer card, or Pierce's latest book. For donors to the Tokyo Crusade, he offered a souvenir record that would, as the radio announcer promised, bring "a real touch of Japan right in your home."[43] Each year, World Vision also brought Asian Christians to America for its

Figure 8. Pierce bringing the Korean Orphan Choir to the United States.
© World Vision, Inc. 2011. All rights reserved. Reprinted by permission.

weeklong Festival of Mission to report on God's work throughout the world in their own voice. It also sponsored "Around the World Tours." Predating short-term missions by decades, these "vacations with a purpose" let travelers tour the sights and World Vision's ministries.[44]

In the 1960s, no other World Vision fund-raiser matched the popularity of the Korean Orphan Choir. Selecting thirty-four of its thirteen thousand Korean orphans, Pierce accompanied the choir he called his "little missionaries" around the world as they raised funds for other orphans. The children in the choir served as goodwill ambassadors, their smiles appearing to convey the effects of Christian compassion as they came "singing their thanks . . . to the people of North America for rescuing them from starvation and loneliness."[45]

The choir packed evangelical churches but was soon booked in larger venues as Pierce hired the same Hollywood publicist who promoted Carol

Burnett and Julie Andrews to give exposure to his choir.[46] They filled Harvard's Holden Chapel and New York's Carnegie Hall. Their diverse repertoire included classical pieces from Strauss and Schubert as well as hymns like "How Great Thou Art" and the "Lord's Prayer." They sang Korean folk ballads but also performed "America the Beautiful" and "God Bless America." After the success of their initial 1961 tour, they came back three more times during the decade. As minor celebrities, they sang for Chicago's mayor Richard Daley and former president Dwight Eisenhower. Young Caroline Kennedy led them on a behind-the-scenes White House tour. One year they rode in the Rose Bowl Parade. The next they cut a Christmas album with Burl Ives and accompanied Billy Graham's crusades. In an age of anti-Western sentiment, World Vision's Korean Orphan Choir offered a message that Americans were eager to hear and few could resist. Pierce reminded Americans that they were compassionate and should continue to be.[47]

World Vision continued to grow as it reflected its founder's energetic, entrepreneurial personality. Pierce was of the opinion that you had to spend money to make money, and so while other evangelical agencies scoffed at decisions such as hiring a Hollywood publicist, he boasted that increasing revenues made his case clear. Others were just jealous. Besides Billy Graham, no other evangelists were getting booked on *The Ed Sullivan Show* except Pierce and his orphan choir. World Vision's founder was all imagination and untamed energy. He took big chances in his marketing at home and was just as brazen overseas, relishing his ability to roam the world with World Vision's checkbook. He trusted that God would provide the resources, but his enthusiasm for the work abroad caused World Vision to neglect oversight of budgets and programs at home. The charisma that served as Pierce's greatest strength often became a liability as the board worried how to cover checks Pierce had already written.[48]

Even Pierce began to see how his growing ministry had become too big for him to manage alone. The organization constantly ran in the red, depending on all-night prayer sessions to meet expenses. In 1963, Pierce hired Youth for Christ president Ted Engstrom as World Vision's executive vice president. A fixture in evangelical parachurch networks, Engstrom had the managerial gifts Pierce lacked.[49] Upon arrival, he found World Vision a half million dollars in debt and delinquent in paying its monthly bills. He let it be known that projects could no longer simply rely on prayer. Budgets also mattered.

World Vision worried about its founder. Engstrom described Pierce as "the most complex, fascinating individual I had ever known or met. In many ways, he was a classic schizophrenic."[50] His compassion was matched by an explosive temper. He frequently prayed that he might "burn out for God," and on several occasions he worked himself into depression and exhaustion that forced him into several extended medical leaves. In 1964, he spent the entire year convalescing alone in Asia.[51] World Vision hid most of Pierce's emotional and physical struggles from the public. It did announce his yearlong leave as necessary medical treatment, and World Vision's evangelical donors never questioned it. They revered his willingness to sacrifice his life for the work of God.[52]

With Pierce increasingly absent from day-to-day operations, Engstrom set about establishing a new culture of professionalism and institutional stability. To bolster its fund-raising efforts and meet rising expenses, World Vision leased an IBM 1401 mainframe computer at six thousand dollars a month. Engstrom boasted that only two other nonprofits, the Billy Graham Evangelistic Association and Catholic Relief Services (CRS), had similar machines in 1962.[53] The new technology streamlined records management and led to new fund-raising techniques. Stored information allowed the organization to personalize appeal letters. "Dear Sir or Madam" became "Dear Mr. Smith." General appeals became targeted requests that matched donors' interests. World Vision rented the mailing lists from like-minded periodicals and bid out its marketing accounts to leading advertising agencies. At the same, time it also built a major donor strategy. Pierce had insisted World Vision relied on the grassroots support of many individual child sponsors, but Engstrom hired his former Youth for Christ associate Evon Hedley as World Vision's first director of development. Hedley courted donors outside World Vision's original evangelical networks. He secured the organization's first grants from the Kresge Foundation, Lilly Endowment Inc., and Pew Charitable Trusts.[54] Increasing scrutiny by donors and government agencies also led World Vision to demonstrate closer oversight of how it raised and dispersed funds.

As World Vision professionalized, leadership carefully insisted how efficiency and accountability did not undercut the organization's Christian identity. In contrast to Pierce's charisma and leadership by fiat, Engstrom adapted American business principles into a style of "Christian management." While World Vision employees attended weekly chapel services, they also embraced time-management seminars. A more active board would no longer permit Pierce to promise funds, hire, and fire staff without proper approval. If Pierce had developed a reputation as highly entrepreneurial, Engstrom recast World Vision's reputation as established, efficient, and strategic. In promoting Christian management through countless books and leadership seminars to evangelical pastors and nonprofit executives, Engstrom made World Vision's organizational development the model for the rapidly expanding parachurch sector.[55]

World Vision's organizational transition also illustrated the tensions of a host of young evangelical agencies entering their second decade. Founded by charismatic, entrepreneurial leaders, these specialized agencies were light on their feet, free to ignore established hierarchies and streamline their ministries to the particular passions of their leaders and constituents. Now, many had grown beyond their capacities. Some dug in to resist change, while others adopted new outlooks wholesale. Most fell somewhere in between, realizing that questions of organization and religious identity intertwined.

Two of the largest, Campus Crusade and the Billy Graham Evangelistic Association, mirrored World Vision's transition by embracing greater professionalization, aggressive fund-raising, and broader appeal. Between these agencies, personal friendships, casual conservations, and staff transitions provided a constant exchange of information and even "organizational secrets." They also produced sibling rivalries.

Among child-sponsorship agencies in particular, World Vision found itself jockeying for market share with a handful of competitors. Pierce had originally "borrowed" the sponsorship concept from one of the oldest agencies, Christian Children's Fund (CCF). While CCF's donor base largely remained within the Protestant mainline, they still advertised in *Christianity Today* and *Eternity* and maintained a number of evangelical donors.[56]

Another agency, Compassion Incorporated, soon emerged to become World Vision's closest evangelical competitor. Compassion was founded as the Everett Swanson Evangelical Association by Everett Swanson himself, and its story initially looked incredibly similar to World Vision. Encountering poverty after visiting Korea as an international evangelist just a few years after Pierce, Swanson started an agency to make Western Christians aware of needs overseas. Swanson established a child-sponsorship model that became the base of his support soon after he saw Pierce's success. Several years after the debut of World Vision's Korean Orphan Choir, Swanson initiated a similar program. By the time that the organization began to transition from its founder and rename itself Compassion in 1963, it looked remarkably similar to World Vision even if it always remained a size smaller and step behind. Over the next few decades, the two organizations would become increasingly keen to distinguish themselves from one another through their mutually distinctive approaches, but during the early 1960s, World Vision's growth in budgets, brand, and institutional capacity came to exceed almost all other competitors.[57]

World Vision's leaders began to feel a responsibility to use their growing influence to shape American evangelicals' global outlook more intentionally. One goal became the professionalization of the missionary enterprise. Even as evangelicals fought to maintain a role for missionaries in an increasingly global world, they realized they too must adapt while empowering indigenous mission models. Among their innovations was the "church growth movement," pioneered by former missionary and founding dean of Fuller Theological Seminary's School of World Mission Donald McGavran, who advocated replacing Western mission models with indigenous church planting aimed at converting entire local cultures. McGavran labeled each culture an "unreached people group."[58]

Church growth required the latest anthropological and sociological research as well as the technology to process data. Evangelicals were comfortable with technology, having flown planes into remote jungles, broadcast the gospel over radio waves, and filmed people and places for Western audiences. Yet some feared research could quench evangelistic zeal; they preferred to rely on the Holy Spirit alone. World Vision's leaders believed the latest management and scientific tools complemented rather than replaced the Spirit. Their refrain became "If we have the resources to put a man on the moon, shouldn't world evangelization also be possible?"[59] In partnership with Fuller Theological Seminary, it brought together NASA aerospace engineers and mission executives to discuss the possibilities. They left optimistic that disciplined planning, research, and development could accomplish the task.[60] In 1966, World Vision and Fuller established the Mission Advanced Research and Communication Center (MARC). In 1967, it became a division of World Vision. MARC served as a clearinghouse and think tank for evangelical missions, collecting information, linking organizations, and applying technical assistance to aid missionaries. To head the new division, World Vision hired Edward Dayton, a former aeronautical engineer turned Fuller seminarian.[61]

MARC offered missionaries a means of greater cooperation, shared data, and rigorous research while seeking to convince them that research and development could only enhance the efficiency of evangelism.[62] It sent questionnaires to every mission agency to catalog what they were doing and where they were working.[63] It offered strategic planning and management consulting to mission executives.[64] World Vision executive Paul Rees reminded fellow evangelicals that if the gospel requires their very best, then "deficiencies in planning, decision making and management" cannot be "accepted and glossed over with spiritualized explanations."[65] Even Pierce, wary of institutions and hesitant to relinquish the centrality of individual missionaries, jumped on board to promote World Vision's strategy: "We are fooling ourselves if we think that the heroic missionary and evangelistic efforts of the past will stir the young people of today. . . . This is fast becoming a world of the super-educated technical leader." Pierce had before filled his staff with pastors, evangelists, and missionaries; now World Vision saw an influx of computer programmers, engineers, and systems analysts eager to utilize "today's satellite communications, global television, the marvels of electronic data processing" for the work of the gospel.[66]

From Missions to Humanitarianism

While professionalizing missions, World Vision also found itself enmeshed in debates over what the task of missions should be. *Christianity Today* editors claimed, "To lose the priority of the Great Commission as the defining force of the witness and work of the Church would mean transfer of trust by the Christian community for the renovation of society from foreign missions to foreign aid, from Christian benevolence to social welfare."[67] Before the 1960s, pragmatism fueled evangelical mission growth and led evangelicals to dismiss the larger conciliar mission debates as irrelevant. By the time they returned to fight what they perceived as an ecumenical watering down of evangelistic convictions, they discovered that the theological debates had moved on without them. In reassessing their own missiology, they were now playing catch-up as they debated the role of social action alongside the primacy of evangelism.[68]

In 1966, two large evangelical conferences sought to agree upon a common missiological identity.[69] Sponsored by the IFMA and EFMA, the first conference brought 938 delegates from seventy-one countries and 150 mission boards to Wheaton College for the Congress on the Church's World-wide Mission. It defended evangelism as the indisputable priority of mission while affirming MARC's recent infusion of new management techniques "to make plain to the world their theory, strategy and practice of the church's universal mission."[70] Several conference delegates acknowledged divisive social issues such as race and poverty in America but offered no solutions. Wheaton settled for reaffirming evangelical standards and attacking the ecumenical movement's drift away from them.[71]

Five months later, even more evangelicals gathered in Berlin, Germany, for the World Congress on Evangelism. Convened by Billy Graham and Carl Henry on the occasion of *Christianity Today*'s tenth anniversary, Berlin's theme, "One Race, One Gospel, One Task," sought to unite evangelicals around the priority of "biblical evangelism."[72] *Christianity Today* called the congress a "breakthrough" for evangelical unity, and Billy Graham's opening address set the stage: "Evangelism is the only revolutionary force that can change our world. . . . If the church went back to its main task of proclaiming the gospel and getting people converted to Christ, it would have a far greater impact on the social, moral, and psychological needs of men than any other thing it could possibly do."[73] Few evangelical mission agencies quibbled with the priority of individual conversion as the key to social transformation, but they were far less certain what that meant for any efforts to address material and political concerns.[74] In the words of another missionary, "In the drive of evangelism, too often we have rushed by the hungry ones to get to the lost ones."[75] Some feared any turn from evangelism toward humanitarian aid. Others saw social ministries as a means to evangelize, while still others included physical needs as part and parcel of their larger mission.[76]

The crises at home and abroad in the 1960s made it increasingly difficult to ignore these social issues. Carl Henry's *Christianity Today* editorials told preachers to say something about material distress in their sermons but rarely offered anything beyond general abstractions.[77] Graham became a convert in support of President Lyndon Johnson's War on Poverty, testifying before Congress and asking its members for their continued support, but he remained a fair-weather fan of government social programs.[78] Evangelicals continued to acknowledge social suffering, but reaching no consensus, they said little about it.

As evangelical debates over the relationship of evangelism and social concerns grew, World Vision balked at efforts to separate the two. Pierce was rarely careful to nuance his theological language; rather he persuaded through pragmatism and folksy piety: "You can't preach to people whose stomachs are empty. First, you have to give them food."[79] He wanted evangelicals to house refugees, feed the hungry, as well as evangelize the world, and he presented World Vision as a means to meet needs comprehensively.

Yet, while Pierce grew impatient with the missiological debates growing among his fellow evangelicals, the managers and marketers within his organization recognized the need to communicate World Vision's unique approach. By 1962, World Vision labeled that approach "total evangelism," "a fully homogenized ministry in which every part is integrated and blended into the whole."[80] In its marketing appeals, staff reworked the concept into Pierce's trademark populism: "We feed the hungry because they're hungry. We give a man a blanket because he needs it. And of course we tell him of the One who died to save him. These things are not just a means to our evangelism—they are a part of it . . . an expression of Christian concern which ministers to body, soul, and spirit—which reaches out to every human need."[81]

In its second decade, World Vision was growing and maturing. While it still specialized in orphan care and missionary support, it realized that longer-term, more systematic humanitarian aid was necessary too. As it looked beyond Korea, Pierce and his lieutenants knew that the global needs were only growing and they could not ignore them. At the same time, they were caught between multiple challenges. Alongside their own often unwieldy expansion, they fretted over fellow American evangelicals' methodical debating of how best to engage social issues. On the other hand, they often faced skepticism and even scorn outside the evangelical fold from government, religious, and secular international agencies engaged in humanitarian aid.

World Vision still identified as a missionary service organization, but it realized it also functioned like a relief agency as well. The problem was that funding and infrastructure were still tied to child sponsorship, indigenous leadership development, and small-scale mission projects. World Vision did not have the budget or know-how for large-scale relief. In the 1950s, when Pierce had encountered an immediate need in the midst of war or natural disaster, an emergency appeal letter would ask supporters for funds to cover what he had already committed. By 1960, World Vision created the Mission of the Month Club. Built on the success of the child-sponsorship model, donors would pledge ten dollars a month that World Vision would reserve to deploy for emergencies. Similar relief efforts became a growing part of World Vision's work even if they remained largely unsustainable within its current structure.[82]

At the same time World Vision's own work was expanding, many denominations and religious agencies were rethinking their approach to missions. While evangelicals continued to boast increases in missionary numbers, the budgets and numbers of mainline mission agencies were shrinking. The size of religious humanitarian agencies, however, mushroomed.[83] Perhaps what evangelicals lamented as the "loss of missionary concern" was more a transfer of allegiances. Still intent on "saving the world," American Christians had begun to substitute relief and development for evangelization.[84]

The transfer of allegiances was not new. The growth of religious private voluntary organizations (PVOs) had been going strong for several decades as they provided significant relief to post–World War II Europe and expanded along with U.S. foreign assistance during the Cold War. As the United States battled the Soviet Union, these agencies served as conduits for U.S. food aid, community development, and technical assistance. When former colonies in Africa and Asia gained independence, American foreign aid became an advertisement for Western democratic values, science, and technology. Religious PVOs largely fell in line alongside diplomats and the Pentagon as relief and development became a tool of statecraft.[85]

A handful of agencies dominated the aid industry. The American Council of Voluntary Agencies for Foreign Service (ACVAFS), established to coordinate relief during World War II, continued to function after the war as an accrediting agency that allowed the oldest and largest religious humanitarian agencies such as Catholic Relief Services (CRS) and Church World Service (CWS) to maintain insider status that few younger agencies could muster. Their registered status also allowed them to receive U.S. surplus food and other commodities that came to dominate their revenue streams. As Cold War pacification and other foreign policies led the United States to pour even more resources into these humanitarian programs, the PVOs, particularly the religious organizations, became even more reliant on such grants. From 1955 to 1965, mainline Protestant agencies received 53 percent of their budgets from Washington while CRS saw an average of

67 percent of its revenue come from the federal government in the same time frame.[86] To refuse government partnership was to languish on the sidelines of the aid industry, yet an overreliance on federal aid often led to underdeveloped fund-raising and less focus on connecting with a broader public.[87]

Most religious Americans, however, supported federal aid to church-related agencies. Both governmental departments and humanitarian agencies promoted their partnerships in the popular press. The United States Information Service showcased American humanitarianism with relief boxes stamped with messages like "from the people of the United States to the People of Vietnam." CARE issued press releases and appeal letters with graphic images of hungry children alongside the arrival of U.S. farmers' foodstuffs. Church World Service promoted CROP Walks to raise awareness of world hunger. The partnership was most often mutually beneficial for all involved.[88]

In 1961, President Kennedy raised the profile of foreign aid even more. He established the Peace Corps to "promote world peace and friendship" and the United States Agency for International Development (USAID) to administer growing foreign assistance budgets. Yet while he continued to support religious PVOs, he refused them the special treatment they had often enjoyed. As USAID shifted its funding priorities from large-scale relief to more localized technical assistance, religious PVOs had to compete for grants and contracts with a number of smaller, specialized, and secular PVOs.[89]

At the same time, the leading religious PVOs were in flux. They favored a move from relief to development but struggled to retrain staff and implement new approaches into their current work.[90] They adapted to the new USAID agenda and won contracts for agricultural projects, industrial training, and the building of roads, schools, and hospitals. At the same time, the government still relied on them as first responders to global emergencies, so they could not afford to abandon the large-scale relief business. If the U.S. government often relied too heavily on PVOs to manage its diplomatic and humanitarian agenda, religious PVOs profited from federal largesse and the USAID contracts that still often matched their vision of saving the world.

In 1961, World Vision made its first foray into government partnership. Pierce had always maintained close ties with the U.S. military—traveling with them, preaching to them, and bunking on their bases—but he was careful to avoid official affiliation. He championed American foreign policy, but he feared that too close a relation to the military might compromise religious identity. Yet in 1961, World Vision established Operation Handclasp to ship hundreds of tons of relief goods in the empty cargo bins of U.S. Navy ships. By 1962, it established a separate, nonsectarian NGO, World Vision Relief Organization (WVRO), to be eligible for ocean freight reimbursements and food surpluses.[91] If it was to grow in providing humanitarian relief, it could not ignore the same grants and subsidies that benefited other organizations.

World Vision registered with USAID but failed to gain membership in the coordinating council (ACVAFS). The accrediting agency continued to fear that new organizations threatened their hard-earned government connections and questioned the motives of agencies that continued to describe themselves as missionary and evangelistic.[92] Despite the snub, World Vision sought to learn from the humanitarian community. WVRO executives visited the offices of USAID and the World Health Organization. They still conferred with NAE leaders, but now they also attended conferences led by secular PVOs on international development.

World Vision's relief budget amounted to a fraction of the budgets of the leading agencies, but by 1965 it valued the commodities it shipped overseas at almost one million dollars, doubling the amount of the previous year. Most of its government aid came in the form of freight subventions, but it also forged relationships with American corporations for in-kind donations. It shipped Campbell's soup, Carnation milk, Gerber baby food, and Johnson and Johnson pharmaceuticals throughout Asia. It insisted that its evangelical identity did not prevent it from distributing material aid, working with government and corporations, and learning from nonevangelical humanitarians.[93]

While World Vision felt it could no longer ignore these new revenue and resource avenues, other evangelicals continued to dislike material aid and identified it as one more sign of a drift away from traditional missions. The overall debate, however, was much more complicated, as evangelicals often saw this as an opportunity to play both sides. Clyde Taylor, elevated to general director of the NAE in 1963, had previously worked for years as the NAE's secretary of public affairs. Over decades in Washington, D.C., he lobbied for greater support of evangelical missionaries abroad and sometimes chastised the government for giving Catholic agencies special treatment or watering down what he considered to be the nation's religious moorings at home and abroad. At the same time, he also came to see "foreign policy as a mission field." He paved the way for World Relief, chartered by the NAE, to rely heavily on federal funding for its programs of refugee resettlement and relief throughout Southeast Asia.[94] Similarly, agencies like the Mennonite Central Committee (MCC) viewed government aid as an opportunity to expand their mission and recognized their expansion required increased development expertise.[95] Other agencies like Compassion admitted they had a biblical responsibility to save body and soul but limited their ability to apply for government support by insisting that any overseas relief go through local churches and missionaries.[96]

In the 1960s, evangelicals were still hashing out the role of material aid within global missions. One issue in which evangelicals fixated was the expansion of the Peace Corps. Initially, they applauded the program, but perceived slights chipped away at their optimism.[97] They complained first that Catholics received an unfair advantage. While the program approved Catholic Georgetown and Notre Dame as training centers, it refused Wheaton College as too sectarian. *Christianity Today* recounted stories of Peace Corps volunteers assigned to teach religion in Catholic mission schools.[98] Beyond interreligious discrimination, they also feared that Peace Corps volunteers undermined Christian missions. They accused the United States of "dumping" volunteers into sites that would lead to the displacement of missionaries and local Christian leaders. Occasionally, they painted volunteers as ugly Americans, culturally insensitive and immoral.[99] Yet most often they affirmed the program's mobilization of Americans for international purposes, and they felt free to copy the model to experiment with their own short-term service programs such as the Christian Service Corps and Southern Baptists' Journeymen program that recruited lay missionaries for two-year assignments.[100]

Even if evangelicals disagreed over their own approaches to international aid, they began to agree that the expansion of the military, aid agencies, and international business marked "the comparative shrinkage of foreign missions to small potatoes in our international relations." As a result, they set out to make "the whole of America's secular contact with the heathen world an informal Christian mission."[101] If America was God's instrument, they must engage debates on foreign policy, international aid, and military intervention. Again, however, they shared no consensus on how. *Christianity Today* feared in the 1960s that emulating the large religious PVOs was a slippery slope and reminded readers that the same groups championing secularization at home gladly accepted government money abroad.[102] Yet as historian Axel Schäfer has argued, even if American evangelicals often argued publicly against liberal public policies and an expanding state, they were often simultaneously expanding in tandem with a "big government conservatism" that depended on their willingness to participate in new U.S. methods of statecraft. If the issues over social welfare programs at home remained contentious, evangelical agencies abroad generally relented to embrace foreign aid as a part of their mission with much less controversy.[103]

American evangelicals also came to expand their global focus beyond the front lines of the Cold War. When a famine struck India in 1966, *Christianity Today* printed images of emaciated bodies, which it often had avoided previously in its pages.[104] It noted the work of World Vision as well as nonevangelical agencies such as CWS and Lutheran World Relief, and it asked its readers to join the united relief efforts. The same article highlighted a rare social statement from Billy Graham urging Americans to share their wealth with the world's underdeveloped countries: "There is a social aspect of the Gospel that many people ignored." Graham's words modeled evangelicals' increased attention and clearer focus on material suffering.[105] Not that evangelism was in danger of being cast aside. *Christianity Today* still insisted that "the best way to improve world conditions is to bring men to Christ and deliver them from the bondage of false religions."[106]

Vietnam Redefines World Vision's Global Engagement

The escalation of the Vietnam War reshaped the international perspective of almost all American Christians in the 1960s. It unintentionally served as a testing ground for playing out American evangelicals' debates over missions and humanitarianism as well as questions over supporting the state at home and partnering with governments abroad. A melding of political and religious rhetoric initially depicted Vietnam as "the new face of an old enemy," the latest site where atheistic communism fought to eliminate a country's right to choose democracy and faith. Despite his hardline political positions and increasing religious persecution of the Buddhist majority of his own people, many Americans saw South Vietnamese president Ngo Dinh Diem, a Christian, as "God's man" for Vietnam.[107] Dating back to

1954–55, the American press had reported how U.S. Navy ships succeeded in rescuing one million Catholic refugees fleeing religious persecution in the North through "Operation Passage to Freedom."[108] Catholic humanitarian doctor Tom Dooley became the American face of the story. Alongside the refugees ferried from North to South, Dooley documented the communist persecution for *Reader's Digest* as well as through his own best-selling books with provocative titles such as *Deliver Us from Evil*. Until his death in 1961, he repeatedly landed on the list of most admired Americans. Just like Bob Pierce in Korea, Dooley shaped Americans' perceptions of Southeast Asia and a righteous rationale for Cold War rhetoric.[109]

Before troop escalation in 1965, Americans perhaps heard as much about the humanitarian efforts to win the hearts and minds of the Vietnamese people as the actual conflict itself. Catholic Relief Services (CRS) had worked alongside the U.S. Navy initially to resettle Catholic refugees, and by 1958 four of the largest religious relief services (CRS, CWS, MCC, and International Voluntary Services [IVS]) administered the bulk of U.S. humanitarian aid.[110] In promoting their work, agencies flooded Americans with heartwarming stories to raise funds as well as convince the public of the rightness of their cause.

For American evangelicals, missionaries became trusted news sources for updates on the "other war" in Vietnam, and their message was consistent: "Alongside the more obvious turmoil that now engulfs Vietnam, there is a war being waged for souls."[111] They claimed that the conflict opened new doors to evangelistic opportunity: "It seems just a matter of time between whether it is Communist guerillas or the Christian gospel that claims the yet unreached tribes of northern South Vietnam."[112] They even claimed that evangelistic success helped to turn the tide militarily, as they made the case that fewer Vietnamese Christians joined the Vietcong than their non-Christian neighbors. In the midst of war, however, missionaries also became martyrs. In 1962, the Vietcong kidnapped three Christian and Missionary Alliance (CMA) workers, and the next year they killed two Wycliffe missionaries. It was clear within the evangelical press that the missionary effort "was inextricably wed to the struggle for freedom in Vietnam."[113]

The 1964 Gulf of Tonkin Resolution escalated and Americanized the war. President Lyndon Johnson authorized air strikes in North Vietnam and committed hundreds of thousands of American soldiers.[114] President Johnson matched military escalation by intensifying humanitarian aid. In 1965, he commissioned an ACVAFS delegation to assess humanitarian needs in Vietnam. CWS, CRS, CARE, MCC, and Lutheran World Relief all agreed to help but cautioned that they would need government resources. Soon USAID was spending a quarter of its annual budget in Vietnam.[115]

Pierce also jumped into Vietnam with both feet, which would lead to significant change within World Vision. By the early 1960s, he was regularly flying into the country with American troops, visiting missionaries, assessing needs, and capturing it all on film. World Vision had sponsored orphans and missionary projects in Vietnam since 1954, but as the war escalated by 1965, so did the organization's work. For the first time, however, instead of funneling all funds through local mission agencies, World Vision instituted its own large-scale distribution networks and relief programs. Soon it was constructing and staffing three Christian refugee centers, two orphanages, a hospital for the blind, a vocational training school for tribal people, and a halfway house for disabled war veterans. It supplied wheelchairs and crutches to Vietnamese hospitals and shipped thousands of pounds of relief aid. Commodities came from local church volunteers who assembled small "Viet Kits" to deliver overseas as well as from expanded USAID grants. World Vision continued to rely on missionaries, military, and local churches, but now it also turned to government resources and the broader aid community.[116]

In 1965, images of Vietnam were not yet ubiquitous on the evening news. To bring the war to Americans, Pierce released his longest film, *Vietnam Profile*. It became an instant success as World Vision booked the film for eight hundred to nine hundred showings a month for over a year. Dozens of network television stations showed the film for free as a public service announcement. The attention garnered Pierce network television interviews, book contracts, and new funds.[117]

The film followed Pierce's typical pattern. He promised that viewers would "fly over the battlefields, witness war's devastation, see the heroic work of the chaplains, thrill to answered prayer with courageous mountain tribespeople, meet the people of Viet Nam, and watch missionaries and Vietnamese Christians in their evangelistic ministry."[118] A tour through Saigon presented an exotic land highlighted by the city's colorful marketplace, modern hotels, and beautiful women. Pierce introduced scenes of abject poverty and disease as well as dead and wounded soldiers. He saw U.S. involvement as righteous, and his narration made clear that the enemy remained an anti-Christian communism. He acknowledged the growing controversy Vietnam provoked at home but stressed that World Vision's purposes were not political. Instead they were "motivated by the desperate needs we find . . . and by the conviction that as a Christian agency we must do all we can to help." He was confident that Christians could not ignore the need to "stand with Viet Nam in its crisis hour."[119]

The film also depicted the diversity of World Vision's work. Pierce's narration highlighted World Vision's weekly evangelistic rallies and Christian literature distribution but also captured the "total evangelism" that World Vision professed. He showed tribal Christians constructing a church as well as a new village school. He interviewed CMA missionaries who led Bible studies but also taught new farming methods. He illustrated how each Viet Kit included emergency relief items as well as the Gospel of John. Pierce felt the combination carried a message: "Yes, we care about your eternal destiny—but we also care about you now."[120]

Pierce praised missionaries as well as the U.S. military. After hitching rides on army helicopters to scout orphanages and deliver aid, he attested to the heroism of American pilots. He witnessed soldiers risking their lives to rescue refugees from the communists and volunteer to assist World Vision medics in treating the wounded Vietnamese.[121] Pierce hoped to demonstrate the true spirit of the American soldier and make viewers think twice before criticizing the war: "Here in Viet Nam, where the 'cream of the crop' of American military 'know how' and experience is concentrated, it is heartwarming and encouraging to meet dedicated men of God in uniform who know why they're here, who brought them here, and what He led them here to do."[122]

Still serving as World Vision's voice, Pierce also increasingly affirmed the humanitarian community. In the past, Pierce had acknowledged mainstream relief agencies only to contrast them with World Vision's work as a missionary service organization. A few years earlier he had called State Department officials and aid workers "ugly Americans." By 1965, however, he was calling USAID workers "dedicated Americans" and the "bravest men I know," willing to live and suffer with the Vietnamese people. While he continued to caution against an overreliance on government support, he now proudly claimed World Vision's status as an accredited USAID agency and acknowledged the good work of all missionary, government, and relief agencies he saw working in Vietnam, from the religious to the secular. He illustrated new partnerships by retelling one of his favorite stories from Vietnam. One local village had prayed for a tractor to farm its land. Missionaries made the request known to Pierce who used World Vision funds to purchase a John Deere. He called in USAID workers to transport the tractor and teach the villagers to use it. Where it once saw competitors and enemies, World Vision now found allies.[123]

Pierce's depictions of World Vision's work in Vietnam demonstrated the subtle shifts in the organization. He continued to see the world through glasses colored by Cold War anticommunism and American exceptionalism, but acknowledged that close association with American politics was no longer universally appreciated and brought liabilities in work overseas. He remained firmly committed to his evangelical identity but grew increasingly frustrated with fellow evangelicals' limited vision abroad as they questioned his willingness to partner with outsiders and engage in social ministries beyond evangelism. Pierce still supported missionaries, but the size of World Vision's Vietnam programs made it necessary to hire its own staff to transport, store, distribute, and account for relief aid.[124] Missions were still number one, but World Vision no longer ignored humanitarian relief while also accessing government aid. As it professionalized alongside expanding budgets and staff, the organization began to take on a more prominent role at home among evangelical parachurch ministries. Abroad, it was well connected among local Christian communities throughout Asia, and it began to garner more attention among the international aid community as well as the global church. By the end of 1967, World Vision recognized that it was entering new territory and continued change was inevitable as new contexts and incredible expansion forced it to grow beyond its founding vision and its founder.

CHAPTER 5

Taking Domestic Debates of God and Country Overseas

WHILE WORLD VISION'S BUDGET and programs continued to expand, by the middle of its second decade, the organization was in trouble. Money was still tight and tensions remained high. Future World Vision president Graeme Irvine described the organization at the time: "Anyone looking at World Vision would see an organization that was action-oriented, centered around Bob Pierce himself, strongly evangelical, innovative, and progressive. As with most things, there was another side to the coin. The apparent strengths had corresponding weaknesses: instability, dependent on the idea and personality of one person, narrow relationships and limited international perspective."[1] Despite extended medical leaves, Pierce remained physically and mentally unhealthy. His uncontrollable temper had severed ties with family and friends. His authoritarianism had become an organizational liability. He made promises on behalf of the organization in his travels around the world that became difficult for World Vision to keep. He rebuffed his board's pleas for more stability and accountability. Believing the organization he built could not survive without him, he tendered his resignation in a fit of rage and dared the board to accept it. The board called his bluff and asked Pierce to leave in October 1967. Again, Graeme Irvine captured the sentiment of World Vision's emerging second generation of leaders: "Without Bob Pierce World Vision would probably not have been born. It is equally true, in my opinion, that with him it probably would not have survived."[2]

Pierce had dreamed of being an international evangelist, the Billy Graham of Asia, and he succeeded far beyond his wildest expectations. He preached to tens of thousands while also championing forgotten missionaries, bringing global need to the attention of American evangelicals, and goading them into responding with material and spiritual support. Yet, the world Pierce brought home to fellow evangelicals, evangelicals themselves, and the organization he had built were changing. Up to a point, Pierce changed along with them, but the leaders that Pierce brought alongside him also came to know that he had taken World Vision as far as he was able to go. World Vision had outgrown its founder.

World Vision publicly announced Pierce's resignation due to medical reasons. Pierce had continually prayed that he might "burn out for God," and his supporters praised and even admired him for his sacrifice. By almost all accounts, World Vision parted ways with its founder fairly and slowly, funding an around-the-world farewell tour for much of the next year in order for him and his wife Lorraine to say goodbye to all those they had helped.

Yet, Pierce's story continued to be one of tragedy and bitterness. On their 1968 farewell tour, his oldest daughter attempted suicide and later succeeded, in her second attempt, while Pierce was again overseas searching for extended medical and psychological treatment in Switzerland. He remained estranged from his family for much of the rest of his life. In the first few years after his resignation, he accused former friends of wresting control of his organization away from him. While often too frail to continue constantly traveling, he knew nothing else but a peripatetic life of preaching, meeting humanitarian needs, and chasing adventure. Within a few years, Pierce would take over a fledgling missionary agency that resembled a young World Vision, renamed it Samaritan's Purse, and took pleasure as long as he could in resuming global travel and measuring his new venture against what had become of the organization he first founded.[3]

If Pierce's departure initially brought financial instability and organizational unrest, it eventually allowed World Vision to emerge out from under its founder's shadow. As the organization searched for Pierce's replacement, board chair Dick Halverson, a longtime World Vision insider who was well regarded among fellow American evangelicals, was named interim president, while Ted Engstrom maintained day-to-day operations. Engstrom was already well respected within World Vision for bringing stability alongside Pierce's sometimes erratic behavior and overzealous charisma. He was also respected among his evangelical peers for his leadership in professionalizing parachurch ministries and redefining the nature of evangelical missions, yet he knew that he was not the man that the increasingly global World Vision needed at the helm long term. World Vision faced an unknown future. What shape would the organization take in its second generation?

A new generation of American evangelicals began to ask the same question of themselves. If Billy Graham, Carl Henry, and Bob Pierce had fostered a neo-evangelical movement that championed itself as the new mainstream within American Christianity, where was the movement headed? Some established leaders feared American evangelicalism was fragmenting as issues such as civil rights, questions of morality, and the role of social action stirred debates at home while a growing distrust of the war in Vietnam and the role of Western missionaries abroad occupied attention overseas. As foreign relations historian Andrew Preston has noted, conservative Christian "views of world order were shaped profoundly by views of domestic order."[4] Evangelicals struggled to find their way in upholding their self-proclaimed role as custodian of conservative, American, and Christian values at home as well as championing the expansion and defense of those values abroad.

While evangelicals contemplated how to use their growing voice in the public square, the powers that be also took greater notice of them. The same year Pierce resigned from World Vision, Richard Nixon launched his bid for the White House with an article in *Reader's Digest* calling for the restoration of America's "national character and moral stamina." Nixon ended his plea by reminding readers that "a nation weakened by racial conflict and lawlessness at home cannot meet the challenges of leadership abroad."[5] Conservative Christians who flocked to Nixon in 1968 and again in 1972 could not have agreed more. Nixon had tapped into the dual impulse of American evangelicals: a custodial impulse on morality at home and a desire to translate those Christian American ideals abroad.[6]

Over the period that became known as the long sixties, the majority of American evangelicals embraced God and country, but as politics came to occupy more and more of evangelicals' attention, it was clear that a single narrative could no longer hold. The melding of faith and fervent anticommunism that had united evangelicals in their outlook at home and abroad since World War II had begun to fracture with an increasingly unpopular war, growing fears of secularism, and the dawning recognition of living intertwined in a globalized world. Established evangelicals disagreed on how best to use their influence to remake America in the image they envisioned. Other younger voices no longer accepted pleas for patience as an answer to their call for social action. Within these new tensions, World Vision often served as a lightning rod as evangelicals sought to define their own relationship with American culture, the U.S. government and its foreign policy, as well as their own global imaginations.

World Vision still championed American virtues, but no longer without reservation. Operations throughout Southeast Asia during the Vietnam conflict became increasingly difficult for World Vision to manage. Facing attacks on all sides, the organization debated the damage to its reputation even as the work served as a proving ground for its staff's growing confidence in faith-based humanitarianism. It fought for a more global and socially engaged evangelicalism even if it did not go as far as a number of those inside and outside the movement would have wished. And many within the organization constantly worried that it was straying from its missionary roots even as it continued to champion the missionary enterprise through research, practice, and its own growing interest in theological reflection. As an action-first agency, World Vision most often came to know what it would become by forging its identity through crises. As those crises mounted over the decade, World Vision was due for significant change. Much of the change mirrored American evangelicals' own debates over their relationship with God and country.

A Fragmenting Evangelicalism

In 1969, World Vision hired its second president, Stan Mooneyham. A rising star within the Billy Graham Evangelistic Association (BGEA), Mooneyham came with Pierce's entrepreneurial and evangelistic spirit, but he had also earned his stripes working his way up through several of evangelicals' most prominent ministries. Reared in Oklahoma and ordained as a Free Will Baptist minister, he launched the Free Will Baptists' magazine as a teenager and became the denomination's youngest executive secretary at the age of twenty-seven. In 1959, he worked for the NAE as editor of its *United Evangelical Action* periodical. He joined the BGEA in 1964, and later became the special assistant to Billy Graham, organizing the World Congress on Evangelism before being named BGEA's vice president of international relations in 1967. As part organizational man, part mission bureaucrat, and part evangelistic globetrotter, Mooneyham seemed a perfect mix of World Vision's past and present. He trusted Engstrom's managerial methods but made sure that World Vision maintained its pioneering mentality. He was much more willing and adept than Pierce at brokering relationships and negotiating compromises, but he too would not be beholden to what he sometimes saw as American evangelicals' limited vision. Mooneyham operated as a bridge between the first generation of establishment evangelicals and the yet uncertain emerging generation both at home and abroad.[7]

As Mooneyham took the helm, he quickly hit the ground running to mend old wounds while also pushing World Vision in new directions. With Pierce gone, World Vision continued to expand. Over the 1970s, it grew from eight to forty countries, and its annual income ballooned from $4.5 million to $100 million. World Vision no longer apologized that its programs had shifted from primarily missionary support to relief and development as it was increasingly clear that it had evolved from a small evangelical mission agency to a leading Christian humanitarian organization with award-winning marketing campaigns and increased government funding.[8]

Over the same period, many American evangelicals felt they had achieved the mainstream success they craved. While they had no singular political position at the beginning of the new decade, they proudly claimed elected officials who identified as evangelicals like Oregon senator Mark Hatfield and Illinois representative John R. Anderson. They relished Billy Graham's close relationship with President Richard Nixon and appreciated the attention Nixon gave them as the moral backbone of his "silent majority." As the majority of evangelicals began to fall more predictably into the Republican camp, some felt that they should play a role in party politics as the rise of a new conservatism began to take shape. The majority, however, found less institutional ways of sustaining a Christian America.

Evangelicals made dramatic inroads through embracing media and engaging popular culture. They produced national best sellers like Kenneth Taylor's *The Living Bible* and Hal Lindsey's *Late Great Planet Earth*.[9] Pat Robertson had begun airing his daily *700 Club* program in 1966 and Robert Schuller's *Hour of Power* first appeared in 1970 as evangelical programming soon became a fixture on local television channels nationwide. The "Jesus People" brought Christian exuberance to one segment of the youth counterculture and ascended into the national headlines as *Time*'s June 21, 1971, cover depicted a "Jesus Revolution."[10] Even Bill Bright's buttoned-up Campus Crusaders planned a weeklong evangelical "Woodstock" in Dallas, Texas. Crusade's Explo '72 brought together evangelical "straights" and born again "far outs" with 85,000 students evangelizing the city's streets by day and rallying at night to hear Billy Graham as well as music icons Johnny Cash and Kris Kristofferson.[11]

Yet, growth did not necessarily dictate a single evangelical voice. In fact, evangelicals expanded as much through diffusion and division as through any united front. This worried some establishment evangelicals who had toiled for decades to build a movement. By 1967, *Christianity Today* editor Carl Henry lamented that evangelicals stood "at the brink of crisis" with debates over sociopolitical involvement, theology, and ecumenism set to fracture the evangelical voice even further.[12] The next year *Christianity Today* financier J. Howard Pew forced Henry to resign over his unwillingness to narrow the magazine's perspective and refrain from publishing articles calling for evangelical social action.[13] New editor Harold Lindsell feigned apoliticism, but he applied President Richard Nixon's description of his "silent majority" to portray evangelicals as conservative Republicans. By 1974, Bill Bright, pastors Jack Hayford and John Hagee, and Amway founder Richard DeVos had hatched a "Plan to Save America" through rallying Christians to engage more explicitly in politics through precinct-level political activism and running for office.[14]

While some voices rallied evangelicals to seek greater entrée into the nation's conservative establishment, others hoped to take the movement in the opposite direction. Having come of age in the turbulent 1960s, a number of "young evangelicals"—urban, educated, and articulate—challenged the evangelical establishment as a cultural Christianity. While establishment evangelicals had prioritized evangelism in order to oppose a "compromising ecumenism," younger evangelicals claimed they had ignored social justice in the process. In 1969, Billy Graham hosted the U.S. Congress on Evangelism in Minneapolis to address their concerns. The agenda gave speakers time to address topics such as Vietnam, revolution, race, and poverty that past evangelical conferences had largely sought to avoid. In registering his support for the gathering, World Vision vice president Ted Engstrom acknowledged that evangelicals had previously been too slow to deal with the "social, political, and economic evils so evident in American life."[15] Of course, the voices were not all favorable. Billy Graham's father-in-law and *Christianity Today* executive editor L. Nelson Bell wrote that he was "afraid that evangelicals were moving away from the primary task of evangelism and developing a new social gospel."[16]

The following year, the triennial Urbana mission convention of the InterVarsity Christian Fellowship (IVCF) gathered twelve thousand students around the theme of "Christ the Liberator." Many nodded as Peruvian Samuel Escobar challenged the "middle-class captivity" of American evangelicalism. They stood and cheered as black evangelist Tom Skinner preached that "any gospel that does not want to go where people are hungry and poverty-stricken and set them free in the name of Jesus Christ—is not the gospel."[17] Carl Henry agreed that "the time is overdue for a dedicated vanguard to move evangelical witness to frontier involvement in the social crisis." He worried that if evangelicals avoided social issues, they would lose the coming generation.[18]

A number of young professors began criticizing the lack of social concern in evangelical publications. Marquette sociologist David Moberg urged evangelicals in *The Great Reversal: Evangelism Versus Social Concern* to consider not only individual but structural sin. Indiana State University historian Richard Pierard's *The Unequal Yoke: Evangelical Christianity and Political Conservatism* and Calvin College philosopher Richard Mouw's *Political Evangelism* criticized the evangelical equation of Christian values with political conservatism. Establishment evangelicals like Denver Seminary president Vernon Grounds and Carl Henry also contributed to the deluge of books with titles like *Evangelicalism and Social Responsibility* (1969), *Revolution and the Christian Faith* (1971), and *A Plea for Evangelical Demonstration* (1971). With dozens of books published, one critic described the late 1960s to early 1970s as an "unmistakable renaissance in evangelical social concern." Many evangelicals at least thumbed through these popular books while others flocked to study under teachers who saw the social implications of the Christian scriptures.[19]

The movement attracted activists as well as academics. In 1965, Fred Alexander and his son John began publishing *Freedom Now*, a journal that urged evangelicals to take up the cause of civil rights, and one of the few spaces where African Americans could confront and question white evangelical assumptions on race. By 1969, the Alexanders renamed their journal the *Other Side* and broadened their mission beyond race to "the other side of America that is hungry, defeated and miserable" in order to "apply the whole gospel to the problems of suffering people."[20]

In 1971, another small group of students from Trinity Evangelical Divinity School formed the People's Christian Coalition, which emerged as the most aggressive voice among the younger evangelicals. Led by Jim

Wallis, they defined themselves as radical evangelicals critiquing the church for ignoring the injustices of American society. In the first issue of their magazine, the *Post-American*, Wallis claimed the church's cultural captivity caused it "to lose its prophetic voice by preaching and exporting a pro-American gospel and a materialistic faith which supports and sanctifies the values of American society."[21]

These young evangelicals represented a minority, and they rarely spoke with a common voice. They taught in universities, lived in alternative communities, and organized political action committees. Few evangelicals were willing to accept their more radical views, but many were open to new perspectives. In the wake of the civil rights movement, the Vietnam War, and the ongoing Watergate scandal, growing numbers of evangelicals knew they could no longer call for evangelism to the exclusion of social engagement. In 1973, fifty leaders came together over Thanksgiving weekend at an inner-city Chicago YMCA to discuss evangelical social responsibilities. They renounced those who either dismissed evangelism or wedded the church to conservative middle-American values. The resulting "Chicago Declaration" called for economic justice, peacemaking, racial reconciliation, and gender equality. It served as a manifesto for the young evangelicals and received broad coverage in the religious and secular press. The *Washington Post* reported that it "well could launch a religious movement that could shake both political and religious life in America." At the least, it demonstrated the surfacing of an evangelical left.[22]

Amid growing evangelical divisions, World Vision proved difficult to categorize as all sides sought to claim the organization. Some young evangelicals referenced World Vision as an example of evangelical social action, and a few joined its staff. Others depicted the organization as part of the establishment, too big and bureaucratized to speak out prophetically Among the few elder evangelical statesmen invited to attend and sign the Chicago Declaration were two from World Vision. Paul Rees had served as a World Vision vice president since 1957. Carl Henry had recently joined World Vision as lecturer at large. In his recollections on the Chicago gathering, Ron Sider, organizer of the gathering and its offshoot Evangelicals for Social Action, recounted that Carl Henry signed his name to the declaration but then removed it. Henry often worried that the younger generation went too far and too quickly papered over core evangelical distinctives, but he had "experienced his own alienation and isolation in recent years because of his forthright demand for social concern among evangelicals." After reconsidering, Henry felt "he must support the call for greater evangelical social concern, whatever the cost." After re-signing his name, he paused to embrace longtime critic Jim Wallis.[23]

Mooneyham was delighted his organization found support within multiple evangelical constituencies, because he realized that raising funds for multimillion dollar budgets necessitated appeals to a broad conservative constituency. While he pressed World Vision to take stands outside its traditional comfort zones and deputized leaders to ensure that his organization had a voice at all of the pressing evangelical debates, he was also a pragmatist who felt he could not afford to spend too much time wordsmithing evangelical treatises. Perhaps the difficulty of categorizing an evolving World Vision was entirely by design. If all sides claimed a piece of the organization, World Vision appealed to each of them. At the same time, it refused to let any one of them define it.

New Outlooks on Vietnam and Americans' Flagging Support

Just as evangelicals' ongoing debates over deeper social engagement led to further fragmentation and an uncertain future, America's deepening involvement in Vietnam was dividing the entire country. The self-immolation of Buddhist monks, South Vietnamese government corruption, and President Diem's assassination had begun to puncture the idealism of many Americans. While popular support for the war peaked at 61 percent in August 1965 with the escalation of American troops, a growing antiwar movement featured national teach-ins at universities, the emergence of the left-wing student organization Students for a Democratic Society (SDS), raucous antiwar demonstrations, and the burning of draft cards.[24]

The antiwar movement did not belong solely to a secular New Left. The churches, especially mainline Protestant leaders, also questioned American foreign policy. The National Council of Churches (NCC) lobbied President Lyndon B. Johnson's administration to halt bombing raids and allow the United Nations to negotiate a peace. In 1965, the Reverend Richard John Neuhaus, Father Daniel J. Berrigan, and Rabbi Abraham Joshua Heschel formed a multifaith grassroots organization, Clergy and Laity Concerned About Vietnam (CALCAV). In 1967, Martin Luther King Jr. condemned the Vietnam War from the Riverside Church pulpit. That same year, Protestant Robert McAfee Brown, Jew Abraham Joshua Heschel, and Catholic Michael Novak co-wrote *Vietnam: Crisis of Conscience.* The simplicities of past Cold War rhetoric no longer held. Vietnam thoroughly fractured the religious landscape.[25]

The vast majority of evangelicals throughout the 1960s continued to support the war. The Judeo-Christian consensus that undergirded the fight against atheistic communism during the previous two decades was fracturing and leading to a politicized civil religion. By the late 1960s, the most prominent civil religion came to stand for the alignment of political and theological conservativism, and both evangelicals and Republican politicians came to use it as a tool for their benefit. They still fervently believed that communism must be stopped wherever possible, but they also were equally clear that they opposed antiwar sentiments as unpatriotic and unbecoming of Christian Americans. Continued support of Vietnam offered evangelicals another opportunity to position themselves as the new mainstream, the voice of America's silent majority.[26] In 1965, L. Nelson Bell assured President Johnson that the "real Christian position in America" was represented by *Christianity Today* and not mainline liberals, "a minority . . . more interested in political and economic matters than in preaching the gospel."[27] Later that year, Billy Graham hosted President Johnson at his Houston crusade to lend the president his support and display his continued loyalty for the war. As Christian patriots, evangelicals trusted that America's motives were pure and labeled antiwar demonstrators as "extremists" perilously close to treason.[28] Evangelicals saved their greatest rancor for antiwar clergy. In 1967, as Carl Henry looked out his Washington, D.C., office window onto an NCC clergy protest, he asked *Christianity Today* readers, "What special wisdom do clergymen have on the military and international intricacies of the U.S. government's involvement in Viet Nam? None."[29]

Evangelicals undergirded their support of the war at home with stories of Christian success overseas. They highlighted missionaries and Vietnamese Christians as well as soldiers, accusing the religious antiwar movement of ministering more to draft dodgers than servicemen. They encouraged local churches to support the troops, encouraged evangelical military chaplains to start a revival, stocked military bases with gospel literature, and led Bible studies. One chaplain expressed what he considered the consensus among his colleagues in Vietnam: "You tell those 'God-is-dead' fellows back home that there is a living God out here in Vietnam!" To counter reports of soldiers losing faith, doing drugs, and brutalizing villages, some evangelicals depicted troops as "disciples in uniform" who could be "the most tremendous missionary force the Christian church has ever had."[30] Their support of the military allowed evangelicals to merge their support of God and country at home and abroad.

By the late 1960s, however, many evangelicals too began to question whether the war in Vietnam was winnable. *Christianity Today* lamented that the combined budgets of all relief agencies were still less than the cost of one B-52 bomber, but editors urged its readers to continue their support of evangelism and humanitarian aid. Evangelicals were warming to the idea of humanitarian aid as another way to continue their support of U.S. efforts in Vietnam, but as the war escalated, humanitarianism grew more complicated. Relief missions became increasingly dangerous as aid workers became targets who had to rely on the military for transportation, supplies, and security. When the United States turned to a policy of pacification to fight the insurgency, some aid workers questioned whether they had become pawns of U.S. policymakers.[31]

In 1967, the United States consolidated all aid programs into the new office of Civil Operations and Revolutionary Development Support (CORDS) under the command of U.S. Army general William Westmoreland. Many of the established ACVAFS agencies complained that such an action politicized and militarized foreign aid. Aid workers in some ecumenical and peace churches spoke out against U.S. policy, specifically condemning the bombing of North Vietnam and the invasion of Cambodia as inhumane.[32] The American Friends Service Committee and Mennonite Central Committee even defied U.S. sanctions to provide aid to the North Vietnamese. The U.S. government responded by slashing funding to aid agencies it now found troublesome.[33]

Many of the largest established agencies decreased their footprint in Southeast Asia in disagreement with U.S. policy or in order to salvage their reputation in an increasingly unpopular war. Newer agencies quickly stepped up to pick up the slack as the U.S. military still depended on aid agencies to "win the hearts and minds" of the Vietnamese. As a result, the number of private voluntary organizations (PVOs) and dollars spent in Vietnam continued to increase even as the collective experience and expertise of aid organizations declined.[34]

With aid to the established ecumenical agencies dwindling, many of the upstart agencies stepping into the gap to benefit from federal funding for the first time self-identified as evangelical. While still less dependent on government support than the mainline Christian organizations, many were becoming more comfortable receiving USAID contracts for their work and working alongside the U.S. government. These new partnerships sustained a version of the melding of faith and foreign policy that evangelicals had enthusiastically supported since the start of the Cold War. As a result, Vietnam served as a proving ground for the first generation of evangelical relief agencies.

Both larger and more involved than any other agency, World Vision again set the pace. Its expanding activities throughout Southeast Asia, however, forced World Vision to reassess its reputation as an American and evangelical mission agency serving the U.S. government in social amelioration projects.[35] As it developed its reputation as an increasingly competent and experienced relief agency, it continued to see how its explicit religious identity affected its reputation abroad not only among peer agencies but among aid recipients as well. At the same time, its simultaneously pro-American and increasingly professional humanitarian identity impacted its reputation among its faith-based supporters back home. In this case, World Vision may not have asked for the extra attention, but its expanding work in Southeast Asia would force the evangelical organization to make choices that would lead both its proponents and critics to find support through the agency's actions for their own political persuasions at home and abroad.

By 1970, most U.S. evangelicals could see that America was failing in Vietnam, but they refused to abandon their patriotic ardor. In 1970, South Vietnam vice president Nguyen Cao Ky visited the United States to lobby against the withdrawal of U.S. troops. World Vision welcomed him with a tour of its headquarters and a private dinner for like-minded religious leaders. Even as antiwar protesters picketed outside and conservative evangelicals, businessmen, and politicians dined inside, World Vision claimed that its work transcended politics. Workers in other agencies called World Vision naive—or worse, complicit in U.S. policy.[36]

World Vision, however, was not alone in seeking to navigate how to apply its principles alongside its newfound power and prestige in the halls of power. Billy Graham, for example, sought firsthand information on the war from missionaries in Vietnam. In the spring of 1970, he reported back to Nixon their misgivings about military policy in the region, but just a few months later, Graham headlined a national "Honor America Day" alongside comedian Bob Hope meant to demonstrate ongoing patriotism at the beginning of another tumultuous decade. His July 4 sermon to the ten thousand gathered at the Lincoln Memorial highlighted American virtues: the nation had opened its doors to the alienated and oppressed, shared its wealth and its faith, and always refused to use its power to subjugate other nations. America, moreover, was a land of faithful believers; it was still "one nation, under God."[37] If ecumenical voices lambasted an embattled White House, evangelicals approved of Nixon's insistence on peace with honor. America should get out of the war, but it should impress its ideals on the world by continuing to be a city on a hill.

A few evangelicals spoke out against Nixon's strategy, and Oregon senator Mark Hatfield led the way. Elected to the Senate in 1966, Hatfield became known for both his faith and his antiwar sentiments. Evangelicals were proud of his voice in government, but the majority disagreed with his stance against the war.[38] Graham had lobbied Nixon to select Hatfield as his running mate in 1968, but after Nixon selected Spiro Agnew, Hatfield became one of Nixon's harshest critics on the war. In cosponsoring the McGovern-Hatfield bill in 1971, he sought to overturn executive power, halt military funding for Vietnam, and immediately withdraw troops. Hatfield also believed that America was a city on a hill, but he feared that aggression in Vietnam was costing the nation its soul. Seated beside President Nixon at the 1973 annual prayer breakfast, Hatfield asked Americans to repent and prayed for God to forgive the nation.[39]

Hatfield feared that evangelicals had capitulated to civil religion, a position that angered the evangelical establishment.[40] If Billy Graham began to distance himself and Bill Bright removed him from Campus Crusade's board, Hatfield won adulation from a number of younger evangelicals. Invited to speak at Fuller Seminary's commencement in 1970, he found that a third of the graduating class wore black armbands on their gowns to protest the war.[41] The following year, chief staffer Wes Granberg-Michaelson put the inaugural issue of Jim Wallis's *Post-American* in Hatfield's briefcase. The cover depicted Christ with a crown of thorns draped in the American flag with a caption reading, "And they crucified him." The next week, Hatfield had Wallis on the phone for a conversation to learn more.[42]

Wallis shared Hatfield's distaste for an American civil religion. To him, America was no Israel and no city on a hill; it was Babylon: "A society blatantly manifesting violence and racism and resigned to the dictates of a corporate military complex, a people drunkenly worshiping the idolatrous

gods of American nationalism, pride, and power, a culture where values of
wealth, property, and security take top priority."⁴³ Wallis claimed that civil
religion squelched the Christian prophetic voice. It also led American
Christians to endorse as holy the evils of an America empire. He argued
that Vietnam was not a war to free oppressed people but a war against
Third World peoples, a proving ground for the military, and an opportunity
for corporate economic interests to continue to exploit underdeveloped
nations. Wallis shared the language of "Two-Thirds World" evangelicals
who were beginning to speak out in the early 1970s to critique the "cultural
Christianity" of the West. If warplanes dropping napalm bombs on North
Vietnamese villages had become the American way of life, Wallis depicted
America as a near totalitarian state fueled by the gods of consumption and
technocratic control.⁴⁴

The main target of the young evangelicals increasingly became Billy
Graham. As chief priest of the American civil religion, Graham played golf
with presidents, endorsed their policies from the pulpit, and failed to condemn the nation's corporate sin. The *Post-American* offered a point-by-
point rebuttal to Graham's 1970 "Honor America Day" sermon.⁴⁵ A few
years later, in response to the patriotic display that Bill Bright and Graham
had orchestrated at Explo '72, honoring military personnel and publicly
reading President Nixon's telegram of support, Wallis and other members
of the People's Christian Coalition disrupted the event by chanting "Stop
the War" and unfurling banners that read, "Christ *or* Country." They were
clear that Christians could not serve two gods.⁴⁶

Carl Henry again sympathized with the younger evangelicals, but he
brought serious reservations. He had spent his career building evangelicalism
into a movement able to turn America into a truly Christian nation. Yet, he
suffered from the haunting fear that just at the moment when evangelicals
had risen to positions of influence with society's power brokers, the nation
had already reached its spiritual and moral peak. The future, he worried,
would bring a downhill slide. Of course, he also felt that his younger critics
were guilty of "cheap judgment." He worried they too quickly condemned
capitalism and patriotism while escaping into utopian enthusiasm. He used
the editorial pages of *Christianity Today* to take on Wallis: if Wallis was "post-
American," Henry claimed to be "supra-American." Henry's increasing international exposure convening global mission conferences along with his teaching and travel on behalf of World Vision allowed him to imagine a faith that
transcended nationalisms of every kind, even the American variety. Yet, he

could not tolerate a vision of America as the incarnation of evil. He was not yet ready to give up on his nation.[47]

World Vision found itself forced to navigate between these two evangelical camps that debated America's place in the world. Hatfield was already serving on World Vision's board when it officially hired Carl Henry to serve as lecturer at large in 1973. Hatfield brought his increasingly radical positions on U.S. involvement in Vietnam along with his inside-the-beltway connections. Henry brought increased intellectual capacity and evangelical establishment credentials as he traveled the world to keynote indigenous pastors' gatherings, lecture at seminaries and Christian colleges, and represent World Vision at theological conferences. The two men often disagreed, but both shared an appreciation for World Vision's pragmatic focus. If evangelical conservatives still hoped that a Christian America could transform the world, and an evangelical left deplored a militaristic American empire, World Vision increasingly saw both as idealistic and naive. In founding World Vision, Pierce may too have been naive about his organization's inherent and narrow American ideals, but World Vision had moved beyond Pierce. As Mooneyham sought to build World Vision as one of the few agencies able to work alongside the full spectrum of evangelicals at home as well as an increasingly diverse set of religious and secular humanitarian agencies abroad, he saw his organization as anything but naive. In defending World Vision's continued work in Southeast Asia and the complications it brought to the organization, he confessed, "I believe in God but not Pollyanna. I am fully aware of the political and military realities."[48] If he was fully aware of the complexities abroad, he purposefully ignored the increasingly polarizing issues at home. By the mid-1970s, grassroots evangelicals were beginning to debate school textbooks, speak out against abortion, and worry about homosexuality, feminism, and the passage of the Equal Rights Amendment. Yet World Vision systematically overlooked domestic debates. Foreign policy and global humanitarianism alone were complicated enough to garner broad evangelical support, and Mooneyham worked hard to turn attention abroad.

Between a Rock and a Hard Place

Alongside its own pragmatism, the World Vision knew its donors would follow the organization's humanitarian efforts undergirding American foreign policy in Southeast Asia. As a result, World Visions expanded its work in the region even when other organizations were pulling out. In 1969–70, it received its first PL 480 Food for Peace grant from the U.S. government to transport supplies to Vietnam. As more experienced agencies left, World Vision received more USAID grants to provide medical care, refugee housing, and education for the South Vietnamese. When the United States began to bomb North Vietnamese sanctuaries in Laos and Cambodia, World Vision received permission to provide relief in these countries as well. By the early 1970s, a third of all World Vision's programs were in Vietnam, Cambodia, Thailand, and Laos.[49]

While Vietnam and Laos remained World Vision's largest operations, Cambodia came to dominate organizational lore.[50] In-country operations also led new president Mooneyham to establish his own reputation as an evangelistic risk-taker in the mold of his predecessor. Like Pierce, Mooneyham was constantly on the road, spending time on the front lines with staff, and rarely taking no for an answer. In 1970, Mooneyham organized a convoy to travel from Saigon to Cambodia's capital, Phnom Penh. When red tape and armed soldiers halted their trip at the Vietnamese-Cambodian border, he ordered the convoy to blitz the checkpoint. When they arrived in the capital with $100,000 in medical supplies and relief aid, Mooneyham gathered the recipient villagers and spoke about the love of God that motivated him to relieve suffering. Having asked God for a sign, he received a verse from Ecclesiastes. Mooneyham quoted it from *The Living Bible*: "If you wait for perfect conditions, you will never get anything done." He often retold the story to encapsulate what he hoped World Vision would stand for: accepting risks, defying bureaucrats, and doing whatever necessary to carry out Christ's mandate to feed the hungry.[51]

As the first NGO in Cambodia, World Vision siphoned medical supplies and food aid through Christian and Missionary Alliance missionaries and the local Khmer Evangelical Church. Persecuted under the previous Sihanouk regime, only six hundred Christians remained in Cambodia. In 1972 and 1973, Mooneyham preached in the country's first evangelistic crusades, which won three thousand Christian converts.[52] The Cambodian government gave World Vision land to build the nation's first pediatric hospital. The organization still raised money from its private donors, but it now also received major USAID grants for feeding centers, mobile health clinics, and refugee resettlement.[53]

Figure 9. World Vision's second president, Stan Mooneyham, revives Pierce's evangelistic crusades as he preaches throughout Southeast Asia. © World Vision, Inc. 2011. All rights reserved. Reprinted by permission.

Alongside Catholic Relief Services and CARE, World Vision joined a small company of agencies willing to work in Cambodia. With the war's unpopularity at home and fear that the Cambodian government would soon fall to the communist Khmer Rouge, most agencies saw Cambodia as too risky, too unpredictable, indeed, a liability. The Asian nation, however, served as World Vision's tutor. In Cambodia, it learned how to function in complex humanitarian emergencies. Politically unstable, the country relied on the U.S. government. As World Vision staffed up to meet the demands of expanding relief programs, many of World Vision's new leaders came with military experience in Southeast Asia. Don Scott, director of World Vision's Vietnam operations, asserted that his service in the Canadian Navy gave him clearance to move in and out of countries in a way that few others could match. World Vision's former military men bragged that they knew the ways of war in Southeast Asia and admitted being less surprised at the devastation they saw because they had been hardened by what they had already seen. Other new staff members also began to come with backgrounds in the aid community from other agencies, and they taught World Vision the language needed to receive USAID grants and the culture necessary to implement them at an increasingly significant scale.[54]

World Vision's Cambodian involvement also brought it more press coverage, and, like his predecessor, Mooneyham rarely turned down the opportunity for free publicity. World Vision's media prowess and popular appeals surpassed almost every other aid agency and solidified its donor base back home. After the United States withdrew combat troops from Vietnam in 1973, the press praised the relief agencies that remained to clean up the humanitarian mess that the military had left behind.[55] Some reporters portrayed World Vision's relief workers as cowboys, plunging into a wild frontier. Others labeled them as relief experts, efficient in preventing waste and overcoming local corruption.[56] World Vision positioned itself as politically neutral, pleading for more U.S. humanitarian aid while also appealing to the Cambodian government for peace.[57]

The commitment to Southeast Asia won plaudits, but it also brought criticisms. From its earliest involvement in Vietnam, World Vision insisted on working with the Vietnamese government and local churches, but that led some missionaries to feel betrayed by World Vision's new insistence on operating its own institutions. On the other hand, some established humanitarian agencies remained skeptical of an evangelical agency that took a "go-it-alone" approach. While it recognized other agencies, World Vision initially worked only with USAID, the Vietnamese government, and the Christian and Missionary Alliance.[58] At the same time, as World Vision's work alongside the U.S. government grew, some of those same established agencies now began to criticize World Vision's naive and unquestioning support for American policies.

Through its ever-increasing work over a decade on the ground throughout Southeast Asia, World Vision was forging a new identity as a professional relief agency, but a great many of its critics ignored its growing local partnerships and frontline experience in humanitarian emergencies and looked at it as both too American and too narrowly evangelical. That identity probably aided fund-raising at home as the majority of evangelicals still positioned themselves as caretakers for a Christian American ideal, but it hurt partnerships overseas. World Vision became more conditioned to expect attacks and readied to fend them off each time they came.

In 1975, after a fact-finding mission for the World Council of Churches (WCC), a Japanese churchman, John Nakajima, attacked World Vision's work in Cambodia. His accusations, reprinted in a number of newspapers, painted the organization as a pawn of the American military, an agency that received 95 percent of its operating budget from USAID while ignoring the needs of local Cambodians. World Vision's chief contribution, Nakajima claimed, was serving as a conduit of information for the CIA.[59]

Mooneyham denied Nakajima's allegations. World Vision, he said, worked with the local government to approve each of its aid programs, and most members of its staff were local Cambodians, not expatriates. He dismissed Nakajima's unsubstantiated accusation of collusion with the CIA and insisted that World Vision supplied only the information required of all voluntary agencies by USAID to account for the funds received. Nonetheless, Najakima's charges damaged World Vision's reputation. Mooneyham appealed for help to Eugene Blake, the former president of the WCC, but Blake refused to get involved. He reminded Mooneyham that evangelical accusations had hurt ecumenical organizations for decades, and if nothing else, this was simply giving evangelicals a taste of their own medicine. Mooneyham insisted his hope was to build a bridge between the evangelical and ecumenical camps. Blake and others could not be persuaded. Representatives of the National Council of Churches' own agency, Church World Service, reminded World Vision that they had refused USAID contracts in Cambodia because they were not willing to be complicit in American foreign policy. If World Vision accepted government contracts, it also had to accept the consequences.[60]

At other times, World Vision switched from defending its actions to going on the offensive. After substantiated reports surfaced that the CIA had indeed used missionaries in Southeast Asia as informants, Mooneyham wanted to get ahead of any additional news cycle to be clear this was not the case for World Vision. He and current World Vision board member Senator Hatfield lobbied President Ford and CIA chief George H. W. Bush to end such practices, but their efforts had little success. While accusations of World Vision's collusion with the U.S. government remained unsubstantiated, they threatened to hinder the reputation of the organization at home and hamper its overseas relief work on the ground. A debate about World Vision's identity and its future was well under way within the organization itself as it embraced its humanitarian role on the front lines of Southeast Asia, but it still seemed to outsiders, especially its critics, that World Vision was simply one more group of evangelical missionaries, fervently anticommunist, capitalist, and naive to political realities.[61]

As the fall of Vietnam and Cambodia to the communists appeared imminent, World Vision grieved the loss of its programs in Southeast Asia. Some of the staff stayed to close down the offices even as troops traded fire in neighboring streets. U.S. Army helicopters evacuated World Vision expatriate staff, but many local workers could not get out, and many of them died at the hands of North Vietnamese soldiers. Cambodian dictator Pol Pot turned the patients out of World Vision's prized pediatric hospital and used the building as a torture chamber. The staff of World Vision despaired, and they asked publicly in their magazine whether the investment had been worth it. Other NGOs had decided these countries were too risky, but World Vision had invested itself heavily. The consensus was that the investment was the right thing to do. Through its work, World Vision had been faithful to God's calling.[62]

"Operation Babylift" served as one response to the loss of World Vision's Southeast Asian programs. Worried about what would become of its sponsored orphans under new political regimes, World Vision decided to airlift as many as possible out of Vietnam and Cambodia. It planned for three hundred but only proved able to rescue forty-seven. Twenty-three of these children came to the United States to be adopted. Normally, World Vision avoided international adoption and advocated keeping children in their home culture. But in this case, passion outstripped its principles. It turned the orphans over to a Christian adoption agency with instructions for children to be placed in evangelical Christian homes. When a nonevangelical prospective parent sued to challenge the policy, World Vision defended itself against accusations of religious discrimination. The case lasted two years in the courts, and the popular media kept the story in the news constantly. According to the settlement, the children were to remain with the original evangelical parents. As the case played out in public opinion, World Vision's position cost it some of its broader constituency but reinforced its evangelical credentials. Mooneyham was clear that when forced to choose, World Vision remained most at home among American evangelicals.[63]

With the closing of its Southeast Asian offices, World Vision lost a third of its programs and 23,000 sponsored children within a few short months. Without children to sponsor, World Vision stood to lose millions in revenue. Without programs, staff had to be reassigned or let go. It hastily set up operations in Latin America and Africa and sought new children to sponsor.[64] New programs in new contexts allowed World Vision to start with a clean slate and adapt what it had learned in Southeast Asia. It continued to broker relationships with local missionaries and evangelical churches, but World Vision knew it had to broaden its relationships as well.

Soon mainline Protestants, Catholics, and Pentecostals vied for influence within the organization. As it moved deeper into humanitarian relief and development, it further professionalized to become more operational, establishing its own programs, hiring staff, and often interacting with other relief agencies.

World Vision's Evangelical Future?

At the same time World Vision scrambled to sustain its rapidly expanding work and revisit how best to be evangelical, mission-minded, and humanitarian in its new contexts, American evangelicals were debating their future amid their own success. As presidential candidate Jimmy Carter declared himself "born-again" and *Newsweek* declared 1976 "The Year of the Evangelical," the Gallup organization reported that this was not a passing fad. While it was up for debate what was meant by the category, "evangelical" described something as a full 34 percent of Americans identified as "evangelical" or "born-again." These polling numbers would climb even higher over the next decade. Even as World Vision recognized that evangelicals' evolving outlooks on God and country could not help but affect the organization's own approach to international humanitarianism, the rest of America was discovering evangelicals and their influence. As historian Steven P. Miller argues, the expanding evangelical impulse was less a rigidly defined subculture. It was at least an "age," influencing politics, theology, and culture alongside general debates in the public square.[65]

In the first half of the 1970s, evangelical politics were still in flux. An evangelical left minority called for America to repent from militarism, consumerism, and neocolonialism. With Nixon's resignation, some evangelical conservatives like Campus Crusade's Bill Bright began to court politicians, businessmen, and philanthropists to build alliances and engage behind the scenes in political maneuvering. Other voices like Virginia Baptist Jerry Falwell tapped into popular evangelicals' moral anxiety through organizing "I Love America" tours around the country to combat secular humanism, pornography, abortion, and homosexuality. Still other evangelicals were fixated on Francis Schaeffer, as he left his intellectual and spiritual retreat center in L'Abri to take his concerns about the sordid state of Western society on the road. In 1976, he was stumping throughout the United States in support of his book and film *How Should We Then Live? The Rise and*

Decline of Western Thought and Culture to raise the alarm for the onslaught of secularism and legalized abortion. A few years later in 1979, alongside future surgeon general C. Everett Koop, Schaeffer released *Whatever Happened to the Human Race?*, making abortion a new wedge issue that compelled evangelicals to fight against *Roe v. Wade.*[66]

By the late 1970s, many evangelicals had grown frustrated with Jimmy Carter, a president who clearly believed and spoke in an evangelical vernacular but whose policies seemed to betray an assumed melding of faith, morals, and politics that defined a conservative Christian America. Their frustration grew as voices like Falwell and Schaeffer grew louder. By the end of the decade, many evangelicals gave tacit support even if they did not aggressively participate in a grassroots political activism that would later emerge by the end of the decade as the Moral Majority and lead to the Reagan revolution. The Christian Right would soon become the dominant voice associated with evangelical politics.[67]

At the same time, other evangelicals feared that popular growth would compromise their distinctive theological positions. The prime issue soon became debates over biblical inerrancy. *Christianity Today* editor Harold Lindsell's *Battle for the Bible* labeled the doctrine of biblical inerrancy nonnegotiable and called out any "so-called" evangelicals who disagreed. Accusations directed against stalwarts like Carl Henry and institutions like Fuller Seminary made Lindsell few friends, and it led to further internal divisions that led some evangelicals to prefer a new retrenchment to their separatist fundamentalist roots.[68]

As evangelicalism emerged in the 1970s as a popular movement subject to increased attention, it appeared as if Carl Henry's initial dream of an evangelical alliance destined to shape the world had come to pass.[69] But with divisions over politics and theology dividing evangelicals at home, Henry instead lamented that the "evangelical lion is nonetheless slowly succumbing to an identity crisis." The same diffuse growth that led to its popular and numeric success was also splintering the movement.[70]

World Vision attempted to position itself above the fray. Mooneyham grew to deplore his fellow evangelicals' penchant for rigid categories. He argued that the world was gray: "one man's evangelical may be another man's liberal."[71] He grew impatient with inner-evangelical squabbles over school textbooks or the Revised Standard Version of the Bible. After spending most of his year in war-torn Southeast Asia, Mooneyham found these disputes petty. American evangelicals remained World Vision's base: the organization's donors, staff, and networks were firmly rooted in the movement. The more time they spent outside the West, however, with new partners and in new contexts, Mooneyham and others recognized that the global outlook of American evangelicalism was not adequate to make sense of what they were experiencing. Evangelicals' debates over God and country said more about domestic debates at home than they did about the role of faith in action abroad. While others argued, Mooneyham claimed World Vision would focus on one thing: feed the poor in Jesus's name.[72]

CHAPTER 6

World Vision Internationalizes

IN 1977, ARNE BERGSTROM came to work for World Vision. He represented a new generation of American evangelicals interested in faith-based humanitarianism. While he heard Billy Graham and Bob Pierce at Youth for Christ rallies as a child and attended conservative Bethel College, he resisted the traditional subculture and instead embraced the counterculture of the late 1960s and early 1970s, eventually joining the "Jesus People" movement. He participated in the antiwar and civil rights movements, and he pursued graduate education in sociology at Marquette to study under David Moberg, a leading voice advocating fellow evangelicals to embrace social action. While a product of evangelicals' foray into social issues and politics, he preferred Ron Sider over Jerry Falwell. He hoped to follow his calling through working overseas but not as a traditional missionary. In the churches of his upbringing, all he ever heard missionaries mention was "soul winning," and he found such language hollow without work for social change. Among evangelical organizations, only World Vision seemed to offer him an outlet to apply his faith to the world's problems as it began to welcome new voices on its staff eager to solve social problems and recalibrate the direction of American evangelicalism.[1]

While some young evangelicals like Bergstrom brought a new optimism and fresh approach with them in their hopes to change the world, many other Americans found global engagement over this same period highly disorienting. Alongside the failures in Vietnam, the United States was trying to make sense of the thawing of relations with the People's Republic of China, a long-standing communist enemy. They grew anxious over heightened politics in the Middle East as they listened to news reporting the 1973 Arab-Israeli War and unrest in Iran while feeling OPEC's power through the 1973–74 oil embargo. Americans were facing dramatic economic fluctuations at home with rising inflation, stagnation, and an increasingly unequal distribution of wealth and income. Many began to link rising globalization to shrinking U.S. manufacturing jobs, growing multinational corporations, declining organized labor, and an increasing trade imbalance as the United States continued to import more than it exported abroad.[2]

As Americans tied forces of globalization to mounting issues at home, they also began to reconsider their support of international humanitarianism. The domestic programs of President Johnson's Great Society had proved largely ineffective in the minds of a majority of Americans. Extending these programs abroad met little enthusiasm. U.S. international aid budgets shrank at the same time development practitioners began to question their own past approaches. Major foundations such as Ford and Rockefeller continued to invest heavily in development through programs focused on particular issues such as population control and environmental conservation. At the same time, international agencies such as the United Nations, World Bank, and International Monetary Fund took on a larger role, often with increasingly distinct and sometimes contradictory approaches. While the approaches to international development remained a hotly debated topic, much of the initial optimism that Americans tied to their efforts to save the world had worn off even as the gap between the North and global South grew.[3]

Yet, despite this growing pessimism and uncertainty, American evangelicals continued to paint a largely optimistic global picture, and they grew increasingly excited about the role they could play in a globalized world. In July 1974, Billy Graham convened the International Congress on World Evangelization in Lausanne, Switzerland. This "Lausanne Congress" gathered 2,700 evangelicals from 150 countries to equip the church for world evangelization, define the relationship between evangelism and social responsibility, and seek evangelical unity. Lausanne proved that evangelicalism had circled the globe. For the first time, half the delegates came from the global South. In his opening, Graham made a distinction that had rarely occurred to evangelicals twenty years earlier: "When I go to preach the gospel, I go as an ambassador for the kingdom of God, not America."[4] American evangelicals' increasingly fraught relationship with politics at home and their experience with global Christian communities abroad had tempered a bit of Graham's earlier civil religion. He exhibited the initial efforts of some American evangelicals to speak in a different register when evangelizing the world and exporting their faith abroad. They knew that global Christianity would lead to change, maybe even some change at home, but American Christians still remained largely unprepared for the number of voices and new realities that would forcibly challenge their global outlook over the next decade.

As these contexts evolved both at home and abroad, World Vision thought it might be best suited to bridge these multiple audiences and transform American evangelicals' global outlook as its own work continued to grow. By the late 1960s, it had opened support offices in Canada, Australia, and New Zealand to raise funds for its operations abroad. At the same time, a few non-Western voices from within the organization began to model new leadership. While the agency hired the bulk of its operational staff from within the local Christian populations in which it worked, senior leadership most often rose from the ranks of its Western offices. By 1974, this began to change as World Vision appointed Indian Sam Kamaleson as its first non-Western vice president. First trained as a veterinarian, Kamaleson fulfilled his passion for ministry by working with street children in Madras (Chennai). Pierce encountered Kamaleson on his initial trips to India decades earlier and asked Kamaleson to help him make connections while in country. Later Kamaleson would come to the United States to earn a master of divinity degree from Asbury Theological Seminary and a doctorate of sacred theology from Emory University. Ordained as a Methodist, he served as a district superintendent throughout South Asia and was helping to launch the local World Vision India office when World Vision tapped him to head its international pastor conferences. If elder statesmen of American evangelicalism such as Paul Rees and Carl Henry had traditionally led these conferences, now World Vision felt the need to indigenize one of its longest running ministries. Kamaleson would travel the world for the next two decades teaching pastors not only throughout Asia but also behind the Iron Curtain in Eastern Europe, South America, and Africa. He would also serve as a resident theologian for World Vision often working to pull back the blinders of American evangelicalism to incorporate a more fully global theology of mission, justice, and shared leadership. Through the 1970s, Kamaleson was just one of dozens of non-Western leaders beginning to find platforms to speak out within World Vision's global networks. While World Vision staff still looked more like Arne Bergstrom than Sam Kamaleson, World Vision slowly began to welcome new voices.[5]

Figure 10. World Vision vice president Sam Kamaleson preaching at World Vision Pastors' Conference in Tamilnadu, India, 1975. Used by permission of the Samuel Kamaleson Collection held in the Archives and Special Collections of B. L. Fisher Library, Asbury Theological Seminary, Wilmore, Kentucky.

During the 1970s, World Vision could not help but begin to see itself differently. While it did not relinquish its moorings as an evangelical missionary service organization, the makeup of evangelical Christianity looked quite different outside its particular American context. Alongside the rapid expansion of World Vision's programs around the world, the increasing necessity of applying for government funding, the integration of its work with other religious and secular humanitarian agencies, and the slow but steady diversifying of its staff would lead to theological and practical changes within the organization. By the late 1970s, World Vision would undergo a reorganization to form World Vision International in efforts to share leadership throughout its many country offices—among the multiple Western nations raising funds but also a first attempt was made to listen responsibly to the needs of both donor and recipient countries. These changes would alter World Vision's work in the field as well as how it marketed to and educated donors in the United States. World Vision realized it still had a lot of on the job training left to do, but simultaneously it was becoming more assured of its own approach. As the size and scope of its budget, staff, and programs began to outdistance rival relief and mission agencies, it felt compelled to take on the mantle of leading evangelical organization shaping a global movement.

World Vision believed growing awareness of new global realities could draw American evangelicals together beyond their growing differences to meet needs abroad. From Pierce's initial formulation of World Vision's mission, he assumed evangelicals could not refuse sharing the gospel alongside a cup of cold water, food, and clothing to the least of these. World Vision began to see itself as out ahead of other Western evangelicals in its efforts to partner with the global church and embrace a broader missiology. As its own programs in places like Southeast Asia and drought-stricken Africa evolved to meet new contexts, World Vision also positioned itself as the most logical common link within a maturing global evangelicalism. As global evangelicals spoke back to the West, World Vision felt they could come alongside as translators to a broad base of American Christians and institutional evangelical leaders. The organization was not immune from critiques, but it was confident it was ahead of the pack. Its growing confidence, warranted or not, would lead it to more directly challenge its donors and partner agencies to change. It began to understand its marketing not only to raise awareness of need and secure funds, but also to educate and change behavior at home. Over time, the result was an evolving World Vision and an American evangelicalism forced to respond to these new global realities that they could no longer ignore.

The Direction of Global Evangelicalism

World Vision's growth occurred alongside an expanding conversation on the future of evangelical missions. At first, Western evangelicals continued to contrast their approach with "ecumenical" Christians'. After the World Council of Churches' 1968 Uppsala meeting, evangelicals lamented what they saw as the WCC's full abandonment of evangelism for social work. They recoiled when the 1973 WCC Bangkok meeting issued a moratorium on missionaries. Just at the moment American evangelicals cornered the missionary enterprise, however, they also began to realize they must reassess their own approaches to mission. The dichotomy between saving souls and feeding bodies no longer made sense to a host of evangelicals, and many recognized that they had let their fixation on communism, theological liberalism, and secularism skew their global vision.[6]

Evangelical self-reflection often began through gatherings around the globe. After the 1966 Berlin World Congress on Evangelism, the Billy Graham Evangelistic Association (BGEA) helped to organize regional conferences outside the West for the first time. In Singapore, Stan Mooneyham convened the 1968 Asia–South Pacific Congress on Evangelism before assuming the presidency of World Vision. He remarked that in allowing Asian leaders to take the lead in planning, he had tried to embody what he had already begun to articulate: Western leaders must now listen to the voices of the global South. During the conference, Asian evangelicals assured the West that they valued evangelism and did not need a "wholly new theology," but they wanted to dissociate the gospel from Western cultural entanglement.[7]

In 1969, Latin American evangelicals convened their regional gathering entitled "Action of Christ in a Continent in Crisis" in Bogota, Colombia. The Medellin conference where Latin American Catholics embraced liberation theology had been held in the same city just the year before. The Evangelical Latin American Conference (CELA), made up of predominantly mainline Protestant denominations, had met just months earlier. Seeking an alternative to Catholic liberation theology and ecumenical liberalism, the Bogota gathering of Latin American evangelicals became known as the First Latin American Congress on Evangelism (CLADE I).[8] They focused on the crises of "underdevelopment, injustice, hunger, violence, and despair," but the main outcome of the congress was the formation of the Fraternidad Teológica Latinoamericana (FTL). Through the FTL, Latin American theologians demonstrated that they would not only make their own way amid religious divisions within their own context, they also would not be beholden to American evangelicals. They criticized Americans' coziness with Western imperialism and its preoccupation with personal salvation at the expense of social issues.[9]

Global evangelicals were finding their voice, and many Western mission organizations were more willing to listen. Without sacrificing their desire for person-to-person evangelism, they realized that postcolonial conditions required attention to non-Western voices, new methods, and social justice. World Vision's executives and field-workers again thought that they could lead the way. Few agencies were better connected. Through their network of pastors' conferences, they knew most of the leaders of the Christian churches in the global South and engaged with many of them to run World Vision's own local programs. World Vision staffed the coordination and underwrote much of the cost of many of the regional congresses in Asia and Africa as well as ongoing support of FTL meetings in Latin America.[10]

Playing the seasoned veteran, World Vision also urged the West to avoid its past mistakes. In 1971, as U.S. relations with China thawed, some Western evangelicals readied a missionary invasion to evangelize the mainland. China had always been the grandest goal of Protestant missions before and after closing its doors in 1949, but Mooneyham preached patience. In an article entitled "Lord, Save China from American Evangelical Opportunists!," he questioned whether evangelical missionaries had learned anything from the past. Instead of sending American missionaries, Mooneyham proposed the "internationalizing of missions, stripped of Western Christian imperialism, would be a magnificent demonstration of the validity of our message in the nonwhite world."[11]

If American evangelicals were beginning to consider what the internationalization of missions would mean for their work, they were also more willing to reconsider social action. Mission agencies heard the critiques from young evangelicals at home, but their experience on the ground overseas was even more persuasive. Larger numbers of American evangelicals traveled for the first time as short-term missionaries. New programs like Wheaton College's Human Needs and Global Resources (HNGR) sent students for field-based service learning around the world. At the same time evangelicals' own international experience increased, magazines like *Christianity Today*, *World Vision*, and InterVarsity's *His* increasingly brought global evangelical voices into American homes. Hearing global voices recalling how the prophets had called for justice and Jesus had fed and healed the poor offered greater impact than another editorial from a familiar voice at home. More evangelicals were increasingly unwilling to hold so tightly to evangelism that they forfeited any mandate to build schools and hospitals and feed the hungry. World Vision had sometimes believed it occupied the fringes of evangelical mission, but by the early 1970s it represented the mainstream of both evangelical missiology and popular opinion.[12]

At the time and in the years to follow, the 1974 Lausanne Congress was cast as a watershed moment for evangelical growth and global reach. Alongside Billy Graham's address that confessed learning that American and Christian ideals are not necessarily one and the same, British leader John Stott asked evangelicals to take a humbler tone, repent for their arrogance and pride, listen to the ecumenical movement and each other, and expand their definition of mission.[13]

While the global context forced Western leaders to reflect on their own positions more carefully, the congress initially failed to integrate the global church. The West and global South may have shared equal counts of delegates, but Western leaders still set much of the agenda and delivered the majority of keynote addresses. The church growth movement led by Fuller Seminary professors Donald McGavran and Ralph Winter took center stage. Their concept of "unreached people groups" became the guiding principle of Lausanne to equip the mission movement with the research and techniques to evangelize the world.

The Latin American theologians and veterans of the FTL, Samuel Escobar and René Padilla, however, made the biggest splash when they denounced American evangelicalism. Escobar claimed American Christianity had generated two attitudes: either Constantinianism, seeing Christianity as a religion of the West, or indifference to embodied persons, seeing the gospel merely as a spiritual message.[14] Padilla attacked evangelicalism as "a cultural Christianity" that equated faith with the American way of life. With the church growth movement (and perhaps World Vision's MARC) in mind, he criticized evangelicalism's penchant for "managerial missions" that turned "the strategy for the evangelization of the world into a problem of technology." Such an obsession with efficiency had made the gospel a commodity, a "product . . . to distribute among the greatest number of consumers."[15]

In the end, the resulting Lausanne Covenant represented an unprecedented international evangelical statement on the need for Christians to resist poverty, hunger, and injustice. It called for missionaries to preach the gospel and get their hands dirty in the streets at the same time.[16] But it left open the question of how to explain the relationship of social action and evangelism. John Stott interpreted the covenant as saying that the two were equal partners. Others, while accepting the need for missionaries to care about daily bread and shelter, still wanted to insist that the proclamation of Christ in word had to be the priority. Escobar and Padilla convened dissenters who thought that Lausanne had spoken too timidly. They published a manifesto on "radical discipleship," endorsed by almost a fifth of Lausanne delegates, that, while released at the same time also, went beyond

Lausanne's official Covenant by saying that the gospel included liberation, restoration, wholeness, and "salvation that is personal, social, global, and cosmic."[17] While Western evangelicals now shared the conviction that Christians cared about the body as well as the soul, many of them were taken aback by the force of the global critique. After Lausanne it was fair to ask: Would evangelical missions continue to be a united movement?[18]

World Vision thought that it had emerged from Lausanne as one of the winners. It had invested more than $125,000 in funding the planning of Lausanne and hundreds of hours of in-kind staff support.[19] It applied its skills in media promotion and research to construct exhibits, and Mooneyham's keynote address highlighted World Vision's potential in a stirring statement that ranged in content from statistics on world evangelization to video clips of his interviews with Christian leaders from every continent.[20]

Mooneyham sought to frame World Vision as an ally of the new global evangelical voices. While some mission executives hesitated to embrace the new rhetoric of what came to be called "Two-Thirds World" evangelicals, Mooneyham spoke as the leader of an organization that had already learned that Jesus wanted his disciples to feed the hungry, heal the sick, and visit the imprisoned while they carried his message of salvation to all the world. He remarked that sometimes he found himself more at home with the impatient voices of the global South than with some American evangelicals. Yet World Vision was also learning to accept its own criticism from those impatient voices. Some viewed the agency as one more "managerial mission," a highly specialized Western organization bent on exporting its technology, business principles, and fund-raising strength to institutionalize—and thereby domesticate—missions in the developing world.[21]

After the congress, the Lausanne movement seemed to travel in two directions. Church growth experts promoted strategies for harvesting souls, while evangelicals in the global South wanted to plant the seeds of social justice.[22] Mooneyham was not naive; he worked both sides of the aisle and continued to pour money into Lausanne.[23] World Vision's MARC division cheered for church growth and outreach to unreached peoples as Donald McGavran handed leadership of the ongoing Lausanne Strategy Working Group to MARC director Ed Dayton. In handpicking congress delegates and directing programs, Dayton (and World Vision) ensured that the Lausanne movement remained committed to the evangelization of the world for years to come.[24]

Yet, World Vision leaders also supported Lausanne because it legitimated the quest for social amelioration and justice as part of evangelical mission. Without providing exact formulas for the division of labor between the evangelists and the activists, Mooneyham believed World Vision left Lausanne with a mandate. As one executive reflected, "The emphasis on social action ministries hand in hand with evangelistic outreach put World Vision in a unique catalytic and leadership position in Evangelical Christianity."[25]

By no means did World Vision abandon the mandate to evangelize. Local missionaries and national church leaders still administered the majority of World Vision–funded programs for orphans, medical care, education, and relief. The agency continued to sponsor conferences to train local pastors, and Mooneyham revived Pierce's large-scale crusades, preaching to thousands in Indonesia, Cambodia, and the Philippines. Without abandoning its roots, World Vision simply believed it supported more than traditional missions. In 1973, World Vision's Project REAL (Revolution, Evangelism, Action, and Love) formed a partnership with the Jesus People to sponsor young adults on ten-month missions to the Philippines. Serving as workers in a nationwide Filipino evangelistic campaign, students learned to maintain the balance between evangelism and social ministry. They dug wells, rebuilt rice paddies, and provided prenatal health care; they also taught Bible classes and went door-to-door proclaiming that Jesus was the way of salvation.[26]

Marketing Famine, Disasters, and Emergency Relief

While World Vision continued to debate its religious identity and mission among fellow evangelicals, leaders also began to extend the organization's reach at the same time by marketing its message to much broader audiences. Much of the tremendous growth in annual budget, staff, and programs through the 1970s came as a result of expanding into large-scale relief work. It had always provided emergency relief through missionaries and local Christian communities, but high-profile disasters in the early 1970s prompted the organization to take on larger challenges. In 1970, it moved into East Pakistan (now Bangladesh), which had suffered from a massive cyclone, tidal wave, and civil war that left 500,000 dead and created ten million refugees. In 1972, it received its first large government grant to coordinate relief after a devastating earthquake in Nicaragua. In Africa, it launched programs to feed people during famines in Biafra (Nigeria) and Ethiopia.[27]

The interventions brought increased media attention and record donations. Disasters and the various responses they trigger remain an understudied topic marking religious, economic, and political history. The coverage of global disasters and Americans' growing willingness to donate to such causes led to the rapid expansion of many relief agencies. Among evangelicals, World Vision grabbed the greatest share of headlines. The new programs allowed World Vision to recoup its losses from closing offices in Southeast Asia, but government funds still made up only a fraction of World Vision's budget. Fund-raising through emergency appeals and monthly pledges became the catalyst for World Vision's explosive growth.

Pierce's movies, direct mail campaigns, and full-page color ads had always made World Vision an innovative fund-raiser, but his target audience remained churchgoing Americans. Mooneyham sought to parlay World Vision's success in social ministries into ongoing partnerships with evangelical denominations and mission agencies, but they considered him more of a threat than a partner. Spurned by traditional religious networks, he decided to bypass the churches and reach out to the American public. These new lines of communication allowed for a continued connection with popular American evangelicals who spent far more time consuming religious and mainstream media than listening to sermons and Christian education at local churches. World Vision's popular forms also clicked with countless other American Christians outside the boundary-defined networks of American evangelical institutions. Mooneyham insisted his organization remained evangelical in both religious identity and activity, but he would no longer allow institutional networks and associations alone to define who counted as an evangelical insider. World Vision was testing a more diffuse definition of American evangelicalism.[28]

In exploring broader audiences through new media, the advertiser Russ Reid steered World Vision to television. As a teenager, Reid had traveled the country showing Pierce's films in local congregations. After working for Youth for Christ and Word Books, he launched an advertising firm to introduce state-of-the-art marketing strategies to Christian agencies. By 1968, the Russ Reid Agency had won World Vision's account.[29] After dominating religious radio, evangelicals had begun experimenting with television. While many pastors bought time to broadcast their worship services, Pat

Robertson had launched his daily religious variety show, *The 700 Club*, on the Christian Broadcasting Network in 1966. After parting over differences with Robertson, on-air hosts Jim and Tammy Faye Bakker announced a rival show, *Praise the Lord*, in 1974. At the same time, Paul and Jan Crouch also launched Trinity Broadcasting Network, which would grow to become the largest religious television empire, with its mix of prosperity preaching, fundraising appeals, and faith-focused talk shows.[30]

Even as religious media was changing, Reid pushed World Vision to try something different: a documentary that would not preach at the audience while also limiting fund-raising appeals to three or four short commercial breaks. World Vision could use images and stories of hungry children to compel viewers to give money. In 1972, World Vision produced its first hour-long documentary, *Children of Zero*, and released it the following year on three hundred stations nationwide to introduce its work in Vietnam. The film's success led to the release in 1974 of a second documentary, *They Search for Survival*, to highlight its work in the African Sahel, Bangladesh, and Cambodia. Aired in 167 markets, it generated 95,000 new names for World Vision's mailing lists.[31]

The documentaries gave World Vision a new platform. Mooneyham believed that the television "put the average American family inside the skin of these Asian kids and let them feel with us what it is like to be born in a developing world."[32] Shot on location, the films gave audiences a sense of intimacy with the children who appeared on their screens. They depicted World Vision staff members as credible experts worthy of support. Celebrities lent even more credibility. Television personality Art Linkletter provided the initial "tune-in value." As audiences watched Linkletter accompany Mooneyham throughout Asia, they traveled alongside a trusted source to see World Vision's work firsthand. The documentary taught, but mainly it motivated. After each segment, a celebrity asked for financial support while images of hungry children flickered in the background. The appeal was emotional, reducing large problems to an image of a single hungry child. "If you don't help that one child," Mooneyham declared, "nobody will." The approach was not new for World Vision, but television heightened the effect.[33]

The medium did not change the message, but it did lead to a shift in rhetorical style that subtly altered the organization's identity. Mooneyham had made a calculated risk when he appealed beyond church walls. The decision led him to drop the "evangelical code words" on which World

Figure 11. Television personality Art Linkletter served as host of multiple World Vision television specials in the 1970s. He filmed these both in television studios and on trips abroad to bring World Vision's work to American audiences. Here he is with a member of the Korean Orphan Choir. © World Vision, Inc. 2011. All rights reserved. Reprinted by permission.

Vision had often relied. In the words of one producer, "World Vision productions couched the organization's Christian motivation in language the average person could understand. We did not want to hide the Christian purpose, but to express it in general terms more appropriate for a television audience."[34] World Vision was beginning to reach an audience outside the evangelical orbit while at the same time challenging any notion that traditional evangelical networks held a monopoly on definitions or modes of operation. World Vision never hid its Christian identity, but explicit language about mission now fell into the background; Mooneyham was adamant that his organization was about hungry children, and its messages, still religious and humanitarian, reached anyone willing to tune in.

By 1975, World Vision's documentaries evolved into multihour hunger telethons. Images of poverty and starvation alternated with upbeat musical numbers by celebrities like its own Korean Children's Choir, the Muppets, and Julie Andrews. Telethons lent themselves to immediate responses from the audience.[35] Rather than writing a check to a PO box, they could phone pledges to toll-free numbers. Productions left little to chance. Scripted programs tested with focus groups allowed World Vision to predict which appeals maximized its return on investment. It collected extensive demographic research about its donors.[36] As it followed professional marketing trends, World Vision became the leader among all relief agencies in television fund-raising.[37]

No longer known simply to evangelicals, World Vision created a television presence that appealed to a broader demographic. Even as it invested millions in setting the directions of evangelical missions through the Lausanne movement, when turning to popular audiences in its marketing, it dropped the word "missionary" from its self-description and referred to itself as a Christian humanitarian organization. World Vision was clear that it was not seeking to be all things to all people, but it strategically spoke in multiple registers as it sought influence among its various audiences: American Christians tuning in to their televisions, leaders of evangelical parachurch networks, mission strategists, critical theologians from the global South, as well as funders and development practitioners from the international relief and development community. World Vision was not just hedging its bets; Mooneyham grew more confident that his organization had a unique role to play in all these spheres. By the mid-1970s, its newfound television income led to annual budget growth of 20, 30, and 40 percent per year. Even as critics questioned its evangelical, missionary, and American identities, World Vision was gaining influence with a larger audience than its critics could ever reach.[38]

From Fund-Raising to Reeducation

World Vision believed that increasing budgets and influence gave it an opportunity and responsibility to offer education to its donors in addition to simply provoking a response through compelling images of children in need. As a twenty-fifth anniversary project, the organization designated 1975 for a yearlong emphasis on world hunger. It announced Project FAST (Fighting Against Starvation Today) to raise funds and public awareness. Having only ramped up operations in Africa over the past few years, it realized it had arrived late to the continent. Missionaries had approached Pierce about working throughout Africa by the early 1960s, but for once, he had turned down expansion. At that time, World Vision was growing too quickly and resolved to focus on Asia. Other relief agencies, however, did begin arriving in the 1960s to provide emergency aid for famine victims in North Africa's Sahel region. By the time World Vision arrived in the early 1970s, the famine was already at its height, as Western newspapers shocked readers with images of malnourished African children. Such images became stock photos of World Vision's famine coverage.[39]

It enlisted recent board member Senator Mark Hatfield as the FAST campaign's honorary chairman. With American troops withdrawn from Southeast Asia, Hatfield had turned his own attention to world hunger. In 1974, he served as an official U.S. delegate to the United Nations' World Food Conference in Rome called to deal with the growing hunger crises in Africa and Asia. Countries pledged to eradicate hunger within a decade and make access to food a basic human right. Hatfield returned home to press for U.S. support. He discovered that U.S. food surpluses given in aid had declined by half since the 1960s with much of it tied as incentives amid Cold War politics. Hatfield noted that Cambodia had received as much aid in 1974 as the entire continent of Africa. His calls for substantial increases in humanitarian food aid met with resistance from President Ford and Agriculture Secretary Earl Butz. Hatfield claimed that they had caved to politicians, corporations, and agribusiness.[40]

What Hatfield could not accomplish through legislation, he publicized through a Senate "Thanksgiving Resolution" in November 1974. For the next year, he challenged Americans to identify with the poor by simplifying their lifestyles and donating a portion of their earnings to help feed the hungry. He resolved to end 1975 with a national day of fasting on Thanksgiving. In announcing the resolution, Hatfield gathered congressional leaders and reporters to a Capitol Hill luncheon. To their surprise, the meal consisted of nothing more than a few ounces of rice, the sixty-seven-calorie daily average intake of the world's hungry. With Mooneyham by his side, Hatfield took the opportunity to announce his partnership with World Vision: "It is my hope the government will respond when it sees that Americans do feel compassion for the millions now starving throughout the world." The resolution served as the kickoff to the FAST campaign, and World Vision followed with its own media blitz. It bought even more time for its television specials, while Mooneyham and Hatfield fielded interviews from the press and flooded evangelical magazines from *Christianity Today* to the *Post-American* with articles on hunger.[41]

The FAST campaign not only sought to raise funds but also challenged Americans to identify with the hungry. Hatfield realized that "until Americans willingly experience hunger, even on a limited basis, they cannot begin to comprehend the condition . . . responsible for the death of more than 10,000 of their fellow men every day."[42] World Vision developed "planned famine" curricula for local churches so that youth groups could raise funds while fasting for forty hours. The Love Loaf campaign asked families to skip a meal each week and give the amount to world hunger as World Vision distributed small loaf-shaped banks as reminders for families to pray for the hungry at each meal.[43]

World hunger resonated with evangelicals, and World Vision offered them acceptable ways to respond. It allowed them to act, indeed, to become social activists within limits. They could provide emergency aid without abandoning evangelism or becoming entangled in unproductive debates about structural change. They could funnel support through mission and parachurch agencies without turning to government programs. World Vision's appeals offered hard facts and statistics, but they made sure that "hunger has a face."[44] Playing to emotion and asking for an immediate response, the hungry child became the face of World Vision.

World Vision emotionalized hunger, but it also began to challenge evangelical audiences to move beyond Christian charity to advocacy. In calling for an "all-out war against world hunger," Mooneyham deemed World Vision a voice for the voiceless: "Who pleads their case to an overfed, affluent world that seems more concerned with gross national product, megatons and horsepower than it does with human beings?"[45] He criticized the premillennial eschatology that led evangelicals to reject this world for the next and contested how pervasive the popular theology was throughout evangelicalism.[46] He also challenged similar approaches from a secular perspective that advocated so-called "life-boat ethics," proposing that since saving everyone was impossible, it was best to let the majority drown. Mooneyham said that no Christian would succumb to an ideology limiting help to "the fittest." Defining himself as a Christian humanitarian, Mooneyham said that World Vision viewed the hungry as persons in need of spiritual as well as physical aid. And he added that the aid would sometimes require social change. World Vision matured in its understanding of poverty; its appeals were religious and emotional, but they also reflected an awareness of the political, economic, and systemic dimensions of hunger.

As World Vision's message began to move beyond primarily emotion and Christian compassion to embrace a level of education and advocacy, the organization's spokespeople also became more comfortable introducing structural topics into its appeals. If evangelicals at home and abroad had once distinguished themselves from their ecumenical rivals by promoting evangelism at the expense of social action, these divisions were less black and white. Younger evangelicals like Jim Wallis and Ron Sider were certain that this was a false dichotomy, and many World Vision staff, new and old guard alike, agreed. Vital global evangelical voices were even clearer that such a dichotomy remained untenable. While still left insufficiently resolved, much of the debate at the Lausanne Congress revolved around this particular issue, and the debate empowered many evangelicals to speak out even more on the structural issues they saw as central to address in order to eliminate social inequities such as hunger, poverty, and discrimination. Finally, more evangelicals at home and abroad were now willing to work across traditional boundaries. While still suspect to some, claiming the evangelical label did not mean automatic refusal to partner with those outside the evangelical camp. For World Vision, this meant retaining its evangelical identity, expanding its religious language to reach a broader audience, and openly affirming secular or ecumenical agencies it previously labeled as suspect now as partners in a shared mission. World Vision no longer apologized for encouraging churches to explore resources from the United Nations, USAID, and Church World Service. It often repackaged statistics from these organizations into its own marketing. Layering the systemic and the individualistic, it began to redraw the lines between evangelical and ecumenical, sacred and secular.[47]

Mooneyham also wanted to expose Americans to broader global perspectives. For two decades, World Vision had defined its missionary agenda in concert with Cold War anticommunism. It now realized that divisions once seen as purely ideological were in fact economic. Turning to America's dependence on foreign oil and cheap coffee, Mooneyham demonstrated how globalization made the West complicit in poverty. He dispelled popular myths that the poor were happy with their current conditions and criticized simplistic population control policies. While curtailing population was popular in the West, he encouraged his audience to consider the issue from the perspective of people in the global South. Not only did they dislike the West telling them what to do, but the poor in the global South also had different reasons for having children. The West viewed children as a cost;

the rest of the world saw them as potential security. World Vision acknowledged its previous captivity to American parochialism, and it challenged its audiences to free themselves from the same prison.[48]

Before long, it was raising hard questions about the American way of life. It remained hopeful that Western technology could boost food production, but it complained that broken systems created hunger in the midst of abundant resources. Mooneyham echoed Hatfield's pronouncement that the United States was far less generous with foreign aid than its citizens believed. He chastised the American military for withdrawing from Cambodia and allowing the Khmer Rouge regime to butcher thousands. But Mooneyham's critique went beyond systems and governments. He told the American public that it shared the guilt. He criticized American overconsumption, challenged Americans to fast in solidarity with the poor, and admonished Christians to join the move toward simple living. "Should not doing good include working for systematic change as well as delivering a Christmas basket, making a contribution on worldwide communion Sunday, or writing a check to the United Way?" World Vision's fund-raising appealed to the "compassionate charity" of American Christians, but it began to teach them that charity was not enough.[49]

A few from the evangelical left adopted simple lifestyles, protested structural poverty, and began to question American innocence. Most evangelicals ignored critiques of American imperialism, demands for structural change, and appeals for simplicity of life, but pleas to feed starving children in the name of Jesus touched their hearts. By 1976, as the worst of the Sahel famine passed and World Vision's campaign ended, the hunger crisis faded from the front pages. World Vision's response to the famine had put the organization on the humanitarian map even as its hunger appeals had introduced Third World poverty to American evangelicals and made alleviating hunger and global poverty, for many, a goal of Christian mission. World Vision's new approach was helping to change evangelical humanitarianism.[50]

World Vision and the Rise of Samaritan's Purse

World Vision was no longer the organization Bob Pierce had founded. Through the 1970s, it remained clearly evangelical, but as identity politics divided American evangelicals, World Vision broadened its message. It could not avoid the internal debates within evangelical missions, but it increasingly presented itself as a humanitarian organization, albeit one that spoke in evangelical accents. It still remained largely an American organization, but it recognized the implications of its global presence: it could no longer be tied to the ideology of a single nation.

Of course, not everyone supported World Vision's growth and new directions. Its founder, Bob Pierce, became one of its chief critics. Pierce remained bitter after his resignation and several years of searching for physical and mental health, but he eventually threw his energy into another fledgling evangelical mission organization, Food for the World. In 1970, with only twelve dollars in the bank, Pierce took control of the organization, renamed it Samaritan's Purse, and set about recreating the World Vision he had founded in 1950.[51]

While World Vision was expanding beyond missions, Samaritan's Purse would remain a missionary service organization. Pierce traveled the world in search of small groups who needed emergency help. Rather than channeling resources through institutions, he delivered funds directly to missionaries. "I'm going to spend my life," he said, "backing up people [who have] proved they care about people and God. When I could no longer do that through World Vision, that's when I resigned and started Samaritan's Purse."[52] Having taken World Vision's mailing list and the loyalty of many missionaries with him, he solicited support through letters filled with "on-the-scene" stories of need.

Pierce feared that the professionalization of World Vision had come at the expense of its evangelical faith, and he did not mind saying so. Often Pierce's appeals would attempt to convince donors of the superiority of his agency's work through thinly veiled comparisons to bigger agencies like his former employer. He told the *Los Angeles Times*, "World Vision has a new complex computer system which diagnoses the failures of Christianity and prints them on a data sheet. . . . I can't stand it. I love the early days when I was walking with widows and holding babies. When I began flying over them and being met by committees at the airport it almost killed me."[53] He felt that World Vision's "slick, market driven" fundraising appeals lost any "personal identification with individual human needs."[54] He drew on the parable of the Good Samaritan to differentiate Samaritan's Purse from other agencies. The priest and the Levite, the two characters indifferent to the wounded traveler on the side of the road, represented the "organizational machinery of relief agencies, charities, and even churches." He cautioned, "You can operate exactly like Sears & Roebuck or General Motors or IBM—but the blessings will all be gone." Instead, he would operate with an account entrusted to him by donors to meet whatever mission need he stumbled across on his global travels. Pierce returned to where he was most at home: traveling the world, often alone, and meeting needs in the most remote places.[55]

While World Vision began to venture outside an exclusively evangelical orbit, Pierce reentrenched himself in conservative evangelicalism. Even as many NGOs still criticized World Vision for bringing evangelism into its humanitarian work, Pierce took the opposite tack. He wore his evangelist credentials as a badge of honor and took aim at those he believed watered down the faith into nothing more than "do-goodism." Samaritan's Purse, he said, would never be ashamed to "fly the banner of Jesus Christ high." He was also clear that he would refuse any government funding. World Vision was his object lesson: "he who pays the piper, calls the tune."[56] He portrayed the path that World Vision had begun even under his tenure in the 1960s as a slippery slope to losing its core religious identity. Pierce was an evangelical, nothing more and nothing less. The priority was preaching the gospel.

Under Pierce's charisma, Samaritan's Purse grew modestly, but his annual budget never exceeded $100,000. Soon after being diagnosed with leukemia in 1975, Pierce sought a potential successor. Billy Graham introduced him to his son Franklin, a man whose story resembled Pierce's. Having rebelled from the faith of his youth, Franklin had little interest in education or Christian gentility, but he shared Pierce's thirst for adventure. In 1975, Franklin Graham accompanied Pierce on an around-the-world tour designed as an excursion into suffering. Soon the two were inseparable. When Pierce died in 1978, twenty-eight-year-old Franklin Graham fought the board for control of Samaritan's Purse and became its president a year later.[57]

Today, Samaritan's Purse has also grown under Graham to become one of the largest charities in the United States. In its first few decades, however, Graham built a small but steadily expanding agency as he adhered to Pierce's principles. Committed to Pierce's notion of "God room," he believed that God would always provide resources beyond his organization's capacities to plan and raise funds. Graham built Samaritan's Purse around his own personality, soliciting support through personal stories of individual and emergency needs encountered through his danger-filled

travels on the front lines of war zones and natural disasters. He held tightly
to wedding his mission to the conservative politics of the day. As a crusade
evangelist, Graham unabashedly touted his core commitment that evangelism and relief must work together without compromise. He often reiterated that Samaritan's Purse is "not just a Christian relief organization. We
are an evangelistic organization . . . and I will take advantage of each and
every opportunity to reach [anyone] with the gospel message that can save
them from the flames of hell."[58]

Pierce was right. World Vision had changed since its founding over
twenty-five years earlier. But he was also wrong. The organization no longer
felt the need to fit into his categories. It had little interest in squabbles
about the mix of evangelism and social action, even less interest in quarrels
about biblical inerrancy, and almost no interest in right-wing politics. It
preferred to present the image of global poverty in the face of an individual
child broadcast to large-scale popular audiences. At the same time, donors
saw in the organization whatever they wanted to see. It straddled divisions.
Was it removing itself, without intending it, from evangelical circles? Or
did it represent an international engagement of American evangelicalism?

Internationalization

Even if expanded among new audiences at home, World Vision did not
mark its own evolution only through domestic debates. Instead, it often
focused on international concerns: the voices of global Christians, the challenges coming from peers within international humanitarianism, and the
concerns from field offices within World Vision's own organization. While
Mooneyham sometimes presented World Vision as both an advocate and a
critic of well-meaning Americans, he also began to develop a heightened
sense of self-reflection. He realized that his own predominantly Western
organization would have to change if it was to live up to the theological
and institutional values that it articulated.

Bob Pierce had referred to his organization as World Vision International since 1966, but it largely remained an American agency, funding
programs run by local missionaries and churches overseas. As early as 1959,
however, when a base of donors in western Canada began sponsoring children after picking up the signal of Pierce's radio program from across the
border, World Vision opened a Canadian office. In 1966, it sent U.S. staff

to open a similar office in Australia. An office in South Africa followed in 1967 to raise funds and implement programs. By 1971, World Vision opened its fifth fund-raising office in New Zealand.[59] Through the 1970s, these new offices sought to help make decisions and plan programs. They were no longer content simply to raise money for World Vision's work with little voice for how it was used. In addition, they realized that a one size fits all fund-raising approach was insufficient. World Vision had to tailor its fundraising and marketing to diverse donor bases. The same letter that might appeal to an evangelical housewife in southern California or Christian businessman in Grand Rapids might not work for an Anglican in New Zealand.

In other parts of the world, both in the West as well as the global South, World Vision's American label had also proven a liability. In its first two decades, the joint identity as Christian and American served its purposes well as it joined U.S. efforts to halt the expansion of a godless communism. But by the 1970s, Vietnam had sullied America's image at home and abroad. Various media, NGOs, and foreign governments criticized World Vision as inexperienced and naive at best and provincial and uncritically pro-American at worst.[60]

Fellow evangelicals from around the world also criticized World Vision's reflex Americanism. Mooneyham supported the social agenda that Two-Thirds World evangelicals defined at Lausanne, but they pushed back when confronting the organization's reliance on Western voices, structures, and technologies. World Vision's own personnel complained of the organization's paternalism and seeming need for rigid control. Staffers in field countries expressed frustration that they had little voice in planning programs, and management in other fund-raising countries complained that it was hard to raise money for an American organization.[61]

Mooneyham saw that World Vision could not turn back the clock, and in 1972 he announced his intention to study internationalization, a process meant to reorganize the partnering countries within World Vision to share funds, leadership, and accountability more fully. Mooneyham recognized his organization had to become a genuinely international agency. It was too large and diverse to follow a single voice. The negative coverage of its work in Southeast Asia taught him that a narrow identification with one culture and one national perspective hurt the organization. To become a peer among international humanitarian NGOs, it must abandon provincial Americanism for global geopolitics. Internationalization would open the way for greater representation and participation; it would also require more democratic structures and the delegating of accountability. Mooneyham worried that if he resisted calls for necessary change, he could prompt national offices to secede and create competing organizations.[62]

For Mooneyham, internationalization was more than a question of organization; it was also a matter of theology. The Western agency that saw itself as sending missionaries to act on behalf of native peoples had become an "anachronism." Evangelical missiology now viewed Western missionaries as partners or servants of indigenous churches. World Vision championed a supranational and supracultural church, but it recognized that its organization was American. Mooneyham saw that he had to lead the organization to change; he also saw that this meant integrating the theology they articulated in their missions and humanitarian work into organizational practice.[63]

Attempts to "express spiritual internationalism in organizational terms" led to real structural change. By 1973, World Vision promised to replace most American expatriate personnel with an indigenous workforce while helping field countries establish autonomous boards.[64] That same year it began its official internationalization process. World Vision searched for an appropriate model to follow as it scoured multinational corporations, international aid organizations, and mission agencies. It built case studies from mission agencies like the Latin American Mission, aid organizations like the Salvation Army and Oxfam, as well as international government outfits like UNESCO and UNICEF, but none met the internationalization criteria that World Vision sought. The organization realized it was taking on internationalization through organizational restructuring before many of its Western peer INGOs. As World Vision's leadership began to see itself as a pioneer, it began to claim its religious identity as the key factor leading to progressive changes outpacing secular development.

To realize World Vision's "big experiment," Western support offices and a handful of field office staff planned for years to implement the organization's first attempts at restructuring. By 1978, the United States office handed over control to create World Vision International (WVI), a new legal entity governed by a board comprising all five support offices. The U.S. office remained the most influential, but now sat at the table as one among several voices making decisions about strategic planning, field operations, and budget.[65] The new organization was not as international as many hoped. Western countries still dominated the governing board while non-Westerners remained underrepresented, but WVI at least united as a single international organization.⁶⁶

If internationalization did not immediately solve World Vision's organizational challenges, it opened the way for new perspectives. The organization celebrated the change, but many still fretted over the question of identity. Some U.S. leaders lamented their loss of authority and worried that increased diversity might lead to watering down evangelical distinctives. Other national offices feared that World Vision U.S. would give lip service to equality but continue to dominate the partnership. Mooneyham could not help worrying about the changes he had helped bring about: "I have either assured the future of World Vision or destroyed it. God have mercy on us."⁶⁷

Throughout the 1970s, new global realities were forcing American evangelicals to reconsider their global imaginations. Refusing to remain passive, new global voices now began to insist that Western Christian agents could not abide by the status quo but must engage internationally in new ways. World Vision often believed that it was situated as the best translator of these new global realities to its loyal American constituents, but it also came to realize that it could not escape the need for change as well. Rapid growth continued as World Vision communicated global need to an even wider audience. The remaining questions left World Vision to ask what was the message that it was sharing, to whom, and how would religious humanitarians accomplish their work around the world? In working out the answers, it stumbled into a new identity.

CHAPTER 7

Evangelical Relief and Development

THROUGH THE 1970S, record budget growth, institutional expansion, and internationalization marked a decade of drastic change. The 1978 Declaration of Internationalization had established World Vision International (WVI). Soon after, Stan Mooneyham, now president of the new global partnership, embarked on a goodwill tour throughout World Vision offices to tout the reconfiguration. Mooneyham hoped that such changes would allow for greater flexibility, sharing personnel and resources, integrating ministries on the ground, and pursuing partnerships that would put its global theology into practice while positioning the organization for future success.[1]

Reorganization amid increased globalization proved to be one concern, but World Vision's evolution from missionary service to relief and development remained the other. As Mooneyham contemplated future directions, he shared a speech throughout the organization that he entitled "Some Thoughts About Two Words." One of those words was "internationalism"; the other was "development." He reiterated the nonnegotiables: "the message we preach, the Bible we believe, and the Christ we serve."[2] The original principles of witness and service remained unchanged. The practices, however, subtly evolved. The organization's operations in contexts such as Cambodia and the African Sahel had already forced it to adapt its traditional programs to a broader humanitarian agenda. Expanded marketing and fund-raising to mainstream audiences as well as increased government aid and grant-seeking also led it to characterize itself more broadly as a Christian humanitarian organization. Pierce had officially chartered World Vision in 1950 as "a missionary service organization meeting emergency needs in crisis areas of the world through existing evangelical agencies."

When the 1978 Declaration of Internationalization rechartered the organization as World Vision International, it now officially listed its purpose as "a humanitarian organization [that] is an interdenominational outreach of Christians concerned for the physical and spiritual needs of people throughout the world."[3] Leaders realized that World Vision was becoming a vast international relief and development agency and could not help but change. Mooneyham would not allow the organization to build an altar to the status quo, even as he refused to sacrifice the organization's religious identity. He insisted that World Vision remain unapologetically evangelical.

It was clear that the organization's leadership intended to remain Christian and even broadly evangelical, but few were sure what that meant for World Vision's religious identity as it transitioned from missionary service to relief and development. While Mooneyham and others lobbied for necessary change across WVI, at the same time, he privately worried that success, the outside influences of secular humanitarianism, and a more inclusive disposition toward diverse faith perspectives threatened to erode World Vision's spiritual values and lead them away from their religious roots.[4]

Again, World Vision's leaders saw themselves as pioneers. They could find few models of others who had grown in scale and scope, reorganized to share leadership, and evolved in organizational mission without succumbing to what those inside and outside the organization most feared, secularization. What secularization meant differed depending on the audience. For some, it was implicit in any success that seemed to limit the need for an abundance of sacrifice, prayer, and reliance on the Holy Spirit. For others, it was more the loss of a particular type of bounded American evangelical identity that intentionally separated itself from other religious, secular, or government partners. Still others worried that in giving up ultimate control, American leaders were relinquishing their role as caretaker of the organization's religious identity in exchange for a watered-down, lowest-common-denominator faith. Finally, many pointed most plainly to the move from missions to religious humanitarianism as a slippery slope that could lead to abandoning evangelical principles in exchange for secular practices. World Vision was not the only organization wrestling with these questions, but as the biggest, it often served as the lightning rod among evangelicals at home and abroad. As its leaders reconsidered the theory, theology, and practices necessary to become an intentionally global, Christian, and respected relief and development agency, it again forced evangelicals in the United States to reconsider their own missionary, American, and global identities.

World Vision Embraces Development

By the 1970s, World Vision realized it remained several steps behind trends within the relief and development community. As it moved beyond orphanages to embrace large-scale relief, other agencies moved beyond relief to experiment with long-term development. Agencies like Church World Service and the Mennonite Central Committee combined their resistance to the politicizing of U.S. aid in Vietnam with efforts to create new development models that empowered local communities rather than serve Western purposes. The same agencies that accused World Vision of naïveté for falling in line with U.S. policy now derided its staff as ambulance chasers who sped in with emergency relief but did not stay around to help with lasting change.[5] World Vision would respond to such criticisms, but its local staffers on the ground had already convinced the organization that emergency relief alone was inadequate.

Some World Vision staffers were already idiosyncratically experimenting with development programs. Gene Daniels, World Vision director for Indonesia, initiated his "Pioneers for Christian Development" program in the early 1970s. When Daniels initially entered Indonesia as one of World Vision's first African American staffers in the early 1960s, Bob Pierce gave him little direction, telling him only to find what God was doing and start there. A decade later, Daniels was bringing trained Indonesian teachers and agriculturalists to teach their fellow countrymen in remote villages to read and provide medical care as well as plant cash crops and raise livestock. Daniels's small-scale village development program proved successful. As World Vision highlighted it across its international partnership, leaders began to notice other field offices launching similar projects.[6]

In 1974, World Vision decided to add development to its core objectives, the first addition since the organization's founding.[7] Development became the organizational buzzword as it sank resources into a newly established relief and development division. Mooneyham hired Hal Barber, a retired Army colonel, to lead. He recruited Bryant Myers, who had a PhD in chemistry, to implement logistics. Myers confessed that "we didn't know a lot about development ourselves then. It was sort of like the teacher who keeps one page ahead of the student."[8]

Even as World Vision lagged behind other agencies that had adopted development principles a decade earlier, development theory itself was relatively new, and the relief and development industry was constantly evolving. Development theory grew out of the reconstruction of Europe after two world wars and expanded as a part of Western assistance to Third World nations during the Cold War. At first, modernization and economic growth were the goals. As the United Nations declared the 1960s the "Development Decade," the United Nations, International Monetary Fund and World Bank poured money into large-scale development projects and brought in Western technical and scientific knowledge to build highways, promote industry, and establish universities. Tackling macro issues, theorists posited that a growing gross national product (GNP) would trickle down to benefit everyone.[9]

The initial development models had more than their share of critics. Latin American dependency theorists claimed that development perpetuated Western domination and reinforced the same systems that created poverty. Other Third World leaders did not refuse Western aid but advocated "self-reliance" that allowed them to make their own choices about how development should proceed in their countries. When the United Nations declared the 1970s the "Second Development Decade," it heeded some calls for change. Development policy moved from investments in governments and an obsession with GNP to the redistribution of wealth and consultation with local communities about their own prioritized needs.[10]

In 1973, the U.S. Foreign Assistance Act, known as "New Directions," aligned USAID's programs with this new approach. Instead of awarding contracts for the distribution of relief goods or the building of infrastructure to a handful of established agencies, it asked all NGOs to propose grants for individual projects. The number of NGOs receiving grants skyrocketed as the United States increasingly came to value grassroots expertise and the capacity to mobilize local resources. NGOs appreciated the ability to shape their own projects while the State Department benefited from limiting direct assistance and in-country U.S. government personnel that sometimes strained international relations.[11]

Most religious NGOs supported these new directions. The dependency theorists' critiques of Western development paralleled the rise of liberation theology among Catholic, ecumenical Protestants, as well as a handful of evangelicals. As religious leaders in the global South came to praise new forms of community development that aligned with prioritizing solidarity with the poor, NGOs birthed from religious networks also highlighted their long-standing relationships with local communities. Smaller religious agencies often lacked the resources for large-scale relief, but many had decades of earned trust working in local towns and villages. The smaller size and local focus that had often served as a liability for religious agencies seeking a seat at the table among the handful of organizations dominating the sector now proved to be their greatest asset in fostering indigenized community development.[12]

In initially adopting development, World Vision's working definition functioned like many agencies: simply a catchall for what it was already doing. Development could mean "ministry to the whole person," self-help, long-term assistance, or community-focused programs. Yet, if it was to become a respected relief and development organization, World Vision knew it had to strengthen both its capacity and expertise. In 1975, USAID awarded it a three-year Development Program Grant (DPG) to facilitate its competence in development practice and technical skill.[13] The funds allowed World Vision to hire relief and development coordinators for each of its global regions, teach field staff the language of development, and implement reporting systems and procedures into its programs.[14] The grant also gave the agency exposure to a new web of humanitarian networks. As it now applied for USAID grants, it would conduct dialogues with foreign governments and interact closely with secular organizations. It still promoted its work at Urbana mission conferences and NAE conventions, but it also now attended gatherings on income generation, sustainable agriculture, and family planning.

Increased institutional capacity and new partnerships led World Vision to expand its development efforts. In 1975, it began with twenty-two programs. The next year, development programs grew by 160 percent. By 1977, it reported 314 projects in thirty-nine countries. While many of these programs were small, their number continued to double annually throughout the decade.[15] As projects expanded, World Vision struggled to staff them with competent development professionals. It still relied on missionaries and indigenous pastors to implement its work on the ground. These leaders knew their local communities, but few had development training. To find staff with the necessary new skills, the organization began to recruit outside traditional evangelical networks. While these professionals still professed a Christian faith, they were hired for their technical expertise over evangelistic prowess. Outside hires began to build institutional capacity and added credibility among new humanitarian peers like the Purdue University professor it hired to head its new agriculture division, but traditional partners sometimes questioned whether new additions eroded evangelical identity.[16]

Even with new expertise, World Vision's professionalization most often proceeded through retraining existing staff. In 1976, it used USAID funding to bring all of its relief and development coordinators to Nairobi, Kenya, for its inaugural development workshop.[17] In 1978, it sent over fifty staff members to a five-week training at the International Institute for Rural Reconstruction (IIRR) in the Philippines. Directed by development pioneer Dr. James Yen, the IIRR played a leading role in shaping the field. While it was important for World Vision that Dr. Yen quietly identified as a Christian, more important, he was respected as a pioneer in global rural development. The training was a watershed moment for World Vision staffers. Yen's approach matched their needs while lending them credibility. They left optimistic that they could now articulate World Vision's hope for its ministry of development.[18]

When Bryant Myers arrived at World Vision, he admitted that he knew little about development. By the end of the 1970s, however, World Vision's confidence in the concept of faith-based development had grown dramatically. Relief and development programs still remained a small part of World Vision's international programming as child-sponsorship funding continued to constitute nearly three-quarters of World Vision's budget over the decade.[19] Yet, a new relief and development identity was catching on throughout the global partnership. By 1979, Myers predicted that over the next ten years development would make up 75 percent of World Vision's work.[20] Explicit missionary language waned as the organization increasingly began to refer to its staff as aid workers. Stories of meeting individual needs with Christian compassion continued to dominate fund-raising appeals, but the organization no longer shied away from describing programs as enterprises in health care, family planning, land regeneration, income generation, and vocational training.[21] Such a shift in self-definition reflected nonevangelical influences. Some saw it as an expansion of evangelical influence into new spheres. Others worried that World Vision was leaving its evangelical heritage behind.

Evangelicals and Development

Although Western evangelicals had often eschewed development as a form of "secularized missions," many now began to see development principles aligning within their own professed missiology. Amid the debates over evangelism and social action, development offered some evangelical advocates more holistic language. Others used it to support a turn toward indigenized non-Western missions.[22] Still others appreciated the ways in which it allowed them to raise questions of structural injustice.[23] Missionaries were no longer afraid to champion their own development projects in local communities, as many evangelical denominations and independent mission agencies incorporated aspects of relief and social ministries within their ongoing work as they saw both shifts in funding as well as a push toward a more holistic missiology.

Evangelical humanitarianism was expanding in earnest from all angles. The separation between evangelism and social action that had so often defined evangelicals and the work of particular organizations in the past diminished as a broad cross-section of evangelical donors found the distinctions insignificant. Overall evangelical giving to Third World poverty grew over the 1970s from $147.7 to $622 million. Many missionary societies had strong connections from decades of work within local communities around the world, but starting broader social ministries took time and expertise not often immediately available. As a result, evangelicals founded a number of new development agencies that had no missionary past. Nine more evangelical relief and development agencies were founded just in the 1970s. With an average annual growth of 17 percent throughout the decade, new agencies like Medical Assistance Program (MAP), World Concern, Institute for International Development, Inc. (IIDI), and Food for the Hungry grew at twice the rate of traditional evangelical mission organizations.[24]

With its ballooning size, several decades of relationships with missionaries and indigenous pastors, and now growing interest in relief and development, World Vision emerged far ahead of most fellow evangelical agencies in scale and sophistication. The organization's traditional competitors grew steadily but fell further behind World Vision's drastic expansion. As an agency committed to relief, development, and refugee resettlement, World Relief was poised to grow as evangelicals increasingly embraced these causes, but its economy of scale remained limited as a subsidiary of the NAE. It received limited support from member denominations and some government funding, but without the marketing engine and media profile of World Vision, it retained its small footprint. Conversely, Compassion International continued to grow rapidly as it sought to match World Vision's marketing and fund-raising prowess through its own focus on child-sponsorship programs, but it resisted any urge toward government funding, large-scale relief, or broader humanitarianism. It had found its niche and remained content to live within it.[25]

In contrast to these established agencies, Food for the Hungry served as an example of an upstart founded in 1971 seeking to outpace World Vision's transition to relief and development. Its founder, Larry Ward, was a World Vision insider who often served as ghostwriter and attaché for Bob Pierce on his global travels. Converted to new systemic models, Ward grew frustrated that World Vision had not moved to address world hunger issues earlier in its own work and left to start Food for the Hungry to expose audiences to these structural issues through education and popular communication while also providing relief and development. Like the others agencies, however, Ward's new organization gathered steam slowly and remained limited in size.[26]

Even as the direction of evangelical missions continued to evolve and a number of agencies came to share World Vision's enthusiasm for development, growing excitement could not hide the continuing tensions over the relationship between evangelism and social action. The 1974 Lausanne Covenant had attested that both were necessary. Evangelism remained primary, but as Lausanne chairman John Stott claimed, "the [Great] Commission itself must be understood to include social as well as evangelistic responsibility, unless we are to be guilty of distorting the words of Jesus."[27] Stott's attempts at mediation failed to end the debate.

The dominant group consisted of those who sought to use Lausanne as the platform for world evangelization. In 1980, the Consultation on World Evangelization (COWE), in Pattaya, Thailand, gathered more than nine hundred attendees to form strategies for the evangelism of unreached peoples. World Vision and its MARC division loaned staff, provided statistical research, and invested hundreds of thousands of dollars to the meeting. Yet the Pattaya consultation left social action off the agenda.[28]

That same year, evangelical theologian Ron Sider gathered a smaller group for an International Consultation on Simple Lifestyle. They called evangelicals to suffer with the poor by pledging "to live on less and give away more." In moving beyond past evangelical statements of social concern, they labeled certain social structures as evil and criticized Western overconsumption.[29]

Two years later, at the Lausanne Consultation on the Relationship Between Evangelism and Social Responsibility (CRESR) in Grand Rapids, Michigan, both sides sat down to mediate the growing rift within evangelicalism.

The consultation allowed for three possible relationships between social action and evangelism. Social action could be a consequence of, a bridge to, or a partner with evangelism. In pitching a big tent, it fell short of providing a definitive solution, but it demonstrated that most evangelicals now found both necessary.[30]

As evangelical missions moved beyond either-or debates, practitioners adopted holistic over dichotomous language. In 1983, the World Evangelical Fellowship sponsored a Consultation on the Church in Response to Human Need in Wheaton, Illinois. It declared that since "evil is not only in the human heart but also in social structures . . . the mission of the church includes both the proclamation of the gospel and its demonstration. We must therefore evangelize, respond to immediate human needs, and press for social transformation."[31] While not theologically far from the earlier Grand Rapids consultation, the Wheaton '83 statement sought to overcome dualisms by integrating evangelism and social concern into a single concept of "transformation." By the 1980s, holistic language infused much of the discourse around evangelical missions.

Advocates for social action applauded the turn to development. In the recent debates, evangelical advocates felt such an approach privileged the dignity of the local person over paternalism and holistic over dualistic language. The International Consultation on Simple Lifestyle, CRESR, and Wheaton '83 all affirmed Christian development. In other circles, however, evangelicals began asking questions that tempered initial enthusiasm. Was development Christian? What made it Christian? Did it inevitably diminish the passion for evangelism? Was there a unique evangelical form of development?

Evangelical relief and development agencies were quickly outpacing the growth of evangelical missions and catching up to mainline and secular humanitarian organizations in size and annual budgets, but new evangelical networks forced them to stop and consider their theology.[32] Some worried that their understandings of development—and their presentations of it to others—were steeped in secular language. Perhaps they had embraced it too quickly. In 1977, after helping to draft the Chicago Declaration and found Evangelicals for Social Action (ESA), Ron Sider wrote *Rich Christians in an Age of Hunger* to encourage evangelicals to live more simply and embrace social issues.[33] He championed development and partnership with agencies outside evangelical networks but acknowledged that "it makes no sense for Christian development agencies to take their basic assumption on the nature of development from secular sources like the United Nations, secular government in developed or developing nations, or private secular development agencies."[34]

Some evangelicals viewed "development" as a loaded term that returned to outdated missionary models privileging Western knowledge while ignoring the experience of underdeveloped peoples.[35] In 1983, Wheaton professor Wayne Bragg introduced the concept of "transformation" as an alternative vision of development. Bragg argued, "Transformation is a particularly Christian concept—to take the existing reality and give it a higher dimension or purpose. . . . Development that is Christian is transformation of the person and social structures that frees persons and societies to move toward a state of increasing wholeness in harmony with God, with themselves, with others, and with the environment.[36] "Transformation" came to serve as the evangelical in-house term that distinguished *Christian* development from the kind practiced by the World Bank or USAID.

Evangelicals struggling to define Christian development in theory also struggled to incorporate it into traditional missions in practice. Despite World Vision hiring its own development professionals, the majority of its staff came from missionary backgrounds. In-country, Western aid workers and missionaries often lived in the same compound, attended the same church, and sent their children to the same boarding school. Yet by the early 1980s, as evangelical relief and development agencies grew more prosperous and professional, theological differences or various resentments sometimes eroded these natural affinities. Arne Bergstrom, the young evangelical who joined World Vision in the late 1970s and then was assigned to establish new development projects in the Philippines, described living between two worlds. Although he attended the same churches as the missionary families—and sent his children to the same Christian schools—other missionary families ostracized him. "We were not true missionaries. We were those development people," Bergstrom remembered. He had even less in common with secular development workers. In its work throughout the global South, World Vision straddled two worlds; the balance was precarious.[37]

Evangelical relief and development agencies faced the same problem at home. People in the pews supported the new agencies. Uninterested in the old debates over social action and evangelism, they responded to appeals to help victims of poverty, famine, or war in the name of Jesus. But traditional missionary executives worried that the new agencies were co-opting their donor base, and they feared losing funds for evangelism.[38] In 1979, evangelical relief and development agencies founded their own umbrella organization, the Association of Evangelical Relief and Development Organizations (AERDO). While AERDO invited evangelical mission organizations for shared conversations, its member agencies were asking different questions. AERDO sought to foster technical expertise, mutual support, and best practices among its members while also lobbying USAID for government grants. Its members had evolved from mission agencies that did social service into relief and development organizations that included evangelism as a part of their holistic mission.[39]

World Vision's Reorganization and Response to Critics

Adopting development affected World Vision's theological outlook and organizational structure. As it continued to professionalize, World Vision vice president Ted Engstrom classified all work into one of three departments: evangelism, childcare, or relief/development. The divisions led to clearer management structures and greater expertise. It also allowed World Vision to maintain that its religious identity had not changed. While the relief and development department developed partnerships with USAID and foreign governments, the evangelism and childcare divisions promoted pastors' conferences and Christian education programs and supported Lausanne's push for world evangelization.[40]

The largest division remained childcare. Sponsorship funds provided the bulk of income while sponsorship programs made up more than 70 percent of field ministries' expenditures. Up until now, each country or mission station decided independently what sponsored children received. As benefits could vary widely, World Vision realized it must standardize childcare activities. In 1973, a new director of childcare ministries established policy and procedures to monitor the status of sponsored children, instituted minimum benefits packages for all children, and required mandatory training of childcare workers. While independent from the relief/development department, the childcare division also bore marks of World Vision's larger transformation as it evolved from an orphanage- to a family-focused model. Acknowledging critiques of institutionalization, World Vision shifted the benefits of sponsorship from individual orphans to extended families to address the long-term goal of community change.[41]

While childcare still anchored World Vision's day-to-day fund-raising and program attention, leaders throughout the organization remained enamored by the promises of development. New staff in field countries as well as administrators at the central office adopted it with wholesale optimism. As the initial enthusiasm wore off, however, some feared they might have moved too fast. They worried the term "development" had become overused and misapplied. Missionaries added it to their list of activities in order to raise funds or as cover to enter countries closed to foreign missions. "Development" had come to mean almost anything: roads and schools built by governments, Land Rovers purchased by humanitarian agencies, or meals served by missionaries. From its founder, World Vision had inherited an action-oriented mentality, but now it realized it had to slow down, reassess, and distinguish its own model of Christian development from those of its secular and religious peers.[42]

World Vision began debating internally what it meant by "Christian development." Some felt that for development to be Christian it required direct evangelism as an aspect of every relief and development program. Saved souls were essential to sound communities. Others described the distinctive characteristic as the Christian commitment of staff—development done by Christians. Still others saw it as simply the motivation behind their activities. If the organization's mission and vision remained Christian, then Christian development would follow.

These various answers failed to satisfy the leaders responsible for shaping World Vision's policy. Eager to champion a biblical language of transformation, some worried development privileged an inherent secularism. At the same time, newly empowered global South voices like Sri Lankan B. E. Fernando critiqued development from another perspective. Through World Vision's recent internationalization process, Fernando had called for mutuality, reminding his fellow World Vision leaders that while they had been very good at giving, now they "need to learn how to receive."[43] These new voices would apply these same calls for mutuality to question the paternalistic practices of Western development overall. World Vision's religious identity allowed many within the organization to turn what they originally conceived of as their lack of experience and expertise into an opportunity to reimagine "Christian" development as a truly "holistic" alternative working to transform the current world into the Kingdom of God.[44]

The effort to articulate a theology of development forced World Vision into organizational restructuring. Separate divisions in the early 1970s allowed for greater efficiency but functioned in ways that countered holistic theology. How could it talk of doing away with dichotomies between evangelism and social concern when it divided the two into separate departments? By 1979, a movement for "ministry integration" once again challenged the organization to adapt to new circumstances. In concert with internationalization, the leaders of the organization gave all regions more autonomy but asked that they integrate evangelism, childcare, and relief/development in each local program.[45]

Ministry integration vaulted relief and development from experimental incubation to front and center for everyone within the organization. World Vision continued to organize pastors' conferences and support local churches' evangelistic crusades, but most of the evangelism now took place within community development programs. Staff still argued that Christian development must offer an opportunity for each individual to respond to the gospel, but most saw evangelism more broadly integrated into every effort to improve the well-being of individuals in building relationships with one other and with God.[46]

Ministry integration also reshaped its childcare ministries to correspond with its holistic theology. In the early 1970s, childcare expanded from institutions to families, but sponsorship still provided fixed assistance packages to individuals. By 1979, World Vision pledged to move 50 percent of its childcare projects to development by 1984. In fund-raising, it slowly shifted models as well. While child sponsors still built relationships through letters and updates with an individual child, World Vision would pool sponsorship dollars for development with children throughout a community. Specific benefits were no longer earmarked for sponsored kids with unsponsored children left out. The new approach allowed for greater flexibility but presented a risky adjustment to the program that brought in the bulk of its annual income. Yet the adjustment helped bring World Vision's organizational structure and fund-raising practices in line with its evolving theology.[47]

As the organization adjusted internally to the ways in which relief and development led it to rearticulate its theological values alongside organizational change, it also faced questions of how success impacted the organization's religious identity. While drastic growth extended World Vision's impact, others worried that it would lead the organization outside of evangelicalism and even perhaps to abandoning its religious roots. While WVI president Mooneyham consistently insisted that the organization remained unapologetically evangelical, World Vision's professionalization, popularity, and new partners demonstrated that an organization's evangelical bona fides extended far beyond simply affirming particular theological beliefs and practices.

Of course, World Vision was not alone in its dramatic growth. Other charismatic and entrepreneurial leaders like Billy Graham and Bill Bright had founded organizations that led to evangelicalism's popular reemergence but also forced new debates about the proper role of ministries outside the church (parachurch). While each had independent streaks, they all proclaimed their ministries as supplements to denominations and local churches. Yet some evangelicals began to worry that they had gone from supplementing to supplanting the church. In 1979, historian Stephen Board noted, "there was a day when newspapers would summarize Sunday's sermons of prominent ministers in their Monday editions; today the media interview and quote from parachurchmen."[48]

When brimming budgets and media attention made parachurch leaders the face of American evangelicalism, detractors questioned their fiscal responsibility and lack of accountability. Some accused them of narrowing the gospel for reasons that served their own self-interest while needlessly duplicating each other's efforts. Others turned to ecclesiology, debating how parachurch agencies should function as a part of the larger church's mission. By 1980, heated exchanges filled the editorials pages of evangelical magazines. At one point, the Lausanne movement brought church and parachurch leaders together to mend strained relationships.[49]

World Vision's leaders took these tensions seriously. Even as they moved from missions to development, they noted their long history with the local church. They admitted the faults of the parachurch, but they also pointed to positives. Greater flexibility and expertise allowed parachurch ministries to respond rapidly to immediate needs while sometimes adding a prophetic voice calling the church to action. World Vision continued to argue that it served as an extension of the church's witness in areas where the church was nonexistent or needed assistance.[50]

World Vision's theology kept it rooted to the church, but increasing professionalization often practically led it in the opposite direction. It decried the inefficiency of the church and brought a corporate management culture into Christian nonprofits. In promoting a "stewardship of results," it claimed that its professional capacities ranked second to none in the evangelical world. World Vision insisted that all employees profess a

Christian faith, but fewer now came with pastoral callings or degrees from evangelical seminaries. With a need for more marketing, development, and management specialists, a new class of technocratic experts entered World Vision's ranks.[51]

New fund-raising strategies also led it away from the local church. Pierce had taken his early films to churches to raise support, but Mooneyham realized that mission offerings in local churches provided a meager return on investment. With rapid income growth in the 1970s and early 1980s coming from television and government grants, local churches became less important. Telethons appealed to mass audiences and allowed World Vision to stay out of contentious theological debates and domestic church politics. The large majority of World Vision's donors remained Christian, but Catholics, mainline Protestants, and generic "born-again Christians" joined World Vision's evangelical base. Even as it reaffirmed its evangelical roots, it moved beyond its older donor base and expanded its identity.[52]

World Vision also moved away from Christian education. In order to raise the largest possible amount of money, the organization used telethons that substituted emotional appeals for education. Market analysis demonstrated that stark images of African children drew more funds than information on systemic development or world evangelization. One World Vision filmmaker voiced his concerns for the organization: "It was abandoning its responsibility to communicate the needs of the world to churches and challenge them to Christian mission. . . . The result? More funds raised, but at the expense of a holistic Biblical message."[53]

While professionalization led to less interaction with local American churches, it also led it away from churches in programs overseas. As it initiated larger development operations, it relied less on local pastors and missionaries to administer them. Isolated cases of local pastors misappropriating funds or proselytizing recipients of government aid worried World Vision. It recognized that its programs had become too complex and the need for accountability too high to trust untrained specialists.

Its commitment to hire an indigenous workforce led to even more conflict with local Christian communities. On entering a new area with big budgets and new programs, World Vision's higher salaries, Land Rovers, and air-conditioned offices led a number of local pastors to leave their churches. Missionary agencies that had spent years building relationships and educating local leaders accused World Vision of arriving late and stealing the best Christian talent. Some missionaries and local Christians questioned World Vision's motives and complained about its success.[54]

At the same time, World Vision's growth made it difficult to implement stated goals of internationalization as well. Fund-raising most often outpaced organizational development. The U.S. office hounded field countries to establish new programs and locate new children to sponsor. Field countries could not recruit and train staff quickly enough. Programs rushed into operation to market to Western donors suffered from inadequate design. Development practitioners in the field felt out of sync with the fund-raisers in Southern California. Tensions grew between the "donor" Western countries and "recipient" field countries. One would hear the same refrain among field staff: "World Vision abided by the golden rule: the one with the gold makes the rules."[55]

Fund-raising success led some to ask again how World Vision's activities related to its new theology of development. Again, its marketers knew that images of starving African children best motivated donors, but practitioners felt such depictions diminished the dignity of those in need. It stereotyped Africans as helpless poor, denied them the opportunity to help themselves, and avoided confronting donors with the need for structural change. As outside critiques of such images mounted, internal debates also raged within World Vision. By the early 1980s, the leaders acknowledged the tensions but decided that for the sake of budgets they had to live with them.[56]

Some critics even used World Vision's financial success to point to a diminished religious identity. They equated impoverished budgets as a sign of living by faith, but Mooneyham made no excuses for excellence. He knew it was necessary to retain the best staff and recruit big donors. Yet in some settings World Vision earned the reputation for lavish lifestyles: jet-setting around the world, staying in fine hotels, and building impressive office buildings. World Vision's own field staff would argue that reported largesse perpetuated its reputation as a Western-dominated agency that stood in contrast to their call to identify with the poor through embracing a simpler lifestyle. World Vision's answer again was to insist on living with the tensions.[57]

Its size and success also forced World Vision to respond to the larger trend across the nonprofit sector calling for greater transparency and accountability. Before the 1970s, Christian nonprofits grew with little oversight, but when reports surfaced in 1977 of suspect agencies pocketing up to 95 percent of funds raised, the public began to demand regulation.

World Vision had already recognized that the climate of charitable giving was changing. It faced stiffer competition for donors' dollars even as donors grew increasingly skeptical of charitable organizations. It could no longer rely solely on its emotional appeals and reputation as a Christian mission. It began to publish its overhead expenses, marketing its efficiency as something that should reassure donors of its reliability.[58]

With Americans' general diminishing confidence in institutions, World Vision board member and sitting senator Mark Hatfield urged evangelical agencies to find ways to monitor themselves or expect to face regulation from Congress. As two of the largest, World Vision and the BGEA convinced thirty others to come together to address the problem. The result in 1979 was the formation of the Evangelical Council of Financial Accountability (ECFA). As the Better Business Bureau for evangelical nonprofits, the ECFA required member agencies to disclose financial statements and implement professional management criteria. Many modeled their professionalization on World Vision's example.[59]

World Vision's Religious Identity Put to the Test

Record budget growth, institutional expansion, internationalization, and the addition of development marked a decade of drastic change. Of course, others saw such success as a slippery slope. The YMCA, Red Cross, and Christian Children's Fund (CCF) became oft-cited examples of how easily organizations lost their religious roots. In embracing government grants, adopting development strategies, and participating in broader humanitarian discourse, religious voices inside and outside World Vision feared peer pressure would lead the organization to relinquish its evangelical identity.

While some critics proclaimed World Vision guilty simply by associating with nonevangelicals, others pointed to a more specific trajectory. In 1979, World Vision opened fund-raising offices in the United Kingdom and Germany, and later in several other Western European countries. From the beginning, these offices appealed to a more secular donor base and hired a more religiously diverse staff than other World Vision offices.[60] The U.S. office as well as leaders within several global South field offices worried about the trend. The World Vision India board publicly questioned whether the international organization was becoming a secular agency.[61]

In response, a few within the organization cautioned that it was time to step back to see how the organizational changes had affected its religious identity. Founded by an evangelist, World Vision had used evangelism as the measure of its religiosity since 1950. Three decades later, however, as it adopted holistic language, ministry integration, and Christian development, measures became more difficult. World Vision vice president Ed Dayton claimed that "evangelism is the umbrella under which we do everything but we didn't define what evangelism was."[62] President Mooneyham agreed, "We put evangelism first and last in our work, but this doesn't mean that everything we do has direct evangelistic connection. We don't stamp Jesus Saves on every vitamin pill."[63]

Without ceding ground to critics accusing World Vision of abandoning its evangelistic roots, Mooneyham saw the importance of reaffirming the role of evangelism within the organization. He responded by declaring 1980 as World Vision's Year of Evangelism. An evangelism task force ensured that the organization did not lose its spiritual heart by requiring existing staff to document how they would implement evangelism in each field program and train new hires in Christian discipleship and appropriate evangelistic techniques.[64] It introduced new assessment tools within its development programs designed to measure the spiritual growth of local communities. It also drafted guidelines to help consider if new partnerships with governments or other agencies might compromise World Vision's mission and prevent evangelistic opportunities.[65]

While at times evangelism itself served as the primary measure of World Vision's evangelical identity, the list of nonnegotiables was always changing. One reporter described Mooneyham "as an evangelical but not the type who walks around with a Bible under his arm and invokes the name of the Lord in every other sentence."[66] The pastor of New York City's mainline Riverside Church, William Sloane Coffin, quipped in 1977, "If you get an Evangelical with a social conscience you've got one of God's true saints."[67] World Vision hoped it fit the bill, but it knew that its public remained undecided.

Yet even as its own evangelical identity remained on trial, World Vision benefited from the popularity of American evangelicalism. As the mainstream media "discovered" evangelical growth in the mid-1970s, they often highlighted World Vision as a prime example. Coverage of evangelicals consisted largely of stories about conflict, personal piety, and popular culture.[68] Yet Mooneyham accused fellow evangelicals of "navel-gazing" and "aping

American culture" at the expense of global issues.[69] As coverage of evangelicals honed in on politics even more with the rise of the Religious Right by 1980, Mooneyham worried that domestic politics and culture wars would only further divide evangelicals into special interest groups that ignored global issues. World Vision wanted to be evangelical; it also wanted to be distinctive.[70]

World Vision faced mounting criticism for the way it expressed its evangelical identity not only from American evangelicals but also from global religious voices. In 1977, the Roman Catholic press accused World Vision's Filipino staff of withholding childcare funds, encouraging contraception in opposition to Catholic teaching, and requiring aid recipients to attend Bible studies before receiving assistance. World Vision dismissed a number of the charges as unfounded but admitted that in four of its ninety-two childcare programs, overzealous pastors did pressure Filipino Catholics to attend Protestant services. While World Vision officially forbade proselytism (defined either as using conversion as an inducement or requirement to receive aid or as enticing individuals to convert from one church to another), the indigenous staff people did not always follow or understand organizational policies. Tensions between evangelical Protestants and Catholics in local communities abroad also sometimes led to efforts to "convert" Catholics. To make amends, World Vision met with Roman Catholic leaders and developed training manuals to educate field staff on Roman Catholicism. In predominantly Catholic countries like the Philippines, World Vision hired a handful of Roman Catholics to fill local staff positions.[71]

The incident led World Vision to reassess its relationship with nonevangelical organizations. It recognized that the Catholic Church was not monolithic and pledged to work with Catholics willing to labor alongside an evangelical organization. In expanding to include ecumenical organizations, World Vision publicly committed itself "to work first with those, regardless of ecclesiastical tradition, whom we identify as combining evangelical fervor with a desire to serve all men in Christ's name."[72] It reaffirmed the NAE statement of faith but argued that its evangelical identity did not prohibit it from cooperating with others who ministered with the poor.[73]

World Vision faced criticism from all sides of the religious spectrum. Not only Catholics but also the ecumenical World Council of Churches used incidents of proselytism to disparage World Vision as a fundamentalist organization ill-equipped to work with other Christian humanitarian agencies.[74] In contrast, World Vision's traditional partners interpreted dialogue with Catholics and partnerships with ecumenical bodies as compromising its evangelicalism. Some of its own local staff resented the pressure put on them by senior management to work with Catholics.[75]

In an effort to find broad consensus, Mooneyham insisted that World Vision remained "evangelical in the historic sense" but "ecumenical in spirit." He defined "evangelical" as allowing for "broad inclusivity" in contrast to a "narrow and exclusive" fundamentalism, and he refused to allow past "evangelical prejudices to establish parameters for World Vision's work." Mooneyham's only criterion for partnership was that "people are exposed to the word of God." Without dismissing real theological differences, Mooneyham had little patience for theological discussions brokered through established ecclesial structures. Instead he sought a "practical ecumenism" that found partners willing to work around a common cause. While some admired his pragmatic approach, others saw his unwillingness to engage theological differences and ecclesial particularities as another example of the go-it-alone approach that they associated with World Vision.[76]

World Vision: Global or American?

World Vision's distance from the identity politics, inerrancy debates, and culture wars that defined American evangelicals showed the effects of its internationalization. In its early history, Pierce had championed evangelical missions and American exceptionalism as he followed the U.S. military to fight for freedom and Christian faith in Korea and Vietnam. As it evolved into a professional relief and development organization, World Vision was more careful to distinguish its mission from an American political agenda. When asked by an evangelical reporter what God was saying to America, Mooneyham answered, "Why should God be saying something special to America that He isn't saying to Canada or Mexico or scores of other countries? When God did speak to other nations other than His people, Israel, it was most often an announcement of judgment."[77]

Despite Mooneyham's critique, World Vision maintained a close relationship with the U.S. government long after other humanitarian agencies had distanced themselves from American foreign policy. It stayed in Vietnam until U.S. military evacuated its staff in 1975. By 1978, however, it returned to Southeast Asia against U.S. advice. As Vietnam returned to war against Cambodia and China, hundreds of thousands of Vietnamese fled

Figure 12. World Vision shared its encounters with Vietnamese refugees during Operation Seasweep through media and marketing to raise awareness and funds for the plight of the Vietnamese people. © World Vision, Inc. 2011. All rights reserved. Reprinted by permission.

their country. Over 277,000 attempted to flee by boat, but with inadequate supplies, piracy throughout the South China Sea, and no countries willing to accept them, the refugees stood little chance of survival. On discovering their plight, Mooneyham appealed to his political connections only to be told to forget the "boat people." Never one to take orders, he decided that World Vision would act on its own.[78]

In 1978, World Vision bought a boat and set sail on the South China Sea looking to rescue Vietnamese refugees. The boat found no refugees and proved unseaworthy. Mooneyham procured a replacement, but no country would grant it registration. Finally, he convinced Honduras to license the vessel. Flying under the Honduran flag, he christened the vessel *Seasweep*. "Operation Seasweep" commenced in July 1979. Since no country would accept the refugees, they could only offer food, fresh water, and medical treatment to the refugees they encountered. They made Bibles available on request. But Operation Seasweep also helped turn the world's attention to the refugees' predicament. Sympathizers called it advocacy. Detractors called it a public relations stunt. Many humanitarian agencies decried the mission as ill-conceived, another example of World Vision's working counter to local and long-term development principles.[79]

Operation Seasweep rescued several boatloads of refugees, but it was even more successful in garnering press coverage. World Vision highlighted the "boat people" in its own fund-raising appeals, magazine, and films, but it received international attention when the British Broadcasting Corporation (BBC) came on board to film its own documentary, *The Desperate Voyage.*[80] Soon Operation Seasweep found its way into newspapers, national newscasts, and even *People* magazine.[81] After four weeks in Southeast Asia, Mooneyham flew back to the United States to capitalize on the media attention. Publicity led to a spike in donations and exposure to new audiences beyond an evangelical base. It also contributed to the decision of the United Nations and sixty-five nations to pledge financial support for the refugees. President Carter reversed course and ordered U.S. Navy ships to assist in rescuing refugees and offering them asylum in the United States. Other Western countries followed suit. World Vision claimed Operation Seasweep not only as a marketing and humanitarian success but also as its first success in shaping public and political opinion.[82]

Operation Seasweep demonstrated World Vision's willingness to second-guess and criticize U.S. policy. Yet among American donors, Mooneyham still appealed to faith and freedom as founding values:

> I keep remembering that our country was conceived in the hearts of a group of families who also prized freedom above everything else, and sailed on a perilous journey to give birth to this nation under God. They too were refugees from tyranny. And they gave us our heritage as the land of the free and the home of the brave. From that day until this, we have never refused to open our hearts, our hands, yes, and our doors to any people who sought to live as free men. . . . God has promised to bless the people who do justly and show mercy. You know I believe He'll bless you if you'll extend a loving and compassionate hand to these homeless and unwanted refugees.[83]

Mooneyham ended his appeal by melding the Beatitudes with Emma Lazarus's poem inscribed on the Statue of Liberty. In tying "blessed are the merciful" with "give me your tired, your poor, your huddled masses," Mooneyham criticized the United States for not living up to its mission. He resorted to the traditional evangelical jeremiad, lamenting America's failure to live as a Christian nation.[84]

World Vision's rhetoric occasionally relapsed into the language of American exceptionalism, but it also began to demonstrate where its Christian mission diverged from American foreign policy. World Vision became one of the first humanitarian organizations to return to Cambodia after the fall of the Khmer Rouge in 1979. It committed itself to reopening the National Pediatric Hospital it built but lost to Pol Pot's totalitarian regime in order to help the new Cambodian government provide health care to its people. Moving beyond the Christian anticommunism of an earlier generation, World Vision assisted a communist regime for the first time.[85]

World Vision's renewed work in Cambodia gave it courage to break from Western interests in other areas. In the early 1980s, it worked with other communist regimes in Ethiopia and funded programs in Sandinista-governed Nicaragua. While American evangelicals deepened their commitment to Israel, World Vision spoke out against Israel's invasion of Lebanon and advocated for Palestinians' human and civil rights. Not only did such positions oppose U.S. policies, they also conflicted with the views of the core evangelical constituency.[86]

World Vision vowed to stick to its Christian principles even if they led to positions that cost it donor support, but it found that putting its principles into practice often led to internal tensions with efforts to maximize income, expand programs, and heighten its professional reputation.[87] Latin America served as one setting for major expansion.[88] World Vision had funded small programs in Latin America for many years, often supporting progressive evangelicals like the Latin American Theological Fraternity (FTL). FTL criticized Western evangelicals for their lack of social engagement, and it conducted dialogues with liberation theologians. World Vision exposed its donors to these positions, even reprinting in its magazine the sermons of martyred Salvadoran bishop Oscar Romero.[89] Yet it raised suspicions when expanding its own programs in Latin America. Latin American evangelicals appreciated that World Vision did not always fit the Western missionary model. It hired locals and worked in grassroots communities, but it also soon earned a reputation as too big, too flashy, and too independent, as other established humanitarian and mission agencies felt that they had been pushed aside. World Vision's rhetoric favored partnerships with all Christians, but local programs seemed to hire only conservative evangelicals.

In 1981, World Vision faced significant criticism for its work in Honduras. Alongside Comité Evangélico de Emergencia Nacional (Evangelical National Emergency Committee, CEDEN), the mainline Protestant relief agency, and Caritas, the Catholic agency, World Vision maintained camps for Salvadoran refugees fleeing El Salvador's civil war. Many suspected that the Honduran government was supplying names of dissidents to the Salvadorans. One journalist reported that in the midst of these pressures, all humanitarian agencies except World Vision refused to provide lists of refugees to the Honduran government. An uproar ensued after World Vision allowed Honduran officials to take two refugees from its camp—refugees who soon turned up dead. The Catholic human rights NGO Pax Christi mounted a public campaign against World Vision, labeling it a "Trojan horse" of U.S. foreign policy and accusing it of collaboration with the CIA and Honduran secret police, the theft of food aid, aggressive proselytism, and subversion of the work of other Christian agencies.[90] World Vision fought back, denying any connection with the CIA or Honduran government, but internally admitted that a number of the accusations had merit and laid the blame at the feet of the local program staff. The project director, labeled a renegade anticommunist Cuban exile, had used the program to promote his own political and theological agenda, stealing food and pressuring Catholics to convert. World Vision shut down the program and fired or transferred much of its local staff.[91]

Pax Christi's unrelenting accusations in the press took a toll on World Vision.[92] Depictions of World Vision as a professional and progressive organization were displaced by renewed characterizations of the organization as a fundamentalist puppet of American foreign policy. World Vision's internal report admitted that outsiders saw it as "active, organized, compassionate, but naïve." The report continued, "In large part we remain not only evangelical, but also conservative, essentially North American, and consciously non-involved with those issues having the most sensitive political ramifications. . . . In trying to remain apolitical, we became frozen around inaction and security. So we communicated that we favored status quo while others more actively defended human rights."[93] World Vision realized that distinguishing itself from American foreign policy was no longer enough. Its work in Latin America served as a wake-up call. It had hoped to avoid politics but it now realized that its Christian identity would no longer allow it to maintain neutrality.

By the early 1980s, World Vision evolved from an American mission agency to the world's largest Christian humanitarian organization. The organization grew savvier as it expanded its marketing to broader demographics and adopted new relief and development methods. It reconfigured its American and evangelical identity as it pursued internationalization and professionalization. Yet despite the changes, World Vision admitted that it had an image problem. Many still saw the organization as inflexible, isolationist, Western, and fundamentalist. From the opposite side of the spectrum, others believed it had abandoned missions and evangelical fidelity. The question among donors, peer agencies, religious leaders, and critics remained "Who is World Vision?" It could not escape the question: how could it retain its evangelical heritage while it was evolving into an international relief and development organization willing to work in ways—and alongside other organizations—that troubled evangelicals attuned to narrowly American identities and traditional beliefs and practices? Was it abandoning evangelicalism or was it redefining what it could mean to be a Christian humanitarian agency?

CHAPTER 8

A Changing World Vision:
A Changing Evangelicalism?

BY THE EARLY 1980S, World Vision cast its lot alongside international relief and development agencies and away from its American, evangelical, and missionary-centered roots. From 1976 to 1984, during the same period it sought to transform itself from missions to humanitarian agency, the organization expanded dramatically. Field staff grew seven times larger while annual income increased fivefold.[1] By 1986, World Vision's budget would double again as it garnered increased government funding and saw its gift-in-kind (GIK) receipts grow astronomically.[2] Disaster philanthropy took center stage as famines in Africa grabbed headlines, humanitarian agencies made dramatic appeals, and everyone scrambled to deliver the aid received from donors and foreign governments. The decade remained a continual roller coaster of ups and down. Dramatic growth one year was met by lean budgets and layoffs the next. Yet by the 1990s, World Vision returned to double-digit annual growth and emerged as a fixture among the ten largest international nongovernmental organizations (INGOs).[3]

New voices emerged from within World Vision to address these new challenges. During the 1970s, World Vision's president Stan Mooneyham had led its evolution from an American mission agency to the world's largest Christian humanitarian organization. While his vision diverged from founder Bob Pierce, the two leaders shared much in common. They emerged alongside a generation of postwar American evangelicals who built new institutions eager to take their message to the rest of the world. Like their peers Billy Graham and Bill Bright, they embraced charismatic leadership that made their own personality the face of the organization. They trusted their gut and the calling they believed God placed on their lives. They also took too much upon themselves. Wearisome travel, constant expansion, and exposure to the world's most difficult areas took a toll. Like Pierce, Mooneyham's marriage dissolved, he adopted a more dictatorial leadership style, refused accountability, and lost the support of the board. He resigned in 1982, another casualty of evangelical sacrifice again fulfilling Bob Pierce's prayer to burn out for God.[4]

With Mooneyham's departure, World Vision entered its third generation. New leaders emerged within the organization who had never known Bob Pierce or his personal vision to support missionaries and evangelize the world. At the same time, the international organization had grown too large and complex to be defined by a single personality, and it would adopt more bureaucratic over charismatic leadership by necessity.[5] Struggling to manage the steep learning curve that tremendous growth demanded, staff fretted that change was coming so fast that the organization left its head behind in following its heart. Mooneyham's successor, new WVI president Tom Houston, admitted the organization was "due for a resetting of the compass."[6]

Who was World Vision going to be? Having toiled at the fringes of the relief and development establishment for years, its growing size and professionalization prompted INGOs to take notice, but World Vision was often at a loss to know how to respond. If the relief and development community sometimes complemented its reach and expertise, at other times it still critiqued its religious identity as undermining development goals. What did it mean to be both Christian and humanitarian? World Vision continued to debate the role of its religious identity internally even while simultaneously defending its approach within the new networks in which it operated. Others within the organization sought to bury the issue to avoid confrontation. Coming to terms with its religious identity, however, remained a constant concern. Later WVI president Graeme Irvine remarked, "If World Vision does not speak about itself with accuracy and truth, others will speak of it out of ignorance and distortion."[7] Yet the desire for clarity collided with increasing diversity and division within the organization.

Describing World Vision's challenges at the end of the decade, Irvine claimed the organization was at a "*kairos* moment . . . at the crossroads of time." He went further to claim the organization mirrored the struggles of the larger world.[8] If World Vision had once found itself embedded in Cold

War anticommunism and debates between East and West, now the fissures grew between the West and the global South. Field offices in Latin America, Asia, and Africa exercised their voices against what they saw as the dominance of the West that gave voice to the ideals of global partnership but proceeded with limited mutuality and shared decision-making. At the same time, other World Vision offices grew without the same evangelical ethos and donor base that defined the U.S. office. Internal debates within World Vision through the 1980s and early 1990s led many to question whether religious identity would serve as the source of unity across the international organization or whether various interpretations of that identity would emerge as WVI's inevitable division.

Within the United States, the religious landscape of the 1980s and early 1990s was often defined by the rise of the Religious Right as well as the popularity of televangelists and other religious celebrities. As World Vision sought to make sense of its work amid this new religious and political landscape, it demonstrated how it continued to be intertwined with American evangelicalism even if not defined by the movement. In fact, World Vision's continued popular support among evangelicals despite its theological evolution, clear divergence from the politics of the Religious Right, and increasing global outlook demonstrated that a defined evangelical movement labeled by pollsters, pundits, and historians may no longer hold if it ever did. World Vision continued to speak within an evangelical vernacular that resonated with American evangelicals' global imaginaries even amid increasingly fragmented institutional networks that had formerly defined the movement.

World Vision grew in size and popularity and evolved into a leading relief and development organization, but many within the organization worried that it was changing too much too fast. It had already adopted an international rather than an exclusively American outlook, a holistic mission, and a broad evangelicalism. Its new role within the culture of international development pushed World Vision to restate its Christian identity as the principle holding the organization together. But what did the Christian identity now mean for the organization? Did it require different practices? Did it mean distinctive methodologies? Did it require structural changes? Such questions produced vigorous debate about its role within relief and development, its own ability to remain a united global agency of dozens of distinct national offices, and its efforts to retain its evangelical roots while not being defined by American ideologies alone. World Vision's leaders often disagreed on the organization's future path and the best way to get there, but they all agreed they no longer had the luxury to maintain the status quo.

African Famines and World Vision Expansion

In 1984–85, famine in Ethiopia dominated international headlines. Before the famine, World Vision's work in Africa lagged behind other regions. After the catastrophe, the continent consumed its attention.[9] In 1981, it released *Crisis in the Horn of Africa*. Like earlier television appeals, it featured celebrities in studio alongside firsthand footage of hungry children. A television crew filmed World Vision president Stan Mooneyham as he transported the sick to medical clinics. The crew flew on a World Vision plane to distribute grain to remote villagers. And they visited an overcrowded feeding center to capture images of children with flies on their faces and mothers with withered breasts, unable to feed their babies. The resulting television film provided the highest return on investment of any World Vision television appeal, and the malnourished African child became the human face of humanitarian relief in the 1980s and 1990s.[10]

Having closed its offices in Southeast Asia in the 1970s, World Vision took part in relief work during the Biafra famine in the African Sahel. By 1980, it established a Relief and Rehabilitation Division, designed for large humanitarian emergencies. With more attention to famines, natural disasters, and international politics, World Vision attempted to deploy resources more quickly, manage complex logistics, and handle large shipments of relief goods while raising its profile among the international aid community.[11]

By late 1983, World Vision realized that severe drought was creating a humanitarian crisis in Ethiopia. The following year, Scotsman Tom Houston succeeded Mooneyham as WVI president. The first non-American president, he retained a ministerial voice from his experience as a pastor in his native Scotland and Nairobi, Kenya. He demonstrated evangelical credentials through his work within the Lausanne movement and moved to World Vision from directing the British and Foreign Bible Society.[12] In his new job, he quickly sensed heightened tensions within the organization. Support and field countries fought over autonomy and control while the staff struggled to implement development programs with necessary technical expertise. Growth had outpaced relationship-building and strategic planning.

Nevertheless, Houston gambled World Vision's reputation on the Ethiopian crisis. He took charge of a new African Drought Project and pledged over $25 million of unbudgeted funds. Some within the organization viewed Houston's move as an attempt to circumvent local control. Others realized that it brought funds, personnel, and expertise that the local World Vision Ethiopian staff could not bring on its own.[13]

World Vision was one of several INGOs providing emergency Ethiopian relief. Agencies attempted to alert donors of the urgent need through direct appeals, but the severity of the famine remained underreported. Ethiopia's Marxist government prevented foreign journalists from entering the country, and few media outlets pressed the issue, but in October 1984, a World Vision plane took two reporters, Mohamed Amin and Michael Buerk, into the country.[14] When the BBC broadcast their footage on October 23, the famine became international news. Amin alternated close-ups of malnourished children with pictures of hungry people in lines that stretched for miles. Buerk's narration depicted Ethiopia as "hell on earth." The original BBC footage garnered an estimated audience of 470 million viewers. *NBC Nightly News* anchor Tom Brokaw picked up the story, and CBS's *60 Minutes* soon followed. Within a month all three major U.S. networks featured the famine. Camera crews flooded every INGO refugee camp.[15]

Funds for famine relief poured into international charities. British musician Bob Geldof established his Band Aid organization and gathered fellow recording artists to raise money. Their song "Do They Know It's Christmas?" climbed to number one on the charts, selling over six million copies and raising over eight million dollars. In 1985, Geldof organized Live Aid, a global concert that attracted 70,000 to London's Wembley Stadium, 80,000 to John F. Kennedy Stadium in Philadelphia, and over 1.5 million others watching live through satellite. The concert raised another $80 million for famine relief and empowered bands like U2 to take up humanitarian concerns.[16]

World Vision capitalized on the media frenzy by producing its own stream of fund-raising appeals, yet aggressive marketing was not necessary. News anchors provided free publicity through interviews with relief workers and doctors. World Vision labeled 1985 "the year the world cared." It raised funds faster than it could create programs to spend them, its income increasing by 80 percent in a single year. Its funds for Ethiopian relief and development grew from $6 million in 1984 to $71 million in 1985 while its in-country staff mushroomed from 100 to 3,650.[17]

Figure 13. World
Vision's coverage
of the Ethiopian
famine, 1985.
© World Vision, Inc.
2011. All rights
reserved. Reprinted by
permission.

World Vision had already edged away from Pierce's fear for governmental funding, but as it learned to handle large gifts in kind, it drew record levels of support. USAID awarded World Vision $13.5 million and 1.5 million metric tons of food aid for Ethiopia. In 1985, 93 percent of World Vision U.S.'s revenue came from federal funding. The percentage dropped to 87 percent in 1986 and 42.3 percent in 1987, but the Ethiopian famine made World Vision a major broker of federal humanitarian aid.[18]

The rise in federal assistance required professionalization. World Vision hired consultants away from USAID and other INGOs to establish new programs almost overnight. New grants created logistical nightmares. Purchasing fleets of trucks, establishing feeding centers, and training short-term staff, World Vision learned to navigate governmental bureaucracies and contract with other INGOs for services it could not yet provide. It scrambled to implement means of evaluation to meet the accounting standards of its government donors.[19]

Even as it took in millions of dollars for emergency aid, World Vision realized that famine relief was not enough. Like other INGOs, it began to move from relief to development. World Vision introduced USAID-funded "food for work programs" that provided agricultural assistance packages (AGPAKs) to Ethiopian families, giving them the seeds and supplies to plant one hectare of land. Farmers received an ox and plow; herdsmen got sheep or goats. World Vision drilled wells and stepped up its work in agricultural training. By 1986, it presented Ethiopia's Antsokia Valley as a model for success. A barren region that only two years earlier had housed 60,000 Ethiopians in a World Vision feeding center now emerged as a "green oasis" with the return of the rains and INGO-led community development projects.[20]

World Vision now moved to large-scale development (LSD), which it defined as projects budgeted over one million dollars, lasting at least three years, and aiding multiple communities. Before the era of rapid budget growth and government aid, World Vision had worked mainly at the village level. Now it believed LSD projects would increase the reach of the organization and draw more funding. LSD projects required higher technical standards for staff members, more complex logistical structures, and closer interaction with local governments. They also required a high level of federal aid. World Vision's leaders knew that few INGOs had succeeded with large-scale programs, but they could capture the attention of USAID, foundations, and other funding agencies. World Vision stood to gain substantial fundraising and publicity if its large-scale approach succeeded, but failure would be costly. The stakes were high but so was World Vision's optimism.[21]

After emergency aid relieved the Ethiopian famine, international attention waned. As crowds of hungry people disappeared from feeding centers, camera crews moved on to other stories. By 1987, World Vision's income had shrunk to almost half its record high two years earlier.[22] The organization had to lay off staff, cut programs, and deplete its reserves to keep commitments. Some ugly realities came to light. The INGOs and media had depicted the famine as a natural disaster from years of drought, but Ethiopia's government had also spent its own money on weapons to fight a counterinsurgency instead of meeting the basic needs of its citizens. For access to the feeding centers, INGOs had been compelled to ignore political irresponsibility in Ethiopia.[23] Work with local governments would become increasingly difficult as INGOs moved from providing emergency relief to implementing long-term development.

World Vision reevaluated its engagement in Ethiopia. While some INGOs still saw the organization as "aggressive and uncooperative," operating more like a fire brigade than a seasoned development agency, it succeeded in making the jump into the select circle of large INGOs, becoming a leader in fund-raising, emergency relief, and cooperation with the U.S. government. But the difficulty of fund-raising and LSD projects entailed a scaling back of effort.[24] Expansion had required hiring staff members who did not share its Christian values. Growth followed by budget slashing also created tensions, often between fund-raisers from Western support countries and development staff in the field offices of the global South. It was not easy to function among the elite echelon of international relief and development agencies, but there was no going back.[25]

INGOs and a Shared World Culture

In the 1980s, the combined budgets of INGOs almost tripled from $2.3 billion to $6 billion as Western governments turned to these agencies to administer most of their humanitarian aid. From 1970 to 1990, government aid to NGOs increased from under $200 million to $2.2 billion.[26] Government funds allowed the biggest agencies to continue to expand while upstarts liked World Vision received substantial federal aid for the first time. World Vision soon learned to speak the common language of an INGO culture.[27]

Models of development also changed as agencies like the World Bank and the International Monetary Fund (IMF) demanded that developing nations make structural adjustments in order to receive foreign aid. Favoring neoliberal economics, they required the reduction of government spending, deregulation of public institutions, and free trade. The theory linked underdevelopment with corruption and inefficiency. If they could privatize the public sector, free markets would benefit everyone. In reality, their demands led governments to cut social services, and Western aid once funneled directly to foreign governments now went to INGOs.[28] Growing numbers of Western expatriates and locals made their living in the humanitarian industry. When one INGO's grant expired, they moved on to another agency. As agencies imitated each other, swapped staff, and worked along-side one another, they began to reflect the contours of a shared culture.

Scholars have pointed to INGO growth to illustrate the effects of global-ization.[29] Without denying either complexity or local diversity, they empha-sized its power to shape an overarching "world culture."[30] Nation-states, transnational corporations, and intergovernmental organizations (IGOs) set the norms for this common culture, but INGOs often mediated them to civil society. This shared world culture appeared rationalized, production-oriented, and professional.[31] As many INGOs came into closer contact with governments, IGOs, and one another, they began to exhibit a homogeniza-tion of language, practice, and organization. Within international relief and development, the desire for federal funding led many INGOs to adopt a minimum level of professionalization and regulation required by govern-ment authorities. At other times, a desire to gain cultural legitimacy among donors or a need to compete with other INGOs served as the impetus for imitation. As a recognized field of international relief and development solidified, the leading INGOs came to look remarkably similar.[32] It seemed to follow that even though an organization like World Vision claimed a religious identity, it would eventually function like any other secular relief and development INGO within its field. In presuming a shared world cul-ture, theorists often ignored religion.[33]

Other scholars pointed to the resurgence of global religion and the plethora of religiously diverse humanitarianism organizations.[34] While a cosmopolitan, transnational elite stratum of international relief and devel-opment agencies shared a common world culture, others resisted it. Work-ing among largely secular organizations, these resisters held on to religious motives that made them more complex than the secularization theorists recognized. They did not see inevitable conflict between religion and humanitarianism. They held on to fluid identities that combined religious values and technical expertise.[35]

Such issues permeated discussions within World Vision. Relief and development agencies combining an evangelical religious identity with humanitarian work expanded throughout the 1980s. By the end of the dec-ade, six of the seven largest evangelical mission agencies were relief and development organizations.[36] World Vision remained distinct by keeping one foot in the evangelical world and the other within the culture of elite INGO agencies. Some within World Vision feared that government funding would silence the evangelistic impulse. They petitioned World Vision to limit reliance on government support so as not to compromise its mission. Others saw federal funding as the ticket to expansive growth and lobbied to create programs in accord with government funding priorities.

World Vision continued its drive toward professionalization. Staff members affirmed its Christian identity, but more now came with experience in other development agencies, university appointments, or government posts.[37] Government funding and large-scale programs led to new layers of logistics and expertise. Some worried that faith did not run as deep in these newcomers as earlier generations, but they could no longer afford to hire pastors and missionaries and give them on the job training. World Vision expected both professionalism and piety, but when forced to choose, some favored technical expertise.[38]

World Vision's leaders also followed the latest in development practice. They translated it through a biblical and Christian vernacular, but many now spoke the language of international humanitarianism fluently. Secular development may not have been their mother tongue, but many had become bilingual. What did it then mean to be a Christian development agency? The discussions produced no consensus.[39]

Nonetheless, World Vision began to pursue partnerships outside its evangelical context. Forging them was not easy. Many still saw World Vision as arrogant, uncooperative, and American. World Vision sometimes perpetuated these stereotypes, and the humanitarian industry's old guard had little incentive to open its doors to "upstarts." Yet, by 1985, World Vision had gained consultative status with the United Nations High Commission for Refugees (UNHCR) and the World Food Programme (WFP). A few years later it added the United Nations Children's Fund (UNICEF) and the World Health Organization (WHO) to the list.[40] When Pierce founded World Vision in 1950, few evangelicals trusted the United Nations. By the mid-1980s, Pierce's organization was making UN initiatives central to its own work.

Many saw these new bilateral partnerships as a necessary response to critics who saw World Vision as narrowly American and too inexperienced. In 1985, World Vision named Australian Graeme Irvine as its first vice president of international relations. Irvine opened a World Vision office in Geneva to be near other INGO leaders. He even lobbied World Vision to move its headquarters there. While he failed to persuade the board, by the end of the decade, World Vision worked consistently with the United Nations, gained a seat at the World Economic Forum in Davos, and initiated bilateral aid programs with the World Bank.[41]

The most difficult partner remained the World Council of Churches (WCC). Despite World Vision's willingness to work closely with ecumenical agencies, the evangelical-ecumenical divide proved difficult to overcome. The WCC still questioned World Vision's theology and accused it of prose-lytism, stealing national church leaders, and Western imperialist tenden-cies.[42] Most often the WCC's accusations reflected past rather than present relationships, but the conflicts were also personal, as in a family feud. Over time, however, the chilly relations thawed, and in 1987 evangelical and ecumenical leaders met in Stuttgart, Germany, to write a shared statement on evangelism. Both admitted past faults and recognized how much they had in common.[43] In many countries, World Vision's staff worked closely with local national church councils. By 1992, the international coordinator of UNICEF as well as the general secretary of the WCC would bring greet-ings to World Vision's international board.[44]

Tensions over World Vision's Organizational Identity and Public Image

World Vision's growth required changes in the organization. For one, World Vision U.S. was no longer the only source of financial support. Other support countries began to contribute more, so that by the end of the 1980s the U.S. office funded little more than half of the international partnership's budget.[45] Yet, other support countries sometimes downplayed their evan-gelical identity. For example, 93 percent of Australians recognized the agency by name, but only 11 percent recognized it as Christian. In Europe, World Vision offices gained favor with international agencies and received government grants but made less headway with the Christian public. As other church-related European NGOs feared World Vision would siphon off their Christian constituents, European offices never held to a strict pol-icy of hiring evangelicals and came to employ a broad range of Christian staff, many of whom did not interpret World Vision's Christian identity as requiring anything different from secular development.[46]

World Vision's field offices administering the programs raised their own concerns. Even as the number of field countries doubled throughout the 1980s, the international organization pushed them to raise their own funds and establish local governing boards. In 1982, Hong Kong became the first field office to support programs outside its borders. Other nations, such as

South Korea, soon followed. In encouraging field countries to take owner-
ship of their programs, World Vision empowered new voices to address
local issues as well as raise questions relevant to the entire partnership.[47]

These new voices pressed World Vision to reposition itself in the midst
of a diversifying world Christianity. In many countries, World Vision was
learning to work with and often hire staff outside of its traditional evangelical fold. While an evangelical ethos still dominated, field countries now
hired staff from Pentecostal, Catholic, Orthodox, and mainline traditions.
Staff had to learn to operate in contexts where no religion or other world
religions dominated, and they found their own colleagues occupied an
increasingly diverse religious spectrum. A single "World Vision story" was
now impossible.

The East-West divisions that defined World Vision throughout the Cold
War now also gave way to divisions of North and South.[48] Throughout
World Vision's history, Western evangelicals celebrated the spread of a
world Christianity that assimilated familiar Western forms. Now Two-
Thirds World evangelicals reminded the Americans that the world had
changed. A global Christianity would require the West to listen and reevalu-
ate its own theology and practice.[49]

Tensions abounded as World Vision expanded. Professionalization
increased efficiency and government funding, but some complained it con-
formed the organization to Western norms. While internationalization led
the U.S. office to give up full control, field offices realized that only the
largest fund-raising countries had a real voice. Southern partners complained that they were treated as second-class citizens and demanded a
more equitable partnership. Northern partners complained that the central
World Vision International office operated unilaterally, focusing on the
field with little regard for the wishes of its financial supporters.[50]

When Houston assumed the WVI presidency in 1984, frustrations were
high. Houston responded with a reorganization plan. Instead of Western
offices making decisions for field countries, he appointed three regional vice
presidents over Latin America, Asia, and Africa. With leaders in each region,
Houston hoped to give national offices a greater voice in decision-making.
The following year, WVI changed its bylaws to balance representation from
field and support countries on its governing International Council.[51]

Organizational changes helped, but they did not solve the problem.
Support and field offices came with different priorities. The common asser-
tion was that northern countries raised the funds while southern countries

administered the programs. Both accused one another of limited vision and lack of understanding. U.S. fund-raisers complained that field staff took too long to develop programs and then offered explanations laden with so much jargon that they held little interest to donors. Field staff complained that support offices clamored for programs that might bring in funds but would not work on the ground. If they were not technically feasible, culturally appropriate, or welcomed by the local community, the relief and development staff argued they ran contrary to World Vision's mission.[52]

A debate over development education illustrated the divisions. Most Western fund-raising offices had little knowledge of development practice and subdivided the mission between the administrative and marketing work they did "at home" and the development work done "in the field." Program staff resented the pictures of malnourished children that World Vision U.S. used to raise funds, arguing that such images implied a call for simple charity that undermined the dignity of the people they served as well as the organization's commitment to development.[53] They claimed that World Vision had a responsibility to educate its staff and donors on development.[54] President Houston defined the conflict as one between idealism and pragmatism.[55] Yes, educating donors about development was important, but marketing studies told fund-raisers that images of hungry children brought in more financial resources than explanations of crop rotation or reforestation. U.S. marketers debated the ethics of their approach, but they knew pragmatically that World Vision evaluated them on money raised over the message portrayed.[56]

Debates over child sponsorship led to even more heated confrontations. In the late 1970s, World Vision made commitments to incorporate development into its childcare ministries and pool child sponsorship resources for the needs of an entire community. By the 1980s, some wanted to get rid of sponsorship all together. In the early 1980s, child-sponsorship agencies faced increased scrutiny and negative publicity. Investigative journalists uncovered isolated cases of negligence or fraud. Other mainstream media sources, including a few evangelical publications, questioned whether child sponsorship was the best way to raise money for humanitarian causes.[57] Internally, World Vision admitted that child sponsorship was difficult to administer and required enormous overhead. It worried that child sponsorship ran counter to its development values, but it also knew that sponsorship remained the most reliable and largest source of annual income.[58]

In 1983, despite having enrolled over 300,000 sponsored children, an internal Sponsorship Task Force recommended that World Vision move away from its sponsorship program.[59] The fund-raising offices in the United States, Canada, and Australia experimented. Instead of assigning donors a specific child, World Vision sent information about a "representative child" and spoke of helping children in community. With its focus on the Ethiopia famine in 1984, World Vision decided to stop acquiring new sponsors altogether. After two years, however, World Vision saw a substantial decline in its sponsor fulfillment rates. Marketers realized that people were not connecting to a "representative child."[60]

By 1985, already seeing budget shortfalls after the height of the Ethiopian famine, World Vision returned to child sponsorship. It still integrated the funds into community development programs, but it realized that donors needed a one-to-one connection.[61] By the end of the decade, they were sponsoring more than one million children. Not everyone was happy with the decision. Some field offices refused to sign up kids for sponsorship despite the money it would bring to their programs.[62]

World Vision learned to live with tension, but some worried that rising discontent would fracture the organization. National offices began to work against one another, form alliances, and hold closed-door meetings. Frustrations came to a head at the annual 1987 Field Directors' Conference in Sierra Madre, California. As executive leaders presented future strategies, local national directors balked. Joining in protest, they took over the agenda to voice their concerns. Manfred Grellert, WVI's vice president for Latin America, recounted that "people were angry and spoke rough things to one another . . . but what looked to be a fiasco created an agenda for authentic partnership."[63] The event propelled World Vision into years of dialogue to repair relationships and revise structures.

Organizational turmoil led to Houston's resignation in 1988.[64] Australian Graeme Irvine took his place in an effort to build consensus and rebuild a fractured organization. Irvine was a longtime World Vision staffer respected for his leadership in the field and his willingness to try new approaches. While affirming an evangelical theology, he presented a new pedigree for World Vision. As an unordained Anglican, he came out of Australia's YMCA movement. He was more at ease with ecumenical traditions, and he brought a contemplative rather than a revivalistic spirituality, introducing employees to the work of Henri Nouwen and Thomas Merton, Catholic spiritual mentors popular in ecumenical seminaries.[65]

By the end of the 1980s, World Vision had recovered from budget cuts and was again expanding programs, but internally it remained in crisis. Brazilian Manfred Grellert pointed to global Christianity's evolution from "a whiter to darker face."[66] Roberta Hestenes, WVI board chair and president of evangelical Eastern University, in St. Davids, Pennsylvania, near Philadelphia, issued a public confession: "The most profound division in the world Church and in World Vision was between those of dominant culture and those who are marginalized. . . . World Vision has been primarily Protestant; we have been primarily evangelical or members of daughter churches of evangelical missions. We have been primarily traditional in our worship patterns. We have been primarily male. We have been primarily members of the dominant cultures, no matter where we are from in the world."[67] World Vision wondered if it could bridge the divide between North and South to become a truly international NGO working "together in authentic partnership.[68]

Over much of the next decade, Irvine led World Vision through the slow and deliberate process of redefining itself.[69] His Partnership Task Force (1988–95) proposed a new system of governance. WVI needed to adapt to its massive growth. In interviewing hundreds of staff members, the task force discovered three key concerns. First, labeling support countries as fund-raisers and field countries as development practitioners perpetuated conflict and made the mission more difficult. Second, southern countries complained that the partnership privileged money as the measure of power, and they demanded more equitable leadership. Third, with growing religious diversity and secular influences, the staff needed guidance as to how World Vision's Christian identity informed its practice.[70]

In debating decentralization and mutuality between northern and southern NGOs, World Vision was not alone. The issue caught fire throughout the international humanitarian community. Yet, alongside organizational studies and management principles, World Vision framed some of its concerns theologically: how could it model a holistic Christian mission and inclusive global Christianity within a growing partnership? By the 1990s, World Vision could say that no single voice defined the partnership. For some, this was a virtue; for others, a lack. Leaders wondered if they had lost a cohesive vision. The national and regional offices marketed different messages, produced their own mission statements, and even carried different logos. They competed for resources, created redundancies, and resisted any cohesive strategy.

Irvine noted that "in an organization of the size, diversity, and geographical dispersion of World Vision, a high degree of decentralization is essential."[71] The Partnership Task Force introduced a new federalism model that allowed national offices to make local decisions; removed the labels of field and support countries in order to repair divisions between fund-raisers and ministry practitioners; and provided for more equitable representation to counter the assumption that money was the measure of power. It even implemented a process of peer review in which national offices shared mutual accountability by evaluating one another.[72]

Within the new federalized structure, a top-down, exclusively Western directed organization was no longer possible. If national offices had often experienced the central International Office (IO) as a "no organization," simply there to implement rules and regulations, now it sought to serve by centralizing services like human resources, accounting, and information technology but allowing the national offices to attend to the local issues distinctive to their context.[73]

At the same time, World Vision encouraged its national offices to see themselves as dual citizens. Without forgoing local priorities, each country had some responsibility for the international work. All national offices adopted the shared documents Core Values, Covenant of Partnership, and Statement of Faith, but WVI leadership realized by the early 2000s that in an age of the internet and twenty-four-hour cable news, there had to be an even stronger central message.[74] While national offices maintained autonomy, the INGO could capitalize on its size by working together.[75] World Vision even suggested coffee retailer Starbucks as a model. Starbucks was ubiquitous in a globalized world, but each local franchise maintained a consistent brand. Countries empowered a representative WVI council to make decisions for the entire organization while adopting a common vision statement, enforcing a single logo, and launching a singular brand strategy. Like Starbucks, it sought to make World Vision's orange trademark synonymous with humanitarian relief and development.[76] All knew that the plan was messy, but they hoped to balance a theological commitment to stewardship with a commitment to diversity within community.

World Vision U.S. and American Evangelicalism

In the midst of the international partnership's increasing diversity and reorganization, World Vision U.S. (WVUS) assessed its own current context in

Figure 14. World Vision's logo, a licensed trademark, serves as a key asset linking together the multiple and somewhat independent national offices of World Vision International. © World Vision, Inc. 2011. All rights reserved. Reprinted by permission.

light of the organization's evangelical past. Many celebrated the 1980s as the height of evangelical success. Televangelists created empires while seeker-sensitive pastors like Rick Warren and Bill Hybels built Saddleback and Willow Creek into the country's largest megachurches. With the election of Ronald Reagan, Christian Right leaders like Jerry Falwell, Pat Robertson, and James Dobson framed evangelicals as a sought-after voting bloc.

Others lamented that evangelicals had become victims of their own success. Televangelism soon suffered from financial misappropriations and sex scandals. Fellow evangelicals accused seeker churches and celebrity pastors of watering down faith for larger numbers. Some worried that right-wing politics drew evangelicals into "culture wars." Carl Henry, by now an evangelical elder statesman, began to lament that the "respectable reputation" for which evangelicals had worked so hard had fallen "into open caricature and ridicule."[77]

Just as an evangelical left splintered in the 1970s, the evangelical establishment further fragmented in the 1980s. The establishment sought to maintain evangelicalism as a single movement united around theological distinctives, even as social, economic, and political issues increasingly scattered evangelicals across a broader conservative-liberal spectrum. By the end of the 1980s, some began to give up any hope for unity.[78] In response to Carl Henry's laments, evangelical historian Nathan Hatch claimed that a single "evangelicalism" was nothing more than an abstraction more accurately identified as a cultural style rather than any set of doctrinal categories. Evangelicalism's success was tied to its "entrepreneurial quality, its populist and decentralized structure, and its penchant for splitting, forming and reforming."[79] Further fragmentation was inevitable as America fostered multiple evangelicalisms with similar, but not identical, practices and institutions.[80]

WVUS still fit within these broad evangelical networks. Stan Mooneyham and Ted Engstrom stood among the who's who of American evangelicalism, yet as the first generation of postwar evangelicals retired, World
Vision joined others in seeking leadership from a new generation.[81] In 1987,
WVUS named Robert (Bob) Seiple as president. Unlike previous leaders
with degrees from evangelical colleges or seminaries, Seiple had an Ivy
League education from Brown University. After flying combat missions
with the U.S. Marines in Vietnam, he made his name as an administrator
and fund-raiser in higher education. When World Vision hired him at the
age of forty-four, he was serving as president of evangelical Eastern College
(now Eastern University). Seiple felt at home within evangelical networks,
but he represented a changing of the guard.[82]

When Pierce founded the organization, he took his films to evangelical
churches, mission conferences, and Bible colleges. In the late 1970s, World
Vision turned to mass marketing through direct mail and television. By
1984, it acquired 86 percent of its donors through television.[83] Pierce's
vision was not only to raise funds for foreign missionaries but also to educate evangelical congregations on global issues. Over time, World Vision
downsized its church relations department to emphasize fund-raising over
education. Building relationships with local churches was expensive and
time consuming. Some congregations began to question their relationship
with the new World Vision. It seemed too cold and too big; they labeled it
the "IBM of the Christian world."[84]

Mass marketing led WVUS to recast its language for a broader demographic, and it succeeded in increasing revenues and new donors. Still, its
vernacular and practices made clear that it felt most at home among evangelicals, and it refused to take its core constituency for granted. Its research
demonstrated that evangelicals were more likely to recognize the organization's reputation and remain long term donors. In 1998, 41 percent of the
U.S. population considered themselves born-again Christians compared to
86 percent of World Vision donors. When using the more stringent definition of the pollster George Barna, evangelicals made up 7 percent of the
American population but 42 percent of World Vision's supporters.[85] While
it still poured the bulk of its marketing into television and direct appeals, it
continued to take out full-page advertisements in *Christianity Today*,
exhibit at InterVarsity's Urbana mission conferences, and create a curricu-
lum that highlighted its work for use by Christian schools and homeschool-
ing parents.

World Vision also turned to the growing contemporary Christian music (CCM) industry. The rival evangelical child-sponsorship agency Compassion International competed to sign artists to endorse its work. Early Christian artists like Sandi Patti and Dino accompanied World Vision on overseas trips and then returned to offer testimonies in television specials or benefit concerts.[86] Most often artists promoted child sponsorship on concert tours. After the artist shared stories of children in need, World Vision staff members gave information packets to concertgoers during intermissions. Artists often received a percentage of a new sponsor's pledge. Bigger artists received up-front tour expenses. By the 1990s, World Vision and Compassion had saturated the CCM market. Almost every Christian concert brought a plug for child sponsorship and further solidified World Vision's evangelical identity.[87]

While World Vision maintained popular support among its evangelical donors, it walked a fine line in balancing evangelical commitments. For instance, as evangelicals began reading an outpouring of books on premillennial eschatology and prophecy in the 1980s, Ted Engstrom praised Billy Graham's latest best seller *Approaching Hoofbeats*, an interpretation of the book of Revelation. He agreed with Graham's interpretation of the Four Horsemen of the Apocalypse as famine, pestilence, war, and death, while also affirming his belief in Christ's imminent return, but he warned evangelicals against isolating themselves from the world in a "cloistered, ecclesiastical compound" from which they pushed "tracts out through knotholes."[88] Engstrom would not allow a particular eschatology to undermine a commitment to social concern.

It was no easy matter to stand between two evangelical cultural spheres. Well-connected World Vision leaders may have attended the annual National Prayer Breakfast, but they avoided direct support of the Religious Right. They criticized the Christian Right for trying to gain political power when Christian humanitarian agencies had already earned credibility. Without dismissing social issues, World Vision's international orientation often kept it above the domestic culture wars as it kept its eye on child poverty, famine, and global evangelism.[89]

Yet, it also kept its distance from the evangelical left. While the voices in *Sojourners*, the *Other Side*, and other publications still served many alternative communities, by the 1980s, they had lost their prominence among evangelicals in the public square. World Vision found other voices to challenge American evangelicals' social consciences. One of these was John

Perkins, widely recognized by fellow evangelicals for his decades of work in racial reconciliation and local community development in his native Mississippi. Perkins joined WVUS's board in 1977 and encouraged the beginnings of WVUS's domestic ministries in order to address the need for holistic development in the organization's own backyard. As a black southerner who spoke out for evangelical issues such as strong families and the necessity of evangelism in working for structural change, Perkins traveled on behalf of World Vision internationally while adeptly bridging theological and political differences among American evangelicals.

Another new voice, Tony Campolo, may have been slightly less successful in bridging divides but even more successful in garnering headlines. Trained as a sociologist who gave up a prestigious post at the University of Pennsylvania to teach at evangelical Eastern University and live among Philadelphia's urban poor, Campolo was a captivating speaker who resonated with young evangelicals. World Vision worked with Eastern University on a new program to train development practitioners, and it joined with Campolo on a film to promote its work in Africa. In preaching to thousands of evangelical youth at the 1987 Urbana mission conference, he questioned whether it was possible to follow Jesus and drive a BMW. "What would Jesus drive" soon became a stock Campolo refrain. After reprinting the sermon in its magazine, World Vision received more letters to the editor than it had received in reaction to any other article, most of them attacking Campolo. The negative responses from donors demonstrated how difficult it was for World Vision to find any single issue where its broad constituency would all agree.[90]

World Vision had already moved beyond its evangelical roots by accepting government aid, adopting professional development, and entering the INGO culture. It expanded its donor base, diversified its staff, and found new partners. Yet American evangelicalism itself was also broadening. Throughout the 1970s and 1980s, evangelicals moved up the social scale through gains in higher education, income, and political power. For increasing numbers of Americans, it became acceptable to be known as an evangelical.[91]

The larger question remained whether it was still important to define who was in and out of the evangelical movement? Evangelical anthropologist and Fuller Seminary missiologist Paul Hiebert introduced the mathematic metaphor of "bounded" versus "centered" sets. Bounded sets made clear who was in and out through moral and cultural codes, ideologies, and institutions, but they offered little definition beyond those boundaries. Centered sets offered a core ideology but fewer boundaries. World Vision appropriated the metaphor of the "centered set" to describe itself. It still claimed an evangelical identity, but it often found American evangelical boundaries constricting.[92]

World Vision Debates Justice, Advocacy, Gender

While WVUS followed the changes within American evangelicalism, it also could not ignore the growth of global evangelicalism. Too many people still saw evangelicalism as a Western export, but WVUS realized that Americans were no longer at that center of evangelical demographic or institutional growth.[93] How would WVUS's work at home have to change if American evangelicalism no longer defined the agenda?

On certain topics, World Vision could no longer avoid controversial decisions. For instance, following evangelicals' traditional distaste for what they saw as ecumenism's unsavory politicking, World Vision often claimed its evangelistic and humanitarian activities remained apolitical. Yet for years critics had suggested that its claims of neutrality were naive and harmful in ignoring unjust political and social structures.[94] Some of its own staff members had privately harbored similar reservations, and by 1982 World Vision's field directors, indigenous staff heading up large-scale development in the global South, made their concerns known in a public document, "World Vision in a Political and Social Context."[95] They agreed that World Vision's work to alleviate the needs of those in poverty must also adequately address the root causes of injustice. The following year, they presented their case before the WVI Council: "We need to recognize the reality that our ministry is political . . . rather than trying to maintain a dangerous fiction that we are non-political, we would be better served by developing far more political expertise."[96] Strict divisions between politics and ministry may have placated evangelical constituencies in the fundraising offices, but practitioners argued that they undermined World Vision's mission on the ground.

President Mooneyham commissioned Anglican priest and World Vision New Zealand board chair John Rymer to prepare a study that began a ten-year focus on justice. In 1983, Rymer presented an initial document, 150 pages long, that gave a biblical and theological argument for justice. He reiterated arguments from global evangelicals such as Orlando Costas and Samuel Escobar as well as information from the World Council of Churches and Latin American Catholic bishops.[97] Few denied the thoroughness of Rymer's work, but some complained that it was too abstract. What they needed was direction for internal decisions and external communications. What they got was a theological position paper.[98]

The majority of those shaping policy came to view justice as indispensable. So what forms should this commitment take? In 1985, World Vision adopted the Universal Declaration of Human Rights. While the United Nations had adopted the declaration in 1948, most evangelicals dismissed it as a secular document ill-suited or even contrary to its missionary work. World Vision's affirmation of universal human rights represented an important first step. In 1987, a revised policy statement on development and a new statement on urban ministry also suggested a need to oppose oppressive and unjust structures. By 1989, the World Vision board adopted a statement on justice. A statement on advocacy followed in 1991.[99]

Some within the partnership complained that taking up questions of justice and advocacy would alienate the organization's donor base and take time away from relief and development. Yet with the support of the Western fundraising and Latin American field offices, in 1992 World Vision added the new statements to its mission: promoting human transformation through relief and community-based development, bearing witness to Jesus Christ, and also working to change unjust structures affecting the poor. Bringing everyone along at the same pace and in the same way was rarely possible, however, as a number of Asian and African evangelicals abstained from the vote.[100]

Even as World Vision pushed ahead to implement justice, it ventured more slowly into advocacy. In the past, it had brought attention to the Vietnamese boat people in the 1970s and the Ethiopian famine in the 1980s but stopped short of outright advocacy. In 1989, however, WVI president Graeme Irvine lobbied the United Nations for changes in Cambodia, where World Vision had a long history. In front of the prison where 20,000 Cambodians were tortured and killed, Irvine pressed the United Nations to reject former Khmer Rouge leader Khieu Samphan as its Cambodian representative, called for free elections, and pushed for religious freedom. The media blitz and political rankling that followed led Cambodia to implement each change.[101]

World Vision's passion for the Palestinians stimulated another early advocacy effort. Having opened an office in the West Bank in 1986, it spoke out against Israel's "oppression" of the occupied territories. Among World Vision's constituency, President Irvine knew that evangelicals often referred to Israel as "the people of God," and "the creation of the Israeli state as the fulfillment of biblical prophecy." Yet he felt that World Vision was obligated to correct misinformation and raise public awareness about the plight of the Palestinian people. "Failure to speak or act on behalf of the poor . . . [would] be inconsistent with World Vision's Christian development stance."[102]

In subsequent years, World Vision would join the Red Cross to ban the manufacture, sale, and use of landmines. It also drew attention to the exploitation of children, particularly in child prostitution. World Vision's initial campaigns met with success across its diverse constituency, yet it chose its issues selectively. Few found banning landmines or protecting children controversial.[103]

Staff assigned to advocacy remained small. In 1985, WVUS hired Tom Getman, former aide to Senator Mark Hatfield, to set up an office in Washington, D.C. As World Vision's director of governmental relations, Getman managed a staff of two. When he left in 1997 for even larger roles within the World Vision international partnership, he managed a staff of forty-seven that kept track of federal grants, implementation, and evaluation.[104] Access to power grew as the organization became larger and more well known, and it soon began to lobby U.S. legislators and UN representatives on foreign aid policy and international relations while also planning future programs in accord with the grant cycles of USAID. Advocacy campaigns to raise public awareness were good, but briefing elected officials often worked even better.

As World Vision explored justice and advocacy as a part of its mission, other voices began to assert that gender was another justice issue the organization had ignored. By the 1970s, the field of development had already shifted its attention with the United Nations, christening 1976–85 as its Decade for Women. New development programs focused on women's health, child-rearing, and economic growth; research showed that women were the linchpin for development success. A few World Vision practitioners experimented with local development initiatives for women, and a handful of staff members attended the 1985 UN World Conference on Women in Nairobi, Kenya. They left enthusiastic but found little built-in support, as World Vision remained on the sidelines of larger gender conversations.[105]

Advocates for women's development initiatives also turned their attention to the lack of women leaders within World Vision. Without claiming intentional gender discrimination, they confronted the "old boys club" culture that kept women out of senior leadership positions. World Vision commissioned a study group that led the partnership to approve a new "Women in Development and Leadership Policy" in 1992. Roberta Hestenes, World Vision International board chair and the only woman among World Vision's senior leaders, posed the question "Is the gospel good news for women?" She linked her own story with that of a female Quechua Indian in Ecuador. Like this forgotten villager, she too had felt invisible and unimportant as her Christian subculture had led her to accept assumptions about male leadership that subordinated her gifts. Yet Hestenes concluded that the gospel not only called Christians to work for change among Quechua villagers, it also called for changing roles for women in ministry.[106] World Vision found the first a much easier sell than the second. Work on behalf of Two-Thirds World women was an issue of biblical justice. Views on women in leadership among its evangelical constituents were much more diverse.

After intense research and debate, the working group adopted a master of divinity thesis, "Women in the Bible and the Implications for Leadership," by Fuller seminarian Katherine M. Hambert, as its text. The paper drew support because it offered a theological reassessment of traditionally conservative understandings while not ignoring troublesome Pauline texts that seemed to restrict women. World Vision sent the paper for review to theologians inside and outside of World Vision, male and female, from widely different theological and cultural traditions. Now insisting that the organization's biblical and theological stance "values the equal worth and dignity of women and men," World Vision advocated a new policy that elevated women both in leadership and as the focus of its development.[107]

The new policy "recognized that the responsibilities of women far outweigh their access to educational, health, material, social, and political resources."[108] In 1992, World Vision launched its Girl Child Initiative to address these inequities. It highlighted its work to donors by running articles focused on women and girls in the developing world.[109] Integration of women into leadership moved more slowly. World Vision set up recruitment and personnel policies that promoted equality and opportunity. Several women ascended to leadership as vice presidents and country directors, but uprooting an evangelical "old boys club" proved difficult.[110]

In the 1990s World Vision sought to expand the reputation it enjoyed among evangelicals to the relief and development community. Alongside its dominance in child sponsorship, it added large-scale government aid and gifts in kind. After Ethiopia, World Vision sought to be a key player on the ground in almost every humanitarian crisis. With the overthrow of Romanian dictator Nicolae Ceausescu in 1989, World Vision staffers flocked to the country and publicized the thousands of children abandoned in orphanages. Beginning in 1991, it delivered relief to war victims in the Balkan civil war. By 1993, it had joined agencies pouring into African hot spots to offer relief to the victims of ethnic fighting in Somalia, Uganda, and Rwanda.

World Vision's Rwanda work illustrated its new comprehensive approach. It provided immediate relief through medical care and food aid while also advocating for greater international responsibility to act. Its graphic images of torched churches, butchered bodies, and mass graves helped compel the public to insist on a response to the genocide.[111] On the ground, it implemented long-term holistic development as well as reconciliation projects between Hutus and Tutsis and centers for child soldiers to rehabilitate and reintegrate them into their communities.[112]

Expansion in size and expertise became the measure of success, but Christian identity remained the organization's defining marker. The majority of donors, particularly in the United States, attested that World Vision's Christian identity alongside the compelling need convinced them to give. Yet internally World Vision debated how its Christian identity affected organizational growth and practice. While some wondered whether it hindered professionalization and development expertise, organizational leaders crafted distinctive approaches to Christian witness and development. It moved further away from the local church and grew more religiously diverse even as leadership remained vigilant to defend the organization against signs of secularization. World Vision continued to change, but what did the change mean? Did it reflect a changing evangelical culture, both abroad and in the United States? Or was the organization now in tension with the evangelical culture that had supported it?

CHAPTER 9

World Vision and the New Internationalists

BY THE 1990S, World Vision claimed to be not only the largest *Christian* humanitarian organization but also the largest privately funded relief and development agency of any kind in the world.[1] Yet growth in the 1980s and 1990s paled in comparison to the expansion in the decade after 2000. In 1995, WVI's budget stood at $300 million. By 2002, it had tripled to over $1 billion, and by 2006, it had doubled again. For fiscal year 2017, WVI reported revenue of over $2.7 billion. It operated in ninety-nine countries and employed 42,000 staff members.[2] If it had once remained on the periphery of the relief and development industry, its size and stature now afforded it a seat at the head table as politicians, mainstream media, and policy experts relied on its global reach and experience on the ground.[3]

World Vision's rise reflected the general growth of fellow Christian relief, development, and mission agencies. Sociologist of religion Robert Wuthnow claimed that American Christians spent $4 billion annually on overseas ministries, a 50 percent increase over the previous decade. Career missionaries and short-term mission trips continued to multiply, evangelical engagement in foreign policy issues intensified, and the size of almost every faith-based relief and development agency ballooned.[4]

As American evangelicals turned to international issues, outsiders took note of their interest. In 2002, *New York Times* editorialist Nicholas Kristof labeled them the "new internationalists."[5] In the wake of Religious Right politics and domestic culture wars, Kristof found evangelicals' international forays refreshing. Many evangelicals also appreciated the attention. While they disputed any claim that evangelicals' interest in global and social issues was new, they agreed that evangelicals were developing a "deepening social conscience."[6]

How then can we account for World Vision's exponential growth? At one level, World Vision expanded as it continued to move beyond its American and evangelical roots. It chose professional development over missions and international governance over American unilateralism. It also embraced a Christian identity that allowed it to partner across ecumenical, interreligious, and even secular divides. At another level, World Vision grew as global issues caught the popular attention of American evangelicals. Over the past decade, World Vision also returned to the American church. It did not offer a new message as much as a hope that evangelicals were entering a new period that put the organization at the forefront of popular Christian social action.

The Rise of Faith-Based Organizations and the Response of the Development Sector

World Vision sought to capitalize on its inclusion within the fraternity of elite international relief and development agencies. If over the previous two decades, it had fought for respect at the World Economic Forum, World Health Organization, and USAID offices, by 2003 it had become the largest distributor of food aid. It trailed only the Red Cross in responding to disasters and complex humanitarian emergencies.[7] Increased capacity meant the ability to apply for multimillion-dollar governmental grants and receive generous gifts in kind, donated commodities that bolstered its bottom line as well as increased its global distribution.[8] Its reputation, record of efficiency, and aggressive marketing attracted the corporate social responsibility (CSR) of major Fortune 500 companies like Coca-Cola as well as upstarts like TOMS shoes.[9] From National Football League T-shirts and U.S. Department of Agriculture grain to Pfizer pharmaceuticals, one group after another off-loaded in-kind gifts that required less overhead than governmental grants or child sponsorship.[10]

Despite the high operating costs, the criticism of child sponsorship from development theorists, and journalistic exposés, individual child sponsors still made up the largest percentage of World Vision's funding.[11] World Vision had spent decades reconsidering child sponsorship, but the steady stream of support was too lucrative to abandon. While other INGOs depended on government grant cycles and the latest development fads, World Vision's devoted base of individual donors afforded it a measure of financial stability.

If in the past, it trailed other INGOs in development expertise, now it sought to be an earlier adopter.[12] Local staff persons had experimented for decades with microlending, small loans to jump-start small businesses, especially to women. World Vision officially implemented microfinance programming in 1993. By 2003, it spun off its own Vision Fund subsidiary to capitalize on the newfound popularity of microfinance among donors.[13] In 2009, it adapted the platform of the popular NGO Kiva to allow individuals to loan money directly to a self-selected project. World Vision understood that its success depended on maintaining both development expertise and marketing prowess.

It also joined other INGOs in making advocacy a larger part of its mission. Its 150 D.C. employees maintained portfolios of issues for which to fund, campaign, and lobby on Capitol Hill, the United Nations, or the G8 summit. While it still felt the need to explain its rationale to some Christian constituencies, it no longer shied away from advocacy. World Vision realized that staff testifying as expert witnesses on global crises and foreign aid bolstered its name recognition and appeal among donors and granting agencies. World Vision came to see advocacy as a tool for marketing, protecting its funding interests, and promoting its expertise.[14]

Throughout this period, faith-based organizations (FBOs) expanded, with evangelical agencies leading the way. In 1946, evangelicals constituted 16 percent of faith-based INGOs. By 2004, they made up 45 percent. Over the same period, the real revenue of evangelical agencies grew from 5 to 41 percent of all FBOs.[15] These evangelical agencies ranged from new small agencies to established industry leaders.[16] Unlike Catholic Relief Charities, which received most of its revenue from federal funding, most evangelical agencies raised the bulk of their funds from private donations. And unlike denominational agencies like Church World Service or the United Methodist Committee on Relief (UMCOR), which served as an arm of denominations with oversight over their budget and programs, independent evangelical agencies had the freedom of entrepreneurs.[17]

In addition, federal regulations became more favorable to faith-based organizations. In 1995, the Canadian International Development Agency (CIDA) endorsed its partnership with Christian NGOs in development.[18] In 1996, the U.S. government passed the Welfare Reform Act that allowed a number of FBOs unable to meet distinctions between religious and secular activities to apply for federal funding. In 2001, Congress consolidated these "charitable choice" provisions with passage of the Faith-Based and

Community Initiatives Act. The same year, President George W. Bush established Centers for Faith-Based and Community Initiatives in five federal departments. A 2004 ruling determined that "USAID can no longer discriminate against organizations which combine development or humanitarian activities with 'inherently religious activities' such as worship, religious instruction, or proselytization."[19]

The new regulations met with mixed reviews, and they did not immediately affect World Vision, which already received millions in federal support and operated by stricter standards. Other more sectarian evangelical agencies like Samaritan's Purse saw the ruling as an opening for expansion. Most international evangelical agencies continued to refuse government aid.[20]

The changes led to robust scholarly debate over the definition of faith-based organizations. Some focused on the religious features of FBOs that distinguished them from secular relief and development.[21] Others emphasized their diversity, locating FBOs along a continuum of "more or less" religious, looking at how religion affected staff hiring, organizational structure, and public identity, or scrutinizing relations to donors and aid recipients.[22] Many either presumed that FBOs remained outsiders to a dominant humanitarian discourse or were forced to accommodate their faith to a shared world culture. In actual practice, FBOs were incredibly diverse. World Vision illustrated the fluid and contested nature of religious identity, for it maintained its religious character even as it evolved. Religion shaped its development practice even as development activities altered the way it presented its religious identity to staff members, donors, and aid recipients.[23]

Scholars and development sector leaders confessed that they had failed to recognize the force of religion. In a content analysis of the three top development journals from 1982 to 1998, sociologist Kurt Ver Beek found not a single article dealing with spirituality and development.[24] Yet, views slowly changed as the sector came to notice and appreciate the size, experience, and expertise of FBOs, as well as the power of public religion. While professional development may have often presumed the hegemony of a "secular world culture," Latin American Pentecostals, the U.S. Christian Right, Hindu nationalists, and Iranian ayatollahs demonstrated that religion was not going away nor was it possible simply to relegate it to the private sphere. Secularism had become the minority view in the world.[25]

In fact, religious advocates often served as the strongest critics of development. Some called for the "end of development," seeing it as "top-down, ethnocentric, and technocratic," reproducing its own form of "secular religion" imposed on local cultures.[26] Andrew Natsios, former WVUS vice president who became head of USAID during the George W. Bush administration, remarked, "While most American and European foreign policy elites may hold a secular worldview, much of the rest of the world lives in one of the great religious traditions."[27] Such criticisms led the field to take a look at itself. Religious values affected both "the actual kind of development that takes place" and the "very meaning of development."[28]

Movements like Jubilee 2000 rallied religious voices to call for debt relief and to criticize intergovernmental agencies like the World Bank. As a result, the World Bank came to recognize the influence of religious voices. An informal staff gathering known as the Friday Morning Group had begun meeting in the late 1980s to discuss the issues, and under new president James Wolfensohn, the World Bank established in 1995 the Development Dialogue for Values and Ethics.[29] In 1998, George Carey, the archbishop of Canterbury, convened the leaders of the world's faiths alongside the World Faiths Development Dialogue (WFDD).[30] Soon the World Bank came to acknowledge that "religion is a central part of the international system. . . . [Even] if it wished to do so, the Bank could not entirely sidestep the faith engagement."[31]

For one thing, the World Bank realized religion was an asset in local communities. Its survey *Voices of the Poor* interviewed sixty thousand poor men and women and found that "churches and mosques, as well as sacred trees, rivers, and mountains were highly valued among the poor."[32] It also noticed that religious leaders were key mediators to empower and motivate developing communities, and FBOs were often able to gain the trust of local leaders and embed themselves at the grass roots far better than World Bank's own secular approach.[33]

Yet, even as it acknowledged religion's power, the World Bank used it instrumentally. It encouraged "good religion" that shared its values. It had no use for "bad religion." Indeed, the World Bank supported religious voices at global conferences that championed its own initiatives, while engaging churches, synagogues, mosques, or temples on the ground. Most often, however, the mainstream development community simply added faith to a largely westernized elite discourse to increase current development capacity. Less often were FBOs viewed as offering new approaches to development or questioning the very meaning of development practice.

Religion and development stimulated a flood of books, lecture series, conferences, and think tanks.[34] Some religious agencies liked the attention; some felt used; and others saw themselves as offering alternatives to the methods of Western development.[35] A few FBOs withdrew when they realized that most people in the secular development community dismissed their normative claims and disdained their evangelistic witness. Yet, however great the cacophony of voices, religion was now on the agenda.

World Vision's Transformational Development

By the 1990s, World Vision realized that its earlier forms of Christian development were insufficient. As it professionalized, the staff came to speak the technical language of development fluently, and it transformed its original scattered community projects into expansive Area Development Programs (ADPs). These ADPs identified pockets of poverty in a geographic area that encompassed multiple communities and populations of 20,000 to 40,000 people. Programmatically, ADPs offered World Vision a model that combined funding from international governmental organizations (IGOs) and the support of individual child sponsors with the stability of long-term planning.[36] It realized that social structures perpetuating poverty often extended beyond a single community and that larger projects would allow it to implement its holistic principles. World Vision pledged to support each ADP for ten to fifteen years until it could turn over complete control to the local communities.[37]

In the 1970s, World Vision entered the relief and development arena by grafting a few development principles onto its missiology; now it attempted to integrate holistic Christian discourse into its primary language of development. But what did that mean for the world's largest Christian humanitarian organization? Now that fellow evangelicals admitted Christian development as a legitimate form of mission, World Vision leaders began to pore over the works of development theorists to articulate the agency's own approach.

After decades of work with the poor, theorists revisited the definition of poverty and the goal of development. Critics questioned a "growth-centered" development that relied on Western assumptions, economic measures, and theories of modernization. Instead, theorists like David Korten and Robert Chambers advocated a "people-centered" approach that concentrated on the needs and capacities of local communities in order to move from welfare to "sustainable development." Beginning in the 1980s, Chambers defined poverty not only as material deficit but as "entangled clusters of disadvantage" and articulated the goal of development not as material wealth but as "responsible well-being."[38] By 1990, Indian economist Amartya Sen introduced measurements to evaluate a people-centered approach. The resulting Human Development Index (HDI) added life expectancy, health, and literacy to the standard economic measure of a nation's gross domestic product (GDP). These new theories and measurements changed the way development agencies designed their programs.[39]

The leaders in World Vision consumed the work of Chambers, Korten, and Sen and hired them as consultants to train staff members and assess World Vision's programs. They adopted Chambers's expansive definition of poverty and introduced participatory evaluation to allow communities to tailor development to their needs.[40] But all of this still left open the question of how to integrate Christian witness. In 1983, World Vision began to publish *Together*, a periodical for its own development practitioners and any others who "ministered to the poor and needy of the world in the name of Jesus Christ." In the first issue, editor John Kenyon claimed that the journal would be unique in combining issues in development, missiology, and Third World dynamics. World Vision believed it was among the few organizations attempting such an endeavor.[41]

At times, World Vision still employed past evangelical dichotomies. Following a *Together* article by David Korten on sustainable development, WVUS president Bob Seiple made sure to highlight that "sustainable development is truly sustainable only when it is rooted in Christian values," which included "naming the Name" and "sharing the Good News in all of its holistic richness."[42] In 1988, World Vision's leading development researcher, Bryant Myers, adopted the language of the Lausanne mission initiatives to highlight World Vision's development among "unreached peoples" in the "10/40 window," the latitude lines that encompassed the majority of people defined by both poverty and lack of access to the gospel.[43]

By the mid-1990s, the rigid divisions between evangelism and social action faded as World Vision and other evangelical relief and development agencies became more self-assured in their ability to work as Christians toward holistic development.[44] World Vision strove to define evangelism as more than assent to a set of Western theological propositions, and it often found fellow global Christians served as its best teachers. Two-Thirds World voices within World Vision were the first to criticize the penchant for modernization and economic growth in Western development programs. They did not need to wait for "people-centered development" to convince them of the need to foreground local experience and address disparities of power and influence. Their contextual theologies had already led them to the same conclusion. World Vision came to realize that development theory was beginning to mirror its own theological positions.

By 1995, transformational development became the new buzzword within evangelical circles. It attended to participatory and sustainable development, local political, environmental, and social problems, as well as culture and religion. World Vision saw transformational development as validation for its own Christian development models, and Bryant Myers's *Walking with the Poor* became the most influential approach.[45] Originally published in 1999 with Orbis Press and expanded in 2011, *Walking with the Poor* became the standard work used by evangelical seminaries and development agencies. Myers couched the entire enterprise in Christian terms, yet he resisted the claim that he was merely spiritualizing secular theory. He sought an expansive definition of poverty that included spiritual deprivation. Arguing that poverty was relational, he claimed that the powerlessness of the poor resulted from sin, broken relationships with God manifested in "relationships that do not work" on personal, social, and structural levels.[46]

Myers charged that Western development agencies ran roughshod over the knowledge and skills of "underdeveloped" peoples by offering unwelcome answers to unasked questions. Modernization also led to the disentanglement of the physical and spiritual worlds that made little sense to many non-Western cultures. Religion and spirituality were not privatized categories. Myers asserted that secular development itself implied a particular culture, set of values, and worldview. In dismissing the myth of a neutral modernity, World Vision could more confidently affirm its particular approach that sought material, social, *and* spiritual change.[47]

World Vision began to create assessments to measure Christian witness, religious change, and spiritual sustainability.[48] By using transformational development indicators, it could measure levels of well-being for children, degrees of transformation in relationships, the impact of Christian witness, and the empowerment of local communities.[49] In its relationships with other INGOs and governments, World Vision now advocated for spirituality in development. It developed guidelines to test the appropriateness of government funding for its Christian mission, and it committed itself to transparency in communicating its religious identity. While it still accepted government funding and the restrictions that such funding sometimes required, it discouraged governments and other agencies from importing a Western worldview that separated the religious and secular. When necessary, it integrated private funds alongside government aid in order to introduce holistic programming.[50]

Putting Christian Witness into Practice

World Vision's evolving development approach drew mostly positive reviews from its humanitarian peers, but it sometimes alienated its own local religious partners. For decades, World Vision had worked on the ground alongside local churches, but as its work expanded, it realized that few local churches had the adequate infrastructure or training to staff Area Development Programs. To involve the entire community, ADPs set up local boards, and church leaders became only one among many stakeholders. Some churches felt betrayed and complained that World Vision had lost touch with local faith communities.[51]

At the same time, World Vision saw itself as a model for practical ecumenism. The organization inherited from its founder an impatience with "academic" ecumenism. It avoided theological dialogue in favor of fostering "grassroots" ecumenism—leveraging its size and resources to incentivize local engagement.[52] Its commitment to working alongside indigenous communities also forced religious encounters that it had often sought to avoid. In the Philippines and Latin America it sought to repair broken relationships with Catholics and attempted to overcome rigid divisions between traditional evangelicals and new prosperity preaching Pentecostals.[53] World Vision grew comfortable partnering with anyone affirming a broad evangelical ethos. Its attempts at practical ecumenism did not always work, but it moved ahead with the idea that Catholics, evangelicals, ecumenical Protestants, Pentecostals, and Orthodox could best undertake solutions to local problems by working together.

World Vision's commitment to practical ecumenism and transformational development also led to a priority of hiring indigenous staff. As it began to grow exponentially in the late 1970s and early 1980s, the need for experienced workers outstripped the number of local evangelicals available.

By necessity, expansion led to a more diverse Christian workforce as staff began to resemble the Christian communities in the countries where they worked. In expanding to Eastern Europe after the Soviet Union's collapse, it hired a number of Orthodox. In Latin America, it hired more Catholics. The percentage of Pentecostal staff grew alongside the movement's growth throughout sub-Saharan Africa.[54] Increasing staff diversity served as another factor leading World Vision to adopt a broader Christian language beyond the particular dialect of an American evangelicalism. Returning to the analogy of a shared center rather than rigid boundaries, World Vision most often interpreted increasing diversity not as the loss of a univocal evangelicalism but rather the broadening of a shared Christian faith.

While World Vision offices agreed that every staff member should be Christian, they debated the degree of permissible ecumenical diversity. Eventually they set the minimum requirement as affirming the uniqueness of Christ and the authority of scripture, personal faith within Christian community, and a commitment to mission.[55] Leadership often reminded staff that attending to Christian identity when hiring was the best inoculation against secularization.[56] Yet they also needed development professionals, and that sometimes created a predicament for the organization: "Some feel that there is a choice to be made between being professional and being Christian. . . . Should we hire good Christians, who are not relief or development professionals, and accept lower quality of ministry? Or, should we hire the best professionals we can find who have some kind of Christian commitment or values similar to ours?"[57]

World Vision realized that in some national offices being Christian had become a box to check rather than a way of life. It was not immune from the challenges of the humanitarian sector where development staff turned over quickly, moving between agencies in accord with grant cycles and project needs.[58] When appointing a Christian Witness Commission to study the issue in the early 1990s, leadership discovered that less than half of World Vision offices referred to the mission statement when screening employees. Only 40 percent asked for a written personal faith statement. Only a third made use of the Statement of Faith. World Vision had originally adopted the NAE's original Statement of Faith, but it realized that some offices avoided it because they found its "old language and fundamentalist feel" no longer applicable. But altering it required a unanimous vote of the council, and World Vision's leaders feared that change would prove divisive. The commission proposed affirming the Nicene Creed or

Lausanne Covenant as an additional option.[59] They were willing to embrace evangelical alternatives, but they worried that the staff's ignorance of its Christian principles would cost the organization its identity.

To address these challenges in the 1990s, World Vision International asked each office to review its practice and establish a department of Christian Witness. Responding to critiques that it relegated religious talk to chapel, devotions, or the occasional retreat, it created programs to train staff how to express their faith in comfortable and culturally appropriate ways. It also promoted spiritual self-care. Recognizing the burnout that often troubled development workers, it cultivated a spirituality that could sustain a "holistic practitioner." It hoped to convince the staff that "being Christian enhances professionalism, rather than detracts from it."[60] Its efforts met with mixed results, but by raising the issue through high level commissions, funding, and required programs, it demonstrated its efforts to maintain a Christian staff.

World Vision, however, also operated in countries where its Christian message was unwelcome. By the 1980s, it had designated more than one-third of the countries where it worked as "restricted contexts," the majority led by socialist governments or dominated by a Muslim majority.[61] In 1995, World Vision affirmed it would register as an official Christian humanitarian organization with every government where it operated and insisted that it be able to describe its work as motivated by the love of Christ. While it agreed to forgo direct evangelism if legally required to do so, it maintained its right for staff members to pray and worship together as well as work directly with any local churches. Even if religious restrictions prevented it from introducing holistic development, its staff members could be open about their Christian faith.[62]

Restricted contexts forced World Vision to weigh its dual commitments to hire Indigenous and Christian staff members. In many countries, there was a limited pool of Christians and even fewer with the necessary skills. In these contexts, it imported experienced Christian expatriates to set up new programs, but it also hired local, non-Christians to operate them. It stipulated that non-Christians would not be able to advance to senior management positions but should be willing to support World Vision's mission and live in accordance with the organization's values. It also made clear that non-Christian staff members would be treated hospitably, invited but not required to attend World Vision's religious gatherings, and given freedom and space to practice their own faith.[63]

The majority of non-Christian staff members came from Muslim majority countries.[64] World Vision's willingness to hire Muslims sometimes tested its support among evangelicals. One philanthropist ruefully remarked that "World Vision is the largest Christian employer of Muslims around the world."[65] Indeed, in the twenty or so Islamic countries where World Vision worked, most of its personnel were Muslim. World Vision had a long history of engagement in the Muslim world.[66] In the early 1960s, Bob Pierce brought relief to Iran and Afghanistan. In 1978, World Vision and the Lausanne movement cosponsored the North American Conference on Muslim Evangelization and published the proceedings, *The Gospel and Islam*, as the text for evangelistic outreach to "unreached" Muslim peoples.[67] In the wake of the Iranian Revolution, World Vision released the video *Islam: Unlocking the Door*, to inform Western evangelicals on Islam's history and growth.[68]

During the 1990s, it continued to evangelize Muslims, but it also recognized the humanitarian needs in many Muslim countries as well. Was work in the Muslim world worth accepting restrictions preventing conversion? Most often World Vision answered affirmatively. The need to be religiously nonsectarian complicated efforts to raise funds through traditional child-sponsorship and mass-market appeals, but in those cases World Vision pursued governmental grants. If it conducted any religious activities, it raised private funds or worked with other independent Christian agencies.[69] World Vision may not have highlighted its hiring of Muslims to its Christian donor constituency, but it did not shy away from acknowledging its work throughout the Muslim world. For example, World Vision maintained a long history of good working relationships in the West African countries of Senegal, Mali, and the Islamic Republic of Mauritania where most local staff members were Muslim. At the same time, World Vision faced tragedy in 2010 when its office in northern Pakistan was bombed and at least six members of its staff were murdered by militants.[70] Almost all of the local staff, including those killed, were Muslim. Through it all, World Vision tried to stay on message, highlighting its efforts to increase the well-being of children. As it expanded to consider more diverse Christian and even non-Christian voices, what emerged was an expansive view of what made it a Christian organization, retaining an evangelical center while accepting diffuse boundaries.

Another challenge WVI faced was defining what it meant by terms such as "transformational development," "holistic ministry," and "Christian witness." In polling the partnership in the early 1990s, World Vision found that 90 percent of senior leaders and the majority of grassroots staff agreed on the necessity of "leading the lost to faith in Christ," yet some worried new language served as a cover for avoiding evangelism.[71] The organization clearly distinguished "evangelism" from "proselytism." As a signatory of the Red Cross Code of Conduct, World Vision explicitly forbade proselytism, defined as "requiring aid recipients first to listen to a religious message as a condition of help or using aid as an inducement for aid recipients to change religions."[72] Beyond that distinction, however, World Vision found no clear consensus. Should every program include an evangelistic component? Should the organization separate evangelistic work into a separate division or turn the task over to local churches?

After three years of official study and debate, World Vision's Christian Witness Commission offered a new policy that replaced the term "evangelism" with "Christian witness." World Vision defined "Christian witness" as "being Christian, living as Christians, doing Christian service, and verbally sharing the good news about Jesus Christ." It hoped to reframe the key question from "Where is the explicit evangelism?" to the broader "What must our ministry look like, and how must we do it so as to create the environment in which the Holy Spirit may encourage people to ask questions to which the gospel is the answer?"[73]

World Vision could not help but continue to debate its Christian identity as it clarified its stance on evangelism. When WVI issued its new strategic action plan in 2005, the first mandate was to reinforce its Christian identity by establishing a new department entitled Christian Commitments.[74] Lingering worries about secularization varied from place to place. African, Latin American, and Asian countries liked the clarity of Christian identification. Europe and Australia were less concerned. WVUS took it upon itself to raise most of the money for Christian Commitments, sometimes with a specific ask to donors to give in order to sustain the organization's religious identity.[75]

The new department of Christian Commitments asked each national office to designate at least one staff person to lead the work locally. Some national offices welcomed the mandate; others buried it in bureaucracy. But with a large budget and buy-in from upper-level management, Christian Commitments proceeded with a threefold mission: the spiritual nurture of staff members, the development of partnerships with local churches, and the integration of Christian witness into every World Vision program.[76] To help form staff members spiritually and educate them about the faith, World Vision commissioned partnership-wide Bible studies and devotionals, spiritual retreats, and weekly chapel services in national offices.

World Vision also sought to rekindle ties with local churches. If it had often dropped local church ties as it evolved from Christian parachurch agency to professional INGO, now it repented of past attempts to see itself as a "substitute, competitor, or replacement for the Church."[77] If it now saw itself as a global expression of the universal church, it wondered if it occupied a unique position to pull diverse churches together.[78]

Integrating Christian witness into its programs proved the most difficult task. The Christian Commitments staff members worked with each World Vision ministry to implement an appropriate Christian witness, one that was sensitive to cultural differences. From drafting vision statements to evaluating outcomes, World Vision tried to measure Christian witness in programs ranging from emergency relief and microfinance to community development and the well-being of sponsored children.[79]

Implementing a core Christian identity across World Vision has remained a continual challenge. The Christian Witness Commission introduced standards that required each office to affirm its Christian identity in fund-raising, grant writing, and program delivery. It also set guidelines for working as a faith-based agency with secular or hostile governments.[80] Yet, it also recognized that its internal religious diversity now required attention to interfaith relations, as staff with strong religious identities could become hostile to interfaith and interreligious partnerships without religious literacy training and theological reflection. In 2006, World Vision hired its first world religions specialist, Chawkat Moucarry. As a Syrian evangelical with a PhD in Islamic studies from the Sorbonne University, Moucarry traveled from one office to another in the World Vision partnership to promote religious reconciliation as well as greater interreligious understanding.[81]

WVUS Operations and Its American Evangelical Base

In the late 1970s, World Vision's U.S. office ceded control to the new international structure. Since then, WVUS largely kept pace with WVI's growth, maintaining market dominance among child-sponsorship agencies even as it became a leading relief and development organization respected for its professional expertise, receipt of government funding, and procurement of

GIK donations. While organizationally separate, WVI and WVUS maintained close ties and even shared office space in Southern California. Despite repeated calls for WVI to relocate abroad to overcome its image as an American agency, it was the U.S. office that moved first. In 1995, while WVI offices remained in Monrovia with a relatively small staff, WVUS pulled up stakes from the San Gabriel Valley to relocate just outside of Seattle to Federal Way, Washington. Citing high taxes, cost of living, and government regulation, WVUS president Seiple explained that relocation would save five million dollars annually to invest in humanitarian programs. Beyond financial incentives, the move also symbolized a mutual willingness for the two offices to move in slightly different directions.[82] It made sense for WVUS to maintain strong ties to a vibrant and prosperous American evangelical subculture. At the same time, WVI needed to focus its attention on a diverse set of constituents abroad.[83]

Both in the United States and abroad, World Vision led the way among evangelical parachurch agencies in adopting corporate techniques of management and marketing. As it moved into relief and development, it often went outside the organization to find expertise, hiring away other agencies' professionals or USAID staffers. By the 1990s, it no longer hoped it could find talent. Now other humanitarian and government agencies had begun to poach its own staff. President George W. Bush selected former World Vision vice president Andrew Natsios as his USAID administrator, replacing Clinton appointee J. Brady Anderson, who subsequently became vice chairman of the World Vision U.S. board.[84]

American evangelicals generally were moving up in the world, gaining positions of power in politics, business, arts, and entertainment. While World Vision's donors represented a cross section of a broad-based American evangelicalism, its staff members represented a more cosmopolitan form of evangelical piety.[85] In selecting Rich Stearns as its president in 1998, WVUS illustrated a transition within evangelical leadership. While its previous president Bob Seiple was a layman with experience in higher education, he did come with credentials as an evangelical insider. Stearns took a different path. Converting to evangelical Christianity while a graduate student at the University of Pennsylvania's Wharton School of Business, he had served as a youth leader at Boston's historic evangelical Park Street Church, but his first language was corporate America. World Vision wanted a leader with business acumen able to oversee a complex organization and expand its reach. While his salary made him one of the highest paid executives of any Christian agency, it was an 80 percent pay cut from his position as CEO of the luxury china maker Lenox. Stearns, however, saw the move as a calling.[86]

World Vision prefigured a trend of fellow Christian nonprofits reaching out to business executives. World Relief and Habitat for Humanity also turned to the corporate world for their new CEOs.[87] One of Stearns's first hires as vice president of donor engagement, Atul Tandon, came with twenty years of experience as a banker for Citigroup. Now he heads the fellow Christian agency Opportunity International.[88] With Stearns's retirement at the end of 2018, Edgar Sandoval Sr. has moved up from his role as WVUS chief operating officer to become the next president of the U.S.-based office. He follows in Stearns's footsteps with decades of for-profit and nonprofit experience.

World Vision knew that its success relied on more than compelling stories. As a multimillion-dollar operation, it had to streamline expenses, reduce overhead, and boost performance. By the early 2000s, World Vision had returned to double-digit revenue growth, increasing its name awareness and donor satisfaction while keeping marketing expenses flat. Stearns's arrival signaled a culture shift. He measured employees' performance in quarterly reviews and bottom-line results. Dozens of staff members unable to meet the new expectations had to go elsewhere.[89]

At the same time, located in the backyard of Microsoft and Boeing, World Vision's new Federal Way offices appealed to computer programmers and graphic designers looking to move "from success to significance."[90] A testimonial on a World Vision web page exemplified the trend: "For 5 years, I rose through the ranks at Microsoft. But I wondered where I was 'storing up my treasure.' Instead of being ambitious for one of the world's largest corporations, now I'm ambitious for the poor and children. Working here is the best-kept secret for ex-corporate types."[91] Although most still identified as evangelicals, they came less frequently with degrees from Christian colleges like Azusa Pacific or Wheaton. They came with Harvard MBAs and years of experience with consulting firms or advertising agencies.[92]

Even if staff bios were changing, WVUS maintained its focus on its evangelical target audience for reasons of religious affinity and fund-raising prowess. In the 1970s, World Vision's move to television issued in record budget growth and exposure to new audiences. By the 1990s, World Vision continued to pour money into television without measuring its return on investment. With advertising costs rising, it sought bargains, buying time in bulk or late at night. The new leaders of the late 1990s forced a reassessment of marketing expenses. It simply cost more to acquire a donor through television than through other media, and television donors were often less reliable. The organization abandoned high-priced television specials and redoubled its direct mailing, returned to advertising on Christian radio and in magazines like *Christianity Today*, and made use of its ties to contemporary Christian music artists. It also created a prominent presence on the web, adapted to social media, and established links with corporations.[93]

American evangelicals remained WVUS's most loyal constituency. From 1999 to 2006, the number of donors identifying themselves as evangelicals actually increased by 50 percent.[94] Evangelicals were far more likely to recognize World Vision's name and to have a favorable impression of it.[95] It had penetrated the evangelical market more than the general public, and it honed its marketing strategies to reach them more effectively. With an expanding evangelical subculture, World Vision could narrow its focus and still maintain double-digit annual growth.[96]

WVUS also saw a focus on the church as a moral and theological obligation. While evangelicals' separation of evangelism and social action had sometimes led World Vision away from its base, evangelicals were now changing, local churches were open to broader views of development, and Stearns thought that a close tie to the church was the best way to maintain the organization's Christian commitment. No longer would it use the church only as a source to raise funds when convenient; Stearns mandated that his organization return to its original objective of educating and inviting the church to help it do God's work in the world.[97]

A New Evangelical Internationalism?

Most evangelicals, like most Americans, still paid more attention to domestic issues than to international affairs.[98] Grassroots organizations like the Christian Coalition rallied evangelicals around local political issues while national evangelicals rejoiced that the 2000 presidential election of George W. Bush put "one of their own" in the White House. While only 30 percent of evangelicals identified themselves with the Religious Right, George W.

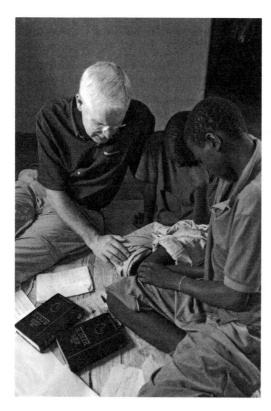

Figure 15. Rich Stearns prays with kids participating in World Vision's programs. © World Vision, Inc. 2011. All rights reserved. Reprinted by permission.

Bush's campaign promises of a "compassionate conservatism" that highlighted the necessity of FBOs to meet domestic social needs resonated with Christian voters.[99]

Nonetheless, American evangelicals were wrapped up in global realities even if they failed to recognize it. They had always sponsored world missions and fervently championed anticommunist foreign policy. Now twenty-four-hour cable news, internet, and social media continued to bring stories of natural disasters, war, and suffering into their living rooms every day. The global awareness of U.S. church members had reached an all-time high.[100] Americans also traveled more and realized their interdependence in the global economy. Transcontinental business flights to Asia, Skype calls to friends overseas, and immigration made globalization a daily reality. In 2009, sociologist Robert Wuthnow reported that 62 percent of active U.S. church members have traveled or lived in another country.[101]

The global missions enterprise has continued to grow while its institutions continued to evolve. According to Wuthnow's research, 74 percent of American congregations had supported a missionary working in another country in the previous year. Even as the mission agency of the largest Protestant denomination (Southern Baptist Convention's International Mission Board) faced dramatic budget shortfalls and layoffs in recent years, the number of overall full-time missionaries has steadily increased, as the majority of new missionaries affiliated with independent agencies.[102]

The greatest growth in missions arguably has come through short-term mission (STM) experiences. Lasting anywhere from a few days to a few weeks, short-term missions have taken an estimated 1.6 million Americans annually into another culture. Wuthnow estimated that 2 percent of all active churchgoers embarked on an STM trip in any given year and 25 percent will probably go at some point during their lifetime.[103] While some critics insist that STMs do more harm than good, others argue that increased international exposure unsettled "a confident American exceptionalism" and troubled "simplistic patriotism."[104] Still others seek a middle ground with Western churches adopting sister churches overseas through long-term commitments and reciprocal exchanges to promote mutuality and a sense of shared mission.[105]

While some American Christians have pointed to evangelical expansion in the global South as a foil for religious decline at home, others welcomed global Christian growth and declared an affinity with born-again believers abroad.[106] As American studies scholar Melani McAlister argues, many Americans evangelicals embraced an "enchanted internationalism" that bolstered global solidarity but reintroduced an "imperialist-style imaginary" that exoticized the other it claimed to embrace.[107] After brief international experiences, Western evangelicals often claimed to "really know" their fellow global Christians, as shared beliefs often trumped real differences.[108] Global awareness, in short, has been a source of both discouragement and enthusiasm—both real and imaginary—but in almost every case, American Christians' increasing internationalism created an audience more susceptible to World Vision's message.

A new generation of evangelicals looked at global issues without rehashing old debates over evangelism and social action. Ron Sider, a longtime evangelical social activist, described the trend as a genuine shift: "The bitter battle between conservative Christians who emphasize evangelism and liberal Christians who stress social action that weakened the church for much of this century has largely ended. Increasingly, most agree that Christians should combine the Good News with good works and imitate Jesus' special concern for the poor."[109] Evangelicals own internal debates over global engagement for most of the last fifty years now seemed to have been resolved enough that former World Vision vice president Bryant Myers could label the dichotomies typified at Lausanne as a "historical footnote."[110] Even Bill Bright's Campus Crusade and televangelist Pat Robertson created relief and development projects.[111]

By the late 1990s, it appeared that increasing international concern might be one of the few issues on which American Christians agreed. The chief lobbyist of the National Association of Evangelicals, Richard Cizik, noted that "the American electorate was split right down the middle on . . . cultural wars [about abortion and school prayer], and nobody was going to win them." But the new international efforts are "going gangbusters."[112]

One such international issue was religious freedom. Popular evangelical agencies like the Voice of the Martyrs had documented the persecution of Christians since the 1960s, but in the 1990s evangelicals refocused attention on the persecuted church.[113] A religious civil war in Sudan, the "underground" house church movement in China, and the prohibitions against Christian worship in Saudi Arabia rallied evangelicals to action.[114] Evangelicals from across the theological spectrum came together to champion religious freedom, even partnering with old enemies like the American Civil Liberties Union (ACLU) and World Council of Churches. Conservative Republicans and liberal Democrats came together to push legislation through Congress.[115] In signing the 1998 International Religious Freedom Act into law, President Bill Clinton established an independent Commission on International Religious Freedom and named outgoing WVUS president Bob Seiple as its first ambassador at large. Seiple's task was to hold countries accountable for their religious rights records.[116] To protect the persecuted church, evangelicals were willing to work through government channels, cross traditional boundaries, and even adopt human rights language.[117]

Evangelicals also attacked child exploitation and global sex trafficking. In 1997, Gary Haugen founded the International Justice Mission (IJM). A former civil rights attorney at the U.S. Department of Justice, Haugen led the UN investigation into the Rwandan genocide. This experience led him to start IJM as "an evangelical social gospel."[118] IJM's core mission was to "stand against violent oppression in response to the Bible's call to justice

(Isaiah 1:17): Seek justice, rescue the oppressed, defend the orphan, and plead for the widow."[119] Haugen spearheaded evangelical lobbying efforts that led to the Victims of Trafficking and Violence Protection Act in 2000.

IJM's accolades extended beyond the evangelical world. Oprah Winfrey promoted Haugen's efforts on her show, and journalist Nicholas Kristof accompanied IJM investigators on raids and recounted them in his *New York Times* editorials.[120] Yet, IJM was most popular among young evangelicals. It has over eighty-five campus chapters, and its internship program overflowed with qualified candidates. Haugen's hope was to entice competent Christian lawyers to work in government and international relations in order to change the world. For Haugen, IJM's mission was to "motivate the evangelical community . . . to care about what's going on in the world beyond [U.S.] borders and to pay attention to the sin of injustice." He knew that "twenty-five years ago, IJM couldn't have made this kind of progress. Previous generations [of evangelicals] thought the social gospel was a distraction to spiritual concerns."[121] Now he claimed that evangelicals "under thirty" understood that "you can still be orthodox . . . and take action."[122]

Alongside religious freedom and sex trafficking, evangelicals came to champion the fight against extreme poverty. In conjunction with the United Nations' Millennium Development Goals (MDGs) that initially pledged to halve global poverty by 2015, new agencies like Micah Challenge emerged to enlist Christian support.[123] A generation ago, most evangelicals saw the United Nations as a liberal or even atheistic enemy. Now a number of evangelical NGOs and denominations integrated the MDGs into their mission goals. In the wake of September 11, 2001, World Vision joined with other humanitarian organizations to form the "Better Safer World Campaign," recognizing that poverty was a factor in rising global instability. In 2004, with celebrities like U2 front man Bono and the funds of the Bill and Melinda Gates Foundation, the agencies reorganized to launch the ONE Campaign to end extreme poverty and fight the global AIDS epidemic. While the campaign's goal was to persuade the U.S. government to allocate 1 percent of its budget to the world's poorest countries, its biggest success was making global poverty an issue for a new generation. Young evangelicals bought "Make Poverty History" wristbands and attended benefit concerts in droves. Few stopped to think about distinctions between structural injustice and individual salvation or whether poverty was a religious or secular issue.

World Vision, AIDS, and the Local Church

In an atmosphere vastly different from the context of its founder Bob Pierce, World Vision sought to capitalize on a renewed interest in global humanitarianism. It introduced its own popular campaigns to fight global poverty, sex trafficking, the selling of "blood diamonds," and exploiting child soldiers. At the same time, it felt some obligation to push American evangelicals beyond their comfort zone. Its AIDS initiative served as a case in point. In the 1990s, the disease was not well understood. Most evangelicals associated it with homosexuality and sexual promiscuity. A World Vision executive characterized the general sentiment: "you play—you pay."[124] After 1990, World Vision's field offices took up the AIDS crisis, providing relief to orphans and their caregivers in Uganda, care for Romanian children infected through unsterilized needles, and help for young women and girls trying to escape prostitution in Thailand.[125] World Vision rarely publicized these programs. Funds often came from intergovernmental sources like the World Bank. After that funding ran out, World Vision struggled to market AIDS care to its donors. Its staff was ill prepared for the epidemic. How would they respect local religious beliefs while debunking misinformation and myths?[126] African development staff members called for help, and a few months after his arrival at WVUS, new president Rich Stearns took a trip to Uganda to see the AIDS crisis firsthand. He returned determined to put AIDS at the forefront of World Vision's agenda.[127]

World Vision arrived later than most other humanitarian agencies to the AIDS crisis, and it worried that the issue had little traction among its evangelical constituency. Stearns remembered the advice of his marketing team: "We're a G-rated ministry getting involved in an R-rated issue. . . . People equate us [with] helping children and families in need. They said if we start talking about AIDS, prostitutes, drug users, long-haul truckers, and sexuality, it would hurt our image."[128] Their marketing hunches proved correct. A 2001 World Vision–sponsored Barna poll found that "evangelical Christians were significantly less likely than non-Christians to give money for AIDS education and prevention programs worldwide." Only 3 percent of evangelical Christians would consider supporting World Vision's AIDS efforts.[129]

Stearns pressed ahead. World Vision established the Hope Initiative in 2000 as its global response to the HIV/AIDS crisis. Marketing costs would be higher and returns on investment much lower, but World Vision decided that education would be as important as the fund-raising. It enlisted celebrities like Bono to turn contemporary Christian artists onto the HIV/AIDS issue.[130] In 2003, WVUS also launched its first Hope Tour to educate American Christians and their churches about AIDS. Taking its message to major cities across the country, it parked its 2,500-square-foot interactive World Vision Experience in church gyms, civic centers, and even New York's Grand Central Station. As people made their way through the exhibit, they followed the story of a child affected by AIDS. At the conclusion, participants had the opportunity to sponsor a Hope Child, a designation given to children awaiting sponsorship in communities devastated by AIDS.[131] In a single year, World Vision saw the percentage of evangelicals willing to support HIV/AIDS work jump from 3 to 14 percent.[132]

While World Vision lobbied governments, bilateral organizations, corporate donors, and celebrities to support its AIDS work, Stearns saw the Hope Initiative as the first big opportunity for World Vision to reconnect with the local church. He started, however, by chastising the church for its indifference: "Where has the church been? If we honestly ask who are the ones who have taken the lead in fighting against AIDS and showing compassion to its victims, we find a surprising list . . . the homosexual community, Hollywood, rock stars, political liberals, the U.S. government, the United Nations, secular humanitarian organizations, the Bill and Melinda Gates Foundation."[133] Speaking in an evangelical vernacular with a revivalist flare, World Vision depicted the AIDS crisis as a pandemic Christians must address. Richard Cizik soon began to label World Vision the "E. F. Hutton" of AIDS work. "When World Vision speaks, people listen."[134] World Vision encouraged evangelical progressives like Tony Campolo, as well as megachurch pastors like Bill Hybels formerly of Willow Creek Community Church and Rick Warren of Saddleback, to speak out. It encouraged evangelicals to lobby for George W. Bush's President's Emergency Plan for AIDS Relief (PEPFAR)—a program that proposed a commitment of fifteen billion dollars to fight the global HIV/AIDS pandemic.[135] A decade earlier, Stearns saw evangelicals as not only apathetic about AIDS relief but "downright hostile toward it." As the tide began to turn, World Vision took part of the credit. Within the organization, the AIDS response became a badge of pride. It had taken a prophetic stance, regained the trust of the churches, and led evangelicals into the midst of a global crisis. That was precisely where it wanted to lead them.[136]

One new convert was Saddleback pastor Rick Warren, founder of one of the country's largest megachurches as well as author of the *Purpose Driven Life,* one of the best-selling nonfiction books in American history. Warren promoted church growth principles and personal discipleship but seemed an unlikely champion for humanitarianism. His wife, Kay Warren, was the evangelist who turned him around. On a conference call with World Vision spokesman Steve Haas, she found herself overwhelmed by the statistics and stories of AIDS orphans. World Vision enlisted her to educate fellow evangelicals.[137] Rick Warren soon confessed, "I have been so busy building my church that I have not cared about the poor." After visiting Africa, he felt God calling him to "the cause of ending global poverty."[138] By 2005, Warren established his PEACE Plan to "Plant churches, Equip servant leaders, Assist the poor, Care for the sick, and Educate the next generation."[139] With an invitation from Rwandan president Paul Kagame, Warren set about to make Rwanda the first "purpose-driven nation."[140] Most development experts questioned Warren's methods if not his motives. Boston College political scientist Alan Wolfe criticized Warren's "considerable naïveté," but at the same time, he claimed historians would likely "pinpoint Mr. Warren's trip to Rwanda as the moment when conservative evangelical Protestantism made questions of social justice central to its concerns."[141]

Bill Hybels, founding pastor of the Willow Creek Community Church, also began to refine his church's mission program. Renamed as "Compassion and Justice Ministries," it combined short-term missions, education, and advocacy with the work of global partners "to fight local and global poverty and injustice." Like Saddleback, Willow Creek's influence extended far beyond its membership. While Hybels resigned in 2018 and the church has been mired in controversy over its handling of multiple accusations against Hybels of sexual harassment and misconduct, the church had claimed over 20,000 members and the Willow Creek Association, a national network of congregations, counted over 11,000 local affiliates. Hybels introduced them all to World Vision. Hybels and his wife, Lynne, have both served as WVUS board members, and in 2009 WVUS president Stearns headlined Hybels's annual Leadership Summit, attended by more than 100,000 church leaders. The same year, Willow Creek teamed up with World Vision to award $100,000 to an outstanding local church program involved in fighting HIV/AIDS.[142] Until Hybels stepped down from the church, the association, and the Global Leadership Summit in spring 2018, he and Lynne remained among World Vision's greatest champions in bringing justice issues to the American evangelical church.[143]

During the early 2000s, the timing was right for World Vision to renew relationships with local churches. Warren and Hybels illustrated local churches' growing interest in justice issues like clean water or health care. At the same time, many megachurches or nondenominational churches did not have reliable partners for accomplishing such work and denomination-ally affiliated churches were becoming less inclined to funnel their mission resources to institutions' hierarchies that gave them little control over where their funds were spent. Churches needed experienced partners; they also wanted to maintain a personal connection to their work. World Vision took this as an opportunity. It had the infrastructure, experience, and con-nections on the ground in one hundred countries. As the world's largest child-sponsorship agency, it excelled at helping people understand vast suf-fering through the story of a single child. World Vision could serve as the link for local churches to mission opportunities overseas.

World Vision employed regional representatives to connect with pastors and invite them to VIP events. It hired a handful of respected evangelicals to speak at mission conferences, pastors' gatherings, and student events.[144] It set up exhibits at mission fairs, denominational meetings, and local churches. Communication staff distributed resources enabling churches to promote World Vision's work in sermon series, prayer guides, and mission experiences. It often took pastors on Vision Trips overseas to see its pro-grams in action, and the returning pastors shared their experiences with congregations. Instead of recruiting a handful of child sponsors, World Vision launched campaigns for congregations to adopt an entire village by sponsoring five hundred or one thousand children.[145] While World Vision used the funds to facilitate large-scale development, the church had a con-nection with a community where it could send mission teams, collect school supplies, or lead Bible school classes. World Vision prospered through its church connections; local churches expanded their vision with the help of World Vision.

World Vision also adapted to transitions in evangelical youth culture. It recognized that television spots and direct mail had little effect on what it labeled the "high touch generation."[146] Turning to "creative activism," World Vision realized that new donors wanted not merely to give money but to *do* something. In 2004, World Vision established Acting on AIDS as a student ministry on college campuses. It also expanded the agenda to include issues of sex trafficking, malaria, and global poverty. Through partnerships with the Council of Christian Colleges and Universities (CCCU), InterVarsity Fellowship, and Urbana mission conferences, it soon had twenty thousand students active on four hundred campuses.[147] With interactive websites and Facebook pages, World Vision provided resources for learning about clean water and microfinance, as well as space for uploading personal stories. Tweets went out encouraging members to call their elected representatives about pertinent legislation. Investment in "creative activism" was costly, and it did not always provide the same returns on investment as other income streams. Yet, World Vision believed it had a mandate to educate and motivate the next generation on faith and justice.

Building a New Evangelical Center

Committed to appealing across a broad cross section of American Christianity, World Vision refused to be monopolized by an evangelical right or left.[148] Dean Owen, director of executive communications at the U.S. office, described World Vision's approach: "On one side, you have Jim Wallis of Sojourners. Over here, you've got Franklin Graham of Samaritan's Purse. In between those two extremes . . . we attempt to present World Vision as a moderate voice."[149] Few evangelical agencies have been able to enlist support across the theological spectrum better than World Vision. Besides plugs by Bono and former secretary of state Madeleine Albright, the lists of endorsements for Rich Stearns's first book, *The Hole in Our Gospel*, included a who's who of evangelicals (Jim Wallis, Ron Sider, Tony Campolo, T. D. Jakes, John Ortberg, Max Lucado, Bill Hybels, Chuck Colson, Kay Warren, Eugene Peterson, just to name a few). Few other evangelicals could appear on the conservative Focus on the Family radio broadcast one month and at a Sojourners rally the next.[150]

In its official communications, World Vision used "Christian" over "evangelical" as its chief descriptor. Not only did the broader term allow it to cast a wider net, but it also allowed World Vision to avoid being lumped into stereotypes of "evangelical" that pollsters and reporters used as shorthand for white, conservative, and Republican.[151] To insiders, World Vision spoke in an evangelical vernacular through all outlets of American evangelical culture. That was sufficient. It had little interest or incentive to define itself too narrowly or take sides in polarizing culture war issues. Instead, it quoted scripture, painted pictures of need, and shared stories of changed lives that touched Christian consciences across the board.

President Richard Stearns modeled this approach in his book *The Hole in Our Gospel*, published in 2009 with the evangelical press Thomas Nelson. The book served as Stearns's public coming out party. After eleven years as an internal CEO focused on day-to-day operations, Stearns became an evangelical celebrity with the book's success. He claimed that "being a Christian requires much more than just having a personal and transforming relationship with God. It also entails a public and transforming relationship with the world."[152]

Stearns's book struck a chord. It was part biography, as Stearns narrated his first conversion to Christianity and his second conversion to the "whole gospel," which combined "proclamation of the good news" with a "compassion for the sick and sorrowful" and a "commitment to justice."[153] It was also part Bible study, compiling and interpreting texts to build a biblical case for a holistic gospel. By the end, he chastised the American church for being "AWOL for the greatest humanitarian crisis of all time."[154] He offered a brief history of evangelical social engagement and challenged the church to do more. The Evangelical Christian Publishers Association named it the 2010 "Christian Book of the Year." Bill Hybels bought ten thousand copies to distribute to his congregation. World Vision followed up on the book's success with its own media blitz of study guides, videos, and press releases. The book elevated the standing of the organization throughout evangelical popular culture.

The acclaim did not inoculate WVUS from criticism. More liberal voices, many coming from within World Vision's own international partnership, lamented what they viewed as a retreat. Stearns spoke the evangelical language, but they claimed he was simplistic and naive. He slid into biblical proof texting and emotional stories rather than educating his readers with sophisticated theology and development theory.[155]

From the other side, some conservatives still accused World Vision of giving up evangelism and chasing after liberal social issues. In 2006, James Dobson and thirty other evangelical leaders lobbied Congress against a proposed increase in U.S. contributions to the Global Fund, an international effort to fight AIDS, tuberculosis, and malaria. Dobson complained that the Global Fund promoted condom distribution as well as "legalized prostitution and all kinds of wickedness around the world."[156] These same evangelicals targeted World Vision as a coconspirator with the Global Fund. If it would not take a stand with evangelicals in the culture wars, how could it claim their support? Stearns answered their attacks carefully in *Christianity Today*: "As Christians we have to have a list of priorities. Sometimes I think we get our priorities turned upside down. . . . I think abortion is on that list. But how can you care about abortion and not care about the 26,000 children that die every day of preventable causes? It dwarfs the abortion problem in America. Five times as many children die around the world of preventable causes than die in abortions."[157] World Vision advocated sexual abstinence for the unmarried in its programs and claimed that it supported condom distribution only as a last resort, but it acknowledged that the complexity of the AIDS epidemic did not allow for simple slogans. "When you're talking to a sex worker in a brothel who has to feed her child and maybe her elderly mother and father through her work," Stearns said, "it's not realistic to say she's going to be abstinent."[158] Bruce Wilkinson, serving at that time as World Vision vice president for southern Africa, said it more bluntly: "Christians keep majoring on the minor. The issue really needs to be: what can the church do to provide love, care, and support."[159]

At the same time, World Vision would not allow its reengagement with the church to undercut its insistence on professionalization. Local churches had the ability to start their own programs overseas and send their own short-term missionaries, but World Vision remained the expert. Stearns acknowledged that there was a tendency to say, "This ain't rocket science. People are hungry: feed them." But he admonished newcomers like Rick Warren and his PEACE Plan: "The deeper you get into relief and development, you realize *it is rocket science*, because you are dealing with all kinds of social, cultural, political, and religious landmines."[160] He admitted World Vision's own mistakes, and he urged zealous evangelicals not to repeat them.

World Vision's response to the publicity that accompanied the distribution of a video called *Kony 2012* illustrated its efforts reeducating American evangelicals. Three young filmmakers, Jason Russell, Bobby Bailey, and Laren Poole, founded an organization named Invisible Children in order to expose the forced conscription of child soldiers by the Lord's Resistance Army (LRA) in Uganda in 2003. In March 2012, Invisible Children released *Kony 2012* with the intent of "making LRA warlord Joseph Kony famous" and generating public pressure on the U.S. government to capture him and hold him accountable for war crimes. The film reached over 40 million views in three days and quickly attracted over 100 million viewers.[161] It also drew critics. Development professionals, foreign policy experts, and African studies scholars criticized the video for manipulating facts, advocating violence, and oversimplifying issues. They also questioned the organization's finances and methods.[162]

World Vision stepped into the debate. Realizing that many of Invisible Children's advocates were the same younger evangelicals it courted for its own work, World Vision praised Invisible Children's good intentions: "People are still talking about Joseph Kony. We'll say it again: That's a good thing."[163] Staff members talked of "seizing the Kony moment," as it saw a spike in its own website traffic and donations. Yet it spoke to the issue as an organization with professional expertise and knowledge. It reminded audiences of complexities that the video ignored. It highlighted its own twenty years in the country rehabilitating child soldiers as well as preventing the current "main killer" in Uganda, malaria. It asked supporters to lobby Congress not for military action but for increased foreign aid. It spoke as an organization that knew the African cultural terrain from decades of painstaking work on the ground.[164]

Still, some advocates of civil liberties accused World Vision of a retrenchment into a separatist Christianity. Criticisms gained steam around the question of religious hiring rights. World Vision claimed a right to hire employees who shared their faith while still receiving federal grants.[165] With its Christian identity already an issue within World Vision's international partnership, WVUS president Stearns argued that "faith-based organizations would not be faith-based if they could not hire employees who share their values and embrace their missions."[166] In Canada, Australia, and many European countries, religious discrimination was illegal. Without the ability to hire only coreligionists, various World Vision offices framed the question of Christian identity in different terms. WVUS, however, continued to require all employees to sign a statement of faith.[167] In 2006, it fired three employees for doubting the divinity of Christ and the doctrine of the Trinity. When the employees sued for wrongful dismissal, World Vision agreed to serve as the test case for other faith-based agencies and fight the suit all the way to the Supreme Court. It organized workshops to advise other Christian NGOs of their rights and argued its point in the court of public opinion.[168]

The 1964 Civil Rights Act allowed for any "religious association, corporation, educational institution or society" to consider religious preference in hiring staff members. The growth of FBOs and the federal funding of faith-based initiatives rekindled the religious discrimination debates. During the 2008 presidential campaign, Senator Barack Obama pledged to end religious discrimination, but once in office, he backpedaled from his pledge. In 2010, the Ninth Circuit of the U.S. Court of Appeals ruled that World Vision qualified as a religious rather than nonsectarian humanitarian organization and therefore had the right to dismiss employees on religious grounds. In October 2011, the Supreme Court declined to hear the case. World Vision announced that if forced to choose between its employment policy and hundreds of millions of dollars in federal funding, it would forgo government funding. World Vision's chief legal adviser, Steve McFarland, claimed that anything less "would start down a slippery slope that would soon dilute and divert World Vision's mission, character, and witness."[169] In court, World Vision won the day. In popular opinion, the results were mixed. Its defense of religious hiring pleased conservatives; it disappointed others who had come to see World Vision as the face of a new kind of religious humanitarianism.

World Vision prided itself in working across traditional boundaries while keeping a foot in multiple worlds. Even as it adopted development methodologies, leading INGOs often looked askance at the agency's faith-based humanitarianism. While they once viewed religion as out of bounds within the practice of relief and development, now religion returned to a place of prominence on the agenda of global civil society. World Vision played a similar role within evangelicalism. If some evangelicals viewed World Vision's work as out of step with traditional theological and missionary outlooks, World Vision saw itself as out ahead of the pack. Its interactions with both relief and development peers as well as its Christian constituencies demonstrated that there was not a single approach to faith-based humanitarianism or a single evangelicalism. While sometimes WVUS took part in building an expanded evangelical center that made room for its faith-based approach, appealed to a broad Christian constituency, and attempted to avoid the more polarizing camps across the religious spectrum, perhaps a united front was too much to ask. Instead of an expanding center, perhaps it functioned within multiple evangelicalisms simultaneously. With its global and child-centered focus, World Vision could operate across boundaries in ways that other domestic agencies could not.

Epilogue

A SINGLE SNAPSHOT CANNOT capture the past or present World Vision. As an international organization made up of almost one hundred countries, each with wide latitude to pursue individual agendas, the organization is simply too big and diverse to tell a single story. The activity and religious identity of each national office differs depending on its historical and current context. I have tried to note the internal diversity within WVI, while focusing on the WVUS office as one case study within the partnership. To paint a full picture of the organization, scholars would need to produce a number of ethnographically informed case studies to demonstrate the organization's diversity and allow for comparative analysis, and each of these studies would convey a small piece of the truth about World Vision. Even its own staff members continue to debate the character of the organization. Yet, I contend that it remains one of the most remarkable Christian institutions of the past century, and its history demonstrates the global turn in American religious history. As World Vision encountered the wider world and brought images and interpretations back to its original Western audiences, it experienced the transformation of its own American, evangelical, and missionary identities. At the same time, it led American Christians to reinterpret their own identities in light of their global encounters—real or imagined.

Through World Vision's rapid response to the 2005 Indian Ocean tsunami and the 2010 Haiti earthquake, WVUS president Rich Stearns observed that being one of the first and largest NGOs on the ground introduced the organization to "millions of Americans who might not have known the depth and breadth of our work."[1] In 2009, President Barack Obama asked Stearns to join the inaugural class of the President's Advisory Council on Faith-Based and Neighborhood Partnerships. World Vision has continued to bolster its popular and professional reputation as it expanded over the past decade.

Throughout its history, World Vision also embodied an evangelical entrepreneurism that often kept it one step ahead of fellow religious and secular humanitarian organizations in reaching popular audiences. Bob Pierce embodied the approach through filming firsthand footage produced into Christian social-action films, launching child sponsorship, and bringing the Korean Orphan Choir on global tours. Stan Mooneyham followed with a turn toward television specials and real-time drama in rescuing Vietnamese refugees at sea. Over the next decade, the attention World Vision received from disasters such as the Ethiopian famine of the 1980s transformed the organization's scale and scope.

In its marketing and fund-raising, World Vision never shied away from experimenting with new approaches. That too has continued over the past decade. While donations were down and budgets tightened during the Great Recession (2008–12), they have now recovered. As television and direct mail largely grew stale for continued fund-raising growth, World Vision shifted to social media, crowd-funding, and action-oriented philanthropy. With clean water emerging as a popular philanthropic interest abroad, a new program, Team World Vision, helps organize donors into teams through churches and other local community groups to run races locally, coach participants to good health, as well as raise money to dig wells in Africa. If marketing innovation and engaging popular culture have defined World Vision from its beginning, those same tools continue to define the organization's success today.

World Vision's story also remains an inherently global one. In 2010, after several decades of debate, World Vision International moved its executive office from Southern California to just outside London in the United Kingdom. In 2009, when current president and CEO of World Vision International Kevin Jenkins came to his new role from leading Canadian Airlines, he announced that it was time for WVI to relocate. London's international airport, proximity to the offices of other international agencies, and a time zone conducive to global communications were key factors in the decision. Demonstrating the global nature of the WVI partnership outside the shadow of the U.S. office was another.

It remains impossible to focus on even the U.S. office of an organization named World Vision without telling an international story. In the past half century, historians have begun to extend their reach by telling the U.S. story in comparative perspective. Regional narratives have helped break down a monolithic American religious history and a search for a single overarching narrative. Renewed interest in the West, the borderlands, and the Atlantic world has allowed for new historical actors and interpretations. Even as transnationalism remains in its early stages, it has served a number of purposes for historians. For some, it removed the nation-state as the historical centerpiece and highlighted a globalized world with a fluid movement of people and resources. For still others, the story of internationalization traced the exchange of ideas and transformation of worldviews.[2]

World Vision's history demonstrates the need for further situating American religious history transnationally. A rash of recent histories have explored the religious values in American foreign relations.[3] Others have prescribed religious understanding as a necessary topic for current diplomatic relations.[4] While World Vision's interactions with the U.S. government, its foreign policy, and international aid are essential to its story, its history also highlights underexplored international faith-based NGOs as key actors in a growing civil society. Yet, it is not only foreign policy, immigration, and international aid that matter in such a history. Increased exposure to a global world has also reshaped Americans' cultural imaginaries. Alongside the recent work of other scholars such as Melani McAlister, Heather Curtis, and David Kirkpatrick, I believe World Vision's history sheds light on the evolving international outlook of American evangelicals from World War II to the present.[5]

Through the Cold War, Vietnam, the downfall of colonialism, the rise of new nation-states, and the current global economy, many American Christians—it is impossible to know how many—have revised their worldview. Whether retaining an American exceptionalism or recasting themselves as global citizens, they also incorporated a religious lens into their interpretation of the world and their place within it. Americans learned about the world through newspaper stories and politicians' press releases, but they also viewed it through the sermons they heard, the missionary magazines they read, the religious infomercials they watched, and the children they sponsored. Organizations like World Vision gained firsthand experience of hunger, poverty, exploitation, and suffering throughout the world. They in turn introduced many American Christians to a world different from the one that they had imagined and that corporations and government agencies had convinced them to accept. For at least some Americans, including some evangelicals, global institutions and movements helped illuminate changing meanings of religion at home and abroad.

World Vision's story also exemplified the growth of evangelical missions after World War II as entrepreneurial parachurch agencies thrived through innovations in fund-raising, corporate organizing, and publicity. Initially, many of these missionaries claimed that being an evangelical meant simply practicing evangelism. They left social action to the World Council of Churches. Yet, their experience overseas with others outside the West led many missionaries from across the theological spectrum to work outside the cultural and theological boundary markers that divided American Christianity at home. As religious historian William Svelmoe has argued, missionaries, more than any other group, moderated and broadened American evangelicalism.[6]

I focus on one example of this shift through the rise of religious relief and development INGOs. Agencies like World Vision have now become the largest mission agencies, and this study has sought to explain how missions are intertwined with evangelicals' increasing encounter with pluralism, embrace of modern methodologies, and rise in social status. It also explored the religious dimension of the relief and development sector. As faith-based agencies have become more influential, the experts in global development have begun to value their size, experience, and expertise. Yet, FBOs drastically differ in size, prestige, and the extent to which their faith influences their work. Religious practice and traditions affect staff hiring, organizational structure, public identity, as well as relations to donors and aid recipients. At the same time, an organization's religious identity is often fluid and contested within multiple fields. For example, even as World Vision fluently speaks the common language of development among its peers, it also participates in wider debates within American evangelicalism, missiology, and the agencies of global Christianity.

Classification of FBOs will grow increasingly difficult as denominations, local churches, short-term missionaries, and new organizations emerge and continue to transform past institutional models. In 2004, the contemporary Christian music band Jars of Clay and twenty-something social entrepreneur Jena Lee Nardella started Blood:Water Mission to work with local African communities to address AIDS and water crises. While a fraction of the size of World Vision, its flexibility and grassroots approach allowed it opportunities to connect with evangelical millennials eager to make a difference.

Another agency, charity: water, claims no religious identity in its public image but emerged out of the faith story of its founder Scott Harrison in 2006. Having forsaken his life as a nightclub promoter to volunteer for faith-based NGO Mercy Ships to bring life-saving surgeries to those without access to medical treatment, Harrison then gave his life over to solving the global water crisis. He started charity: water to revolutionize fundraising in the nonprofit sector. With a guarantee that 100 percent of donations would go to the work of providing clean water, his model challenged traditional overhead and management structures of NGOs. The majority of charity: water donors do not give to the organization out of religious motivations, but Harrison openly speaks not only at tech conferences and New York City fund-raising galas but also to churches and Christian conferences about his faith and passion in ways that resonate with American evangelicals' global imagination and impulse to change the world. The move from missions to humanitarianism and beyond and the role of faith in these processes has not only transformed American Christians' global engagement, it has also served to transform the larger nonprofit sector.[7]

Finally, World Vision's history forces scholars to reflect upon their histories and current interpretations of evangelicalism. World Vision initially grew alongside the rise of a post–World War II American evangelicalism. Evangelicalism has always been difficult to define, even more so in recent years. After the 2016 presidential election where a record 81 percent of white evangelicals voted for Donald Trump, scholars and evangelicals themselves have questioned what to do with the term.[8] Some have continued to wear the label proudly, others have openly renounced it, and still many more continue to debate whether the term holds any meaning beyond pollsters' predictions and party affiliations.[9] Yet, these definitional debates have almost always been a part of American evangelicals' history. In fact, as World Vision's history demonstrates, precisely as evangelicals erected, maintained, and transgressed their boundaries, they imbued the term with various meanings. They fought over doctrine and practice, but in many ways, they defined themselves by a cultural style that scholar Nathan Hatch characterized by its "entrepreneurial quality, its populist and decentralized structure, and its penchant for splitting, forming and reforming."[10]

Sprouting from a fertile evangelical subculture and expanding throughout the height of what historian Steven P. Miller has called the "age of evangelicalism," World Vision modeled an evangelical cultural style even if it did not necessitate a singular theological or political position.[11] Its pragmatic approach demonstrated that even as it moved in, out, and beyond evangelical networks, it most often retained the cultural style and language comfortable to American evangelicals.

World Vision's story also helps to move historians beyond the "two-party" narrative of twentieth-century American Protestantism.[12] Martin Marty popularized the dualism in 1970 when he distinguished between public and private parties among American Protestants. The public party (liberal or mainline or ecumenical Protestants) pursued social reform while the private party (fundamentalists or evangelicals) sought individual conversions.[13] Sociologist Robert Wuthnow similarly argued in 1988 that the cultural changes of the 1960s, the demise of denominationalism, and the rise of single-issue special-purpose groups resulted in a renewed conservative and liberal divide.[14] Sociologist James Davison Hunter split Protestants into orthodox and progressives and linked their antagonisms to a broader "culture war."[15]

The dualistic narrative captured one feature of twentieth-century Protestantism. World Vision began as an evangelical organization that defined itself against mainline Christianity and the secular left, but as it began to work with Christians throughout the world, it crossed over traditional boundaries. It pursued justice and social reform without dismissing the need for individual conversion. It broadened to embrace mainline and Catholic mission agencies as well as non-Christian and nonreligious partners. These new associations—driven in large part by institutional imperatives both inside and outside American evangelicalism—produced a different kind of Christian organization. In the United States, it retained its evangelical style and language even if it no longer used the label, but it did not understand itself simply as an alternative to some imagined "other" in a competitive religious marketplace. The dichotomies departed as new alternatives emerged.

In recent years, advocates of the two-party approach have admitted the need to recalibrate their thesis, and several have even used World Vision as their example.[16] Martin Marty pointed to World Vision's advocacy for increased federal funding for foreign aid to demonstrate how evangelicals are not necessarily beholden to small government principles and afraid of addressing public social debates. *New York Times* editorialist Nicholas Kristof followed suit and chastised his "secular liberal" readership for copping to stereotypes and told them to take notice of World Vision and the changes it represented among American evangelicals.[17]

Of course, it would be simplistic to portray World Vision as a prototype of evangelicals trending toward a particular trajectory—moving from private to public issues or from conservative to progressive theology and politics. As noted throughout this history, the categories were never so clear, and they rarely were taken as evolutionary (that is, moving from less to more enlightened). Such interpretations often do a disservice to the history itself and the historical actors it seeks to interpret.

Over the past several years, debates on same-sex marriage have complicated World Vision's religious identity once again. Staff hiring remained a major public concern that has continued to define perceptions of organizations' religious identity, whether debating corporations' rights to deny contraception in health-care coverage or nonprofits' rights to decide whom to hire based on their beliefs and practices.[18] In March 2014, World Vision U.S. president Rich Stearns announced the organization would employ Christians in same-sex marriages.[19] The Assemblies of God, one of the country's largest Pentecostal denominations, quickly encouraged all its members and churches to end support for World Vision. Evangelical celebrities throughout the blogosphere declared "farewell" to World Vision, claiming Stearns's announcement confirmed what many already knew: World Vision had long since ceased being truly evangelical.[20] The criticism from conservative voices was so intense and the threat of lost financial support so significant that WVUS reversed its decision two days later.[21] Disappointed in the organization's subsequent reversal, several World Vision U.S. board members resigned.[22] Some evangelicals and other Christian leaders who had applauded what they described as World Vision's courageous initial decision grew frustrated and felt used by the organization for their support after WVUS reversed its decision. Many other non-U.S.-based World Vision country offices distanced themselves from the U.S. policy in response to their own organizational values and donor inquiries.[23]

While World Vision U.S. now markets itself with the broader "Christian" over a narrower "evangelical" label, its reversal in the face of intense pressure from American evangelicals demonstrated that its networks and donor base remain decidedly evangelical. In the aftermath of the public relations debacle, World Vision invested even more heavily in traditional evangelical media markets such as *Christianity Today*. While WVUS's leaders may have been surprised by the backlash, they realized they still remained dependent on their evangelical constituency no matter what their relationship with board members from Fortune 500 companies and contracts with USAID might suggest. Multiple constituencies continue to be invested in World Vision's religious identity and interpreting that identity can serve as a litmus test on multiple fronts.

Alongside World Vision, various other leading religious humanitarian agencies demonstrate the diversity of approaches within the U.S. evangelical context. The most likely organization to have benefited from WVUS's media relations turmoil over their hiring decision was Compassion International. While still significantly much smaller than World Vision, Compassion is a major player in child sponsorship and has traditionally remained closer to the local church both among donors in the United States and in working exclusively through the local church in its provision of programs overseas. Compassion only hires Christian staff and works through local churches to ensure the opportunity for evangelism alongside education, health care, and nutrition. In addition, while Compassion focuses the majority of sponsors' funding on individual children, World Vision has moved completely to an area development model that pools funds to benefit the children and families of entire communities together. The two organizations often work alongside one another around the world, but their different approaches lead to different reactions of governments, donors, and other nonprofits. Most notably Compassion was forced to withdraw from India in 2017 after India's conservative Hindu nationalist faction accused it of proselytizing. While Compassion has vehemently denied the accusation, the persecution narrative has continued to gain traction for the organization amid American evangelical donors.[24] Those who find World Vision's approach not religious or evangelical enough often find Compassion as the alternative.

While Compassion's differences with World Vision are significant but subtle, Franklin Graham makes Samaritan's Purse differences much more apparent. Bob Pierce infused a sense of competition from the beginning, as he established Samaritan's Purse in contrast to the increasingly professionalizing and internationalizing World Vision. Franklin Graham followed in Pierce's footsteps in resisting the typical CEO persona while building a reputation as adventurous globetrotter. He has also made his name in recent years in strident criticism of Islam, attacks on gay marriage, and support for right-leaning political candidates. After the election of Donald Trump, he claimed the victory was God's answering the prayers of hundreds of thousands of people intervening "to stop the godless, atheistic progressive agenda from taking control of our country."[25] If World Vision's public leaders have largely tried to avoid weighing in on partisan issues and particular candidates, Graham has relished his political persona, which has made him a Fox News icon and a lightning rod in the public sphere.

When it comes to the actual work of Samaritan's Purse, the story is more complex. Its most visible ministry, Operation Christmas Child, enables individuals and families most often through local churches to pack a shoebox full of small gifts and religious messages for a child affected by disaster, famine, and disease in another part of the world. In 2017, Samaritan's Purse reported collecting over 9.1 million shoeboxes from U.S. donors over the past year.[26] Development practitioners uniformly critique the program as ill-informed and counterproductive to standards of development, but donors love the simplicity and the chance to give easily to a child in need in the name of Jesus. The goodwill that Samaritan's Purse has received and the connection to local churches as a result of shoebox campaigns demonstrates that the organization has no plans to stop despite criticism from the development community.

Yet, at the same time that it fills shoe boxes, Samaritan's Purse has also expanded drastically in its size, budgets, and relief and development capacities. Samaritan's Purse began to pursue federal funding after the George W. Bush administration intentionally worked to foster funding opportunities to faith-based NGOs working domestically and abroad. In 2017, *Forbes* ranked it as the twenty-second largest U.S. charity—just a few spots behind Compassion and World Vision.[27] If Franklin Graham speaks out on hot-button political topics, he has also taken stands on other controversial topics that have galvanized evangelicals' response to issues like HIV/AIDS. If World Vision takes credit for playing a major role in changing the minds of American evangelicals, Franklin Graham does too. Pulling together strange bedfellows like North Carolina Republican senator Jesse Helms and U2 front man Bono, Graham encouraged conservative evangelicals to support PEPFAR and funding to alleviate the African AIDS crisis.[28]

Samaritan's Purse has continued to professionalize its relief and development operations. Like World Vision, it strives to be one of the first organizations on the ground after a disaster. It has helped to fund and establish hospitals in some of the world's most difficult areas, such as in Liberia during the 2014 Ebola crisis. Samaritan's Purse staff member Kent Brantley, one of the first American health-care workers to contract the disease while working on the front lines, lobbied to draw international attention to the crisis.[29] Throughout its field staff, it recruits highly competent professional development practitioners. Alongside Graham's political persuasions and evangelist identity, no one doubts Samaritan's Purse evangelical commitments, but that complicates how to make sense of the religious identity and practice of the organization at home and abroad.

Finally, World Relief's contemporary context serves as one more contrast to World Vision. As the elder evangelical relief agency founded alongside the birth of the NAE, it emerged to meet the need for humanitarian action in the aftermath of World War II. Yet as an agency underneath the larger umbrella network of evangelical denominations, it remained limited in size without the marketing prowess of World Vision or opportunities for child sponsorship like Compassion. However, it took part in providing relief and development in the midst of the same wars and natural disasters that defined other agencies over the past seventy years. By the late 1970s and in the wake of the Vietnamese boat people crisis that World Vision publicized, World Relief began to focus on refugee resettlement. World Relief was authorized as a resettlement agency through the U.S. government, and work with refugees came to define a significant amount of its ministry. As World Relief's resettlement reached new numeric highs in 2017, Donald Trump's executive orders banning the travel and resettlement of many refugees from Muslim-majority countries drastically reduced its caseload and led to the closure of five U.S. regional offices and layoffs of over 140 staff members. World Relief leaders spearheaded a letter condemning the ban, which was signed by several thousand evangelicals across the theological spectrum. While their budget and staff size have not recovered from the loss of federal funding tied to refugee resettlement, World Relief has redoubled its public efforts to encourage fellow evangelicals to advocate for change.[30]

The work of these leading evangelical humanitarian organizations as well as countless others demonstrate that telling the history, making sense of the present, or predicting the future of a diverse evangelicalism and global humanitarianism is never a straightforward or simple task. At the same time, organizations like World Vision might possibly register significant shifts within American evangelicalism as it constantly worked to build bridges over long-established divides. World Vision staff worked with feet planted in first one world and then another, functioning sometimes as insider, sometimes as outsider. Its innovations created tensions among evangelicals uneasy with its work alongside ecumenical missions, its devotion to the solving of social problems, and its decision to share leadership with Christians outside the United States. Critics on one side chastised what they saw as a narrow form of evangelism, while critics on the other worried that the organization had lost its evangelistic moorings. Nonreligious relief and development agencies worried that it could not measure up to the standards of a demanding international enterprise. Christians outside the West sometimes accused it of propagating an aggressive American exceptionalism. Recent decisions have led World Vision to refocus its efforts in appealing to American evangelicals around traditional cultural and theological issues even as it has continued to press ahead in its development practice. World Vision has never escaped the multiple tensions inherent in its work or its religious identity.

A look at World Vision's history helps explain how it came to rearticulate and retain its Christian identity even as it expanded beyond a limited American evangelical subculture, how the ethos of evangelical missions has shifted from evangelism alone to creative forms of Christian humanitarianism, and how exposure to global influences affected the reflection and effected change in the self-understanding of many American evangelicals at home. As leading evangelicals and their institutions continue to debate whether the term has lost its meaning, the broader "age of evangelicalism" and born-again culture that captured the attention of an American political and popular culture for several decades may be waning. Yet as historian Steven P. Miller claims, "the recent history of American evangelicalism looks different—and, in many respects, a lot more interesting—when it is not solely about evangelicals themselves."[31] Perhaps what is emerging is something different, broader, unpredictable, and uncertain. Whatever emerges will extend beyond what labeling voters in election exit polls or the leaders standing beside political figures on the dais can capture.

Historian David Hollinger has argued that both twentieth-century Protestant liberals and Protestant missionaries sought to change America and the world. If evaluated by their own measures of success, they often failed; however, their efforts dramatically changed history in the process.[32] Historians may one day soon say the same for American evangelicals. If measured by the bold vision of the first generation of post–World War II evangelicals, such as Billy Graham, Carl Henry, and Bob Pierce, seeking to save the world while reshaping American culture and global civil society in the process, they fell short. Yet, the dramatic impact of American evangelicals at home and abroad cannot be overlooked. While scholars have examined American evangelicalism primarily as an American movement, manifest in politics, theology, or popular culture, many have missed the effect of global forces on American evangelicals and their impact on the world.

Over the past half century, evangelicals have moved into the public square, but they have occupied different corners, addressed a variety of issues, and spoken in multiple dialects. While it is impossible to understand twenty-first-century evangelicalism without politics, the political dimension is only part of the evangelical ethos. The landscape continues to evolve, but global issues remain front and center. Despite ongoing uncertainty on evangelicalism's future and the complexities of individuals' and institutions' religious identities and practices, as more American Christians embrace a global vision, perhaps a new form of practical ecumenism may lead to transcending or transgressing past theological and political boundary markers. And perhaps upstart religious relief agencies and established faith-based nonprofits like World Vision may lead the way.

NOTES

Introduction

1. Rachel M. McCleary, *Global Compassion: Private Voluntary Organizations and U.S. Foreign Policy Since 1939* (New York: Oxford University Press, 2009), 25–34. By 2005, World Vision's revenue dwarfed that of all other religious NGOs—evangelical or not. It had also become the second largest of any international humanitarian organization.

2. Steven P. Miller, *Billy Graham and the Rise of the Republican South* (Philadelphia: University of Pennsylvania Press, 2009); John Turner, *Bill Bright & Campus Crusade for Christ: The Renewal of Evangelicalism in Postwar America* (Chapel Hill: University of North Carolina Press, 2008); Darren Dochuk, *From Bible Belt to Sunbelt: Plain-Folk Religion, Grassroots Politics, and the Rise of Evangelical Conservatism* (New York: W. W. Norton, 2011); Darren E. Grem, *The Blessings of Business: Corporate America and the Rise of Conservative Evangelicalism* (New York: Oxford University Press, 2016; Daniel K. Williams, *God's Own Party: The Making of the Christian Right* (Oxford: Oxford University Press, 2010).

3. Michael Hamilton, "The Financing of American Evangelicalism Since 1945," in *More Money, More Ministry: Money and Evangelicals in Recent North American History*, ed. Larry Eskridge and Mark Noll (Grand Rapids, MI: Eerdmans, 2000), 134.

4. Nicholas D. Kristof, "Following God Abroad," *New York Times*, May 21, 2002, http://www.nytimes.com/2002/05/21/opinion/following-god-abroad.html?pagewanted=2.

5. Rachel M. McCleary, "Private Voluntary Organizations Engaged in International Assistance, 1939–2004," *Nonprofit & Voluntary Sector Quarterly* 37, no. 3 (September 2008): 518–19.

6. Heather Curtis unearths the earlier forms of popular religious, humanitarian appeals. Heather D. Curtis, *Holy Humanitarians: American Evangelicals and Global Aid* (Cambridge, MA: Harvard University Press, 2018).

7. Daniel H. Bays and Grant Wacker, eds., *The Foreign Missionary Enterprise at Home: Explorations in North American Cultural History* (Tuscaloosa: University of Alabama Press, 2003); Dana L. Robert, "The Influence of American Missionary Women on the World Back Home," *Religion and American Culture* 12, no. 1 (2002): 59–89; Sarah E. Ruble, *The Gospel of Freedom and Power: Protestant Missionaries in American Culture After World War II* (Chapel Hill: University of North Carolina Press, 2014); David A. Hollinger, *Protestants Abroad: How Missionaries Tried to Change the World but Changed America* (Princeton, NJ: Princeton University Press, 2017).

8. Andrew Preston, Bruce J. Schulman, and Julian E. Zelizer, eds., *Faithful Republic: Religion and Politics in Modern America* (Philadelphia: University of Pennsylvania Press,

2015); William Inboden, *Religion and American Foreign Policy, 1945–1960: The Soul of Containment* (Cambridge: Cambridge University Press, 2008); Cara Lea Burnidge, *A Peaceful Conquest: Woodrow Wilson, Religion, and the New World Order* (Chicago: University of Chicago Press, 2016); Kevin Michael Kruse, *One Nation Under God: How Corporate America Invented Christian America* (New York: Basic Books, 2016).

9. Andrew Preston, "Bridging the Gap Between the Sacred and the Secular in the History of American Foreign Relations," *Diplomatic History* 30, no. 5 (2006): 783–812.

10. Gilbert Rist, *The History of Development: From Western Origins to Global Faith* (New York: Zed Books, 2008); Michael Barnett, *Empire of Humanity: A History of Humanitarianism*, repr. ed. (Ithaca, NY: Cornell University Press, 2013); David Ekbladh, *The Great American Mission: Modernization and the Construction of an American World Order* (Princeton, NJ: Princeton University Press, 2010).

11. The six largest are World Vision, Feed the Children, MAP International, Compassion International, Food for the Hungry, and Christian Aid Ministries. Michael Hamilton, "The Financing of American Evangelicalism Since 1945," 134.

12. Conrad Hackett and D. Michael Lindsay, "Measuring Evangelicalism: Consequences of Different Operationalization Strategies," *Journal for the Scientific Study of Religion* 47, no. 3 (2008): 499–514.

13. David Bebbington, *Evangelicalism in Modern Britain: A History from the 1730s to the 1980s* (London: Unwin Hyman, 1989).

14. George M. Marsden, "The Evangelical Denomination," in *Evangelicalism and Modern America* (Grand Rapids, MI: Eerdmans, 1984), vii–xix; Steven P. Miller, *The Age of Evangelicalism: America's Born-Again Years* (New York: Oxford University Press, 2014).

15. Mark Noll, "Defining Evangelicalism," in *Global Evangelicalism: Theology, History, and Culture in Regional Perspective*, ed. Donald M. Lewis and Richard V. Pierard (Downers Grove, IL: IVP Academic, 2014), 19.

16. Wilbert M. Shenk, "The Theological Impulse of Evangelical Expansion," in Lewis and Pierard, *Global Evangelicalism*, 45–46.

17. Scholars have noted the transnational nature of American religious history in earlier periods in several recent works, including Christine Leigh Heyrman, *American Apostles: When Evangelicals Entered the World of Islam* (New York: Hill and Wang, 2015); Emily Conroy-Krutz, *Christian Imperialism: Converting the World in the Early American Republic* (Ithaca, NY: Cornell University Press, 2015).

18. See Kendrick Oliver et al., introduction to "Exploring the Global History of American Evangellcallsm," special Issue, *Journal of American Studies* 51, no. 4 (2017). 1019–42, which offers a helpful overview as well as introduces the important articles making up the special issue.

19. For versions of the embourgeoisement, popular culture, and demographic argument, see Bethany Moreton, *To Serve God and Wal-Mart: The Making of Christian Free Enterprise* (Cambridge, MA: Harvard University Press, 2010); Shayne Lee and Phillip Luke Sinitiere, *Holy Mavericks: Evangelical Innovators and the Spiritual Marketplace* (New York: NYU Press, 2009); Michael Hout, Andrew Greeley, and Melissa J. Wilde, "The Demographic Imperative in Religious Change in the United States," *American Journal of Sociology* 107, no. 2 (2001): 468–500. Focusing on politics, see Randall Balmer, *The Making of Evangelicalism: From Revivalism to Politics and Beyond* (Waco, TX: Baylor University Press, 2017); David P. Gushee, *The*

Future of Faith in American Politics: The Public Witness of the Evangelical Center (Waco, TX: Baylor University Press, 2008); Frances FitzGerald, *The Evangelicals: The Struggle to Shape America*, repr. ed. (New York: Simon & Schuster, 2018). Of course, many others combine these viewpoints to demonstrate evangelicals' uniqueness. For example, see Christian Smith, *American Evangelicalism: Embattled and Thriving* (Chicago: University of Chicago Press, 1998).

20. Paul J. DiMaggio and Walter W. Powell, "The Iron Cage Revisited: Institutional Isomorphism and Collective Rationality in Organizational Fields," in *The New Institutionalism in Organizational Analysis*, ed. Walter W. Powell and Paul J. DiMaggio (Chicago: University of Chicago Press, 1991), 63–82.

21. Brian Foster, "In Medicine We Trust," *Slate*, October 2, 2014, http://www.slate.com/ articles/health_and_science/medical_examiner/2014/10/missionary_doctors_treating_ebola _in_africa_why_people_are_suspicious_of.html; Ross Douthat, "Pagans and Christians," *New York Times*, October 3, 2014, http://douthat.blogs.nytimes.com/2014/10/03/pagans-and -christians/; Nicholas Kristof, "A Little Respect for Dr. Foster," *New York Times*, March 28, 2015, http://www.nytimes.com/2015/03/29/opinion/sunday/nicholas-kristof-a-little-respect -for-dr-foster.html?_r = 0.

22. For critiques of those separating religious and secular development, see Elizabeth Olson, "Common Belief, Contested Meanings: Development and Faith-Based Organisational Culture," *Tijdschrift voor economische en sociale geografie* 99, no. 4 (2008): 393–405; Gerard Clarke and Michael Jennings, eds., *Development, Civil Society and Faith-Based Organizations: Bridging Sacred and the Secular* (Basingstoke, England: Palgrave Macmillan, 2008). For examples of those arguing for a general institutional isomorphism, see John Boli and David V. Brewington, "Religious Organizations," in *Religion, Globalization, and Culture*, ed. Peter Beyer and Lori G. Beaman (Boston: Leiden, 2007), 203–31.

23. Wendy Tyndale, *Visions of Development: Faith-Based Initiatives* (Aldershot, England: Ashgate, 2006); Katherine Marshall and Lucy Keough, *Finding Global Balance: Common Ground Between the Worlds of Development and Faith* (Washington, DC: World Bank, 2005); Scott M. Thomas, "Faith and Foreign Aid: How the World Bank Got Religion and Why It Matters," *Brandywine Review of Faith and International Affairs*, Fall 2004, 21–29.

24. See, for example, broadly just within Western evangelical history, Ian R. Tyrrell, *Reforming the World: The Creation of America's Moral Empire* (Princeton, NJ: Princeton University Press, 2010); Melani McAlister, *The Kingdom of God Has No Borders: A Global History of American Evangelicals* (New York: Oxford University Press, 2018); Curtis, *Holy Humanitarians*. Also see articles included in "Exploring the Global History of American Evangelicalism," special issue, *Journal of American Studies* 51, no. 4 (2017).

25. For an overview of the global engagement of American evangelicals, see McAlister, *The Kingdom of God Has No Borders*.

Chapter 1

1. For a fuller account of Pierce's travels to China via the Philippines, see Marilee Pierce Dunker, *Man of Vision: The Candid, Compelling Story of Bob and Lorraine Pierce, Founders of World Vision and Samaritan's Purse* (Waynesboro, GA: Authentic Media, 2005), 65–67.

2. Billy Graham had presented the Bible to Pierce to carry to China at a Youth for Christ rally at the Hollywood Bowl just before he embarked on his trip. The full inscription read, "To Chiang Kai-shek, President of the Republic of China, from Youth for Christ and the

young people of America who are praying for you and for the great country of China that it may come to know Christ." Franklin Graham and Jeanette Lockerbie, *Bob Pierce: This One Thing I Do* (Waco, TX: Word Books, 1983), 59.

3. Bob Pierce to Lorraine Pierce, August 3, 1947, quoted in Dunker, *Man of Vision*, 85.

4. There are several biographical treatments of Pierce's life. I have drawn basic details from the following: Graham and Lockerbie, *Bob Pierce*; Dunker, *Man of Vision*; Norman Rohrer, *Open Arms* (Wheaton, IL: Tyndale House, 1987); Richard Gehman, *Let My Heart Be Broken* (Grand Rapids, MI: Zondervan, 1960); "Dr. Bob Pierce Biography," undated, Folder 23, Box 6, Collection 506, Records of *Decision* Magazine, Archives of the Billy Graham Center, Wheaton, IL.

5. Tona J. Hangen, *Redeeming the Dial: Radio, Religion, and Popular Culture in America* (Chapel Hill: University of North Carolina Press, 2002), 75.

6. Darren Dochuk identifies this new Sunbelt culture as plain folk Americanism primarily founded on race but also constructed by gender, codes of manliness and womanhood, and family often articulated through the populist impulse of evangelical Protestantism. See Dochuk, *From Bible Belt to Sunbelt*; see also Gregory H. Singleton, *Religion in the City of Angels* (Ann Arbor, MI: UMI Research Press, 1978), 119–34.

7. Dunker, *Man of Vision*, 21–23.

8. Pierce often made fun of his own lack of intellect. He remarked, "I'm one guy who got through high school and most of four years of college without ever learning basic grammar. But don't blame my teachers. Bob Pierce was lookin' out the window." Graham and Lockerbie, *Bob Pierce*, 29.

9. Dunker, *Man of Vision*, 29.

10. Ibid., 33–35.

11. "Dr. Bob Pierce Biography."

12. From a handbill circulated for a Pierce revival meeting, quoted in Dunker, *Man of Vision*, 37.

13. Ibid., 52–53.

14. I have not found further reference to the Jubilee Singers to ascertain whether their audiences were mixed, segregated, or all white and how both they and Pierce may have responded to segregation throughout their travels.

15. Graham and Lockerbie, *Bob Pierce*, 50–51.

16. John R. Rice, "And He Gave . . . Some Evangelists," *Sword of the Lord*, January 19, 1940, 1–3, and "Evangelistic Preaching," *Sword of the Lord*, September 20, 1940, 1–4, quoted in Margaret Lamberts Bendroth, *Fundamentalism and Gender, 1875 to the Present* (New Haven, CT: Yale University Press, 1993), 77.

17. Graham and Lockerbie, *Bob Pierce*, 51.

18. James C. Hefley, *God Goes to High School: An In-Depth Look at an Incredible Phenomenon* (Waco, TX: Word, 1970), 25.

19. Forrest Forbes, *God Hath Chosen: Story of Jack Wyrtzen and the Word of Life Hour* (Grand Rapids, MI: Zondervan, 1948).

20. Joel Carpenter, *Revive Us Again: The Reawakening of American Fundamentalism* (New York: Oxford University Press, 1997), 161–64.

21. Joel Carpenter, *The Youth for Christ Movement and Its Pioneers* (New York: Garland, 1988); Billy Graham, *Just as I Am: The Autobiography of Billy Graham* (San Francisco: Harper SanFrancisco, 1997), 87–94; William Martin, *A Prophet with Honor: The Billy Graham Story* (New York: W. Morrow and Co., 1991), 91.

22. "Interview of Torrey Johnson," February 13, 1984, Tape T4, Collection 285, Records of Torrey Johnson, Archives of the Billy Graham Center, Wheaton, IL; Hefley, *God Goes to High School*, 22.

23. Joel Carpenter, "The Fundamentalist Leaven and the Rise of an Evangelical United Front," in *The Evangelical Tradition in America*, ed. Leonard I. Sweet (Macon, GA: Mercer University Press, 1984), 257–88.

24. The NAE did successfully maintain a number of "trade associations" that served the needs of particular constituencies like missions, relief work, broadcasting, and publishing (Carpenter, *Revive Us Again*, 154).

25. In a 1986 letter to George Marsden, Carl Henry, a leading architect of the neo-evangelical movement, wrote: "In the 1930s we were all fundamentalists. . . . The term 'evangelical' became a significant option when the NAE was organized (1942). . . . In the context of the debate with modernism, fundamentalist was an appropriate alternative; in other contexts (of the debate within the fundamentalist movement), the term evangelical was preferable." In the same letter, he wrote, "Nobody wanted the term 'evangelical' when NAE was formed in 1942; in social context and in ecumenical context it implied what was religiously passé." Carl Henry, to George Marsden, February 24, 1986, quoted in George Marsden, *Reforming Fundamentalism: Fuller Seminary and the New Evangelicalism* (Grand Rapids, MI: Eerdmans, 1987), 10.

26. For a selection of the many books seeking to define early neo-evangelicals and fundamentalists, see Garth M. Rosell, *The Surprising Work of God: Harold John Ockenga, Billy Graham, and the Rebirth of Evangelicalism* (Grand Rapids, MI: Baker Academic, 2008), 89; D. G. Hart, *Deconstructing Evangelicalism: Conservative Protestantism in the Age of Billy Graham* (Grand Rapids, MI: Baker Academic, 2004), 113; George Marsden, *Understanding Fundamentalism and Evangelicalism* (Grand Rapids, MI: Eerdmans, 1991), 69.

27. The organization wanted to be, as it said in its motto, "geared to the times but anchored to the rock." Joel A. Carpenter, "'Geared to the Times but Anchored to the Rock': How Contemporary Techniques and Nationalism Helped Create an Evangelical Resurgence," *Christianity Today*, November 8, 1985, 44–47; Hefley, *God Goes to High School*, 18.

28. Mark A. Noll, "Where We Are and How We Got Here," *Christianity Today*, October 1, 2006, 46.

29. Carpenter, *Revive Us Again*, 167–68.

30. Hefley, *God Goes to High School*, 13.

31. "Interview of Torrey Johnson." While cooperation at a regional or national level was rarely the case between mainline Protestants, fundamentalist evangelicals, and Pentecostals, the local structure of rallies allowed for uncharacteristically wide support from the diverse civic and church communities.

32. Of particular importance was Herbert Taylor, head of the Club Aluminum Company in Chicago and one of the chief philanthropists of evangelical causes, including Youth for Christ and later World Vision.

33. Carl F. H. Henry, "Accent on Youth," *Sunday* 6, no. 10 (January 1945): 20.

34. Mel Larson, *Young Man on Fire: The Story of Torrey Johnson and Youth for Christ* (New York: Youth Publications, 1945), 87. Larson notes the specific outline of each Saturday's program: It starts at 7 p.m., with congregational singing, musical numbers; reports on how YFC is spreading through the country; offers testimonies from servicemen; the main speaker delivers a message for about twenty-two minutes; and ends promptly at 9:30.

35. Torrey Johnson and Robert Cook, *Reaching Youth for Christ* (Chicago: Moody Press, 1944).

36. Joel A. Carpenter, "Youth for Christ and the New Evangelicals," in *Reckoning with the Past: Historical Essays on American Evangelicalism from the Institute for the Study of American Evangelicals*, ed. D. G. Hart (Grand Rapids, MI: Baker Books, 1995), 364; Carpenter, *Revive Us Again*, 168–69.

37. Hearst also contributed to Billy Graham's rise to fame through positive exposure during his 1949 Los Angeles crusade. Before Hearst gave the message to "puff Graham," he had given the same message to "puff YFC." "William Randolph Hearst's Editorial Endorsement of 'Youth for Christ,'" *United Evangelical Action*, July 16, 1945 13; "Hearst Papers Now Boast Youth for Christ," *United Evangelical Action*, July 2, 1945, 1.

38. "Youth for Christ," *Time*, February 4, 1946, 46–47, quoted in Carpenter, "'Geared to the Times,'" 46.

39. In 1900, "former president Benjamin Harrison, New York governor Theodore Roosevelt, and President William McKinley all gave speeches at the Ecumenical Missionary Conference in New York City." Soon after, missionary leader John R. Mott served as a leading foreign diplomat under President Woodrow Wilson. Ruble, *The Gospel of Freedom and Power*, 12.

40. Denton Lotz, "'The Evangelization of the World in This Generation': The Resurgence of a Missionary Idea Among the Conservative Evangelicals" (PhD diss., University of Hamburg, 1970), 35–36; Gerald H. Anderson, "American Protestants in Pursuit of Mission: 1886–1986," *International Bulletin of Missionary Research* 12, no. 3 (July 1988): 104; Brian Stanley, *The World Missionary Conference, Edinburgh 1910* (Grand Rapids, MI: Eerdmans, 2009).

41. Dana L. Robert, "The First Globalization? The Internationalization of the Protestant Missionary Movement Between the Wars," in *Interpreting Contemporary Christianity: Global Processes and Local Identities*, ed. Ogbu U. Kalu (Grand Rapids, MI: Eerdmans, 2008): 93–130.

42. William Hutchison, *Errand to the World: American Protestant Thought and Foreign Missions* (Chicago: University of Chicago Press, 1987), 146–75; James A. Patterson, "The Loss of a Protestant Missionary Consensus: Foreign Missions and the Fundamentalist-Modernist Conflict," in *Earthen Vessels: American Evangelicals and Foreign Missions, 1880–1980*, ed. Joel A. Carpenter and Wilbert R. Shenk (Grand Rapids, MI: Eerdmans, 1990), 73–91.

43. Carpenter, "Youth for Christ and the New Evangelicals," 368.

44. Torrey Johnson, "God Is in It!," Minutes of the First Annual Convention, Youth for Christ International, July 22–29, 1945, quoted in Carpenter, *Revive Us Again*, 171.

45. Mel Larson, *Youth for Christ: Twentieth Century Wonder* (Grand Rapids, MI: Zondervan, 1947), 29.

46. Hefley, *God Goes to High School*, 13, 29.

47. Carpenter, "Youth for Christ and the New Evangelicals," 369; Hefley, *God Goes to High School*, 29, 34.

48. Military and crusade language was common and the growth of evangelical mission in the 1940s and 1950s built upon a connection with American nationalism. Many new missionaries were former American GIs. YFC founder Torrey Johnson spoke of the need to "invade England with the Gospel." They talked of "beachheads" being planted, opening up opportunities for further "invasions." Evangelists were "Christian commandos" with "arsenals" for worldwide evangelization. Carpenter, *Revive Us Again*, 178–79; Richard V. Pierard, "Pax Americana and the Evangelical Missionary Advance," in Carpenter and Shenk, *Earthen Vessels*, 155–79.

49. Conquest language built upon the biblical text of 2 Chronicles 7:14. Merv Rosell, "God's Global 'Go!,'" *Winona Echoes* 51 (1945): 260–65; F. D. Whitesell, "God's Purposes in World War No. 2," *Voice* 23 (September 1944): 8.

50. "How Bob Pierce Got His First Orphan: As Told by Pierce to Steve and Mary Nicholson," December 20, 1977, 12–13, Box 1, Bob Pierce Collection, 1950–1978, David Allan Hubbard Library Archives, Fuller Theological Seminary, Pasadena, CA; Dunker, *Man of Vision*, 62–63.

51. *Youth for Christ*, September 1947, 53.

52. Dunker, *Man of Vision*, 65–66; Graham and Lockerbie, *Bob Pierce*, 58–67.

53. In addition to missionary personnel, the movement invested millions of dollars in Asia. In 1939, the mainline invested over $2.5 million just in Japan and Korea. See "God and the Emperor," *Time*, September 9, 1940, http://www.time.com/time/magazine/archives/.

54. Kenneth Scott Latourette, "The Real Issue in Foreign Missions," *Christian Century* 48 (April 15, 1931): 506; "Nationalism Is Throttling Missions," *Christian Century* 50 (September 13, 1933): 1140; Robert E. Speer, "True and Abiding Basis of Foreign Missions," *Missionary Review of the World*, October 1929, 757.

55. Patricia Neils, *China Images in the Life and Times of Henry Luce* (Savage, MD: Rowman & Littlefield, 1990); Robert Herzstein, *Henry R. Luce, "Time," and the American Crusade in Asia* (Cambridge: Cambridge University Press, 2005); Thomas Jespersen, *American Images of China, 1931–1949* (Stanford, CA: Stanford University Press, 1996).

56. "Chiang and His Wife Laud Christianity," *New York Times*, April 13, 1943, 6; Chiang Kai-shek, "The Spirit of the Christian Soldier," *Christian Century*, March 15, 1944, 331–32.

57. More liberal publications like the *New York Times* and *Christian Century* began to waver in supporting Chiang Kai-shek after 1947 due to charges of corruption as well as meager success. While evangelicals largely remained with Chiang, many Americans read the handwriting on the wall and prepared for a Communist mainland China.

58. Graham and Lockerbie, *Bob Pierce*, 66.

59. Ken Anderson and Bob Pierce, *This Way to the Harvest* (Grand Rapids, MI: Zondervan, 1949), 56.

60. Graham and Lockerbie, *Bob Pierce*, 72.

61. Ken Anderson, "Her Community Is Called Death," *Youth for Christ*, April 1949, 16–17, 69.

62. Pierce retold this story so often that he often conflated the details with other stories. This meeting probably occurred in 1948 on his second trip to China even if Pierce often framed it as having happened on his initial trip. "How Bob Pierce Got His First Orphan."

63. Graham and Lockerbie, *Bob Pierce*, 73.

64. World Vision highlights this story as the origin of its child-sponsorship program. In 2010, on the occasion of World Vision's sixtieth anniversary, Pierce's daughter Marilee Pierce Dunker returned to Amoy (now known as Xiamen) looking for White Jade but was not able to locate her. Marilee Pierce Dunker, "In My Father's Footsteps," *World Vision*, August 27, 2013, http://archive.worldvisionmagazine.org/story/my-father-s-footsteps. See also Graham and Lockerbie, *Bob Pierce*, 74–75; Bob Pierce, *Orphans of the Orient: Stories That Will Touch Your Heart* (Grand Rapids, MI: Zondervan, 1964), 55–60.

65. This served as the last line of Pierce's first book on his travels in China (Anderson and Pierce, *This Way to the Harvest*).

66. Bob Pierce quote, *Youth for Christ*, June 1948, 54.

67. Dunker, *Man of Vision*, 85.

68. Ken Anderson, "Ambassador on Fire," *Youth for Christ*, June 1948, 16.

69. Hefley, *God Goes to High School*, 41–42; also see "World Congress Report," *Missionary Digest*, January 1949, 6–7.

70. Bob Pierce and Ken Anderson, "China as We Saw It," *Youth for Christ*, September 1948, 68.

71. *China Challenge: Miracle Miles in the Orient*, directed by Dick Ross (1949), 16 mm.

72. Mel Larson, review of *This Way to the Harvest*, by Anderson and Pierce, *Youth for Christ*, August 1949, 51; "Interview Between Lee Bernard and Robert Pierce," January 10, 1978, Box 1, Bob Pierce Collection, 1950–1978, David Allan Hubbard Library Archives, Fuller Theological Seminary.

73. Anderson and Pierce, *This Way to the Harvest*, 5; John Robert Hamilton, "An Historical Study of Bob Pierce and World Vision's Development of the Evangelical Social Action Film" (PhD diss., University of Southern California, 1980), 38–48.

74. Carl F. H. Henry, *The Uneasy Conscience of Modern Fundamentalism* (Grand Rapids, MI: Eerdmans, 1947), 32.

75. Pierce and Anderson, "China as We Saw It," 67.

76. Hamilton, "An Historical Study of Bob Pierce," 20. Of course, Graham's ministry also came to be defined by international as well as domestic crusades.

77. Bob Pierce, *The Untold Korea Story*, second ed. (Grand Rapids MI: Zondervan Publishing House, 1951), 7–8. The missionaries extending the invitation, the Kilbournes, served with the Oriental Missionary Society, a large faith mission, and had originally served in China where they had met Pierce. Both mainline Presbyterian and faith missionaries supported Pierce's early Korean tours.

78. Dunker, *Man of Vision*, 85–93.

79. Graham and Lockerbie, *Bob Pierce*, 153.

80. Dunker, *Man of Vision*, 99–100.

Chapter 2

1. "News Report," *Youth For Christ*, July 1950, 53.

2. "How Bob Pierce Got His First Orphan," 34.

3. "Dr. Bob Pierce Biography"; "Bob Pierce: Missionary Ambassador," *Youth for Christ*, April 1951, 9–10.

4. World Vision's records of its finances are noted from 1950 to 1959 in its files of Missionary Disbursements, World Vision International (WVI) Central Records, Monrovia, CA (hereafter cited as WVI Central Records). Bob Pierce, "Message Given at Missionary Conference of American Soul Clinic," October 12, 1952, WVI Central Records.

5. "How Bob Pierce Got His First Orphan," 39–40.

6. "Bob Pierce: Missionary Ambassador," 10; Bob Pierce, "Thankful in Korea," *Youth for Christ*, November 1951, 10.

7. World Vision 1956 Pictorial, Folder 40, Box 35, Collection 236, Records of the Latin American Mission, Archives of the Billy Graham Center, Wheaton, IL (hereafter cited as LAM Records).

8. "Interview Between Robert Pierce and Dick Ross," January 7, 1978, Box 1, Bob Pierce Collection, 1950–1978, David Allan Hubbard Library Archives, Fuller Theological Seminary.

9. Bob Pierce, *The Untold Korea Story*, 7–8; Hamilton, "An Historical Study of Bob Pierce," 61–65; "Report," *Youth for Christ*, June 1950, 44; "Report," *United Evangelical Action*, April 15, 1950, 8.

10. "Laboring Together," *Youth for Christ*, August 1953, 37.

11. Billy Graham Center Archives Exhibit, "Madison Sq. Garden, 1957 NY Crusade: Welcome to the Exhibit," accessed September 25, 2017, http://www2.wheaton.edu/bgc/ar chives/exhibits/NYC57/00welcome.htm; Reinhold Niebuhr, "Differing Views on Billy Graham," *Life* 43, no. 1 (1957): 92.

12. "Protestants: The Evangelical Undertow," *Time*, December 20, 1963, 57, referenced in Dennis Hollinger, *Individualism and Social Ethics: An Evangelical Syncretism* (Lanham, MD: University Press of America, 1983), 94; Martin, *A Prophet with Honor*, 213–17.

13. Most scholars see the neo-evangelical label taking root with the formation of the NAE, but this remains a debated historiography. For the best synopsis of the issue, see Douglas A. Sweeney, "The Essential Evangelicalism Dialectic: The Historiography of the Early Neo-Evangelical Movement and the Observer-Participant Dilemma," *Church History* 60, no. 1 (1991): 70–84; see also Jon R. Stone, *On the Boundaries of American Evangelicalism: The Postwar Evangelical Coalition* (New York: St. Martin's Press, 1997).

14. Pierce, *The Untold Korea Story*, 5, 78. For a discussion of postwar evangelical missions and a Pax Americana, see Pierard, "Pax Americana and the Evangelical Missionary Advance." Pierce affirmed Jesus's second coming, and his rhetoric sometimes mentioned his belief that it may come in his lifetime, but his work was not defined by eschatology.

15. Will Herberg, *Protestant, Catholic, Jew: An Essay in American Religious Sociology* (Chicago: University of Chicago Press, 1983); Inboden, *Religion and American Foreign Policy, 1945–1960*, 77.

16. Robert S. Ellwood, *1950, Crossroads of American Religious Life* (Louisville, KY: Westminster John Knox Press, 2000), 11.

17. Henry Luce, "A Path to Peace Through Prayer," *Life*, September 13, 1954, 48, quoted in Seth Jacobs, *America's Miracle Man in Vietnam: Ngo Dinh Diem, Religion, Race, and U.S. Intervention in Southeast Asia, 1950–1957* (Durham, NC: Duke University Press, 2004), 48.

18. Joanne Sharp, *Condensing the Cold War: Reader's Digest and American Identity* (Minneapolis: University of Minnesota Press, 2000).

19. "In marrying faith and freedom," Truman claimed, "both religion and democracy are founded on one basic principle, the worth and dignity of the individual man and woman." Richard Gid Powers, *Not Without Honor: The History of American Anticommunism* (New York: Free Press, 1995), 5–6; Inboden, *Religion and American Foreign Policy, 1945–1960*, 1–2, 109.

20. Buckley's quote is from his 1951 *God and Man at Yale*, referenced in Ellwood, *1950*, 61. Stevenson's quote is from an October 1952 speech referenced in Mark Silk, *Spiritual Politics: Religion and America Since World War II* (New York: Simon and Schuster, 1988), 87.

21. Inboden, *Religion and American Foreign Policy, 1945–1960*, 259.

22. Dulles, "The Importance of Spiritual Resources," January 27, 1950, referenced in Inboden, *Religion and American Foreign Policy, 1945–1960*, 236. Dulles would go on to say later that same year, "Our people, as a whole, believe in a spiritual world, with human beings who have souls and who have their origin and destiny in God," but "Russia, on the other hand, is run by communists who deny the existence of God, who believe in a material world

where human beings are without souls and without rights, except as government chooses to allow them." Dulles, "Our International Responsibilities," June 4, 1950, referenced in Inboden, *Religion and American Foreign Policy, 1945–1960*, 230. The Federal Council of Churches would be renamed the National Council of Churches in 1950.

23. In 1953, *Reader's Digest* wrote, "What President Eisenhower wants for America is a revival of religious faith that will produce a rededication to religious values and conduct. . . . He is determined to use his influence and his office to help make this period a spiritual turning point in America, and thereby to recover the strengths, the values, and the conduct which a vital faith produces in a people." Stanley High, "What the President Wants," *Reader's Digest*, April 1953, 2–4.

24. McCarthy, February 20, 1950, quoted in Ellwood, *1950*, 83.

25. J. Edgar Hoover, "Secularism, Breeder of Crime," speech delivered to Conference of Methodist Ministers, Evanston, IL, November 26, 1947, Office of Congressional and Public Affairs, FBI, quoted in Powers, *Not Without Honor*, 254; Thomas Aiello, "Constructing 'Godless Communism': Religion, Politics, and Popular Culture, 1954–1960," *Americana: The Journal of American Popular Culture* 4, no. 1 (Spring 2005).

26. Jacobs, *America's Miracle Man in Vietnam*, 77–84; Stephen J. Whitfield, *The Culture of the Cold War*, 2nd ed. (Baltimore: Johns Hopkins University Press, 1996), 96.

27. Inboden, *Religion and American Foreign Policy, 1945–1960*, 73.

28. Billy Graham, "Prepare to Meet Thy God," in *Revival in Our Time: The Story of the Billy Graham Evangelistic Campaigns* (Wheaton, IL: Van Kampen Press, 1950), 124, quoted in Martin, *A Prophet with Honor*, 115.

29. Donald Grey Barnhouse, editorial in *Eternity*, August 1952, p. 1, cited in Paul S. Boyer, *When Time Shall Be No More: Prophecy Belief in Modern American Culture* (Cambridge, MA: Belknap Press of Harvard University Press, 1992), 117–18. In my own historical analysis, I would argue apocalypticism was slightly less influential in explicitly shaping evangelicals, politics, and international engagement in contrast to Boyer as well as most recently by Matthew Avery Sutton, *American Apocalypse: A History of Modern Evangelicalism* (Cambridge, MA: Belknap Press of Harvard University Press, 2017).

30. Graham, "Satan's Religion," *American Mercury*, August 1954, 42, and "Our World in Chaos: The Cause and Cure," *American Mercury*, July 1956, 21, quoted in Aiello, "Constructing 'Godless Communism.' "

31. *The Red Plague*, directed by David Wisner (1957), 16 mm, WVI Central Records, quoted in Hamilton, "An Historical Study of Bob Pierce," 97.

32. Bob Pierce, "Too Late for America?," *Eternity*, May 1958.

33. Bob Pierce sermon, n.d., ca. 1956–57, WVI Central Records.

34. Quote comes from *Dead Men on Furlough*, directed by Dick Ross (1954), 16 mm; also see *This Gathering Storm*, directed by Dick Ross (1953), 16 mm; *38th Parallel, the Story of God's Deadline in Korea*, directed by Dick Ross (1950), 16 mm; all located in World Vision United States Archives, Federal Way, WA (hereafter WVUS Archives).

35. There has been a plethora of recent books investigating the ICL, which has been known by many names, including National Committee for Christian Leadership, National Leadership Council, Fellowship Foundation, the Fellowship, and the Family. Most of this research does little to explore the organization's history but focuses on its contemporary political and cultural influence. See Jeff Sharlet, *The Family: The Secret Fundamentalism at the*

Heart of American Power (New York: HarperCollins, 2008); D. Michael Lindsay, "Is the National Prayer Breakfast Surrounded by a 'Christian Mafia'? Religious Publicity and Secrecy Within the Corridors of Power," *Journal of the American Academy of Religion* 74, no. 2 (June 1, 2006): 390–419; D. Michael Lindsay, "Organizational Liminality and Interstitial Creativity: The Fellowship of Power," *Social Forces* 89, no. 1 (2010): 163–84. There has also been a revival of interest in Moral Re-Armament. See especially Daniel Sack, *Moral Re-Armament: The Reinventions of an American Religious Movement* (New York: Palgrave Macmillan, 2009).

36. Dunker, *Man of Vision*, 123; "L.A. Evangelist Tells About Pflimlin's Faith," *Los Angeles Times*, June 7, 1958, 14.

37. Letters between Dick Halverson (World Vision Board chair and later executive director of the Fellowship) and Abraham Vereide discuss the impact World Vision pastors conferences were having on ICL's hope for a "worldwide spiritual offensive." Abraham Vereide to Dick Halverson, September 26, 1956, and Dick Halverson to Abraham Vereide, October 4, 1956, Box 509, Collection 459, Records of the Fellowship Foundation. Archives of the Billy Graham Center, Wheaton, IL (hereafter Fellowship Records). While ICL was made up of evangelicals, Halverson wondered if it was evangelical enough. As an evangelical insider, he understood that ecumenical cooperation remained a barrier to many evangelicals. Kenneth Strachan, head of the conservative Latin American Mission, voiced his concerns for ICL's positions but found himself able to work alongside the organization on issues of anticommunism. Kenneth Strachan to Donald Gill, November 28, 1955, Folder 9, Box 105, Records of the Evangelical Fellowship of Mission Agencies, Archives of the Billy Graham Center, Wheaton, IL (hereafter cited as EFMA Records). ICL's own board discussed if Halverson himself was too evangelical for the organization at the same time Halverson questioned whether ICL was losing its past evangelical moorings (Folder 2, Box 509, Fellowship Records).

38. Inboden, *Religion and American Foreign Policy, 1945–1960*, 97–99.

39. Evangelicals also promoted these pieces in popular periodicals such as *Christianity Today*. See J. Edgar Hoover, "Communism: The Bitter Enemy of Religion," *Christianity Today*, June 22, 1959, 3–5; Walter S. Robertson, "Meeting Communism in the Far East," *Christianity Today*, April 13, 1959, 9–11; Fred Schwarz, "Can We Meet the Red Challenge?," *Christianity Today* April 13, 1959, 13–14.

40. John C. Broger, "'Liberty Militant,' a Condensation by ICL from Militant Liberty," 1955 ICL Annual Conference Folder 3, Box 551, Fellowship Records.

41. Fred Schwarz, *You Can Trust the Communists (to Be Communists)* (Englewood Cliffs, NJ: Prentice-Hall, 1960); Lisa McGirr, *Suburban Warriors: The Origins of the New American Right* (Princeton, NJ: Princeton University Press, 2001), 61; Powers, *Not Without Honor*, 294–95; Sarah Posner, "McCarthy, Born Again and Retooled for Our Time," *Religion Dispatches*, December 13, 2010, http://religiondispatches.org/mccarthy-born-again-and-retooled-for-our-time/.

42. Kevin M. Kruse, "Beyond the Southern Cross: The National Origins of the Religious Right," in *The Myth of Southern Exceptionalism*, ed. Matthew D. Lassiter and Joseph Crespino (New York: Oxford University Press, 2010), 290–91; McGirr, *Suburban Warriors*, 63. For the classic work tracking the "Old Christian Right," see Leo P. Ribuffo, *The Old Christian Right* (Philadelphia: Temple University Press, 1983).

43. Carl Henry, "Fragility of Freedom in the West," *Christianity Today*, October 15, 1956, 8–10, 17; Henry, "Where Do We Go from Here?," *Christianity Today*, November 12, 1956,

16–18; Henry, "The Christian Pagan West," *Christianity Today*, December 24, 1956, 3–5, 34; Henry, "America's Future: Can We Salvage the Republic?," *Christianity Today*, March 3, 1958, 3–7; Henry, "The Spirit of Foreign Policy," *Christianity Today*, April 29, 1957, 20–23.

44. Pierce, "The Greatest Danger," January 1958, WVI Central Records.

45. George Burnham, "World Vision Updates," *World Vision*, October–November 1957, 9.

46. Bob Pierce, "The Iron Curtain Is Raised," *World Vision*, August 1958, 5–6, 10, 15, 20–22; Pierce, "Message Given at Missionary Conference of American Soul Clinic"; Pierce, "Address to the NAE Convention," 1960, WVI Central Records. See also "Pasadena Evangelist Cited for Korean Work," *Los Angeles Times*, May 24, 1959, A5; "Koreans Honor World Vision Head, Dr. Pierce," *Los Angeles Times*, November 30, 1958.

47. Advertisement for *This Gathering Storm*, in *Youth for Christ*, September 1953, 70; and *Cry in the Night*, directed by William E. Brusseau (1958), 16 mm, WVI Central Records.

48. American studies scholar Christina Klein has advocated for a cultural integrationist outlook of Cold War ideology alongside political containment. The United States also saw its rise to global power less through a lens of white man's burden and more through assisting in modernization and development. See Christina Klein, *Cold War Orientalism: Asia in the Middlebrow Imagination, 1945–1961* (Berkeley: University of California Press, 2003), 5. Pierce demonstrates Klein's theory in the realm of evangelical missions and religious philanthropy.

49. Jacobs, *America's Miracle Man in Vietnam*, 95–102.

50. Michener quoted in Jacobs, *America's Miracle Man in Vietnam*, 89–90; Klein, *Cold War Orientalism*, 51.

51. American authors penned multiple biographies to introduce Asian leaders to American readers. See Robert Tarbell Oliver, *Syngman Rhee, the Man Behind the Myth* (New York: Dodd, Mead, 1954); Oliver, *Syngman Rhee and American Involvement in Korea, 1942–1960: A Personal Narrative* (Seoul: Panmun Book Co., 1978); Syngman Rhee, *An Asian Leader Speaks for Freedom* (New York: American-Asian Educational Exchange, 1958).

52. Demonstrating their loyalty to the Chiang Kai-sheks and their anticommunism impulses, midcentury American evangelicals continued to refer to Taiwan as Formosa or Nationalist China for several decades.

53. Pierce, "Address to NAE Convention," 1960; description of Rhee was by the U.S. ambassador to South Korea James Cromwell.

54. Pierce, *The Untold Korea Story*, 30.

55. Billy Graham quoted in Paul Rees, "The Remaining Life or the Removed Candlestick," *World Vision*, April 1960, 4.

56. Dick Ross, quoted in Hamilton, "An Historical Study of Bob Pierce," 72.

57. Hutchison, *Errand to the World*, 175; Rodger C. Bassham, *Mission Theology, 1948–1975: Years of Worldwide Creative Tension—Ecumenical, Evangelical, and Roman Catholic* (Pasadena, CA: William Carey Library, 1979), 21–50.

58. Joel A. Carpenter, "Propagating the Faith Once Delivered: The Fundamentalist Missionary Enterprise, 1920–1945," in Carpenter and Shenk, *Earthen Vessels*, 128–30; Joel Carpenter, *Missionary Innovation and Expansion* (New York: Garland, 1988); Harold Lindsell, "Faith Missions Since 1938," in *Frontiers of the Christian World Mission Since 1938: Essays in Honor of Kenneth Scott Latourette*, ed. Wilber C. Harr (New York: Harper & Brothers, 1962), 211–14.

59. Robert T. Coote, "The Uneven Growth of Conservative Evangelical Missions," *International Bulletin of Missionary Research* 6, no. 3 (1982): 118–23; Ralph W. Winter, *The 25 Unbelievable Years: 1945–1969* (Pasadena, CA: William Carey Library, 1970), 51–57; Mark Noll, *The New Shape of World Christianity: How American Experience Reflects Global Faith* (Downers Grove, IL: IVP Academic, 2009), 82–85; Joel Carpenter, "Appendix: The Evangelical Missionary Force in the 1930s," in Carpenter and Shenk, *Earthen Vessels*, 335–42.

60. Andrew Walls has demonstrated how the missions movement became shaped through the twentieth century not only by the number of U.S. missionaries but also by American over European technologies, optimism, and motivations. Andrew F. Walls, "The American Dimension in the History of the Missionary Movement," in Carpenter and Shenk, *Earthen Vessels*, 1–25.

61. Alan Whaites, "Pursuing Partnership: World Vision and the Ideology of Development—a Case Study," *Development in Practice* 9, no. 4 (1999): 412.

62. Gehman, *Let My Heart Be Broken*, 184; Lee Grant, "He Only Wants to Save the World," *Los Angeles Times*, January 22, 1975, G6.

63. Bob Pierce, Quoted from Presentation at YFC Winona Lake Mission Conference, *Youth for Christ*, September 1949, 17.

64. Soong-Chan Rah and Gary VanderPol, *Return to Justice: Six Movements That Reignited Our Contemporary Evangelical Conscience* (Grand Rapids, MI: Brazos Press, 2016), 52–53.

65. Bob Pierce, "Sermon Given in Orchestra Hall," Chicago, November 5, 1954, WVI Central Records.

66. Ibid.

67. See the films *38th Parallel* (1950) and *The Flame*, directed by Dick Ross (1952), 16 mm, WVUS Archives; Hamilton, "An Historical Study of Bob Pierce," 64.

68. "Stirred Graham Stirs Orient," *Youth for Christ*, February 1953, 28; Martin, *A Prophet with Honor*, 150.

69. Pierce, "Message Given at Missionary Conference of American Soul Clinic"; see also Harold Lindsell, "Today's Missionary—A New Breed of Man," *World Vision*, March 1964, 6.

70. Dunker, *Man of Vision*, 137, 155.

71. "World Vision Appeal Letter," December 1956, WVI Central Records.

72. Bob Pierce sermon, n.d., ca. 1956–57, WVI Central Records; Dunker, *Man of Vision*; Gary F. VanderPol, "The Least of These: American Evangelical Parachurch Missions to the Poor, 1947–2005" (ThD diss., Boston University School of Theology, 2010), 42; Hamilton, "An Historical Study of Bob Pierce," 121.

Chapter 3

1. Rohrer, *Open Arms*, 77; Gehman, *Let My Heart Be Broken*, 176.

2. Booth quoted in Rohrer, *Open Arms*, 77.

3. Grant Wacker, "The Waning of the Missionary Impulse: The Case of Pearl S. Buck," in *Foreign Missionary Enterprise at Home*, ed. Daniel H. Bays and Grant Wacker (Tuscaloosa: University of Alabama Press, 2003), 191–205; Hollinger, *Protestants Abroad*, 33–47.

4. From 1955 to 1961, Tom Dooley's name consistently ranked among the most admired Americans as he introduced Americans to Vietnam by promoting Catholic Vietnamese as persecuted refugees and martyrs. World Vision had a few short-term medical teams that worked alongside Dooley for a brief time with his MEDICO nonprofit. For a critical look at

the reception of Dooley's message by Americans, see Jacobs, *America's Miracle Man in Vietnam*, 126–67. For a sample of the popular biographies and autobiographies, see Agnes W. Dooley, *Promises to Keep: The Life of Doctor Thomas A. Dooley* (New York: New American Library, 1964); Thomas A. Dooley, *The Edge of Tomorrow* (New York: Farrar, Straus and Cudahy, 1958); Thomas A. Dooley, *The Night They Burned the Mountain* (New York: Farrar, Straus and Cudahy, 1960); Thomas A. Dooley, *Before I Sleep* (New York: Signet Book, 1961).

5. Roy Robertson, *Developing a Heart for Mission: Five Missionary Heroes* (Singapore: NavMedia, 2002), 156–57; "Bob Pierce Interviewing Billy Graham," *Haven of Rest* radio program, February 28, 1956, transcription in Folder 5, Box 6, Collection 74, Records of Billy Graham Ephemera, Archives of the Billy Graham Center, Wheaton, IL; George Burnham, *To the Far Corners: With Billy Graham in Asia* (Westwood, NJ: Revell, 1956).

6. "Seoul Crusade," *World Vision*, August–September 1957, 7; "Why We Are Going to Osaka for Next Crusade," *World Vision*, February 1959, 3; "Pierce Preaching in Osaka Crusade," *World Vision*, July 1959.

7. "World Vision News," Summer 1955, 4.3, Folder 11, Box 7, Collection 5, Papers of Vernon William Patterson, Archives of the Billy Graham Center, Wheaton, IL (hereafter cited as Patterson Records).

8. "Operation Now: 1958 World Vision Pastors' Conferences," Patterson Records; Paul Rees, "Purpose of World Vision's Pastors' Conferences," *World Vision*, January 1960, 4.

9. "World Vision News," Summer 1955. Patterson Records. In promoting 1955 pastors' conferences in Indonesia, Pierce claimed, "Indo-China is a powder keg with the Communists ready to take over the entire country. Six months from now the pastors there may be martyrs just as the Koreans became martyrs a few years ago. Pray that God will use these days to His glory."

10. Ellsworth Culver, "A World-wide Impact for Christ," *World Vision*, April 1958, 11; George Burnham, "Special Report from Far East," *World Vision*, October–November 1957, 3–4.

11. Burnham, "Special Report from Far East," 3–4; also see Carl F. H. Henry, *Confessions of a Theologian: An Autobiography* (Waco, TX: Word Books, 1986), 197.

12. Burnham, "Special Report from Far East," 4; Culver, "A World-wide Impact for Christ," 4; J. Christy Wilson quoted in World Vision Annual Report, 1956, WVI Central Records.

13. "Korea: Shining Star for Christianity," *United Evangelical Action*, February 1, 1954, 3.

14. Bob Pierce sermon, n.d., ca. 1956–57, WVI Central Records.

15. Brad Watson, "Origins of Child Sponsorship: Save the Children the 1920s," in *Child Sponsorship: Exploring Pathways to a Brighter Future*, ed. Matthew Clarke and Brad Watson (Basingstoke: Palgrave Macmillan, 2014), 18–40; Hillary Kaell, "How Asking and Giving Beget Distrust in Christian Child Sponsorship," in *The Request and the Gift in Religious and Humanitarian Endeavors*, ed. Frederick Klaits (New York: Palgrave Macmillan, 2017), 93–116.

16. A "private voluntary organization" (PVO) is one of the most accepted terms used for a voluntary agency (religious or secular) engaged in overseas relief and development. Edmund Janss and Christian Children's Fund, *Yankee Si: The Story of Dr. J. Calvitt Clarke and His 36,000 Children* (New York: Morrow, 1961); Larry Tise, *A Book About Children: The World of Christian Children's Fund, 1938–1991* (Falls Church, VA: Hartland Pub., 1993).

17. "How Bob Pierce Got His First Orphan."

18. "Missionary Disbursements, 1950–59," WVI Central Records; "WVI Factbook" (1982), WVI Central Records. Child sponsorship continues to make up the largest source of World Vision's annual income.

19. Ken Anderson, "The Story Behind Christian Films," *Youth for Christ*, January 1954, 20–22. The only major studies of Christian films remain Terry Lindvall, *Sanctuary Cinema: Origins of the Christian Film Industry* (New York: New York University Press, 2007); Terry Lindvall and Andrew Quicke, *Celluloid Sermons: The Emergence of the Christian Film Industry, 1930–1986* (New York: New York University Press, 2011).

20. "Interview Between Robert Pierce and Dick Ross."

21. Advertisement for *This Gathering Storm* (1953), referenced in Hamilton, "An Historical Study of Bob Pierce," 74.

22. Anderson, "The Story Behind Christian Films," 22; "Interview Between Lee Bernard and Bob Pierce," *World Vision*, June 1957, 4.

23. Larry Ward would become Pierce's right-hand man and ghostwriter for the rest of his tenure. He would later leave World Vision to establish Food for the Hungry. Rohrer, *Open Arms*, 77.

24. "Interview Between Robert Pierce and Dick Ross."

25. Hamilton, "An Historical Study of Bob Pierce," 32; Graham, *Just as I Am*, 174, 294.

26. "Introduction to Holt," accessed September 29, 2017, http://www.holtinternational .org/historical.shtml.

27. Rohrer, *Open Arms*, 69–70; Greg MacGregor, "Oregonian Takes 8 Seoul Orphans," *New York Times*, October 2, 1955, 124; Malcolm Bauer, "Korean Orphans Find U.S. Homes," *Christian Science Monitor*, April 9, 1956, 3; "Rancher Brings 89 More Korean Orphans to U.S.," *Washington Post and Times Herald*, December 18, 1956, A1.

28. Franklin Graham, *Rebel with a Cause* (Nashville, TN: Thomas Nelson, 1995), 141.

29. Herbert Taylor was president of Club Aluminum and funded a number of evangelical agencies, from YFC to Campus Crusade. J. Howard Pew initially served as the financial bank-roller for *Christianity Today*. Sarah Ruth Hammond, *God's Businessmen: Entrepreneurial Evangelicals in Depression and War*, ed. Darren Dochuk (Chicago: University of Chicago Press, 2017).

30. Gehman, *Let My Heart Be Broken*, 179.

31. McCleary, *Global Compassion*, 47–53; J. Bruce Nichols, *The Uneasy Alliance: Religion, Refugee Work, and U.S. Foreign Policy* (New York: Oxford University Press, 1988), 10–11; Rist, *The History of Development*, 71–75.

32. Several significant relief agencies were founded earlier in response to conditions after World War I. They included the American Friends Service Committee (1917) and the Mennonite Central Committee (1920)

33. CARE was the only secular international PVO among the eight largest between 1950 and 1960. While CARE is now a secular agency, it was originally a coalition of religious and secular organizations such as Church World Service, American Friends Service Committee, American Jewish Joint Distribution Committee, and International Rescue and Relief Committee. The religious agencies pulled out in the 1950s because they felt CARE's objectives had become too closely aligned with U.S. politics and were infringing on their own individual agencies' work. McCleary, *Global Compassion*, 25–28; Wallace J. Campbell, *The History of CARE: A Personal Account* (New York: Praeger, 1990), 25–28.

34. For particular organizational histories from this period, see Eileen Egan, *Catholic Relief Services: The Beginning Years* (New York: Catholic Relief Services, 1988); Ronald Stenning, *Church World Service: Fifty Years of Help and Hope* (New York: Friendship Press, 1996). See also Joshua H. Mather, "Citizens of Compassion: Relief, Development, and State-Private Cooperation in U.S. Foreign Relations, 1939–1973" (PhD diss., St. Louis University, 2015).

35. Axel R. Schäfer, "Evangelical Global Engagement and the American State After World War II," *Journal of American Studies* 51, no. 4 (November 2017): 1069–94.

36. In an ad in the March 15, 1957, issue of *United Evangelical Action*, the periodical of the NAE, World Relief articulated its identity against other mainstream agencies even more clearly:

> Why does NAE have its own relief agency—NAE relief is different—it is Christian relief. With every gift of food and clothing distributed overseas by reliable established evangelical Christians, goes a Gospel message in printed from. It is not enough for Christians to relieve the physical suffering of men and women and children, while their souls go to hell. On the other hand, evangelicals cannot preach Christ to people whose stomachs are empty and whose bodies are weak from exposure to cold when Christians have it within their power to feed and clothe them. Through the food, clothing and Gospel testimony distributed by NAE's World Relief Commission every year, thousands and thousands of people find relief from acute physical suffering and spiritual starvation.

37. World Relief's income rose from $52,000 in 1955 to $114,000 (not including gifts in kind [GIK]) in 1960, according to the 1961 NAE Annual Report, Folder 17, Box 4, Collection 165, EFMA Records.

38. Missionaries also praised Pierce for the attention he showed them overseas. He not only funded needs for the mission, but he would also donate funds to make missionary families' lives easier: tuition for school, new clothes, radios, transportation, even a night at a nice restaurant.

39. IFMA's records contain correspondence between World Vision executive director Frank Phillips and IFMA leadership detailing their reason for declining World Vision's membership application. The IFMA had formally denied World Vision's application for membership by 1957. Officially, the IFMA claimed World Vision was a service rather than a missionary-sending organization, but additional communications indicate that World Vision's fund-raising, social ministries, and diverse cooperation across denominations also affected its decision. Folders 3–4, Box 70, Collection 352, Records of the Interdenominational Foreign Mission Association, Archives of the Billy Graham Center, Wheaton, IL (hereafter IFMA Records).

40. Graham and Lockerbie, *Bob Pierce*, 142.

41. The EFMA Mission Executives Retreats began in 1953; World Vision first attended in 1959 (Folder 2, Box 18, Collection 165, EFMA Records). World Vision's records note its funding of Clyde Taylor's EFMA travel as well as other needs ("Missionary Disbursements, 1950–59").

42. Harold Lindsell, *Missionary Principles and Practice* (Old Tappan, NJ: Fleming H. Revell, 1955), 18.

43. Mission Executives Retreat, 1953, Folder 22, Box 3, EFMA Records.

44. Arthur Glasser, "Communism—A Missionary Problem," 1955 EFMA Convention, Folder 13, Box 2, Collection 192, Papers of Harold Lindsell, Archives of the Billy Graham Center, Wheaton, IL (hereafter cited as Lindsell Papers); Arthur Glasser, "An Evangelical Approach to Communism," 1959 Mission Executives Retreat, Folder 9, Box 4, EFMA Records.

45. R. Kenneth Strachan, "New Emphasis in Missions," address to Mission Executives Retreat, 1954, Folder 23, Box 3, EFMA Records; Juan M. Isais, "How Nationals Feel About Missions," March 17, 1958, Folder 12, Box 2, EFMA Records.

46. IMC officially merged with WCC in 1961, but the impending merger was announced years earlier.

47. "Conferences Prepare Far East Pastors," *Christianity Today*, October 8, 1957, 30–31. Both IFMA and EFMA executives expressed some reservations about Pierce's methods; for examples of conservative missions' criticisms of World Vision, see Jack Percy to S. L. Boehmer, April 6, 1961, Folder 3, Box 70, IFMA Records.

48. Pierce, "Message Given at Missionary Conference of American Soul Clinic," October 12, 1952; see also Lindsell, "Today's Missionary,"6.

49. World Vision sponsored Gladys Aylward's tour of American and Canada from April 26–December 16, 1959, and later an Australian tour. Pierce invested heavily in her ministry financially and through publicity. Rohrer, *Open Arms*, 83.

50. Bob Pierce, "Cost of Being a Missionary," World Vision radio broadcast, September 27, 1959, WVI Central Records.

51. Bob Pierce, "Missionary Education in the Sunday School," *World Vision*, November 1958, 6; Rah and VanderPol, *Return to Justice*, 48.

52. Pierce, "Message Given at Missionary Conference of American Soul Clinic," October 12, 1952.

53. William J. Lederer and Eugene Burdick, *The Ugly American* (New York: Norton, 1958); Clive Christie, *"The Quiet American" and "The Ugly American": Western Literary Perspectives on Indo-China in a Decade of Transition, 1950–1960*, Occasional Paper no. 10 (Canterbury: University of Kent at Canterbury, Centre of South-East Asian Studies, 1989), 38.

54. Pierce argued that since the United States benefited from missionaries, missionaries should receive the same privileges and prestige that aid and military workers received, such as no income tax, reduced shipping and postage rates, and admittance to the commissary. Bob Pierce, "We Need More 'Ugly' Americans," *Washington Post and Times Herald*, April 12, 1959; Carl Henry, "A Footnote to the Ugly American," *Christianity Today*, November 9, 1959, 21–22; Paul Phealn, "A Call for Christian Zeal," *Second New York World-Telegram*, March 28, 1959.

55. World Vision 1956 Pictorial, LAM Records; World Vision 1961 Pictorial, WVI Central Records.

56. Graham and Lockerbie, *Bob Pierce*, 18. For Pierce's harsh words toward Billy Graham and colleagues within the BGEA at the end of his life, see "Interview Between Robert Pierce and Dick Ross."

57. *Cry in the Night*, 1958, WVI Central Records.

58. George Burnham, "Choice Seat on Aisle at NAE Meet," *World Vision*, May 1959, 10.

59. Rohrer, *Open Arms*, 77–78.

60. "President's Report," World Vision Board of Directors' Meeting, October 7, 1958, WVI Central Records.

61. World Vision Board of Directors' Meeting, August 18, 1959, WVI Central Records; "Missionary Disbursements, 1950–59."

62. "Interview Between Robert Pierce and Dick Ross."

63. Dunker, *Man of Vision*, 144–45.

64. The initial order of *Let My Heart Be Broken* was 15,000 copies. World Vision recruited Gehman to write the book and gave him $10,000 for expenses. In exchange, Gehman would give 20 percent of profits to World Vision. See World Vision Board of Directors' Meeting, November 17–18, 1958, WVI Central Records. At the end of *Let My Heart Be Broken*, Gehman acknowledges his own Christian conversion as the result of the trip (243–45), in contrast to his initially articulated journalistic objectivity and religious skepticism (4).

Chapter 4

1. "World Vision Financial Reports, 1960–1970," WVI Central Records; Ken Waters, "How World Vision Rose from Obscurity to Prominence: Television Fundraising, 1972–1982," *American Journalism* 15, no. 4 (1998): 69.

2. Nathan Hatch with Michael S. Hamilton, "Epilogue: Take the Measure of the Evangelical Resurgence, 1942–92," in *Reckoning with the Past*, ed. D. G. Hart (Grand Rapids, MI: Baker Books, 1995), 397.

3. John Carter, "A Sociological Analysis of *Christianity Today* and Society," Folder 39, Box 8, Collection 8, Records of Christianity Today International, Archives of the Billy Graham Center, Wheaton, IL (hereafter cited as CTI Records).

4. In 1958, *Christianity Today*'s own poll found Protestant ministers classified themselves as: 35 percent fundamentalist; 39 percent conservative; 12 percent neo-orthodox; 14 percent liberal. See "What Protestant Ministers Believe," *Christianity Today*, March 31, 1958, 30.

5. Harold J. Ockenga, "Resurgent Evangelical Leadership," *Christianity Today*, October 10, 1960, 11–14; "An Evangelical Protestant Strategy for the Late 1960s," Outline Document, Folder 1, Box 15, CTI Records.

6. Richard Quebedeaux coined the term "establishment evangelicals" in the 1970s to identity one strand of an increasingly diverse American evangelicalism. Richard Quebedeaux, *The Young Evangelicals: Revolution in Orthodoxy* (New York: Harper and Row, 1974), 50–51. See also James Alden Hedstrom, "Evangelical Program in the United States, 1945–1980: The Morphology of Establishment, Progressive, and Radical Platforms" (PhD diss., Vanderbilt University, 1982), 8, 107.

7. George Kennan, *Foreign Policy and Christian Conscience* (Philadelphia: Peace Education Program American Friends Service Committee, 1959), 6.

8. Graham preached these words at the 1960 NAE Convention; they were reprinted in *United Evangelical Action*, June 1960, 10.

9. While Schwarz managed to avoid the more sensationalist rhetoric of the Far Right that alienated mainstream evangelicals, during the early 1960s, the Christian Far Right also regained a level of popular support. Fundamentalists Carl McIntire and Billy James Hargis saw contributions skyrocket in the early 1960s as they partnered with other fringes of the Far Right such as the John Birch Society and Young Americans for Freedom. Schwarz saw his CACC contributions double every year between 1957 and 1960 and quadruple in 1961. Daniel K. Williams, *God's Own Party: The Making of the Christian Right* (Oxford: Oxford University Press, 2010), 59–61; Kruse, "Beyond the Southern Cross," 291; *World Vision*, October 1961, 3.

10. The 1960 NAE Convention launched the Emergency Christian Mobilization program to stop the spread of communism at home and abroad. "NAE Reaffirms Strong Anti-Communist Stand," *Christianity Today*, May 9, 1960, 30; Harold Ockenga, "The Communist Issue Today," *Christianity Today*, May 2, 1961, 9–12; "Better Red Than Dead?," *Christianity Today*, April 27, 1962, 47.

11. J. Edgar Hoover, "Communism: The Bitter Enemy of Religion," *Christianity Today*, June 22, 1959, 3–5; Hoover, "The Communist Menace: Red Goals and Christian Ideals," *Christianity Today*, October 10, 1960, 3–5; Hoover, "Soviet Rule or Christian Renewal?," *Christianity Today*, November 7, 1960, 8–11.

12. Evangelicals disagreed on a response to the Supreme Court cases. Some supported legislative measures amending the Constitution to allow for prayer in schools. Others insisted that the proper place for prayer and Bible reading remained the home and the church. All agreed, however, that the cases pointed to the growing secularization of government, education, and public life. See debates in Mark G. Toulouse, "*Christianity Today* and American Public Life: A Case Study," *Journal of Church and State* 35, no. 2 (1993): 241–84.

13. Billy Graham, "The Event of the Year," *Christianity Today*, January 1, 1965, 45.

14. "Lawlessness: A Bad Sign," *Christianity Today*, April 29, 1966, 29–30. *Christianity Today* argued that the solution for civil rights would be gained through "infusing both cultures [white and black] with the mind and spirit of Jesus Christ." See editorials "The White Conscience and the Negro Vote," *Christianity Today*, March 28, 1960, 22; "Civil Rights Legislation," *Christianity Today*, November 22, 1963, 32–33; "Civil Rights and Christian Concern," *Christianity Today*, May 8, 1964, 28–29.

15. Evangelicals continually echoed the refrain calling America back to its Christian heritage. "Low Tide in the West," *Christianity Today*, December 24, 1956, 20–24; William K. Harrison, "Is America's Spiritual Vigor Waning?," *Christianity Today*, January 20, 1958, 24–25; "The American Malaise," *Christianity Today*, June 20, 1960, 20–21; Edward L. R. Elson, "Has America Lapsed into a 'Post-Protestant' Era?," *Christianity Today*, June 5, 1961, 3–5; "Can We Weather the Storm?," *Christianity Today*, November 23, 1962, 26–27; "National Need—Righteousness," *Christianity Today*, December 6, 1963, 26–27; "Light Out of Darkness," *Christianity Today*, December 20, 1963, 20–21; "Freedom and Morality," *Christianity Today*, January 17, 1964, 26–27.

16. Grassroots evangelicals showed less interest in the councils and statements of the ecumenical movement. It was up to the establishment leaders to persuade the broad conservative Christian constituency that these issues mattered.

17. From 1963 to 1968, *Christianity Today* carried at least fourteen articles and editorials specifically castigating ecumenical mixing of church and politics (Hollinger, *Individualism and Social Ethics*, 138).

18. Norval Hadley, "Christian Liberty," *World Vision*, July 1964, 11, 54–55.

19. See Sherwood Eliot Wirt, "The World Mission Situation," *Christianity Today*, August 1, 1960, 6–7; Coote, "The Uneven Growth of Conservative Evangelical Missions," 120. While evangelicals affiliated with the IFMA/EFMA grew more slowly through the 1960s, the greatest growth began to occur in the late 1960s by unaffiliated evangelicals, specifically the Wycliffe Bible Translators and the Southern Baptist Convention.

20. Howard E. Kershner, "Church and Social Problems," *Christianity Today*, March 4, 1966, 34–35.

21. F. Dale Bruner, "A New Strategy: Statesmanship in Christian Missions," *Christianity Today*, August 1, 1960, 3; see also Eric S. Fife and Arthur F. Glasser, *Missions in Crisis: Rethinking Missionary Strategy* (Chicago: InterVarsity Press, 1961).

22. C. Ralston Smith, "Billy Graham's Evangelistic Thrust: The Crusaders and Changing Times," *Christianity Today*, November 10, 1961, 3.

23. Wirt, "The World Mission Situation," 6.

24. Ralph E. Dodge, *The Unpopular Missionary* (Westwood, NJ: F. H. Revell, 1964); James A. Scherer, *Missionary, Go Home!* (Englewood Cliffs, NJ: Prentice-Hall, 1964). *Christianity Today* actually reviewed both books positively. See P. C. Moore, review of *Missionary Go Home*, by James A. Scherer, *Christianity Today*, May 8, 1964, 36; Henry Cornell Goerner, review of *The Unpopular Missionary*, by Ralph E. Dodge, *Christianity Today*, July 8, 1964, 26.

25. "Congo: 2000 Protestant Missionaries Imperiled," *Christianity Today*, August 1, 1960; "Terror in the Congo," *Christianity Today*, February 14, 1964, 36; "Martyrdom in the Congo," *Christianity Today*, December 18, 1964, 24–25; McAlister, *The Kingdom of God Has No Borders*.

26. "Africa: The Congo Massacre," *Time*, December 4, 1964, http://www.time.com/time/magazine/article/0,9171,830872,00.html; "Congo Massacre," *Life*, December 4, 1964, 32–46, http://books.google.be/books?id = olEEAAAAMBAJ&printsec = frontcover&hl = en& source = gbs_atb#v = onepage&q&f = false; "Dr. Paul Carlson: A Life at Stake," *Christianity Today*, December 4, 1964, 46–47; McAlister, *The Kingdom of God Has No Borders*.

27. Paul Rees, "Publicity Pluses and Minuses," *World Vision*, February 1965, 1; L. Arden Amquist, "Carlson of Congo," *World Vision*, February 1965, 22–23; also see "Unfinished Task of the Congolese Churches," *Christianity Today*, December 18, 1964, 25–26.

28. World Vision ad for Tokyo Crusade, *Christianity Today*, February 27, 1961, 36.

29. Larry Ward, World Vision radio program, June 11, 1961, broadcast live from Tokyo, Japan, WVI Central Records; Rohrer, *Open Arms*, 168.

30. Rohrer, *Open Arms*, 166–67; "Crusade in Tokyo: Smoke of Battle Still Hangs over Tokyo, but Light of God Shines Through," *Christianity Today*, June 5, 1961, 27.

31. "Southland Evangelist to Open Tokyo Crusade," *Los Angeles Times*, May 6, 1961, 14. The crusade was sponsored by the National Christian Council and Evangelical Federation. While not representing all of Japanese Protestants, this was a large majority of the Christian population, claiming 740 churches from forty-one denominations. Bob Pierce, "Tokyo Crusade," World Vision radio broadcast, May 14, 1961, WVI Central Records.

32. While the ecumenical movement advocated that greater church unity would offer a more persuasive Christian message, evangelicals felt it both compromised Christian mission and also targeted evangelical-leaning church unions. Sarah E. Johnson, "Almost Certainly Called: Images of Protestant Missionaries in American Culture, 1945–2000" (PhD diss., Duke University, 2007), 35–36. The divergence also demonstrated the different ecclesiological structures between mainline institutions and evangelical parachurch groups.

33. Conservative missionary societies like the Latin American Mission and Overseas Missionary Society (formerly the China Inland Mission) successfully incorporated indigenous leadership and shared their story to guide other evangelical missions in the process. Arthur Glasser, "The 'New' Overseas Missionary Fellowship," and Horace Fenton of Latin American Mission, "Discussion of the Use of Nationals Within the Framework of the Mission," addresses presented at the 1965 Mission Executive Retreat (the theme of which was the "Development of International and Interracial Missions"), Folder 4, Box 18, EFMA Records.

34. R. S. Nicholson Jr. (chair of World Vision's planning committee) to Clyde Taylor, March 23, 1961; and "Comments on the Tokyo Christian Crusade Appraisal," *Japan Harvest* (Summer 1961); both in Folder 5, Box 105, EFMA Records.

35. Milton Baker to Clyde Taylor, August 15, 1961; Milton Baker and Clyde Taylor to Bob Pierce," November 1, 1961; Bob Pierce to Clyde Taylor, EFMA, December 6, 1961; all in Folder 12, Box 4, EFMA Records. The more conservative IFMA went even further attempting to dissuade donors from supporting World Vision by attacking Pierce for supporting a liberal Presbyterian missionary's orphanage that it believed could prevent children from any opportunity to hear the gospel. Jack Percy to S. L. Boehmer, April 6, 1961, Folder 3, Box 70, Collection 352, IFMA Records.

36. "Pierce Address," 1962 NAE Convention, Denver, CO, April 12, 1962, Folder 16, Box 5, EFMA Records.

37. Paul Rees, "Where We Stand," *World Vision*, September 1964, 3.

38. Ward reported over 22,000 people attended just on the last day with thousands more turned away. "Tokyo Crusade," *Christianity Today*, June 19, 1961, 25, 30; "Report of Crusade in Tokyo," *World Vision*, July 1961, 3–6; "Pierce Calls Crusade, 'Biggest Battle of My Life,'" *World Vision*, June 1961, 3.

39. "Tokyo Crusade," *Christianity Today*, June 19, 1961, 25, 30.

40. Carl Henry, "Step up the Evangelical Thrust," *Christianity Today*, October 13, 1961, 33.

41. Robin Klay, John Lunn, and Michael S. Hamilton, "American Evangelicalism and the National Economy, 1870–1997," in Eskridge and Noll, *More Money, More Ministry*, 36.

42. World Vision Annual Report, 1964, WVI Central Records.

43. Bob Pierce, "Tokyo Crusade," World Vision radio broadcast, May 14, 1961, WVI Central Records.

44. "Vacation with a Purpose," brochure, WVI Central Records.

45. "Orphans Sing Their Thanks," *Christian Science Monitor*, November 16, 1961, 6; World Vision ad in *Christianity Today*, November 23, 1962, 23; Helen Kim, "Transpacific Piety and Politics: Cold War South Korea and the Rise of Modern American Evangelicalism" (PhD diss., Harvard University, 2017).

46. "Interview Between Robert Pierce and Dick Ross," January 7, 1978.

47. The choir toured in 1961, 1962, 1963, 1965, and 1968. In 1963, their itinerary included twelve countries before headlining sixty concerts in the United States (3,500 came to hear them in Carnegie Hall on December 6). Venues included churches, civic auditoriums, and even a mosque. See *World Vision*, June 1963, 5; "34 Orphans from Korea to Sing Here for Suppers of Other Waifs," *Washington Post, Times Herald*, March 6, 1963, A15; "Korean Orphans Win City's Heart," *Los Angeles Times*, October 25, 1961, 3.

48. Franklin Graham, *Rebel with a Cause*, 140–41; one of Pierce's maxims was "faith isn't required as long as you set your goal only as high as the most intelligent, most informed, and expert human efforts can reach" (140).

49. Engstrom was a layman. He had been managing editor for Zondervan's *Christian Digest* before joining Youth for Christ. For more information on Engstrom, see Ted Engstrom, *Reflections on a Pilgrimage: Six Decades of Service* (Sister, OR: Loyal, 1999); Bob Owen, *Ted Engstrom: Man with a Vision* (Wheaton, IL: Tyndale House, 1984).

50. Engstrom, *Reflections on a Pilgrimage*, 85.

51. Ibid., 83; World Vision Board of Directors' Meetings, April 22 and September 22, 1964, WVI Central Records; Engstrom, "Monthly Memo," *World Vision*, March 1964.

52. Gordon MacDonald et al., "When the Ministerial Family Caves In," *Leadership Journal* 4, no. 2 (Spring 1983): 97–113; "Imperfect Instrument," *Christianity Today*, March 2005, 56.

53. Rohrer, *Open Arms*, 86.

54. Evon Hedley, telephone interview with author, April 20, 2011; see "$25,000 Gift from Lilly Endowment to Build New International Center," *World Vision*, March 1965.

55. Ted Engstrom, *The Making of a Christian Leader: How to Develop Management and Human Relations Skills* (Grand Rapids, MI: Zondervan, 1976); Ted Engstrom, *The Art of Management for Christian Leaders* (Waco, TX: Word Books, 1976); Ted Engstrom, *The Pursuit of Excellence* (Grand Rapids, MI: Zondervan, 1982).

56. CCF was also undergoing greater professionalization and financial accountability as it fought against the unilateral control of its charismatic founder (Tise, *A Book About Children*, 61–71).

57. Swanson died in 1965, soon after the organization was renamed Compassion Incorporated (Rah and Gary VanderPol, *Return to Justice*, 42).

58. Donald A. McGavran, *Church Growth and Christian Mission* (New York: Harper and Row, 1965); Arthur Glasser, "The Evolution of Evangelical Mission Theology Since World War II," *International Bulletin of Missionary Research* 9 (January 1985): 10; Bassham, *Mission Theology*, 188–94.

59. Edward R. Dayton, "Computerize Evangelism," *World Vision*, March 1966, 4–5.

60. World Vision adopted the program evaluation and review technique (PERT) systems approach from NASA in order to track world evangelization. PERT had originally been developed by Apollo space program manager Ed Lindaman to assist missile development during the Cold War; it had then been applied to multiple complex management projects in both the government and private sectors.

61. "World Vision Launches New Program Aimed at Global Evangelism," *World Vision Scope*, October 1967, 6–7; "What MARC Is and Is Not," pamphlet, 1966, Folder 1, Box 74, EFMA Records.

62. MARC's directory of "unreached peoples" became a direct precursor to David Barrett's *World Christian Encyclopedia* (David B. Barrett, George Thomas Kurian, and Todd M. Johnson, *World Christian Encyclopedia: A Comparative Survey of Churches and Religions in the Modern World* [Oxford: Oxford University Press, 2001]). See Rohrer, *Open Arms*, 112; Dayton, "Computerize Evangelism," 4–5; David Lundquist, "Missions Need R and D," *World Vision*, October 1966, 18–19; Edward R. Dayton, "Research, a Key to Renewal," *Journal of the American Scientific Affiliation* 21 (March 1969): 15–17.

63. MARC, *Mission Handbook: North American Protestant Ministries Overseas*, 10th ed. (Monrovia, CA: MARC, 1973). MARC took over publication of the *Directory of Mission Agencies* from the Mission Research Library, eventually handing over production of the *Mission Handbook* to the Billy Graham Center at Wheaton College in 2000.

64. Ed Dayton and Ted Engstrom offered PERT management training for many mission organizations as well as publishing the free monthly *Christian Leadership Newsletter* (WVI Central Records).

65. Paul Rees, "Support Disciplined Planning," *World Vision*, May 1966, 3.

66. Pierce, "They Belong Together . . . Communication with Imagination," *World Vision,* March 1966, 6–7.

67. Editorial, "From Mission to Missions," *Christianity Today,* August 1, 1960, 20–21; Wirt, "The World Mission Situation," 6.

68. Raymond B. Buker Sr., "Where Are We Going?," address presented at the 1964 Mission Executive Retreat, Folder 4, Box 18, EFMA Records; Charles Edward Van Engen, "A Broadening Vision: Forty Years of Evangelical Theology of Mission, 1946–1986," in Carpenter and Shenk, *Earthen Vessels,* 213.

69. Billy Graham employed the term "evangelical ecumenicity" to describe attempts at a common evangelical language.

70. Harold Lindsell, "Precedent-Setting in Missions Strategy," *Christianity Today,* April 29, 1966, 43.

71. Harold Lindsell, *The Church's Worldwide Mission: An Analysis of the Current State of Evangelical Missions and a Strategy for Future Activity* (Waco, TX: Word books, 1966); Don Gill, "They Played It Safe in Wheaton," *World Vision,* June 1966, 31; also see Efiong S. Utuk, "From Wheaton to Lausanne: The Road to Modification of Contemporary Evangelical Mission Theology," *Missiology* 14 (1986): 218.

72. C. René Padilla, "How Evangelicals Endorsed Social Responsibility, 1966–1983," *Transformation,* July/September 1985, 28; Utuk, "From Wheaton to Lausanne," 210.

73. Billy Graham, "Opening Greetings" and "Why the Berlin Congress," in *One Race, One Gospel, One Task: World Congress on Evangelism, Berlin, 1966,* ed. Carl F. H. Henry and W. Stanley Mooneyham (Minneapolis, MN: World Wide Publications, 1967), 8, 22; "Good News for a World in Need," *Christianity Today,* October 4, 1966, 34.

74. While the Congress made little official space for addressing the relationship of evangelism and social concern, evangelical commentary after the congress regretted that more attention was not paid to this topic. Notably, the main official exception to this lack of social concern was the address by World Vision vice president Paul Rees. He contended that there were close ties between the two with racial prejudice in the United States and abroad serving as his chief example. See Rees, "Evangelism and Social Concern," in Henry and Mooneyham, *One Race, One Gospel, One Task,* 307–8; and Uta A. Balbier, "The World Congress on Evangelism 1966 in Berlin: US Evangelicalism, Cultural Dominance, and Global Challenges," *Journal of American Studies* 51, no. 4 (November 2017): 1171–96.

75. Horace Fenton, "Social Implications of the Gospel," address presented at the 1962 Mission Executive Retreat, Folder 3, Box 18, EFMA Records; C. Peter Wagner, "Evangelism and Social Action in Latin America," *Christianity Today,* January 7, 1965, 10–12; Wagner's reflections on evangelism and social action, in *World Vision,* June 1965, 26.

76. Articles debating the balance of evangelism/social concern dominated evangelical periodicals for several years. For example, see Willard A. Scofield, "What Is the Missionary's Message?," *Christianity Today,* November 9, 1964, 16–17; Harold Lindsell, "Who Are the Evangelicals?," *Christianity Today,* June 18, 1965, 3–5; L. Nelson Bell, "The Seal of Faith," *Christianity Today,* October 8, 1965, 30–31; Carl Henry, "Evangelicals in the Social Struggle," *Christianity Today,* October 8, 1965, 3–11; L. Nelson Bell, "The Great Counterfeit," *Christianity Today,* August 19, 1966, 26–27.

77. Henry, "Evangelicals in the Social Struggle," 11.

78. David P. King, "Preaching Good News to the Poor: Billy Graham and Evangelical Humanitarianism," in *Billy Graham: American Pilgrim,* ed. Andrew Finstuen, Grant Wacker, and Anne Blue Wills (New York: Oxford University Press, 2017), 119–42.

79. "Bob Pierce Reports: Total Loss for Thousands in Vietnam," *World Vision Frontline News*, August 1965, WVI Central Records.

80. "Total Evangelism," *World Vision*, January 1962, 7.

81. Bob Pierce, World Vision appeal letter, May 1966, WVI Central Records.

82. "Mission of the Month Club," *World Vision*, May 1960, 3–4; "Pierce in Iran After Earthquake," *World Vision*, October 1962, 3, 8.

83. Secular humanitarian agencies also grew, but religious agencies still dominated, making up eight of the top ten agencies. CARE remained the leading secular agency. It ranked second among all INGOs (McCleary, *Global Compassion*, 27).

84. My thesis here follows Hollinger, *Protestants Abroad*.

85. McCleary, *Global Compassion*, 77–78; Nichols, *The Uneasy Alliance*, 85.

86. McCleary, "Private Voluntary Organizations Engaged in International Assistance," 523–24. Over the same time period, registered evangelical organizations received 33 percent of their revenue from the federal government. The Mennonite Central Committee (MCC) and World Relief represented the two largest evangelical organizations.

87. Scott Flipse, "The Latest Casualty of War: Catholic Relief Services, Humanitarianism, and the War in Vietnam, 1967–1968," *Peace & Change* 27, no. 2 (April 2002): 248.

88. Humanitarian agencies' popular public presence often differed based on their need to raise funds. As an independent specialized agency like World Vision, CARE was dependent on individual contributions outside its government support. The majority of other leading humanitarian agencies maintained different institutional structures. For example, CWS, CRS, and World Relief were arms of larger denominations that distributed percentages of aggregate funds received to their work. Denominations frowned on direct soliciting of congregations and individuals that might take away from other local needs. Therefore, they issued fewer fund-raising appeals. Less fund-raising led to less shaping of popular opinion.

89. Nichols, *Uneasy Alliance*, 95; McCleary, *Global Compassion*, 82–84.

90. Delia T. Pergande, "Private Voluntary Aid and Nation Building in South Vietnam: The Humanitarian Politics of CARE, 1954–61," *Peace & Change* 27, no. 2 (April 2002): 174–76; Stenning, *Church World Service*, 35. CWS and other agencies debated whether to continue receiving PL 480 surpluses from the late 1950s through the early 1960s. They worried that surpluses caused them to rely too heavily on U.S. resources and influenced their work toward relief over self-help community development.

91. World Vision felt it necessary to form WVRO to distinguish evangelistic from social welfare work to meet separation of church and state restrictions. Although governed by the same board, WVRO remained a subsidiary of World Vision for many years. With Charitable Choice provisions signed into law under President Clinton in 1996 and expanded by executive order under President George W. Bush's Faith-Based Initiative in 2001 as well as after comfortably working alongside the federal government for several decades, World Vision eventually deemed the separate organizations no longer legally necessary and folded WVRO into its larger World Vision U.S. operations. See Rohrer, *Open Arms*, 139; "Operation Handclasp," *World Vision*, January 1961, 5; also see "Million Dollar Missionary Barrel: Review of World Vision's Relief Procurement Ministries," brochure, WVRO files, WVI Central Records.

92. ACVAFS allowed World Vision membership in 1983. Because of ACVAFS's protection of its relief monopoly, the majority of new agencies founded in the 1960s and 1970s formed another agency, Private Agencies in International Development, in 1980. This new

umbrella organization remained a unique mix of evangelical and secular agencies. McCleary, *Global Compassion*, 119, 195.

93. In 1964, World Vision valued its USAID subventions at $28,860.56. In 1965, they totaled $55,194.53. In 1964, the value of commodities it procured was $584,192.77. In 1965, it was $966,181.26. Evangelical agencies relied on corporate in-kind donations more heavily than secular or nonevangelical relief agencies probably because of skepticism of government partnership as well as limited access to PL 480 resources, which were dominated by the few established humanitarian agencies. McCleary, *Global Compassion*, 101; "World Vision Fiscal Year Annual Report," 1964–65, 1965–66, 1968–69, WVI Central Records.

94. World Relief was a member of ACVAFS since 1956. In 1960, it was the sixteenth largest PVO and received only 2.6 percent of its budget from federal revenue. McCleary, *Global Compassion*, 27.

95. Executive Secretary of MCC, "Training of Personnel for Material Aid Work," 1965 Mission Executive Retreat, in Folder 4, Box 18, EFMA Records. As relief veterans, the MCC made themselves available to advise evangelical mission agencies interested in material aid. In 1960, it was the tenth largest PVO and received 17.3 percent of its budget from federal support.

96. Axel R. Schäfer, *Piety and Public Funding: Evangelicals and the State in Modern America* (Philadelphia: University of Pennsylvania Press, 2012), 110–22.

97. "Interview with Bill Moyers (Associate Director of Peace Corps)," *Christianity Today*, June 5, 1961.

98. "Signs of Religious Favoritism in the Peace Corps Program?," *Christianity Today*, December 21, 1962): 26–27; "Is the Peace Corps Compromising on the Religious Issue?," *Christianity Today*, January 18, 1963, 25; "Peace Corps Aids Sectarian Expansion," *Christianity Today*, August 28, 1964, 31; "Peace Corps in West Cameroon," *Christianity Today*, January 1, 1965, 29.

99. "Religion and the Peace Corps," *Christianity Today*, April 24, 1964, 27–28.

100. Robert N. Meyers, "The Christian Service Corps," *Christianity Today*, July 17, 1964, 8–10.

101. H. Daniel Friberg, "Shifting Balances: Missionaries or Marines?," *Christianity Today*, August 3, 1962, 3–5.

102. *Christianity Today* claimed those supporting a secular public sphere (i.e., removing prayer and Bible reading in public schools) like mainline Protestants and Catholics were the same ones relying on U.S. funding abroad. See "Uneasy Protestant Conscience over Surplus Food to Taiwan," *Christianity Today*, June 8, 1962, 25–26; "Baring Religious Ties," *Christianity Today*, December 7, 1962, 31–32; "US Government Aid Funds Steeped in Religious Compromise," *Christianity Today*, June 21, 1963, 26–27.

103. Schäfer, *Piety and Public Funding*, 214.

104. For discussion of how evangelicals depicted suffering in an earlier era, see Heather D. Curtis, "Depicting Distant Suffering: Evangelicals and the Politics of Pictorial Humanitarianism in the Age of American Empire," *Material Religion* 8, no. 2 (July 2012): 154–83.

105. Joan Kerns, "Famine Stalks India," *Christianity Today*, April 1, 1966, 52–54.

106. "Some Social Consequences of Evangelism," *Christianity Today*, May 13, 1966, 32.

107. One of Diem's most ardent supporters was Henry Luce, missionary kid and editor of *Time* and *Life*. He portrayed Diem as "a resilient, deeply religious Vietnamese nationalist." Jacobs, *America's Miracle Man in Vietnam*, 197.

108. William Lederer, "They'll Remember the Bayfield," *Reader's Digest*, March 1955, 1–8. Lederer was a leading Asian correspondent for *Reader's Digest* and author of *The Ugly American* referenced in Chapter 3.

109. Thomas A. Dooley, *Deliver Us from Evil: The Story of Viet Nam's Flight to Freedom* (New York: New American Library, 1961). Dooley remains a complex figure. He founded his own medical humanitarian agency, MEDICO, but there is evidence that he was used by the CIA and U.S. government to "market" the Cold War in Southeast Asia. His flamboyant life-style contrasted with his devout Catholicism. See Jacobs, *America's Miracle Man in Vietnam*, 139–59; T. Jeremy Gunn, *Spiritual Weapons: The Cold War and the Forging of an American National Religion* (Westport, CT: Praeger Publishers, 2009), 170–72; James T. Fisher, *Dr. America: The Lives of Thomas A. Dooley, 1927–1961* (Amherst: University of Massachusetts Press, 1997).

110. IVS was an ecumenical organization started by the Church of the Brethren. It focused less on relief and more on technical assistance. While founded as religious, it soon lost its religious identity and became a proving ground for many aspiring State Department staffers and new forms of community development. Scott Flipse, "To Save 'Free Vietnam' and Lose Our Souls: The Missionary Impulse, Voluntary Agencies, and Protestant Dissent Against the War, 1965–1971," in *The Foreign Missionary Enterprise at Home*, ed. Grant Wacker and Daniel A. Bays (Tuscaloosa: University of Alabama Press, 2003), 208–10; Hollinger, *Protestants Abroad*, 261–65.

111. The Christian and Missionary Alliance (CMA) dominated Vietnamese missions. In 1911, they founded the Evangelical Church in Vietnam, the church to which most of the 100,000 Vietnamese Protestants belonged. Their one hundred in-country missionaries dwarfed the size of other in-country groups, which included the Adventists, Southern Baptists, Wycliffe Bible Translators, and Navigators. See "Vietnam: The Spiritual War," *Christianity Today*, September 25, 1964, 53–54; the article reviews Homer E. Dowdy's *The Bamboo Cross: Christian Witness in the Jungles of Viet Nam*, Harper Jungle Missionary Classics (New York: Harper and Row, 1964). Dowdy's book was one of several popular missionary hagiographies stemming from the Christian and Missionary Alliance's work in Vietnam. Also see "Missions in Vietnam," *Christianity Today*, February 26, 1965, 45; "Unheadlined Victories in Vietnam," *Moody Monthly*, September 1966, 30–31, 58–59; Grady Mangham as told to Phill Butler, "New Optimism in Viet Nam," *Moody Monthly*, September 1967, 30–31, 43–45.

112. Miriam G. Cox, "Vietnam Up-to-Date: The Race with the Reds," *Eternity*, August 1965, 35.

113. Miriam G. Cox, "Vietnam Report: Murders, Miracles, and Missions," *Christianity Today*, December 1964, 29–30; "Report: Missions in Viet Nam," *United Evangelical Action*, April 1965, 25.

114. In 1964, the United States began with 16,300 personnel in Vietnam. By the end of 1965, there were 184,000 soldiers. The number rose to 383,000 in 1966, 485,000 in 1967, and peaked in 1969 with 543,000 troops. Andrew LeRoy Pratt, "Religious Faith and Civil Religion: Evangelical Responses to the Vietnam War, 1964–1973" (PhD diss., Southern Baptist Theological Seminary, 1988), 383.

115. Flipse, "To Save 'Free Vietnam' and Lose Our Souls," 207–8; McCleary, *Global Compassion*, 92; Flipse, "The Latest Casualty of War," 251.

116. "Aid for Vietnam," *Christianity Today*, October 8, 1965, 53; "Bob Pierce Reports: Total Loss for Thousands in Vietnam." The Viet Kit program resembled CARE's relief packages. The kits provided emergency food and hygiene needs, but they also helped publicize

World Vision's work at home. In its first year between 1965 and 1966, World Vision shipped 133,680 kits. That number grew to 512,727 by 1969–70. World Vision Annual Reports, 1965–70, WVI Central Records.

117. Running eighty-eight minutes, World Vision edited it to fifty-five minutes for television. World Vision allowed ads but not for alcohol or cigarettes. Television statements then allowed World Vision to make its own appeal at the film's conclusion. *Vietnam Profile*, David Wisner, 1965, WVUS Archives.

118. Pratt, "Religious Faith and Civil Religion," 184.

119. Bob Pierce, *Big Day at Da Me* (Waco, TX: Word Books, 1968). "Bob Pierce Reports: Total Loss for Thousands in Vietnam."

120. Pierce, *Big Day at Da Me*, 70; Viet Kit brochure, WVUS Archives.

121. *Vietnam Profile*.

122. Pierce, *Big Day at Da Me*, 49.

123. *Vietnam Profile*; Pierce, *Big Day at Da Me*, 13–15.

124. Doug Cozart, longtime staffer of World Vision and the Navigators, became the first field director of World Vision's Vietnam office in 1966. Linda Cozart, *The World Was His Parish: The Life and Times of Doug Cozart, Missionary Statesman* (Charleston, SC: BookSurge, 2006).

Chapter 5

1. Graeme Irvine, *Best Things in the Worst Times: An Insider's View of World Vision* (Wilsonville, OR: BookPartners, 1996), 22.

2. Ibid., 24. For accounts of Pierce's resignation, see World Vision Board of Directors' Minutes, October 9, 1967, December 4, 1967, December 6, 1967, WVI Central Records; Norman Rohrer, *This Poor Man Cried: The Story of Larry Ward* (Wheaton, IL: Tyndale House, 1984), 100.

3. Dunker, *Man of Vision*, 166–88.

4. Andrew Preston, "Evangelical Internationalism: A Conservative Worldview for the Age of Globalization," in *The Right Side of the Sixties: Reexamining Conservatism's Decade of Transformation*, ed. Laura Jane Gifford and Daniel K. Williams (New York: Palgrave Macmillan, 2012), 229.

5. Richard M. Nixon, "What Has Happened in America?," *Reader's Digest*, October 1967, 49– 54, quoted in Daniel K. Williams, "Richard Nixon's Religious Right: Catholics, Evangelicals, and the Creation of an Antisecular Alliance," in Gifford and Williams, *The Right Side of the Sixties*, 149.

6. Seth Dowland, *Family Values and the Rise of the Christian Right* (Philadelphia: University of Pennsylvania Press, 2015), 17.

7. "Mooneyham Bio," WVUS Archives; Herb Pasik, "Meet Stan Mooneyham: The World Is His Mission," *Palm Desert (CA) Post*, August 22, 1986; VanderPol, "The Least of These," 105.

8. World Vision Annual Reports, 1969–80, WVI Central Records. WVUS annual income under Mooneyham's tenure (1969–82) grew 649 percent. Child sponsorship grew 530 percent, from 30,735 to 332,826 children. Waters, "How World Vision Rose from Obscurity to Prominence," 69; Linda D. Smith, "An Awakening of Conscience: The Changing Response of American Evangelicals Toward World Poverty" (PhD diss., Washington University, 1987), 288–89.

9. First published by Wheaton's Tyndale House in 1971, *The Living Bible* was the best-selling book in America in 1972–73. Lindsey's *Late Great Planet Earth* produced an entire new genre of books predicting end-time scenarios in current events. (It is a precursor to the popular Left Behind series). Originally published by evangelical Zondervan, its success led to secular Bantam press republishing it in 1973.

10. Larry Eskridge, *God's Forever Family: The Jesus People Movement in America, 1966–1977* (Stirling: University of Stirling, 2005); "The Alternative Jesus: Psychedelic Christ," *Time*, June 21, 1971, 56–63; "The Jesus Movement Is upon Us," *Look*, February 9, 1971, 15–21.

11. For more information on Explo' 72, see Larry Eskridge, "'One Way': Billy Graham, the Jesus Generation, and the Idea of an Evangelical Youth Culture," *Church History* 67, no. 1 (March 1998): 83–106; Turner, *Bill Bright & Campus Crusade for Christ*, 1–2, 139–46. Billy Graham became a huge supporter of the Jesus Movement. His 1971 book *The Jesus Generation* sold over 500,000 copies. By the end of 1972, however, the Jesus Movement had reached its zenith. Its short popular success had a lasting effect on evangelicalism as many of the Jesus People came to staff successful evangelical operations such as Maranatha Music, Chuck Smith's Calvary Chapel, and even World Vision.

12. Carl Henry, *Evangelicals at the Brink of Crisis: Significance of the World Congress on Evangelism* (Waco, TX: Word Books, 1967).

13. Henry, *Confessions of a Theologian*, 270–71.

14. DeVos said, "The plan, among other things, was designed to help elect 'real Christians' to government" and "get rid of those so-called liberal Christians like Mark Hatfield." Quoted in "Giving God 'The Business,'" *Mennonite Brethren Herald*, September 14, 1979; Turner, *Bill Bright & Campus Crusade for Christ*, 163–65.

15. Leighton Ford, interview with author, Durham, NC, March 24, 2011; George W. Wilson, *Evangelism Now: U.S. Congress on Evangelism; Official Reference Volume, Papers, and Reports* (Minneapolis, MN: World Wide Publications, 1970); see also Ted Engstrom, "US Congress on Evangelism," *World Vision*, November 1969, 36–37; "U.S. Congress on Evangelism: A Turning Point?," *Christianity Today*, October 10, 1969, 32.

16. L. Nelson Bell, "Beware!," *Christianity Today* 14, October 24, 1969, 24–25.

17. Samuel Escobar, "Social Concern and World Evangelism," in John R. Stott, *Christ the Liberator* (Downers Grove, IL: InterVarsity Press, 1971), 107–8; Keith Hunt and Gladys Hunt, *For Christ and the University: The Story of InterVarsity Christian Fellowship of the U.S.A./ 1940–1990* (Downers Grove, IL: InterVarsity Press, 1991), 274–78.

18. Carl Henry, *A Plea for Evangelical Demonstration* (Grand Rapids, MI: Baker Book House, 1971), 22; Carl Henry, "The Tensions Between Evangelism and the Christian Demand for Social Justice," *Fides et Historia* 4, no. 2 (Spring 1972): 8.

19. See Robert Booth Fowler, *A New Engagement: Evangelical Political Thought, 1966–1976* (Grand Rapids, MI: Eerdmans, 1982), 189; David Moberg, *The Great Reversal: Evangelism versus Social Concern* (Philadelphia: Lippincott, 1972); Richard V. Pierard, *The Unequal Yoke* (Philadelphia: J. B. Lippincott, 1970); Richard Mouw, *Political Evangelism* (Grand Rapids, MI: Eerdmans, 1973); Vernon Grounds, *Evangelicalism and Social Responsibility* (Scottdale, PA: Herald Press, 1969); Vernon Grounds, *Revolution and the Christian Faith* (Philadelphia: J. B. Lippincott, 1971); Henry, *A Plea for Evangelical Demonstration*. Brantley W. Gasaway, *Progressive Evangelicals and the Pursuit of Social Justice* (Chapel Hill: University of North Carolina Press, 2014), 42–44, outlines all the major books in this new genre.

20. [Fred Alexander and John Alexander], "The Other Side," *Other Side*, September–October 1969, 31.

21. Jim Wallis, "Post-American Christianity," *Post-American*, Fall 1971, 3. The publication was renamed *Sojourners* in 1975. The *Other Side* (circulation 13,000) and the *Post-American* (55,000) were only two of many new periodicals to address similar issues. Others included the *Reformed Journal*, *Eternity* (46,000), *Vanguard* (2,000), *Right On* (65,000), *HIS* (90,000), and *Wittenburg Door*. See David R. Swartz, "Identity Politics and the Fragmenting of the 1970s Evangelical Left," *Religion and American Culture: A Journal of Interpretation*, January 2011, 82.

22. For the text of the declaration and commentary on the event, see Ronald J. Sider, *The Chicago Declaration* (Carol Stream, IL: Creation House, 1974); see Marjorie Hyer, "Social and Political Activism Is Aim of Evangelical Group," *Washington Post*, November 30, 1973, D17. Few establishment evangelicals demeaned the Chicago Declaration. In fact, Billy Graham, in a post-Watergate interview with *Christianity Today* claimed, "We have a social responsibility, and I could identify with most of the recent Chicago Declaration of Evangelical Social Concern. I think we have to identify with the changing of structures in society and try to do our part" ("Watergate: Interview with Graham," *Christianity Today*, January 4, 1974, 17–18).

23. Sider, *The Chicago Declaration*, 9, 29.

24. Pratt, "Religious Faith and Civil Religion," 383.

25. Flipse, "To Save 'Free Vietnam' and Lose Our Souls," 213; Jill K. Gill, "The Political Price of Prophetic Leadership: The National Council of Churches and the Vietnam War," *Peace & Change* 27, no. 2 (April 2002): 271–300; Mitchell K. Hall, *Because of Their Faith: CALCAV and Religious Opposition to the Vietnam War* (New York: Columbia University Press, 1990); Martin Luther King Jr., "Beyond Vietnam: A Time to Break Silence," April 4, 1967, Riverside Church, New York City, http://www.americanrhetoric.com/speeches/mlkatimetobreaksilence.htm; Robert McAfee Brown, Abraham Joshua Heschel, and Michael Novak, *Vietnam: Crisis of Conscience* (New York: Association Press, 1967).

26. Miller, *The Age of Evangelicalism*, 11–12; Andrew Preston, "Tempered by the Fires of War: Vietnam and the Transformation of the Evangelical Worldview," in *American Evangelicals and the 1960s*, ed. Axel R Schäfer (Madison: University of Wisconsin Press, 2013), 191–92.

27. L. Nelson Bell to Lyndon B. Johnson, April 2, 1965, Executive PR4/FG 216, Lyndon B. Johnson Presidential Library, Austin, TX.

28. Richard V. Pierard, "Billy Graham and Vietnam: From Cold Warrior to Peacemaker," *Christian Scholar's Review* 10, no. 1 (1980): 42; *Ecumenical News Service*, December 9, 1965, 8. A 1966 NAE resolution affirmed it was possible to trust the government's position on Vietnam in the name of security and a strong anticommunist position against China. "The Ground of Freedom," *Christianity Today*, July 3, 1964, 20–21; Lt. Gen. William K. Harrison, "Is the United States Right in Bombing North Viet Nam?," *Christianity Today*, January 7, 1966, 25–26; "Viet Nam: Where Do We Go from Here?," *Christianity Today*, January 7, 1966, 30–31.

29. In contrast to the NCC protesting the war, the fundamentalist American Council of Christian Churches (ACCC) demonstrated on behalf of winning the war. Henry did not join either protest. He did, however, mutter to both sides, "Preacher, go home," transposing the common "Missionary, go home" quip used to critique the missionary enterprise. "Rival Churchmen in Vietnam," *Christianity Today*, July 1967, 1012; also see "Dodging the Draft,"

Christianity Today, November 5, 1965, 36; "The New Spirit of Defiance," *Christianity Today,* December 23, 1966, 19–20; "NCC Skirmish over Viet Nam," *Christianity Today,* January 7, 1966, 50; "Ignorance Often Has a Loud Voice," *Christianity Today,* February 12, 1965, 35; "A Time to Speak," *Christianity Today,* May 21, 1965, 26; "Religious Coalition in Washington," *Christianity Today,* May 21, 1965, 38; "Clergy Press Role in Peace Talks," *Christianity Today,* February 18, 1966, 51–52; "The WCC and Viet Nam," *Christianity Today,* March 4, 1966, 31.

30. "The Church and the Viet Nam-Bound Soldier," *Christianity Today,* May 13, 1966, 30–31; Anne Loveland, *American Evangelicals and the U.S. Military, 1942–1993* (Baton Rouge: Louisiana State University Press, 1996), 143, 151.

31. Nichols, *Uneasy Alliance,* 102–7.

32. On September 19, 1967, staff of International Voluntary Services published an open letter to President Johnson in the *New York Times.* The next year, several leading IVS staff resigned and took their critique of U.S. military policy on the road to American audiences. By 1971, the United States would ask IVS to leave Vietnam completely. Flipse, "To Save 'Free Vietnam' and Lose Our Souls," 218.

33. Vietnam Christian Service (VCS) united the established agencies of Lutheran World Relief, Church World Service, and the MCC for work in Vietnam. By 1971, MCC left VCS to provide aid to North Vietnam. The United States unilaterally cut VCS feeding programs in 1971, and VCS would later refuse all USAID contracts. By 1974, VCS had turned its community development projects over to the Vietnamese and pulled out of the country. Perry Bush, "The Political Education of Vietnam Christian Service, 1954–1975," *Peace & Change* 27, no. 2 (April 2002): 198; Flipse, "The Latest Casualty of War," 264; Flipse, "To Save 'Free Vietnam' and Lose Our Souls," 221.

34. By 1967, thirty-seven PVOs had registered in Vietnam. Twenty of these had only arrived since 1965. At the height of the U.S. military buildup in 1969, there were fifty PVOs. McCleary, *Global Compassion,* 93–94.

35. The one exception to evangelical relief agencies' alliance with the U.S. government was the MCC. Its peace church tradition caused it to question greater association with the U.S. government. "Halting Red Aggression in Viet Nam," *Christianity Today,* April 23, 1965, 32; "Aid for Vietnam," *Christianity Today,* October 8, 1965, 53; "Churches Hike Vietnam Relief," *Christianity Today,* February 4, 1966, 48. "Waning Surpluses Curb Church Relief," *Christianity Today,* January 20, 1967, 42; "Compassion Gap in Viet Nam," *Christianity Today,* April 14, 1967, 40–41.

36. "Ky to Arrive Today; Demonstrations Set," *Los Angeles Times,* December 2, 1970; Ted Sell, "Ky Says America Must Decide if Vietnam Is Worth Supporting," *Los Angeles Times,* December 3, 1970; John Dart, "Ky, Religious Leaders Visit During Trip," *Los Angeles Times,* December 6, 1970. Dart noted that World Vision "considers itself a Protestant agency but it draws heavily for its support on evangelical, often conservative Protestant churchmen." He also noted the private gathering of religious leaders included one Roman Catholic and a handful of nonevangelical Protestants, but local Southern Californian religious conservatives made up the majority. Stan Mooneyham to Grady Wilson, November 24, 1970, Folder 11, Box 27, Collection 544, Grady Baxter Wilson Papers, Archives of the Billy Graham Center, Wheaton, IL.

37. William Martin, *A Prophet with Honor: The Billy Graham Story* (New York: W. Morrow, 1991), 365–71; Quebedeaux, *The Young Evangelicals,* 84–85; Quebedeaux quotes Joe

Roos's response to Graham's "Honor America Day" sermon (Joe Roos, "American Civil Religion," *Post-American*, Spring 1972); Pratt, "Religious Faith and Civil Religion," 292–95.

38. As Oregon governor, Hatfield was the lone opposing vote against American intervention in Vietnam at the 1965 National Governors' Conference. For examples of evangelicals' fascination with him as a Christian leader, see Mark O. Hatfield, "The Vulnerability of Leadership," *Christianity Today*, June 22, 1973, 4–6; John Warwick Montgomery, "Washington Christianity," *Christianity Today*, August 8, 1975, 37–38; Mark Hatfield, *Conflict and Conscience* (Waco, TX: Word Books, 1971); Mark Hatfield, *Between a Rock and a Hard Place* (Waco, TX: Word Books, 1976).

39. Robert Eells and Bartell Nyberg, *Lonely Walk: The Life of Senator Mark Hatfield* (Chappaqua, NY: Christian Herald Books, 1979), 49–51, 82–83; Robert James Eells, "Mark Hatfield and the Search for an Evangelical Politics" (PhD diss., University of New Mexico, 1976), 218.

40. Hatfield was a Republican and committed member of the Fellowship and close friend with its director Doug Coe, but his political agenda put him at odds with almost every position of the Religious Right. Recent scholarship on the Fellowship has most often avoided these finer distinctions. Randall Balmer, "The Breakfast Club," review of *The Family: The Secret Fundamentalism at the Heart of American Power*, by Jeff Sharlet, *Washington Post*, July 13, 2008, http://www.washingtonpost.com/wp-dyn/content/article/2008/07/10/AR2008071001 924.html.

41. In addition to Fuller, Hatfield gave another often reprinted address, "The Path to Peace," at the 1969 United States Congress on Evangelism that criticized evangelicals for their lack of social compassion. Eells and Nyberg, *Lonely Walk*, 72–76. George Marsden's surveys of Fuller Seminary students substantiate younger evangelicals' support of Hatfield. In the 1950s, three-fourths of Fuller students said social justice was less important than evangelism; at the end of the 1960s, only a little more than half still agreed that social justice was less important (Marsden, *Reforming Fundamentalism*, 254).

42. Cover, *Post-American*, Fall 1971. Granberg-Michaelson served on Hatfield's staff from 1969 to 1975. He would then become the editor of *Sojourners* magazine from 1975 to 1979. Wesley Granberg-Michaelson, *Unexpected Destinations: An Evangelical Pilgrimage to World Christianity* (Grand Rapids, MI: Eerdmans, 2011), xii.

43. Jim Wallis, "The Issue of 1972," *Post-American*, Fall 1972, 2; Jim Wallis, "Babylon," *Post-American*, Summer 1972; William Stringfellow, "The Relevance of Babylon," *Post-American*, January–February 1973; referenced in Gasaway, *Progressive Evangelicals and the Pursuit of Social Justice*, 37–38.

44. C. René Padilla, "Evangelism and the World," in *Let the Earth Hear His Voice: International Congress on World Evangelization, Lausanne, Switzerland; Official Reference Volume, Papers and Responses*, ed. J. D. Douglas (Minneapolis, MN: World Wide Publications, 1975), 126; Fowler, *A New Engagement*, 133; in Fowler's analysis of the *Post-American*, he found that half the articles deal with the faults of institutions.

45. Jim Wallis, "The Movemental Church, *"Post-American*, Winter 1972, 2; Roos, "American Civil Religion," 9–10.

46. Turner, *Bill Bright & Campus Crusade for Christ*, 144; Brantley W. Gasaway, "An Alternative Soul of Politics: The Rise of Contemporary Progressive Evangelicalism" (PhD diss., University of North Carolina at Chapel Hill, 2008), 33–34; Peter Ediger, "Explo '72,"

Post-American, Fall 1972, 13; Jim Wallis, *Revive Us Again: A Sojourner's Story* (Nashville, TN: Abingdon Press, 1983), 83–85; "The Jesus Woodstock," *Time*, June 26, 1972, 66.

47. "Revolt on Evangelical Frontiers," *Christianity Today*, April 26, 1974, 4–8; Jim Wallis, "'Revolt on Evangelical Frontiers': A Response," *Christianity Today*, June 21, 1974, 20–21; Henry, "The Judgment of America," *Christianity Today*, November 8, 1974, 22–24; see also Ron Sider to Carl Henry, June 10, 1974; Donald Dayton to Carl Henry (copied to Richard Quebedeaux, Ron Sider, Jim Wallis), July 10, 1974; Carl Henry to Jim Wallis, July 31, 1974; Carl Henry to Jim Wallis, August 6, 1974; Jim Wallis to Carl Henry, undated; all in Box 6, Carl F. H. Henry Papers, Trinity Evangelical Divinity School, Deerfield, IL.

48. W. Stanley Mooneyham, "My Intensely Personal Encounter with the Cambodian People," *World Vision*, April 1975, 7.

49. Jerry Ballard, "Mountain People on the Run," *World Vision*, June 1972, 4–6; Gordon Diehl, WVRO Report, World Vision Annual Report, 1970, WVI Central Records.

50. World Vision Annual Reports, 1970–75, have records of budgets and descriptions for all Southeast Asian programs (WVI Central Records).

51. Ecclesiastes 11:4; Mooneyham, "My Intensely Personal Encounter with the Cambodian People," 4–8; W. Stanley Mooneyham, *Come Walk the World: Personal Experiences of Hurt and Hope* (Waco, TX: Word Books, 1978), 17.

52. "Cambodia Report," *World Vision*, January 1972, 15; Billy Bray, "Evangelistic Explosion in Cambodia: The Church Triples in Three Days," *World Vision*, May 1972, 4–6. World Vision leaders were excited by Cambodia's openness to the gospel. One claimed, "Cambodia is wide open to the gospel now, but with the military activities increasing, opportunities for a Christian witness may be cut off in the near future" (*World Vision*, November 1972, 14).

53. Donald E. Warner, "Cambodia: A Gentle People Trapped in War," *World Vision*, July–August 1973, 4–6; Stan Mooneyham, "Cambodia: Brittle and Delicate" *World Vision*, November 1973, 4–8.

54. "Don Scott Bio," *World Vision*, June 1972, 19.

55. David K. Shipler, "For Cambodia, Rehabilitation Is Painful, Lonely Effort," *New York Times*, October 21, 1973, 3; Fox Butterfield, "As G.I.s Fade, So Does Help for Vietnam's Orphans," *New York Times*, May 16, 1973, 3; Daniel Southerland, "Cambodian Refugees: U.S. Ups Aid Fourfold," *Christian Science Monitor*, March 11, 1974, 1.

56. Philip A. McCombs, "Paying Cambodia's Middlemen," *Washington Post*, February 24, 1974, A18.

57. H. D. S. Greenway, "Hunger Stalks Phnom Penh," *Washington Post*, February 15, 1975, A1; Daniel Southerland, "Cambodia Suffering Mounts," *Christian Science Monitor*, February 19, 1975, 2; "Urgent Appeal for Peace in Cambodia," *World Vision*, June 1974, 22.

58. Technical Assistance Information Clearing House, *Vietnam Programs: U.S. Voluntary Agencies, Foundations, and Missions* (New York: American Council of Voluntary Agencies for Foreign Service, 1966), 15.

59. John Nakajima, "Cash for Services Rendered," *Far Eastern Economic Review*, April 25, 1975.

60. W. Stanley Mooneyham to John Nakajima, June 23, 1975; John Nakajima to W. Stanley Mooneyham, July 4, 1975; W. Stanley Mooneyham to John Nakajima, August 5, 1975; Mark Hatfield to Eugene Carson Blake, July 14, 1975; Eugene Carson Blake to Mark Hatfield, July 19, 1975; W. Stanley Mooneyham to Eugene Carson Blake, August 4, 1975; Robert

McAfee Brown to W. Stanley Mooneyham, July 7, 1975; William Needham to Brown, July 15, 1975; also see Board of Director Minutes, July 24, 1975; all in WVI Central Records.

61. Edward E. Plowman, "Conversing with the CIA," *Christianity Today*, October 10, 1975, 62–66; Plowman estimated that 10–25 percent of missionaries had given info to the CIA. See also " 'Valuable Sources': Missionaries and the CIA," *Sojourners*, January 1976, 8–9; "Hatfield Urges Ban on CIA Use of Missionaries," *Eternity*, March 1976, 9; Joseph Bayly, "Missionaries and the CIA: Succumbing to Mammon or Patriotism," *Eternity*, April 1976, 51–52; Brian Eads, "Charity Groups 'Ran Out' Saigon Returnee Charges," *Washington Post*, August 9, 1976, A18; Mooneyham, "Open Letter to President Ford," *World Vision*, March 1976, 3.

62. Whaites, "Pursuing Partnership," 416; Sydney H. Schanberg, "U.S. Starting to Evacuate Relief Aides in Cambodia," *New York Times*, March 18, 1975, 1; J. Don Scott, "In Vietnam: Preparing for the Worst, Serving the Last," *World Vision*, July–August 1975, 12–13; Mooneyham, "Southeast Asia: God Still in Control," *World Vision*, May 1975, 4–8; Carl Henry, "Grief, Grace, and Grist," presented at World Vision staff retreat, *World Vision*, April 1976, 16–19. *World Vision's* May 1976 cover reminded donors not to forget Southeast Asia even after it was forced to leave. See Mooneyham, "No Place Left to Run," *World Vision*, May 1976, 4–8; and William L. Needham, "Many Tears, Muted Hope," *World Vision*, May 1976, 10–11.

63. "Saigon Halts Orphan Airlift," *Chicago Tribune*, April 7, 1975, 1; Robert Rawitch, "Religious Group Sues to Keep Orphans," *Los Angeles Times*, November 12, 1975, E3; Edmund W. Janss, "Operation Babylift: Handling Precious Cargo," *World Vision*, May 1975, 10–11; Cliff R. Benzel, "The Babylift: Confronting the Objections," *World Vision*, May 1975, 12; Richard L. Wilson, "Court Case Affects 20 Cambodian Orphans," *World Vision*, November 1975; "Cambodian Orphans . . . Home at Last," *World Vision*, October 1976, 16–17; Engstrom, "Monthly Memo," *World Vision*, August 1977, 18.

64. Other records claim the loss at 30,000 children. World Vision expanded to nine new Latin American countries: Brazil, Haiti, Jamaica, Mexico, Honduras, Guatemala, El Salvador, Colombia, and Ecuador. It began adding one thousand children from Latin America per month to its system. Irvine, *Best Things in the Worst Times*, 53; Whaites, "Pursuing Partnership," 414.

65. Miller, *The Age of Evangelicalism*, 3–8, 19.

66. Barry Hankins, *Francis Schaeffer and the Shaping of Evangelical America* (Grand Rapids, MI: Eerdmans, 2008).

67. Among the many books citing the rise of the Religious Right, one of the best resources remains Williams, *God's Own Party*.

68. Donald W. Dayton, "The Battle for the Bible: Renewing the Inerrancy Debate," *Christian Century*, November 10, 1976, 976–80; Harold Lindsell, *The Battle for the Bible* (Grand Rapids, MI: Zondervan, 1976); Marsden, *Reforming Fundamentalism*, 279–80.

69. "Born Again!," *Newsweek*, October 25, 1976, 76.

70. Carl F. H. Henry, *Evangelicals in Search of Identity* (Waco, TX: Word Books, 1976): 22; Carl F. H. Henry, "American Evangelicals in a Turning Time," *Christian Century*, November 5, 1980, 1060.

71. Mooneyham, "The World: Color It Gray," address given to Religion Newswriters' Association, Anaheim, CA, July 5, 1975, WVI Central Records; Mooneyham, "Some Thoughts About the Bandwagon." *World Vision*, May 1978, 23; Mooneyham, "The Affliction of Adjectivitis," *World Vision*, June 1979, 23; Mooneyham, "United We Fall," *World Vision*, April 1980, 23.

72. W. Stanley Mooneyham, *What Do You Say to a Hungry World?* (Waco, TX: Word Books, 1975), 31–32.

Chapter 6

1. Arne Bergstrom, interview with author, November 16, 2010, Federal Way, WA.

2. Thomas Borstelmann, *The 1970s: A New Global History from Civil Rights to Economic Inequality* (Princeton, NJ: Princeton University Press, 2013), 62.

3. Ekbladh, *The Great American Mission*, 244–51.

4. Graham, "Why Lausanne?," quoted in Timothy Yates, *Christian Mission in the Twentieth Century* (Cambridge: Cambridge University Press, 1994), 203. Also see Pierard, "Billy Graham and Vietnam"; Pierard describes how international crusades and Vietnam altered Graham's view of the Cold War and American exceptionalism.

5. Sam Kamaleson, telephone interview with author, July 10, 2007.

6. Donald A. McGavran, "Will Uppsala Betray the Two Billion?," in *The Conciliar-Evangelical Debate: The Crucial Documents, 1964–1976* (South Pasadena, CA: William Carey Library, 1977), 233–41; Donald H. Gill, "WCC's New Thrust for Mission," *World Vision*, April 1968, 20–23; Paul Rees, "Uppsala Reflections," *World Vision*, November 1968, 47; Rees, "Bangkok Beckons (What Will It Say)," *World Vision*, May 1972, 23.

7. Carl Henry, "An Assessment," in *Christ Seeks Asia: A New Note Is Struck in Asia*, ed. W. Stanley Mooneyham (Hong Kong: Rock House, 1969), 11; Sherwood E. Wirt, "A New Note Is Struck in Asia," *Decision* 10, no. 2 (1969): 9; Paul Rees, "Where Half the World Lives," *World Vision*, November 1968, 47; Valdir Steuernagel, "The Theology of Mission in Its Relation to Social Responsibility Within the Lausanne Movement" (ThD diss., Lutheran School of Theology at Chicago, 1988), 111–14.

8. "Evangelical" has most often referred to all Protestants in Latin America. The divide between the more ecumenical CELA conference and the new evangelical CLADE demonstrated some of the Western categories thrust upon Latin American Protestants. American Christians were concerned about the direction of the Latin American evangelical church. See Dayton Roberts, "Latin American Protestants: Which Way Will They Go," *Christianity Today*, October 10, 1969, 14; "Evangelical Declaration of Bogota," *Evangelical Missions Quarterly* 6, no. 3 (1970): 174.

9. The FTL is alternately known in the United States as the Latin American Theological Fraternity (LATF). Samuel Escobar, "The Bible and the Social Revolution in Latin America," Folder 1, Box 8, Collection 358, Charles Peter Wagner Papers, Archives of the Billy Graham Center, Wheaton, IL; David Kirkpatrick, *A Gospel for the Poor: Social Christianity and the Rise of the Latin American Evangelical Left* (Philadelphia: University of Pennsylvania Press, 2019).

10. David Stoll, *Is Latin America Turning Protestant? The Politics of Evangelical Growth* (Berkeley: University of California Press, 1990), 141.

11. W. Stanley Mooneyham, "Lord, Save China from American Evangelical Opportunists!," *World Vision* (June 1971): 4; John Dart, "Missionaries Warned China Won't Be Easy," *Los Angeles Times*, June 19, 1971. Having spent thirteen weeks in China in 1970, the following year Mooneyham initiated a new Asia Information Office to target China for future mission work. World Vision covered Chinese political and cultural events heavily in its magazine and published Mooneyham's full commentary on the future of China (W. Stanley Mooneyham, *China: The Puzzle* [Pasadena, CA: World Vision International, 1971]). Mooneyham's interest

is significant for both his critique of "evangelical missionary hucksters" as well as World Vision's own continued missionary impulse.

12. David R. Swartz, *Moral Minority: The Evangelical Left in an Age of Conservatism* (Philadelphia: University of Pennsylvania Press, 2012), 129.

13. John Stott, "The Biblical Basis of Evangelism," in Douglas, *Let the Earth Hear His Voice*, 65–79.

14. Samuel Escobar, "Evangelism and Man's Search for Freedom, Justice, and Fulfillment," in Douglas, *Let the Earth Hear His Voice*, 304–5.

15. Padilla went on to say that such a "fierce pragmatism" was found not in scripture but "in the political sphere [that] has produced Watergate" (Padilla, "Evangelism and the World," 125–26, 132, 139–40).

16. Section 5, which addressed social concern, was by far the longest section of the Lausanne Covenant. See Douglas, *Let the Earth Hear His Voice*, 4–5.

17. See "Theology Implications of Radical Discipleship," in Douglas, *Let the Earth Hear His Voice*, 1294–96; the "radical discipleship" statement "repudiate[d] as demonic the attempt to drive a wedge between evangelism and social concern" (1294). John Stott, chair of the writing group for the Lausanne Covenant, signed both statements. See also Carl F. H. Henry, "The Gospel and Society," *Christianity Today*, September 13, 1974, 67; C. René Padilla, *The New Face of Evangelicalism: An International Symposium on the Lausanne Covenant* (Downers Grove, IL: InterVarsity Press, 1976); Brian Stanley, *The Global Diffusion of Evangelicalism: The Age of Billy Graham and John Stott* (Downers Grove, IL: IVP Academic, 2013); Kirkpatrick, *A Gospel for the Poor*.

18. Harold Lindsell, "Lausanne 74: An Appraisal," *Christianity Today*, September 13, 1974, 21–26; Yates, *Christian Mission in the Twentieth Century*, 207; Mark Hutchinson, "The Global Turn in American Evangelicalism," and Darren Dochuk, "Lausanne '74 and American Evangelicalism's Latin Turn," both in *Turning Points in the History of American Evangelicalism*, ed. Heath W. Carter and Laura Rominger Porter (Grand Rapids, MI: Eerdmans, 2017), 203–25 and 247–81, respectively; Melani McAlister, "The Global Conscience of American Evangelicalism: Internationalism and Social Concern in the 1970s and Beyond," *Journal of American Studies* 51, no. 4 (November 20): 1197–1220. Yates, Hutchinson, Dochuk, and McAlister exemplify several historians debating the impact of Lausanne, with some questioning whether the rhetoric of Lausanne outdistanced its actual effects. The style of American evangelicalism continued to dominate. Yates claimed there were twice as many to the right of John Stott and the global evangelicals as ones that joined them.

19. World Vision Board of Directors' Meeting, December 10, 1974, WVI Central Records.

20. Dominating the exhibit hall was a digital clock that calculated the increasing world population to remind delegates of the need for world evangelization. See W. Stanley Mooneyham, "Acts of the Holy Spirit '74," in Douglas, *Let the Earth Hear His Voice*, 428–48, excerpted in *World Vision*, July–August 1974, 8–10. At the last minute, the BGEA paid for Bob Pierce to attend Lausanne. While still grieving from his ouster at World Vision, he noted Mooneyham's speech as the highlight: "World Vision's accelerated growth and increasing influence is sometimes terrifying to me. Yet it was most reassuring to sense the Holy Spirit's anointing and the true spiritual passion evident in the ministry of World Vision's president that night" (Pierce, "Lausanne in Retrospect: A Personal View," *World Vision*, October 1974, 10–11).

21. In a letter from leading Australian evangelical A. J. Dain to World Vision MARC director Ed Dayton, Dain remarks that Fuller's church growth strategies and MARC's research are "frankly largely meaningless to many of our brethren in the Third World." A. J. Dain to Ed Dayton, April 26, April 1974, Folder 47, Box 33, Collection 46, Records of the Lausanne Movement, Archives of the Billy Graham Center, Wheaton, IL. For a similar critique, see Kwame Bediako, "World Evangelisation, Institutional Evangelicalism and the Future of the Christian World Mission," in *Proclaiming Christ in Christ's Way: Studies in Integral Evangelism*, ed. Vinay Samuel and Albrecht Hauser (Oxford: Regnum Books, 1989), 52–68.

22. Robert Hunt and Samuel Escobar differentiate three trajectories within the Lausanne movement: postimperial (European evangelicals like John Stott); managerial (American evangelicals of the church growth school like McGavran and Dayton); and the critical (global South evangelicals such as Padilla and Escobar). See Robert Hunt, "The History of the Lausanne Movement, 1974–2010," *International Bulletin of Missionary Research* 35, no. 2 (April 2011): 83–84; Samuel Escobar, "A Movement Divided: Three Approaches to World Evangelization Stand in Tension with One Another," *Transformation*, October 1, 1991, 7–13.

23. In a 1986 internal report, Ed Dayton estimated World Vision had invested $4.5 million in the Lausanne movement. See Ed Dayton, "World Vision and LCWE: An Analysis," April 28, 1986; and Dayton, "World Vision Support for LCWE," International Affairs Committee, July 1, 1986, WVI Central Records.

24. In the late 1970s, Ed Dayton served on the Lausanne Executive Committee as well as chairing the Strategic Working Group and Program Review and Planning Committee. Dayton negotiated with World Vision to invest 50 to 75 percent of his time with World Vision into his positions with Lausanne as a strategic investment. See Dayton, "World Vision Support for LCWE."

25. William Newell, director of World Vision Canada, speaking as a member of a World Vision committee to assess the organization's position at Lausanne; see World Vision Annual Report, 1973–74, WVI Central Records.

26. "Philippines: Nation Struggling to Stay on Its Feet," *World Vision*, November 1972, 7; "Project REAL," World Vision fund-raising appeal to Herb Taylor of the Christian Workers' Foundation, Folder 48, Box 28, Collection 20, Herbert John Taylor Papers, Archives of the Billy Graham Center, Wheaton, IL.

27. Bill Kliewer, "Joi Bangla: Birth Cry of a Nation," *World Vision*, April 1972, 4–6; Mooneyham, "Longest Walk of Their Lives," *World Vision*, January 1973, 4–6; Mooneyham, "Managua Aftermath—Caricature of Reality," *World Vision*, March 1973, 4–8; "Six Million in Upper Volta Drought," *World Vision*, September 1973, 20.

28. Marty Lonsdale, interview by author, November 16, 2010, Federal Way, WA.

29. Walter Bennett and Russ Reid remained the two main evangelical advertising firms; Reid handled World Vision, and Bennett's main account was the BGEA. See Hamilton, "An Historical Study of Bob Pierce," 183–84; Waters, "How World Vision Rose from Obscurity to Prominence," 74.

30. Stewart M. Hoover, *Mass Media Religion: The Social Sources of the Electronic Church* (Newbury Park, CA: Sage Publications, 1988); Quentin James Schultze, *American Evangelicals and the Mass Media: Perspectives on the Relationship Between American Evangelicals and the Mass Media* (Grand Rapids, MI: Academie Books/Zondervan, 1992); John Wigger, *PTL: The Rise and Fall of Jim and Tammy Faye Bakker's Evangelical Empire* (New York: Oxford University Press, 2017).

31. Hamilton, "An Historical Study of Bob Pierce," 185–204; Waters, "How World Vision Rose from Obscurity to Prominence," 74–75.

32. "*Children of Zero*: A 'Special' Special for the Whole Family," news release, May 22, 1972, WVI Central Records.

33. Waters, "How World Vision Rose from Obscurity to Prominence," 74–75.

34. Ibid., 70.

35. *One to One* (1975), WVUS Archives; Hamilton, "An Historical Study of Bob Pierce," 205–18.

36. World Vision produced five telethons and a number of additional television documentaries through the 1970s. The first telethon garnered $700,000 in one-time and first pledge gifts over a three-month period. Sheryl Watkins, ed., "Understanding Child Sponsorship: A Historical Perspective," 1996, WVUS Archives.

37. Soon many other humanitarian organizations sought to copy World Vision's success. Christian Children's Fund began to focus not on multihour telethons but short commercials in 1976. Sally Struthers became its public voice and image. Tise, *A Book About Children*, 85.

38. Richard Halverson, "A History of Service," *World Vision*, November 1976, 6–8; World Vision Annual Reports, 1970–78, WVI Central Records.

39. For critiques of these practices of fund-raising through images of suffering, see Alex de Waal, *Famine Crimes: Politics and the Disaster Relief Industry in Africa* (Bloomington: Indiana University Press, 1997); Susan D. Moeller, *Compassion Fatigue: How the Media Sell Disease, Famine, War and Death* (New York: Routledge, 1999).

40. From 1968 to 1972, PL 480 funds averaged nine million tons. By 1974, the average was only 4.3 million. In 1975, Congress passed Hatfield's measure that allowed no more than 30 percent of concessional aid to be used for political purposes to countries not seriously affected by food shortages. Another bill limited U.S. aid to any one country to 10 percent of the total. See Eells, "Mark Hatfield and the Search for an Evangelical Politics," 359, 370–74; Mark Hatfield, "World Hunger: More Explosive Than Atomic Weaponry," *World Vision*, February 1975, 4–7.

41. "Joint Senator Hatfield and World Vision Press Release," November 26, 1974, Folder 10, Box 20, CTI Records; Hatfield, "Responses to a Hungry World," *World Vision*, January 1975, 20; "Hatfield Urges National Fasting Day," *Washington Post*, November 26, 1974, A4; Mooneyham, "Ministering to the Hunger Belt," *Christianity Today*, January 3, 1975, 6–11; Ted Engstrom, "Lo the Black Horse Cometh! As Christians, How Shall We Respond to Famine?," *World Vision*, January 1975, 9–11; Hatfield, "Thanksgiving 1974: Feast or Famine?," *Eternity*, November 1974, 35–36, 40–41; Hatfield, "The Greed of Man and the Will of God," *Other Side*, November–December 1974, 8–13, 62–64; Hatfield, "And Still They Hunger," *Post-American*, January 1975, 20–24; Hatfield, "The Shadow of Global Hunger," *Moody Monthly*, January 1975, 30–31, 71–73; Hatfield, "An Economics for Sustaining Humanity," *Post-American*, March 1975, 16–21; Carl Henry, "Spectre of Famine," *Christianity Today*, August 8, 1975, 26–27; J. D. Douglas, "Awakening to a Hungry World," *Christianity Today*, October 24, 1975.

42. "Joint Senator Hatfield and World Vision Press Release."

43. Mooneyham, "The Year Ahead: Focus on a Hungry World," *World Vision*, December 1974, 8. Mooneyham and Hatfield hoped the campaign would raise $5 million for World Vision programs in 1975 (Rah and VanderPol, *Return to Justice*, 80–84).

44. "FAST Project," Mooneyham Papers, WVI Central Records.

45. Ibid.; Fowler, *A New Engagement*, 182–83.

46. Mooneyham's position provides a counterexample to the thesis most recently argued by Matthew Sutton (*American Apocalypse*) that focuses on the centrality of premillennial eschatology in shaping American evangelicalism. While certainly such premillennial eschatology filled the genres of pop theology and religious fiction of the day as well as highlighted the talking points of various religious leaders and politicians, I believe the rise of religious relief and development demonstrates that in practice, the eschatology's influence was less influential than many other scholars have recently argued.

47. Ed Norman, "Our Hunger Program—Not Either/or but Both/And," *World Vision*, May 1975, 16; William Needham, "Where to Learn More About Our Hungry Planet," *World Vision*, May 1975, 17.

48. Mooneyham, *What Do You Say to a Hungry World?*, 137–50.

49. Ibid., 122, 178–79; Rah and VanderPol, *Return to Justice*, 55. The simple living movement gained steam among many Americans in the 1970s. See David Shi, *The Simple Life: Plain Living and High Thinking in American Culture* (New York: Oxford University Press, 1985). It also gathered steam among evangelicals in the late 1970s. See Ronald J. Sider, *Rich Christians in an Age of Hunger* (Downers Grove, IL: InterVarsity Press, 1977); Ronald J. Sider, *Living More Simply: Biblical Principles and Practical Models* (Downers Grove, IL: InterVarsity Press, 1980).

50. World Vision reported its 1975 income was up 57 percent over the previous year, and it also claimed its hunger appeals led to increased contributions to Church World Service, Food for the Hungry, and World Relief as well. Mooneyham, "Where Did the Hunger Crisis Go?," *World Vision*, October 1976, 10–11.

51. Dunker, *Man of Vision*, 193–94.

52. Graham and Lockerbie, *Bob Pierce*, 77.

53. Grant, "He Only Wants to Save the World."

54. Pierce, *Samaritan's Diary*, 1973, vol. 1, Folder 4, Box 1, Collection 593, Records of Lillian Dickson, Archives of the Billy Graham Center, Wheaton, IL.

55. Graham and Lockerbie, *Bob Pierce*, 53.

56. Graham, *Rebel with a Cause*, 149; Graham and Lockerbie, *Bob Pierce*, 83.

57. Graham, *Rebel with a Cause*, 165; Graham and Lockerbie, *Bob Pierce*, 81–85.

58. Graham, *Rebel with a Cause*, 187.

59. Along with the United States, these became known as World Vision support countries in contrast to field or national countries that received funds to operate programs. "Report of World Vision Internationalization Study Committee" (1976), WVI Central Records.

60. Whaites, "Pursuing Partnership," 414.

61. "Report of World Vision Internationalization Study Committee" (1976); Bryant Myers, "Journeying Toward Interdependence: The Unfinished Story of World Vision," n.d., WVI Central Records.

62. Whaites, "Pursuing Partnership," 414; "Report of World Vision Internationalization Study Committee." In his unpublished memoirs, former World Vision Canada president Bernard Barron remembers a conversation with Stan Mooneyham at the 1972 National Prayer Breakfast. While one U.S. board member declared that World Vision Canada must "get back in line" with the U.S. vision of the organization, Mooneyham was more charitable in trying to mend tense relationships with the Canadian office.

63. Paul Rees, "Theology of Internationalization," and Sam Kamaleson, "Theology of Internationalization," in "Report of World Vision Internationalization Study Committee," Minutes of Combined Meetings Boards of Directors of WVI, Pattaya Beach, Thailand, March 22–25, 1974, WVI Central Records; Mooneyham, "Some Thoughts About Two Words"; Irvine, *Best Things in the Worst Times*, 78.

64. W. Stanley Mooneyham, "Remarks on Aspects of Internationalization Prepared Especially for Presentation to Australia/New Zealand Boards," February 1, 1978, WVI Central Records.

65. Because World Vision U.S. contributed the greatest proportion of funds to the partnership (75 percent), it held a higher proportion of board seats: United States, four; Canada, two; Australia, two; New Zealand, one; and six to eight, at large. In early 1975, World Vision reported an income of $15 million; $11 million came from the United States, $2 million from Australia/New Zealand, $1.5 million from Canada, and $250,000 from South Africa. McCleary, *Global Compassion*, 117.

66. Irvine, *Best Things*, 83. For the specifics of World Vision's reorganization, see the "Report of the Internationalization Study Committee," "Declaration of Internationalization," and the "Minutes of World Vision's Joint Board and International Councils," 1974, 1976, 1978, and 1980, WVI Central Records.

67. Bryant Myers, "Journeying Toward Interdependence"; Roberta Hestenes, "Laying the Foundations: Brief Reflections on WV History," n.d., WVI Central Records.

Chapter 7

1. Mooneyham, "Remarks on Aspects of Internationalization Prepared Especially for Presentation to Australia/New Zealand Boards."

2. W. Stanley Mooneyham, "Some Thoughts About Two Words," *World Vision*, January 1974, draft copy in Mooneyham Papers, WVI Central Records.

3. "Declaration of Internationalization," reprinted in *World Vision*, September 1978, 2.

4. Whaites, "Pursuing Partnership," 415; "Declaration of Internationalization"; also World Vision Annual Reports, 1970–80, WVI Central Records.

5. Bernard Barron, "Memoir," unpublished manuscript, WVI Central Records; Barron remembers one Oxfam executive making the accusation to him in 1972 that World Vision waits at the bottom of the cliff with an ambulance for the accident to occur but never looked to preventive measures.

6. Gene Daniels, telephone interview by author, June 6, 2010; Rohrer, *Open Arms*, 150–51.

7. The six objectives were: (1) ministering to children and families; (2) providing emergency aid; (3) developing self-reliance; (4) reaching the unreached; (5) strengthening leadership; (6) challenging to mission. See Graeme Irvine, World Vision vice president of field ministries, "Ministry Integration: What Is Meant by It and Why We Need It," October 7, 1978, Irvine Papers, WVI Central Records.

8. Bryant Myers, interview by author, June 20, 2007, Pasadena, CA; Rohrer, *Open Arms*, 149–52.

9. W. W. Rostow, *The Stages of Economic Growth: A Non-Communist Manifesto* (Cambridge: Cambridge University Press, 1960). Rostow proposed development as a tool to help counter the rise of communism; he hypothesized that traditional societies would reach a point

of economic growth that would allow them to "take-off" and modernize, and it was up to the West to bring Third World societies to this point.

10. Tanzanian president Julius Nyerere became best known for popularizing "self-reliance" into development parlance. In the Arusha Declaration in 1967, he also called for autonomy and auto-centered development. See Rist, *The History of Development*, 123–68; Tara Hefferan, *Twinning Faith and Development: Catholic Parish Partnering in the US and Haiti* (Bloomfield, CT: Kumarian Press, 2007), 46.

11. McCleary, *Global Compassion*, 103–5.

12. Liberation theologians Gustavo Gutiérrez and Leonardo Boff both highlighted how the poor were dignified when they participate in their own liberation. Kevin Norman York-Simmons, "A Critique of Christian Development as Resolution to the Crisis in U.S. Protestant Foreign Missions" (PhD diss., Vanderbilt University, 2009), 75.

13. Rachel M. McCleary, "Taking God Overseas: Competition and Institutional Homogeneity Among International Religious Private Voluntary Organizations," paper presented to the International Studies Association, March 2004, Montreal, Quebec, Canada, 20; McCleary, *Global Compassion*, 105. As USAID began to fund development grants to NGOs over awarding contracts to meet humanitarian mandates, it had a vested interest in facilitating leading NGOs to build institutional capacity as development organizations. Between 1973 and 1979, it awarded forty DPGs to NGOs for this purpose. Initially, all relief and development programs and government funding went through the subsidiary World Vision Relief Organization to avoid questions of government funding of religious programs. WVRO Annual Report to USAID (April 1975 to March 1976), WVI Central Records.

14. World Vision Board of Directors Meeting, March 23, 1974; Rohrer noted that from 1976 to 1978, for each region of world, World Vision had one relief and development staff member whose salary, travel, office budget, and teaching materials were paid by the US government. Rohrer, *Open Arms*, 152.

15. World Vision Annual Reports, 1970–79, WVI Central Records.

16. The Purdue scientist, Robert C. Pickett, had already consulted in over ninety countries in international crop management. In one article to World Vision donors, Pickett articulated his commitments: "As a scientist, I know that much can be done about many of the conditions and situations that allow hunger, malnutrition and inadequate nutrition to exist. My purpose in coming to World Vision was and is to do something about the situation." See Robert C. Pickett, "Hope for the Hungry," *World Vision*, March 1978, 10–11; "World Vision Hires Robert Pickett," *World Vision*, September 1977, 20.

17. "Relief and Development Conference in Nairobi," *World Vision*, October 1976, 19; "Ken Tracy to Gottfried Osei-Mensah," Folder 32, Box 23, Collection 46, Records of the Lausanne Committee on World Evangelization, Archives of the Billy Graham Center, Wheaton, IL.

18. World Vision staffers often replicated Yen's development approach verbatim in articulating their own approach. While offering more information on each step, the approach was: "go to the people; live among them; learn from them; work with them; plan with them; build on what they have; teach by showing; learn by doing; not a showcase, but a pattern; not odds and ends, but a system; not relief but release." See, for example, Bryant Myers, "Bible and Development," Burundi Development Seminar, 1979,WVI Central Records; see also "Engstrom with Dr. Yen," *World Vision*, May 1978, 17; Bryant Myers, "World Vision Policy on

Development," revised 1987, WVI Central Records; Rohrer, *Open Arms*, 152; Daniels interview, June 6, 2010.

19. In fiscal year 1975–76, childcare made up $11,237,391 of its $15,328,704 budget. Africa proved the only exception. World Vision only established an operational office there in 1974–75, and Africa lacked the structures already in place elsewhere for the dominant fund-raising mechanism of child sponsorship. In fiscal year 1975–76, development made up $1,853,886 of the $2,641,942 of Africa's budget. These percentages would later change as World Vision implemented sponsorship in Africa. See World Vision Annual Report, 1975–76, WVI Central Records.

20. Myers, "The Directions for the Next Ten Years," *World Vision*, quoted in Rohrer, *Open Arms*, 153.

21. "Engstrom on Relief and Development," *World Vision*, January 1978, 17.

22. American evangelicals engaged in development during the 1960s, but it took neoliberal economic forms. Development Assistance Services, later renamed International Development Association, became an affiliate of the World Evangelical Fellowship. It sought to use Western businessmen to help train national Christians in economic development so that churches and missionaries could focus on evangelism. Folder 8, Box 28, Collection 338, World Evangelical Fellowship, Archives of the Billy Graham Center, Wheaton, IL (hereafter cited as WEF Records).

23. Carl Henry, lecturing for World Vision on a Latin American tour, retold a story of being accused as another Westerner only interested in giving aspirin and Band-Aids over working against injustice. Henry criticized his accuser's eagerness to embrace Marxism but admitted that attacking unjust social structures was an important part of the gospel. Ronald J. Sider, ed., *Evangelicals and Development: Toward a Theology of Social Change* (Philadelphia: Westminster Press, 1982), 99.

24. Smith, "An Awakening of Conscience," 95, 104–8, 312–16; Smith reports that of the eighty-five evangelical relief and development organizations she studied, average growth rate was 17 percent while the evangelical missions agencies averaged only 8–10 percent.

25. Rah and VanderPol, *Return to Justice*, 90.

26. Yujun Mei, "The Changing Discourse of International Humanitarian Charitable-Relief NGOs" (PhD diss., Arizona State University, 2003); Norman Rohrer, *This Poor Man Cried: The Story of Larry Ward* (Wheaton, IL: Tyndale House, 1984).

27. John R. W. Stott, *Christian Mission in the Modern World* (Downers Grove, IL: Inter-Varsity Press, 1975), 23.

28. Similar to the Radical Discipleship statement at the 1974 Lausanne Congress, those advocating for social action and the voices of Two-Thirds World evangelicals on the Lausanne agenda drafted a "Statement of Concern on the Future of the Lausanne Committee on World Evangelization." See C. René Padilla and Chris Sugden, eds., *Texts on Evangelical Social Ethics, 1974–1983* (Bramcote: Grove, 1985), 22–24; see also David J. Bosch, "In Search of Mission: Reflections on 'Melbourne' and 'Pattaya,'" *Missionalia* 9, no. 1 (1981): 3–18; Waldron Scott, "The Significance of Pattaya," *Missiology* 9, no. 1 (January 1981): 57–76; Steuernagel, "The Theology of Mission," 189–95; Ed Dayton, "World Vision and LCWE: An Analysis," April 28, 1986, and Dayton, "World Vision Support for LCWE," International Affairs Committee, July 1, 1986, both in WVI Central Records.

29. International Consultation on Simple Lifestyle, "An Evangelical Commitment to Simple Lifestyle," Lausanne Occasional Paper 20 (1980), www.lausanne.org/all-documents/

lop-20.html; Ronald Sider, *Lifestyle in the Eighties: An Evangelical Commitment to Simple Lifestyle* (Philadelphia: Westminster Press, 1982).

30. The conference emerged out of a bitter feud within the evangelical movement. Arthur Johnston's 1978 book *The Battle for World Evangelism*, traced the decline of the World Council of Churches to its loss of commitment to missions, and he predicted Lausanne was moving in the same direction. John Stott countered Johnston's accusations in an open letter in *Christianity Today*. They put together the CRESR conference to sort out their differences. The resulting statement defined social action and evangelism as equal partners. It described the relationship as "two blades of a pair of scissors or the two wings of a bird." "Evangelism and Social Responsibility: An Evangelical Commitment," Lausanne Occasional Paper 21 (1982), http://www.lausanne.org/en/documents/lops/79-lop-21.html; see also John R. W. Stott, "Twenty Years After Lausanne: Some Personal Reflections," *International Bulletin of Missionary Research* 19, no. 2 (April 1995): 51–52; Arthur Johnston, *The Battle for World Evangelism* (Wheaton, IL: Tyndale House Publishers, 1978); Bruce J. Nicholls, *In Word and Deed: Evangelism and Social Responsibility* (Grand Rapids MI: Eerdmans, 1986).

31. "Transformation: The Church in Response to Human Need," in *The Church in Response to Human Need*, ed. Vinay Samuel and Chris Sugden (Grand Rapids, MI: Eerdmans, 1987), 254–65, quote at sec. 5.26; also at https://www.lausanne.org/content/statement/transformation-the-church-in-response-to-human-need.html.

32. Edward R. Dayton, "Social Transformation: The Mission of God," in Samuel and Sugden, *The Church in Response to Human Need*, 53. Evangelicals convened a number of conferences on development in the late 1970s through the early 1980s. In 1977, Carl Henry convened a symposium on the "the ministry of development in the life of the church," for Development Assistance Services. The World Evangelical Fellowship (WEF) convened a Consultation on the Theology of Development the week prior to Sider's 1980 International Consultation on Simple Lifestyle. They featured presentations like "Development That Is Christian" and "The Contribution of the Evangelical Relief and Development Agency to the Mission of the Church in Today's World." See Carl F. H. Henry and Robert Lincoln Hancock, *The Ministry of Development in Evangelical Perspective: A Symposium on the Social and Spiritual Mandate* (Pasadena, CA: William Carey Library, 1979); Sider, *Evangelicals and Development*. Also see minutes for WEF Consultation of Development in the 1980s, Folder 267, Box 37, WEF Records.

33. Despite its somber themes, Sider's book (*Rich Christians in an Age of Hunger*) became a cult classic for many evangelicals through multiple revised and expanded editions.

34. Ron Sider, "Toward a Theology of Community Development," Development Assistance Services (DAS) conference, Haiti, 1978, Folder 7, Box 32, EFMA Records.

35. Tom Sine, "Development: Its Secular Past and Its Uncertain Future," in *The Church in Response to Human Need*, ed. Tom Sine (Monrovia, CA: MARC, 1983), 9–36. The World Council of Churches and ecumenical mission also took issue with development as undermining indigenous principles and promoting Western visions of modernization. See Kenith A. David, "Development Is Not Our Word," *International Review of Mission* 73, no. 290 (April 1984): 185–90.

36. Wayne Bragg served as a missionary to the Caribbean, and in 1976 came to Wheaton College to coordinate the Human Needs and Global Resources program that trained many evangelical students in development principles. See Wayne Bragg, "Beyond Development," in

Sine, *The Church in Response to Human Need*, 37–95; Wayne G. Bragg, "Beyond Development to Transformation," *International Review of Mission* 73, no. 290 (April 1984): 157, 165. Bragg consulted for World Vision on numerous occasions, and its own development policies readily acknowledge his approach. See Geoff Renner, "Position Paper on a View of Development," May 11, 1978, WVI Central Records; Bryant L. Myers, *Walking with the Poor: Principles and Practices of Transformational Development* (Maryknoll, NY: Orbis, 1999), 95; also see York-Simmons, "Critique of Christian Development," 87–89.

37. Bergstrom interview, November 16, 2010.

38. Wade Coggins, "The Administrator's Dilemma in Confronting Development Needs," 1978 Haiti Development Assistance Services Conference, Folder 7, Box 32, EFMA Records.

39. AERDO charter members were World Relief; Food for the Hungry, Compassion, World Concern, MAP International, Institute for International Development, Inc., and World Vision International. In 2010, AERDO renamed itself the Accord Network.

40. Graeme Irvine, "Program and Ministry Integration," Relief and Development Conference in Nairobi, Kenya, November 1976; and Irvine, "Ministry Integration," Irvine Papers, WVI Central Records.

41. "Understanding Child Sponsorship: A Historical Perspective," WVUS Archives; Bruce Davis, associate director of the Latin America Regional Office (LARO), "Observations and Some History of the Childcare Holistic Method from the Latin America Region," September 1980, WVI Central Records; Rohrer, *Open Arms*, 121.

42. Bryant Myers, "Bible and Development," Burundi Development Seminar, 1979, WVI Central Records; Ted Ward, address to World Vision staff, February 13, 1981, WVI Central Records.

43. B. E. Fernando quoted in Irvine, *Best Things in the Worst Times*, 115.

44. Edward R. Dayton, "Christian Development," August 1977; Geoff Renner, "World Vision and Its View of Development," May 11, 1978; Hal Barber, "World Vision's View of Development," January 22, 1979, WVI Central Records. In 1979, World Vision approved its first Development Policy Statement. It amended the policy under Bryant Myers's leadership in 1987.

45. Irvine, "Program and Ministry Integration" and "Ministry Integration," WVI Central Records.

46. Edward R. Dayton, "Some Introductory Thoughts on Evangelization and Development," MARC Newsletter, November 1977; Dayton, "Development as Evangelism," MARC Newsletter, January 1979; Dayton, "World Vision and Evangelization," International World Vision Staff Conference, 1978, WVI Central Records.

47. "Understanding Child Sponsorship: A Historical Perspective," WVUS Archives; Fram Jehangir, "Holistic Development Approach in Childcare," 1979, World Vision Position Paper, WVI Central Records; "World Vision Childcare Position Paper," 1985, WVI Central Records.

48. Stephen Board, "The Great Evangelical Power Shift: How Has the Mushrooming of Parachurch Organizations Changed the Church?," *Eternity* 30 (1979): 17–21; see also Christopher P. Scheitle, *Beyond the Congregation: The World of Christian Nonprofits* (Oxford: Oxford University Press, 2010); Michael S. Hamilton, "More Money, More Ministry: The Financing of American Evangelicalism Since 1945," in Eskridge and Noll, *More Money, More Ministry*, 104–38.

49. Ron Wilson, "Parachurch: Becoming Part of the Body," *Christianity Today*, September 19, 1980, 18–20; J. Alan Youngren, "Parachurch Proliferation: The Frontier Spirit Caught

in Traffic," *Christianity Today*, November 6, 1981, 38–41; "Cooperating in World Evangelization: A Handbook on Church/Para-Church Relationships," Lausanne Occasional Paper 24,
1983, http://www.lausanne.org/en/documents/lops/67-lop-24.html.

50. See Mooneyham, "Church vs. Para-Church—a Non-Issue?," discussion paper presented to WVI Council, 1978; Paul Rees, "Response to Mooneyham," June 2, 1978; and
William J. Newell, "Responses to Mooneyham," October 4, 1978; all in WVI Central Records.

51. Mooneyham, "Remarks on Aspects of Internationalization Prepared Especially for
Presentation to Australia/New Zealand Boards." Mooneyham did not apologize for the need
to recruit Christians from the secular marketplace.

52. Bill Kliewer, "Report on World Vision's Constituency," August 12, 1980, WVI Central Records. Kliewer, then World Vision's marketing director, reported to fellow marketing
executives that it was not up to them to decide who were the "wheat and tares" among its
donors but only to control what it could—World Vision's own identity. Kliewer's comments
were in response to growing internal fears of the organization's secularization. From 1974 to
1984, the percentage of funds World Vision U.S. received from local churches went from a
high of 7.6 percent to 4 percent. In the early 1980s, it worked with only 2,000 churches; two
decades earlier, it had worked with 2,500 just in its Northwest office. "World Vision and
Church Relations," 1984, WVI Central Records.

53. Waters, "How World Vision Rose from Obscurity to Prominence," 87–89. James
Greenelsh, director of film and audiovisual productions for World Vision offered this critique
in 1979; quoted in Hamilton, "An Historical Study of Bob Pierce," 273.

54. The accusation of stealing Christian leaders for its staff became a constant refrain
against World Vision. From World Vision's perspective, it insisted on paying nationals a fair
wage so that they would not be considered second-class citizens to the expatriate staff who
received far more. Rohrer, *Open Arms*, 157.

55. Manfred Grellert, interview by author, June 9, 2010, Monrovia, CA; Lonsdale interview, November 16, 2010; Hestenes, "Laying the Foundations"; Myers, "Journeying Toward
Interdependence."

56. Stanley Mooneyham interview, *Wittenberg Door*, February–March 1975, 8–15; Peter
Stalker, "Please Do Not Sponsor This Child," *New Internationalist*, May 1, 1982, http://www
.newint.org/features/1982/05/01/keynote/. Stalker's article was among the first wave of exposés
that grew to critique child-sponsorship programs as ineffective development. World Vision
had already begun to debate these questions. See "Fundraising and the Dignity of People,"
August 31, 1980; and "WV Promotion and Dignity of People" (1981), WVI Central Records.

57. John Rymer, "World Vision and Lifestyle," paper presented at 1983 World Vision
International Council, WVI Central Records.

58. See Ted Engstrom's "Monthly Memo" columns, *World Vision*, February 1976, p. 9,
January 1977, p. 17, February 1979, p. 16, and April 1979, p. 19; also see "Evangelical Agencies
Meet to Discuss Regulation," *World Vision*, February 1978, 22.

59. Engstrom, *Reflections on a Pilgrimage*, 126–27; Mooneyham, "History of ECFA,"
speech delivered at Inaugural ECFA Membership Meeting, September 11, 1979, WVI Central
Records; *Enhancing Trust: The ECFA Story* (Winchester, VA: ECFA Press, 2016).

60. The establishment of World Vision's European offices presented their own problems.
Established Christian charities such as Oxfam and the relief, development, and mission arms
of other denominations resented World Vision expanding on their turf. World Vision UK

committed to avoid fund-raising in churches for fifteen years to assuage the fears of competition from other charities. As a result, it attracted a far more secular support base even as it continued to be attacked by the church establishment as fundamentalist. Whaites, "Pursuing Partnership," 416–517.

61. Irvine, *Best Things in the Worst Times*, 187.

62. Dayton, "World Vision and Evangelization."

63. Mooneyham continued, "We simply try to demonstrate Christian love in tangible ways. I feel it would be phony and manipulative to provide help to suffering people only because they are potentially evangelistic statistics." Sue Avery, "World Vision—Food and Faith," *Los Angeles Times*, December 25, 1980, SG1.

64. Edward R. Dayton, Gene Daniels, and J. Paul Landrey, "World Vision Evangelism Task Force," 1980, WVI Central Records; "Report on World Vision and World Evangelization," January 1981; Sam Kamaleson, "Use of Dialogue in Evangelism," 1979; Sam Kamaleson, "History of Evangelism in World Vision," 1985; also see Ted Engstrom's comments to the International Affairs Committee, February 14–17, 1983, WVI Central Records. Engstrom had just assumed the interim role of WVI president after Mooneyham resigned in 1982. At the meeting, Engstrom expressed his concern that World Vision not let social concerns obscure the need of personal conversion and the importance of holy living.

65. "Relationship to Governments and Supra-Governmental Bodies," WVI policy statement, originally approved June 3, 1978, revised March 13, 1985, WVI Central Records.

66. Avery, "World Vision—Food and Faith."

67. "Back to that Old Time Religion," *Time*, December 26, 1977, 58.

68. Ken Woodward, "Born Again!," *Newsweek*, October 25, 1976, 68–78; "Protestants: Away from Activism and Back to the Basics," *U.S. News & World Report*, April 11, 1977, 58.

69. Mooneyham, "The Day of Missions Has Hardly Begun," address to World Vision New Zealand, November 1979, WVI Central Records.

70. Mooneyham, "Some Thoughts About the Bandwagon," *World Vision*, May 1978, 23; Mooneyham, "The Affliction of Adjectivitis," *World Vision*, June 1979, 23; Mooneyham, "United We Fall," *World Vision*, April 1980, 23.

71. Graeme Irvine, "World Vision Programs in the Philippines," June 14, 1978; Irvine, "Relationships with Roman Catholic Church," September 16, 1983; Irvine, "Guidelines for Field on Roman Catholic Relationships," 1983; all in WVI Central Records.

72. World Vision's policies went on to say that when a Christian community is divided and World Vision perceived it could not work with both parties, it would cooperate with those closest to its own evangelical position. Edward R. Dayton, "World Vision's Relationships to Roman Catholics," prepared for Field Review Meeting, August 21, 1978, WVI Central Records.

73. "Relationships with Other Christian Organizations," World Vision policy statement, approved June 3, 1978 (this policy would be revised March 13, 1985); Edward Dayton, "Discussion of Policy," World Vision Board of Directors Meeting, September 16–17, 1979, WVI Central Records.

74. Michael Lee, "World Vision, Go Home!," *Christian Century*, May 16, 1979, 542–44; Mooneyham, "World Vision: A Different Opinion," *Christian Century*, July 4, 1979, 707–8.

75. Irvine, "Relationships with Roman Catholic Church."

76. World Vision's International Affairs Committee, February 19–20, 1980, and February 15–19, 1981, WVI Central Records. Mooneyham reflected at the end of his career after leaving

World Vision, "We've been ecumenical from day one; we will continue to be ecumenical. It sometimes isn't easy to work with people who claim it in name, and believe it in theory but don't practice it in reality." Mooneyham, "Keep Marching Off the Map," March 13, 1991, WVUS Archives.

77. Mooneyham to John Kenyon, associate editor of *Christian Herald*, April 2, 1980, Mooneyham Papers, WVI Central Records.

78. J. A. Eckrom, "Operation Seasweep: When World Vision Went to Sea," WVUS Archives; W. Stanley Mooneyham, *Sea of Heartbreak* (Plainfield , NJ: Logos International, 1980).

79. Lee, "World Vision, Go Home!"

80. The Desperate Voyage, BBC, 1979; World Vision produced its own film, *Escape to Nowhere*, in 1978 and a revised edition in 1979, both in WVUS Archives. For coverage in World Vision's magazine, see "One Family's Ordeal," *World Vision*, September 1978, 12–13; Burt Singleton, "Operation Seasweep: Our First Encounters," *World Vision*, September 1978, 11–13; "We Knew We Were All Going to Die," *World Vision*, December 1978, 14–15; Kenneth L. Wilson, "On the Edge of Freedom," *World Vision*, April 1979, 11; Kenny Waters, "1400 'Tons of Compassion,' 93 Faces of Joy," *World Vision*, August 1979, 3–7; Kenneth L. Wilson, "Seasweep's New Mission," *World Vision*, October 1979, 3–7; "Seasweep II Begins," *World Vision*, May 1979, 16.

81. Sally Koris, "Stan Mooneyham Gets Help at Last in His Fight to Save the Boat People," *People*, August 6, 1979; James Quig, "One Man's Mission to Save Refugees," *Montreal Gazette*, July 19, 1979, 1, 10; Gerald Utting, "Captain Courageous Leads Fight for Life in Voyage from Hell," *Montreal Gazette*, July 18, 1979, 1, 10; Paul Dean, "Coming to the Aid of the Boat People," *Los Angeles Times*, July 23, 1979, E1; "Refugees: More Trials for the Boat People," *Time*, August 13, 1979; "Interviewing Boat People Survivors," *60 Minutes*, June 24, 1980.

82. Eckrom, "Operation Seasweep." World Vision staff disagreed over the significance of Operation Seasweep. While it had little impact on organizational development and program implementation, it did raise World Vision's public profile. Bill Kliewer, interview by author, June 27, 2007, Monrovia, CA; Dave Toycen, telephone interview by author, May 28, 2010.

83. *Escape to Nowhere* (1979, rev. ed.); Hamilton, "An Historical Study of Bob Pierce," 241–42.

84. *Escape to Nowhere* (1979 rev. ed.).

85. Mooneyham, "Cambodia: Does the World Care?," *World Vision*, November 1979, 3–7; Paul Jones, "Inside Cambodia Wounds Only God Can Heal," *World Vision*, February 1980, 3–6; Mooneyham, "Kampuchea: It Is Worth Beginning Again," *World Vision*, March 1980, 3–9.

86. Whaites, "Pursuing Partnership," 416–17; Lee Huhn, "Dateline Nicaragua," *World Vision*, October 1979, 18–19; Alan Maltun, "Israel Accused of Halting Mercy Ship," *Los Angeles Times*, July 4, 1982, SG1; "Press-Time Report: Inside Lebanon," *World Vision*, August 1982, 12–13, 18; W. Stanley Mooneyham, "Shattered Buildings, Broken Lives," *World Vision*, September 1982, 3–11; Jean Bouchebel, former WVI national director for Lebanon, interview by author, June 10, 2010, Monrovia, CA; Hestenes, "Laying the Foundations."

87. Stoll, *Is Latin America Turning Protestant?*, 284; WVUS Annual Reports, 1978–80, WVI Central Records.

88. The budget for World Vision's Latin American programs grew from $400,000 in 1975 to $27.2 million by 1983. In 1977, the budget expanded by 70 percent in a single year. It grew by 59 percent in 1978, 48 percent in 1979, 44 percent in 1980, 46 percent in 1981, 26 percent in 1982, and 21 percent in 1983. World Vision Board of Directors' Minutes, September 14–15, 1982, WVI Central Records.

89. Oscar A. Romero, "Taking Risks for the Poor," *World Vision*, June 1982, 6–7; Stoll, *Is Latin America Turning Protestant?*, 285.

90. "Human Rights Reports of the Mission Honduras/Salvadorian Refugees," Pax Christi International, 1981, WVI Central Records.

91. Stoll, *Is Latin America Turning Protestant?*, 286–90.

92. Kenneth L. Woodward, "Missionaries on the Line," *Time*, March 8, 1972, 69–70; Maria Rodriguez Araya, "U.S. Relief Agency Accused of Complicity with Honduran Military," *Latinamerica Press*, February 25, 1982, 7–8; Steve Askin, "Hostility, Conflict Engulf World Vision," *National Catholic Reporter*, April 23, 1982, 9ff. World Vision continued to call for Pax Christi to issue a retraction throughout the 1980s, including private meetings with leadership throughout the Catholic Church. See "A Summary of the Pax Christi World Vision Controversy Prepared for His Eminence, Cardinal Franz Koenig by World Vision," July 1986; and Graeme Irvine, "A Statement to the Executive Committee of Pax Christi International," April 1988, both in WVI Central Records.

93. "A Report on the Refugee Relief Program of World Vision in Honduras," Pax Christi, December 1981—World Vision International," December 1981, Pax Christi USA Records (PAX), University of Notre Dame Archives (UNDA), Notre Dame, IN. World Vision did its own extensive investigation of the Honduran program. See Tony Atkins, "Report of an Investigation of the Refugee Relief Program of World Vision in Honduras," November 24, 1981, WVI Central Records.

Chapter 8

1. WVI's 1976 income totaled $27,358,000 and grew to $127,400,000 by 1984. Field staff grew from 260 to 1,800 over the same period. WVI Annual Reports, 1976 and 1984, WVI Central Records; "Commission on Internationalization, 1978–1983, Interim Report," September 1984, WVI Central Records.

2. WVI only began to record any significant GIK funding in 1981, and that had grown by 100 percent by 1984. The following years, GIK funding grew astronomically from $US945,000 in 1984 to $80 million in 1986. Tom Houston, WVI president, "Partnership in Transition," International Council Address, September 16, 1986, WVI Central Records; International Affairs Committee, August 22–24, 1984, WVI Central Records.

3. World Vision cracked the top ten as the ninth largest INGO in 1990 and never again fell out of the top ten. McCleary, *Global Compassion*, 96.

4. "President's Report," Board of Directors' Minutes, September 14–15, 1982, WVI Central Records; Irvine, *Best Things in the Worst Times*, 94.

5. Max Weber, *Max Weber on Charisma and Institution Building: Selected Papers* (Chicago: University of Chicago Press, 1968); Mark Chaves, "Secularization as Declining Religious Authority," *Social Forces* 72, no. 3 (March 1994): 749–74.

6. Houston, "Partnership in Transition."

7. Graeme Irvine, "Relationships Require Work," May 4, 1993, WVI Central Records; Roberta Hestenes, WVI International Council moderator, "How Do Others See Us?," International Council Address, September 18, 1986, WVI Central Records.

8. Irvine, "At the Crossroads of Time," presidential address at WVI International Council, September 22, 1989, WVI Central Records.

9. In 1983, World Vision spent $28,949,766 in the Americas, $18,244,509 in Asia, $17,854,388 in Europe and the Middle East, and $13,312,280 in Africa. "World Vision 1983 Field Report," WVI Central Records.

10. *Crisis in the Horn of Africa*, 1981, WVUS Film Archives. See Waters, "How World Vision Rose from Obscurity to Prominence," 81–83; Waters notes that *Crisis in the Horn of Africa* produced $9.23 pledged for every dollar spent in production and purchasing air time. World Vision magazine articles and direct appeals reiterated the stories and images. See Stan Mooneyham, "A Disturbing Silence," *World Vision*, July 1981, 3–8; Mooneyham, "Life Revived, Laughter Restored," *World Vision*, November 1981, 3–8. One World Vision staffer noted, "Today, through television and such magazines as this one, you and I look into Ethiopian eyes whose glaze expresses as much agony as those of Nain's poor widow or the Jericho road's beaten robbery victim" (*World Vision*, June 1983, 2).

11. Dean Hirsch, "World Vision's Relief Ministry," 1986 International Council Records, WVI Central Records.

12. "Tom Houston Bio" and "World Vision News Release," September 19, 1983, WVI Central Records.

13. Houston, "African Drought Project," WVI Central Records; "Africa's Agony: Drought Withers a Mighty Continent," *World Vision*, August–September 1984; Irvine, *Best Things in the Worst Times*, 98; Grellert interview, June 9, 2010.

14. Irvine, *Best Things in the Worst Times*, 99.

15. Moeller, *Compassion Fatigue*, 111–17; Jonathan Benthall, *Disasters, Relief, and the Media* (London: I. B. Tauris, 1993), 84–85.

16. Subsequent royalties have brought in over $200 million for Band Aid to invest in relief and development work. Benthall, *Disasters, Relief, and the Media*, 84–85; Nina Shapiro, "The AIDS Evangelists," *Seattle Weekly*, November 15, 2006, http://www.seattleweekly.com/2006-11-15/news/the-aids-evangelists/.

17. WVI Annual Report, 1985, WVI Central Records; Irvine, *Best Things in the Worst Times*, 100.

18. McCleary, *Global Compassion*, 134. WVI noted that GIK contributions made up 27.3 percent of its income in 1984, 61.9 percent in 1985, and 59.4 percent in 1986 (WVI Annual Report, 1986, WVI Central Records). Food and pharmaceutical donations make up the majority of World Vision's GIK contributions, which do not include U.S., UN, and other bilateral aid as well as financial contributions from corporations. Between 2015 and 2017, GIK donations made up 15–25 percent of WVUS's revenue.

19. Hirsch, "World Vision's Relief Ministry."

20. "Ethiopia: The Nightmare Begins," World Vision appeal letter, 1988, WVI Central Records; Rachel Veale, "Dignity amid Poverty in Ethiopia: From Relief to Development," *World Vision*, April–May 1986, 12–14; "Ansokia Valley," *Together*, October–December 1985, 18; Irvine, *Best Things in the Worst Times*, 104–5.

21. John A. Kenyon, "Moving from Relief to Development," *Together*, October–December 1985, 12–13; Stephen K. Commins, "Big Goals, Big Problems," *Together*, October–December 1985, 20–23; Cliff Benzel, "Large Scale Development: A New Ministry for World Vision," World Vision International Affairs Committee, February 1986, WVI Central Records; Irvine, *Best Things in the Worst Times*, 106.

22. In 1985, World Vision's annual income was $231.5 million dollars. In 1986, it had slipped to $164 million. By 1987, it totaled $127 million. WVI Annual Report, 1987, WVI Central Records.

23. Alex de Waal, "Humanitarianism Unbound?," *African Rights* Discussion Paper No. 5, November 1994; Ken Waters and Sandy Young, "The Art & Ethics of Fundraising," *Christianity Today*, December 3, 2001, 50–52.

24. World Vision quickly scaled back initial projections of $200 million over five years to $6–10 million per year. Staff cutbacks and turnover eventually led the project to raise a total of $18 million. Sam Voorhies, "Large Scale Development: A Review of World Vision's Large Scale Development Programs," World Vision Staff Working Paper No. 11, 1991, WVI Central Records; Cliff Benzel, "LSD History, Analysis, and Status," memo to Hal Barber, February 13, 1986, WVI Central Records.

25. Irvine, *Best Things in the Worst Times*, 101.

26. Roger Riddell, *Does Foreign Aid Really Work?* (Oxford: Oxford University Press, 2007), 48; Tara Hefferan, Julie Adkins, and Laurie A. Occhipinti, *Bridging the Gaps: Faith-Based Organizations, Neoliberalism, and Development in Latin America and the Caribbean* (Lanham, MD: Lexington Books, 2009), 4.

27. McCleary, *Global Compassion*, 106–8; McCleary, "Taking God Overseas," 22.

28. Sharon Harper, ed., *The Lab, the Temple, and the Market: Reflections at the Intersection of Science, Religion, and Development* (Ottawa: IDRC, 2000), 71–72; Rist, *The History of Development*, 176; Colin Leys, "The Rise and Fall of Development Theory," in *The Anthropology of Development and Globalization: From Classical Political Economy to Contemporary Neoliberalism*, ed. Marc Edelman and Angelique Haugerud (Malden, MA: Blackwell, 2005), 113.

29. According to Peter Beyer, globalization is connected to "the spread of certain vital institutions of Western modernization to the rest of the globe, especially the modern capitalist economy, nation-state, and scientific rationality in the form of modern technology." Peter Beyer, *Religion and Globalization* (London: Sage Publications, 1994), 8. See also José Casanova, "Religion, the New Millennium, and Globalization," *Sociology of Religion* 62, no. 4 (2001): 423.

30. Peter Berger names four cultural forms of globalization: (1) an international business culture; (2) an intellectual elite and progressive NGO culture; (3) popular culture; and (4) popular religious culture in the form of a global evangelicalism or Pentecostalism. All four of Berger's formulations help us analyze an international NGO such as World Vision. Peter L. Berger and Samuel P. Huntington, eds., *Many Globalizations: Cultural Diversity in the Contemporary World* (Oxford: Oxford University Press, 2002), 6–8.

31. Boli and Brewington, "Religious Organizations"; Joshua J. Yates, "To Save the World: Humanitarianism and World Culture" (PhD diss., University of Virginia, 2006), 7–9.

32. Paul J. DiMaggio and Walter W. Powell, "The Iron Cage Revisited: Institutional Isomorphism and Collective Rationality in Organizational Fields," in *The New Institutionalism in Organizational Analysis*, ed. Walter W. Powell and Paul J. DiMaggio (Chicago: University of Chicago Press, 1991), 63–82.

33. See José Casanova, *Public Religions in the Modern World* (Chicago: University of Chicago Press, 1994), 19–38. Casanova notes the frequent linkage of globalization to secularization, which he defines primarily as (1) a differentiation of religious and secular spheres; (2) a decline of religion; or (3) a privatization of religion.

34. Ibid., 17–38. Casanova recognizes the differentiation of religious and secular spheres but dismisses claims about religious decline. He insists that there has been a revival of public religions that cannot be defined simply as a reaction against modernity.

35. Evelyn L. Bush, "Measuring Religion in Global Civil Society," *Social Forces* 85, no. 4 (2007): 1645–48.

36. Hamilton, "More Money, More Ministry," 118, 130; McCleary, "Taking God Overseas."

37. Stephen Commins served as an example of a new type of World Vision employee. Commins served as director of policy and planning at WVI and implemented much of World Vision's integrated development policies. An Episcopal priest, Commins came to World Vision from directing the Development Institute at the UCLA African Studies Center. He held a doctorate in urban planning and later went on to work for the World Bank.

38. WVI vice president Manfred Grellert described the perpetual tensions between piety and professionalism within World Vision: "You may have a bunch of pious folks who are stupid, and a bunch of technocrats who are shallow. And neither exemplify our aspirations to have both of them put together" (interview by author, June 22, 2007, Monrovia, CA).

39. Bryant Myers, "World Vision's Development Ministry: Issues for the Future," presented to World Vision's International Council, 1986. Myers's paper would lead to a revision of World Vision's development policy in 1987.

40. Irvine, *Best Things in the Worst Times*, 116–17.

41. Even after he became WVI president in 1989, Irvine continually advocated for WVI to move its operational headquarters to Geneva to demonstrate its international character without success. See Irvine, "How Can World Vision Become More International?," n.d. (ca. 1986); Irvine, "International Office Location Study," March 3, 1987; and Irvine, "Locating the International Office—Geneva Question," May 3, 1991; all found in Irvine Papers, WVI Central Records. See also Irvine, "The World Bank and World Vision: A Status Report," January 19, 1987, WVI Central Records; Stephen Commins, "World Vision International and Donors: Too Close for Comfort?," in *NGOs, States, and Donors: Too Close for Comfort?*, ed. David Hulme and Michael Edwards (New York: St. Martin's Press, 1997), 149–51.

42. "Report on Europe Program," June 17, 1986; "International Relations Update," WVI Newsletter, August 1987; "Relationship with the WCC," Global Leadership Team Report, March 2–4, 1988; all in WVI Central Records.

43. Irvine was one of forty-six attendees invited to the Stuttgart gathering. Irvine, "International Relations Update," WVI Newsletter, August 1987; "Statement of the Stuttgart Consultation on Evangelism," and John Stott, "A Note About the Stuttgart Statement on Evangelism," in Samuel and Hauser, *Proclaiming Christ in Christ's Way*, 212–25 and 208–11, respectively.

44. WVI International Council Records, 1992, WVI Central Records.

45. Mike Still and Bryant Myers, "Financial Growth of the World Vision Partnership," January 27, 1989, WVI Central Records; "Chronology: Expenditures and Staffing Since 1979," Partnership Review Committee, December 9–10, 1988, WVI Central Records.

46. "Strategy Working Group Records," February 20–22, 2001, WVI Central Records. World Vision's main European offices were located in Germany, the United Kingdom, Switzerland, Austria, Finland, and the Netherlands. See Whaites, "Pursuing Partnership," 416–17.

47. "Chronology: Expenditures and Staffing Since 1979"; Kliewer interview, June 27, 2007; "WVUS Timeline," WVUS Archives.

48. Myers, "Journeying Toward Interdependence."

49. At the 1986 World Vision International Council, Manfred Grellert called for WVI to allow for unique regional strategies to "contextualize the ethos of WVI in the Latin scene." Grellert interview, June 9, 2010; Samuel Kamaleson, interview by author, July 10, 2007.

50. Christopher A. Bartlett and Daniel F. Curran, "World Vision International's AIDS Initiative: Challenging a Global Partnership," Harvard Business School Case Study, May 17, 2005, 3–4, www.stthom.edu/Public/getFile.asp?File_Content_ID = 5545.

51. Houston, "World Vision Reorganization," January 5, 1985, WVI Central Records.

52. Myers, "Journeying Toward Interdependence"; Hestenes, "Laying the Foundations."

53. Under pressure from the field offices, World Vision's marketers undertook a major study in the early 1980s to develop a fund-raising philosophy that respected the dignity of people. See "Fundraising and the Dignity of People," August 31, 1980; "World Vision Promotion and the Dignity of People," December 2, 1981; Bill Kliewer, "World Vision Fundraising Philosophy," October 2, 1981, WVI Central Records.

54. World Vision devoted the entire October–December 1990 issue of its *Together* magazine to debating the issue of development education. It interviewed field staff and marketers in donor countries. It included articles with titles such as "Knowledge That Leads to Enthusiasm," "What I Want Donors to Understand—A Field Perspective," "Development Education: Nicety or Necessity? Bridging the Human Gap," and "Let's Begin with the Fundraisers." Marty Lonsdale, vice president of marketing, noted a World Vision study that found "after six to twelve months . . . sponsors can articulate the community development story clearly." Development staffers were not so sure. Waters and Young, "The Art & Ethics of Fundraising."

55. Houston, "Idealism vs. Pragmatism," n.d., WVI Central Records.

56. Through World Vision's research into its donor base, marketers knew that appeals for immediate relief and impoverished children proved most successful, but they also felt pressure to negotiate this knowledge with the overarching vision to become an integrated, ethical development agency. Ed Gruman, "1984–5 Donor Research Study," 1985; Ross Arnold, "Marketing Study Final Report," August 8, 1986, WVI Central Records. By the 1990s, World Vision and other agencies studied the impact of positive versus negative images for fund-raising and found that positive images actually garnered a greater response. World Vision later drafted guidelines on what it could and could not film (for example, unclothed women and children, flies in the eyes). Theology, development methodologies, and fundraising potential came together as World Vision began to display more positive images of children in need. Evelyne J. Dyck and Gary Coldevin, "Using Positive vs. Negative Photographs for Third-World Fund Raising," *Journalism & Mass Communication Quarterly* 69, no. 3 (September 1, 1992): 572–79; Joan Mussa, WVUS senior vice president, Donor Engagement, Advocacy and Communications, interview by author, November 19, 2010, Federal Way, WA.

57. Stalker, "Please Do Not Sponsor This Child"; also see David Johnston and Jennifer Leonard, "TV Charities: Let the Giver Beware," *Los Angeles Times*, January 20, 1985; Kathleen Hayes, "Child Sponsorship: Mything the Mark," *Other Side*, March 1983, 36–37.

58. "Understanding Child Sponsorship: A Historical Perspective"; Bryant Myers, "Development with Sponsorship Funds," WVI International Affairs Committee, August 16–19, 1982, WVI Central Records.

59. "Report on Sponsorship Task Force," WVI International Affairs Committee, February 14–17, 1983, WVI Central Records.

60. "Understanding Child Sponsorship: A Historical Perspective."

61. Bryant Myers, "Childcare Position Paper," drafts from 1985–87. It culminated with a new World Vision childcare policy approved by the International Board in 1987; Myers, "World Vision's Sponsorship Ministry: The Ministry and the Money," report to World Vision International Council's Ministry Review and Evaluation Committee, March 11, 1989, WVI Central Records. WVUS donor surveys indicated that despite attempts at describing the benefits of community development, a majority of U.S. sponsors preferred their contribution go directly to their sponsored child and family. This proportion climbed to 62 percent among evangelical sponsors. "World Vision: 1999 Comprehensive Donor Survey," August 1999, WVUS Archives.

62. Peter McNee, "Sponsorship: Can It Be a Two-Way Street?," *Together*, April–June 1989, 8–10; John Kenyon, "Child Sponsorship: Getting to the Real Questions," *Together*, April–June 1989, 1–2.

63. "1987 Field Directors' Conference Notes," WVI Central Records; Grellert interview, June 9, 2010; Grellert, "Following Jesus," moderator's address, 1992 WVI International Council, WVI Central Records.

64. Houston, "Resignation Message to the International Office Staff," August 26, 1988, WVI Central Records.

65. Grellert interview, June 9, 2010.

66. Grellert, "Moderator's Address at 1989 WVI International Council," WVI Central Records.

67. Roberta Hestenes, "Beyond Sentimentality: Reflections on Christian Unity," 1989 WVI International Council, September 22, 1989, WVI Central Records. Before arrival at Eastern, Hestenes became the first tenured female faculty member at Fuller Theological Seminary. She was also an ordained Presbyterian Church (USA) pastor.

68. "Partnership Review Committee Report to WVI International Council," September 1989, WVI Central Records.

69. Irvine, *Best Things in the Worst Times*, 134–42, and see appendixes B, C, D for three WVI documents—Core Values (approved in 1990), Mission Statement (1992), and the Covenant of Partnership (1995)—which all remain binding today (271–85).

70. "Partnership Task Force Report and Recommendations," 1995, WVI Central Records.

71. Irvine in Whaites, "Pursuing Partnership," 419.

72. World Vision integrated a federalized structure with the help of Harvard business professor Charles Handy. Manfred Grellert recounts that because Handy was the son of a pastor and believed in World Vision's mission, he offered his consulting pro bono. See Charles Handy, "Balancing Corporate Power: A New Federalist Paper," *Harvard Business Review* 70, no. 6 (November 1992): 59–72; Grellert interview, June 22, 2007; "Partnership Task Force Report and Recommendations," 1995; Tim Burgett, WVI general counsel, interview by author, June 15, 2007, Monrovia, CA.

73. Myers interview, June 20, 2007.

74. Burgett interview, June 15, 2007. In addition to affirming these core documents, each World Vision entity must work toward legally establishing a local board. It must also sign a trademark agreement and agree to peer review and open itself to regular integrated audits. Bartlett and Curran, "World Vision International's AIDS Initiative," 5–6.

75. In a survey of senior leadership, over 90 percent called for (1) a central partnership strategy; (2) changes in governance and decision rights; (3) a process of strategic allocation of resources; (4) improved performance culture; (5) better efficiency, effectiveness, and quality ("Newsline," May 25, 2005, WVI Central Records). Its visioning process commenced at its 2003 National Directors' Conference, which led to a "Big Goals Summit" in 2004; in 2005, it began to implement the strategic mandates of the "Our Future" campaign ("Our Future," overview brochure, WVI Central Records; Grellert interviews, June 22, 2007, and June 9, 2010).

76. Bonnie Jensen, WVI director of brand strategy, telephone interview by author, December 7, 2010; "Strategy Working Group Minutes," August 19–21, 1996, WVI Central Records. World Vision saw the orange color as helpful in emergency relief situations. Easily recognizable, people could associate orange with safety and help. It also stood out in its marketing efforts from other relief and development agencies. The cross/starburst also was a matter of intense debate. For many of World Vision's Christian constituents, the symbol connotes a cross, but it is not so recognizable as a Christian symbol that is off-putting to non-Christians. Trevor Roberts, Cross & Crown, "How to Use a Great Logo: World Vision," September 28, 2011, http://cacpro.com/educational/how-to-use-a-great-logo-world-vision.

77. Carl F. H. Henry, "Foreword," in *Evangelical Affirmations*, ed. Kenneth S. Kantzer and Carl F. H. Henry (Grand Rapids, MI: Academie Books, 1990), 20; Carl F. H. Henry, "American Evangelicals in a Turning Time," *Christian Century*, November 5, 1980, 1058–62.

78. Donald W. Dayton and Robert K. Johnston, eds., *The Variety of American Evangelical-ism* (Knoxville: University of Tennessee Press, 1991); D. G. Hart, *Deconstructing Evangelical-ism: Conservative Protestantism in the Age of Billy Graham* (Grand Rapids, MI: Baker Academic, 2004).

79. Nathan Hatch, "Response to Carl Henry," in Kantzer and Henry, *Evangelical Affir-mations*, 97.

80. On defining evangelicalism as a "cultural imaginary," see James K. A. Smith, "Who's Afraid of Sociology?," *The Immanent Frame* (blog), August 15, 2008, http://blogs.ssrc.org/tif/2008/08/15/whos-afraid-of-sociology/.

81. When Stan Mooneyham became president of WVI in 1980, longtime World Vision vice president Ted Engstrom assumed the presidency of WVUS (Engstrom, *Reflections on a Pilgrimage*, 127).

82. "Seiple Announcement," *World Vision*, April–May 1987, 1. Chuck Colson, former Watergate conspirator turned evangelical insider, first recommended Seiple to World Vision. Russell Chandler, "New World Vision President Named: Robert A. Seiple, 44, Will Replace Ted W. Engstrom, 70," *Los Angeles Times*, December 13, 1986.

83. "1984 Source/Motivation Donor Value Study," May 22, 1985, WVI Central Records.

84. Joe Ryan, "Report on World Vision's Church Relations," November 1984; "World Vision's Ministry to the Church, Executive Summary," March 10, 1986, WVI Central Records.

85. "1984 Source/ Motivation Donor Value Study"; "World Vision: 1999 Comprehensive Donor Survey"; "Americans' Awareness and Perceptions of World Vision," July 2001; "World Vision: 2006 Comprehensive Donor Survey," July 5, 2006, WVUS Archives. World Vision's surveys use Barna's definitions of both "born-again" and "evangelical." Barna defines "evangelical" not as a synonym but a subset of "born-again" that also requires seven additional criteria: (1) saying their faith is very important in their life; (2) believing they have a responsibility to share their faith in Christ with non-Christians; (3) believing in the existence of Satan;

(4) believing that eternal salvation is gained through God's grace alone, not through human efforts; (5) believing that Jesus Christ lived a sinless life while on earth; (6) believing the Bible is accurate in all that it teaches; and (7) affirming God as an omnipotent, omniscient, and perfect creator of the universe who rules the world today. For further discussion on the sociological definition of "evangelicalism," see Conrad Hackett and D. Michael Lindsay, "Measuring Evangelicalism: Consequences of Different Operationalization Strategies," *Journal for the Scientific Study of Religion* 47, no. 3 (2008): 501–2.

86. For example, see World Vision's 1982 *Together* album that featured CCM artists Amy Grant, Andrae Crouch, Dino, Keith Green, Walter Hawkins, the Imperials, Evie Karlsson, and country singer Barbara Mandrell. See *World Vision*, March 1983, 19; see also *World Vision*, October–November 1984, 2; *World Vision*, August–September 1986, 7.

87. Paul Diedrich, director of business development, Artists' Associates, interview by author, November 17, 2010.

88. Engstrom, "As the Hoofbeats Draw Near," *World Vision*, December 1984–January 1985, 23; Billy Graham, *Approaching Hoofbeats: The Four Horsemen of the Apocalypse* (Waco, TX: Word Books, 1983).

89. In the wake of *Roe v. Wade* and the rise of the evangelical pro-life movement, World Vision did make explicit its antiabortion position in all family planning policies. "Family Planning," WVI Board Policy Statements, originally approved June 3, 1978, and revised March 13, 1985, WVI Central Records.

90. "Joining Up with Campolo: Africa in Crisis," *World Vision*, April–May 1989, 22; "Will the Real Jesus Please Stand Up," *World Vision*, October–November 1988; Tom Sine, "Will the Real Cultural Christians Please Stand Up," *World Vision*, October–November 1989; Lauralee Mannes, "God's Catcher in the Rye," *World Vision*, October–November 1991, 2–4.

91. See Hout, Greeley, and Wilde, "The Demographic Imperative in Religious Change in the United States," 468; the authors claim that while in the past, social advancement meant often moving from Baptist to Presbyterian to Episcopal, "the conservative power brokers' prayer breakfast may well have supplanted the need some once felt to align their congregational affiliation with their socioeconomic status."

92. Paul Hiebert, "Conversion, Culture and Cognitive Categories," *Gospel in Context* 1, no. 4 (October 1978): 24–29; Robert Seiple, former president of WVUS, interview by author, November 8, 2007; Bryant L. Myers, "A Funny Thing Happened on the Way to Evangelical-Ecumenical Cooperation," *International Review of Mission* 81, no. 323 (July 1992): 297–407. More recently, Darrell Guder and Alan Hirsch have also employed the concept more popularly in conversations on the nature of the "missional church"; see Darrell L. Guder, ed., *Missional Church: A Vision for the Sending of the Church in North America* (Grand Rapids, MI: Eerdmans, 1998); and Michael Frost and Alan Hirsch, *The Shaping of Things to Come: Innovation and Mission for the 21st-Century Church* (Peabody, MA: Hendrickson Publishers, 2003).

93. World Vision's research noted 70 percent of evangelicals lived in the developing world by the turn of the twenty-first century. Bryant L. Myers, Don Brandt, and Alan Whaites, *Global Context for Action 2001* (Monrovia, CA: World Vision, 2001).

94. John Rymer, "The Church in Search of Justice," September 1983, WVI Central Records.

95. Irvine, *Best Things in the Worst Times*, 146–47.

96. Cliff Benzel, "Justice and Human Rights in an Age of Turbulence," WVI Council, 1983, WVI Central Records.

97. "Conversing with John Rymer on Justice," *Together*, July–September 1990, 6–7.

98. Rymer, "The Church in Search of Justice"; Harold Henderson, "World Vision's Justice and Reconciliation Ministry: Directions for the Future," WVI Council, 1986. In critiquing Rymer's report, Hal Barber, WVI vice president, wrote to Tom Houston, president, to complain, "We don't need any more philosophers on the justice committee." Letters between Houston and Rymer also point to the frustrations they experienced in translating theological proposals into applicable procedures. See Hal Barber to Tom Houston, December 12, 1985; Tom Houston to John Rymer, September 9, 1984, WVI Central Records.

99. "World Vision's Development Ministry," April 15, 1987; "World Vision's Urban Ministry," April 15, 1987; "WVI Policy Statements World Vision and Justice Policy Statement," 1990; "World Vision and Advocacy Policy Statement," 1991; all in WVI Central Records.

100. Grellert interview, June 22, 2007; "World Vision and Justice Study Guide," 1989; "World Vision Mission Statement," 1992, WVI Central Records.

101. Irvine, *Best Things in the Worst Times*, 157–60; Graeme Irvine, "Cambodia: An Occasion to Speak," *Together*, July–September 1990, 4–5.

102. Graeme Irvine, "Beyond Anger," *Together*, July–September 1990, 1–4; "World Vision Advocacy Policy Statement," 1991.

103. Irvine, *Best Things in the Worst Times*, 178–79. The case of apartheid in South Africa did raise controversy within World Vision South Africa. Because South Africa was a support and field country, it raised funds mostly from white donors while the recipients of aid were almost all black. The interracial World Vision South Africa staff had to find a way to raise funds while speaking out for justice. "On the Side of the Poor," World Vision UK Advocacy Paper, February 6, 1997, WVI Central Records.

104. Tom Getman, "Away from Evangelicalism: Reflections on Changes at World Vision," interview by Katherine Marshall, May 1, 2009, http://berkleycenter.georgetown.edu/events/away-from-evangelicalism-reflections-on-changes-at-world-vision. Getman notes that in 2009, there were over 150 employees in the Washington, D.C., office.

105. Linda Tripp, "Getting Beyond Lip Service," *Together*, October–December 1992, 4–5.

106. Roberta Hestenes, "Is the Gospel Good News for Women?," *World Vision*, June–July 1988, 10–11; Hestenes, "Is the Gospel Good News for Women?," *Together*, October–December 1992, 3; Charles Clayton, "Building a Better Theology," *Together*, October–December 1992, 5–7; John Kenyon, "Agreeing on the Theology," *Together*, October–December 1992, 8.

107. Charles Clayton, "Building a Better Theology," *Together*, October–December 1992, 5–7; John Kenyon, "Agreeing on the Theology," *Together*, October–December 1992, 8.

108. "World Vision's Women in Development and Leadership Policy," *Together*, October–December 1992, 8.

109. "Bangladesh: The Girl-Child Initiative," *Together*, October–December 1992, 16–17; "Signs of Hope: Women of the Developing World," *World Vision*, June–July 1992, 18–19; Barbara Thompson, "Coming Out of the Shadows: Women in the Third Word," *World Vision*, February–March 1993, 2–7. World Vision's *Together* periodical gave its entire January–March 1996 issue over to the issue of "The Girl Child." These initiatives gained support among evangelical audiences. Tim Stafford, "Where Are the Men?," *Christianity Today* 49, no. 8 (August 2005): 38–41.

110. Joan Levitt, chair of the Women in Development and Leadership Commission, was the first woman to become a vice president of WVI; Linda Tripp was the first woman to become a vice president of World Vision Canada. Linda Tripp, "Gender and Development from a Christian Perspective: Experience from World Vision," *Gender and Development* 7, no. 1 (March 1, 1999): 62–68; "World Vision Partnership Office Gender Self-Assessment Results," November 2002, WVI Central Records.

111. World Vision employees filming these images also noted their own flashbacks to these events (Mussa interview, November 19, 2010).

112. World Vision established the Gulu Children of War Rehabilitation Center in northern Uganda in 1995; World Vision has stated that since the center opened, nearly 11,000 former abductees and their children have been helped through its services. See Irvine, *Best Things in the Worst Times*, 169–81.

Chapter 9

1. While its revenue includes millions in federal and international government aid, the majority of its funds still come from private individuals, corporations, and foundations. Robert Seiple, "De-Seiple-ing World Vision," *Christianity Today*, June 15, 1998, 51.

2. World Vision International Annual Report, 2016, https://www.wvi.org/accountability; 2017 World Vision Partnership Update, https://www.wvi.org/publication/2017partnership update.

3. After the 2010 Haiti earthquake, World Vision was the first humanitarian agency interviewed by CNN and NPR. During her research on World Vision in the early 2000s, anthropologist Susan McDonic noted that the North American press mentioned World Vision an average of 150 times a day. Susan Mary McDonic, "Witnessing, Work and Worship: World Vision and the Negotiation of Faith, Development and Culture" (PhD diss., Duke University, 2004), 117.

4. Robert Wuthnow, *Boundless Faith: The Global Outreach of American Churches* (Berkeley: University of California Press, 2009), 1. WVUS's 2017 annual revenue was $1,044,000 billion.

5. Kristof, "Following God Abroad."

6. Joseph Loconte and Michael Cromartie, "Let's Stop Stereotyping Evangelicals," *Washington Post*, November 8, 2006, http://www.washingtonpost.com/wp-dyn/content/article/2006/11/07/AR2006110701228.html.

7. World Vision measured its global position in various "product lines" within the humanitarian industry, including sponsorship, humanitarian response, food aid, advocacy, and development. Specifically, in regard to food aid, it was the largest recipient of World Food Programme commodities. Bryant Myers, "Our Future Orientation," March 2005, WVI Central Records.

8. Organizations like World Vision often have come to monetize many of the in-kind gifts they receive by selling the product on the open market and using the income generated for other program expenses. This is standard practice for many agencies. "AERDO Interagency Gift-in-Kind Standards," December 2009, http://www.dochas.ie/Shared/Files/4/Gift_in_kind_Standards.pdf.

9. Blake Mycoskie founded TOMS shoes in 2006 with the pledge to give away one pair of shoes to a child in need for every pair purchased. When Mycoskie needed help fulfilling his pledge, he turned to World Vision to help identify and distribute TOMS shoes. By 2011, World Vision had helped distribute over two million pairs. Steve Haas, WVUS vice president, interview by author, November 16, 2010, Federal Way, WA.

10. In 2010, World Vision U.S. received about $251 million in gifts in kind, around 25 percent of total revenue. Critics claim an overabundance of GIK contributions leads to bad development practice and misleading reporting of revenue. Revised federal regulations and negative publicity have led World Vision and other agencies to reconsider the values it assigns to gifts in kind. The valuations of pharmaceuticals are a major source of debate. See William P. Barrett, "Donated Pills Make Some Charities Look Too Good On Paper," *Forbes*, December 19, 2011, http://www.forbes.com/sites/williampbarrett/2011/11/30/donated-pills-makes-some-charities-look-too-good-on-paper/. World Vision also received negative press for accepting unused Super Bowl merchandise from the National Football League (NFL) branded with the losing team's logo. The NFL writes off the donated merchandise for a tax deduction while World Vision values the merchandise as revenue while receiving free positive publicity. Laura Freschi, "World Vision Super Bowl Shirts: The Final Chapter," Aid Watch blog, March 15, 2011, http://aidwatchers.com/2011/03/world-vision-super-bowl-shirts-the-final-chapter/.

11. Michael Tackett and David Jackson, "Myths of Child Sponsorship: The Miracle Merchants," *Chicago Tribune*, March 22, 1998; Erica Bornstein, "Child Sponsorship, Evangelism, and Belonging in the Work of World Vision Zimbabwe," *American Ethnologist* 28, no. 3 (2001): 595–622.

12. World Vision even set up a "skunk works" outside normal channels of operations to test new programs (McCleary, *Global Compassion*, 135).

13. Charis M. Bracy, "A History of Microenterprise Development: An Examination of MED's Beginnings in Latin America and Its International Expansion, 1970–Present," August 17, 2006, WVI Central Records. Bracy traces World Vision's first involvement in microenterprise to the early 1980s in Sri Lanka.

14. World Vision's website, http://www.worldvisionadvocacy.org/, offers a list of its advocacy efforts, transcripts of World Vision testimonies, legislative victories, as well as speaking points for key issues and contacts on how individuals can call their own elected officials.

15. See McCleary, *Global Compassion*, 14–16: McCleary defines the evangelical category based on doctrine (inerrancy of the Bible, deity of Jesus Christ and personal salvation through him, necessity of evangelism, and pre- or post-millennium belief); she identifies World Vision as moving from "evangelical" to "faith-founded" in the 1980s. With that being the case, McCleary's categorizations may even understate the growth of evangelical INGOs. See also McCleary, "Private Voluntary Organizations Engaged in International Assistance, 1939–2004," 521–22, where McCleary notes that in 1946, the "distribution of faith-based organizations was 38 percent Jewish, 19 percent Mainline Protestant, 16 percent Evangelical, 12 percent Faith-Founded, and 3 percent Catholic. . . . In 2004, the breakdown was 45 percent Evangelical, 13 percent Faith-Founded, 11 percent Mainline Protestant, 9 percent Catholic, 7 percent Ecumenical, 5 percent Jewish, 2 percent Muslim, and 1 percent Orthodox."

16. Based on McCleary's analysis, if counting World Vision as an evangelical organization, evangelical agencies made up three of the top six largest INGOs and four of the top ten in terms of real revenue in 2004. (The others are Feed the Children, MAP International, and Samaritan's Purse.) See McCleary, *Global Compassion*, 25.

17. The private income of evangelical INGOs was 4.6 times that of Catholic organizations and 7 times that of mainline Protestants. In 2000, out of fifty-three evangelical agencies registered with the government, twenty-eight received federal assistance. There are hundreds more unregistered evangelical INGOs who do not take federal funding. See McCleary, "Taking God Overseas," 5.

18. Tripp, "Gender and Development from a Christian Perspective," 63–64; Ray Vander Zaag, "Canadian Faith-Based Development NGOs and CIDA Funding," *Canadian Journal of Development Studies* 34, no. 2 (June 1, 2013): 321–47; Ray Vander Zaag, "Trends in CIDA Funding to Canadian Religious Development NGOs: Analysing Conflicting Studies," *Canadian Journal of Development Studies* 35, no. 3 (July 3, 2014): 458–74.

19. Gerard Clarke, "Agents of Transformation? Donors, Faith-Based Organisations and International Development," *Third World Quarterly* 28, no. 1 (February 2007): 82–83.

20. A *Boston Globe* 2006 study found that between 2001 and 2005, USAID funneled $1.7 billion to FBOs. While the article's intent was to note the significance of Bush's new policies, it did not note what percentage of these agencies already received significant government funding. "Bush Brings Faith to Foreign Aid," *Boston Globe*, October 8, 2006. Another study found that while increased funding to evangelical agencies may have been Bush's intent, most agencies still avoided federal funding. Helen R. F. Ebaugh, Janet Saltzman Chafetz, and Paula F. Pipes, "The Influence of Evangelicalism on Government Funding of Faith-Based Social Service Organizations," *Review of Religious Research* 47, no. 4 (June 2006): 380–92.

21. Clarke and Jennings, *Development, Civil Society and Faith-Based Organizations*.

22. Thomas H. Jeavons, "Identifying Characteristics of 'Religious' Organizations: An Exploratory," in *Sacred Companies: Organizational Aspects of Religion and Religious Aspects of Organizations*, ed. N. J. Demerath III et al. (New York: Oxford University Press, 1998), 79–95; Ronald J. Sider and Heidi Rolland Unruh, "Typology of Religious Characteristics of Social Service and Educational Organizations and Programs," *Nonprofit & Voluntary Sector Quarterly* 33, no. 109 (2004): 109–34; Helen Rose Ebaugh, Janet S. Chafetz, and Paula E. Pipes, "Where's the Faith in Faith-Based Organizations? Measures and Correlates of Religiosity in Faith-Based Social Service Coalitions," *Social Forces* 84, no. 4 (June 2006): 2259–72.

23. Tamsin Bradley, "A Call for Clarification and Critical Analysis of the Work of Faith-Based Development Organizations (FBDO)," *Progress in Development Studies* 9, no. 2 (April 2009): 101–14; Olson, "Common Belief, Contested Meanings"; Fred Kniss and David Todd Campbell, "The Effect of Religious Orientation on International Relief and Development Organizations," *Journal for the Scientific Study of Religion* 36, no. 1 (1997): 93–103; Jenny Lunn, "The Role of Religion, Spirituality and Faith in Development: A Critical Theory Approach," *Third World Quarterly* 30, no. 5 (July 2009): 937–51.

24. Kurt Alan Ver Beek, "Spirituality: A Development Taboo," *Development in Practice* 10, no. 1 (February 1, 2000): 31–43.

25. Casanova, *Public Religions in the Modern World*; *The Desecularization of the World: Resurgent Religion and World Politics* (Washington, DC: Ethics and Public Policy Center, 1999).

26. Arturo Escobar, *Encountering Development: The Making and Unmaking of the Third World* (Princeton, NJ: Princeton University Press, 1995); Heffernan, *Twinning Faith and Development*, 62; Harper, *The Lab, the Temple, and the Market*, 80.

27. Andrew Natsios, "Faith-Based NGOs and U.S. Foreign Policy," in *The Influence of Faith: Religious Groups and U.S. Foreign Policy*, ed. Elliott Abrams (Lanham, MD: Rowman & Littlefield, 2001), 200.

28. Thomas, "Faith and Foreign Aid," 23.

29. David Beckmann, one of the founders of the Friday Morning Group, would later become the head of the U.S. Christian advocacy group Bread for the World. See David M.

Beckmann et al., *Friday Morning Reflections at the World Bank: Essays on Values and Development* (Washington, DC: Seven Locks Press, 1991).

30. There are a number of accounts of the World Bank's encounter with religion. For an insider account and conference proceedings, see Katherine Marshall, "Development and Religion: A Different Lens on Development Debates," *Peabody Journal of Education* 76, nos. 3–4 (October 2001): 339–75; and Marshall and Keough, *Finding Global Balance*. For outsider accounts, see John A. Rees, *Religion in International Politics and Development: The World Bank and Faith Institutions* (Cheltenham: Edward Elgar, 2011); Harper, *The Lab, the Temple, and the Market*, 72–79; Thomas, "Faith and Foreign Aid."

31. Duncan McDuie-Ra and John A. Rees, "Religious Actors, Civil Society and the Development Agenda: The Dynamics of Inclusion and Exclusion," *Journal of International Development* 22, no. 1 (January 2010): 25.

32. Deepa Narayan, "Voices of the Poor," in *Faith in Development: Partnership Between the World Bank and the Churches of Africa*, ed. D. G. R. Belshaw, Robert Calderisi, and Chris Sugden (Washington, DC: World Bank, 2001), 45–46. The *Voices of the Poor* study was published as a three-volume work by the World Bank; see vol. 1, *Can Anyone Hear Us?*, by Deepa Narayan et al. (New York: Oxford University Press, 2000); vol. 2, *Crying Out for Change*, by Deepa Narayan et al. (New York: Oxford University Press, 2000); vol. 3, *From Many Lands*, ed. Deepa Narayan and Patti Petesch (New York: Oxford University Press, 2002).

33. Judith M. Dean, *Attacking Poverty in the Developing World: Christian Practitioners and Academics in Collaboration* (Waynesboro, GA: Authentic Media, 2005), 243–48.

34. As the World Bank's program was dying down, it moved the WFDD to Georgetown University's Berkley Center for Religion, Peace, and World Affairs. The facilitator of the World Bank program, Katherine Marshall, came to lead the concentration on religion and global development (http://berkleycenter.georgetown.edu/programs/127). For an overview of research and other programs, see Anne Marie Holenstein, "Governmental Donor Agencies and Faith-Based Organizations," *International Review of the Red Cross* 87, no. 858 (2005): 367–374. In addition to religion in development, other fields like international relations and foreign policy have embraced renewed discussions of religion's role. See Scott M. Thomas, *The Global Resurgence of Religion and the Transformation of International Relations: The Struggle for the Soul of the Twenty-First Century* (New York: Palgrave Macmillan, 2005); Douglas Johnston, *Faith-Based Diplomacy: Trumping Realpolitik* (New York: Oxford University Press, 2003).

35. Wendy Tyndale, "Idealism and Practicality: The Role of Religion in Development," *Development* 46, no. 4 (2003): 22–28; Tyndale, *Visions of Development*.

36. World Vision's initial attempts at large-scale development (LSD) in the wake of the Ethiopian famine largely failed, but it felt ADPs offered a more sophisticated approach as the organization had achieved exponentially more sophistication in its development strategy.

37. Grellert interview, June 22, 2007; Kliewer interview, June 27, 2007; McDonic, "Witnessing, Work and Worship," 66; World Vision Australia, "Transforming Lives in Area Development Programs," accessed March 26, 2012, http://www.worldvision.com.au/issues/Transforming_Lives___Child_Sponsorship/Why_is_it_happening_/Transforming_lives_in_Area_Development_Progra.aspx.

38. Myers, *Walking with the Poor*, 164; Robert Chambers, *Rural Development: Putting the Last First* (London: Longman, 1984); Robert Chambers, *Whose Reality Counts? Putting the First Last* (London: Intermediate Technology, 1997); David C. Korten and Rudi Klauss, *People-Centered Development: Contributions Toward Theory and Planning Frameworks* (West

Hartford, CT: Kumarian Press, 1984); David C. Korten, *Getting to the 21st Century: Voluntary Action and the Global Agenda* (West Hartford, CT: Kumarian Press, 1990).

39. Amartya Sen, *Development as Freedom* (New York: Knopf, 1999).

40. See Myers, *Walking with the Poor*, 116. World Vision used Chambers's list of aspects of poverty: (1) material poverty; (2) vulnerability; (3) physical weakness; (4) isolation; (5) powerlessness. Its only addition to his five categories was a "spiritual poverty." This list appeared in a number of World Vision documents as they reflect on the nature of its Christian identity within its development principles.

41. John A. Kenyon, "Where We Come from and Where We Are Going," *Together*, October–December 1983, 7. World Vision published the magazine quarterly from 1983 to 2000. The magazine debated liberation theology and theories of sustainable development, as well as offering case studies and instructions on building technologically appropriate water pumps and irrigation systems.

42. David C. Korten, "The Sustainable Project: A Contradiction," *Together*, July–September 1991, 3; Bob Seiple, "As Sustainable as Eternal Grace," *Together*, July–September 1991, 8–9.

43. The "10/40 window" refers to those peoples in the region located between ten and forty degrees north latitude. Evangelical missiologists Luis Bush coined the phrase at the Lausanne II Conference in Manila, Philippines, in 1989. See Bryant Myers, "Where Are the Poor and the Lost?," *Together*, October–December 1988, 8; John Robb, "The Power of People-Group Thinking," *Together*, October–December 1988, 4.

44. Myers, *Walking with the Poor*, 2; Bryant L. Myers, "What Makes Development Christian? Recovering from the Impact of Modernity," *Missiology* 26, no. 2 (1998): 143.

45. While the irony was lost on the professional development community, "transformation" was the original term that Wayne Bragg introduced to evangelicals at the Wheaton 1983 consultation. They were attempting to find an alternative term for Christian development that did not privilege secular approaches. Later Ron Sider and other evangelical social ethicists would publish a journal, *Transformation*, to address these same concerns. See Myers, *Walking with the Poor*, 153–54.

46. Myers, *Walking with the Poor*, 86; Jayakumar Christian, *God of the Empty-Handed: Poverty, Power, and the Kingdom of God* (Monrovia, CA: MARC, 1999).

47. Myers, *Walking with the Poor*, 6–7; Myers, "What Makes Development Christian?," 145; Jayakumar Christian, "Worldviews Should Be Analyzed," *Together*, July–September 1992, 4; William van Geest, "Development and Other Religious Activities," *Together*, July–September 1997, 1–9.

48. Myers, *Walking with the Poor*, 239–85. Myers highlighted a number of respected development evaluation techniques ("Participatory Learning and Action," "Appreciative Inquiry," "Logical Framework" analysis) that relied on local communities to express their own desires for development.

49. Ibid., 299–302. Ethnographer Emily Hogue described a World Vision Peru Area Development Program that saw its holistic development as striving for the "inseparable physical, spiritual, and psychological well-being of participants." Emily Hogue, "God Wants Us to Have a Life That Is Sustainable: Faith-Based Development and Economic Change in Andean Peasant Communities," in *Bridging the Gaps: Faith-Based Organizations, Neoliberalism, and Development in Latin America and the Caribbean*, ed. Julie Adkins and Tara Hefferan (Lanham, MD: Lexington Books, 2009), 136–37.

50. Malcolm Caruthers, "World Vision's Relations with Governments," August 1986, WVI Central Records.

51. World Vision saw the transition as a positive "twenty-year journey from working through the church to working with the church and now to working directly with the community." Graeme Irvine, "World Vision and Evangelism: Paper in Process," March 1991, WVI Central Records"; "Christian Witness Commission Report," 1995, p. 20, WVI Central Records.

52. Ricardo Ramírez, "Toward a More Perfect Union: The Challenge of Ecumenism," *Ecumenical Trends* 25 (November 1996): 155–60.

53. Gene Daniels, "Strategic Considerations for a Catholic Initiative," June 1992, WVI Central Records. I distinguish Pentecostals here as separate from evangelicals in the same way that World Vision did historically to draw attention to the particular divisions these communities maintained around the world. Presently, World Vision follows the general categorization of Pentecostals as a subset of evangelicals.

54. The survey conducted in 1999 claimed 57 percent of staff members identified themselves as evangelical, 19 percent as mainline, 16 percent as Catholic, 1 percent Orthodox, and 7 percent "other." The other included several thousand Muslim, Buddhist, and Hindu staff members. It does not clarify if Pentecostals are included in the evangelical category or other. World Vision instituted a number of sensitivity training seminars to help staff dispel false preconceptions and better appreciate each traditions' commonalities as well as distinctions. "Commission of the Church Report," 2002, p. 48, WVI Central Records. In an informal poll of WVUS staff, Cindy Waple, spiritual formation director of WVUS, estimated 68 percent identified as evangelical/Pentecostal and only 6 percent as mainline. Cindy Waple, interview by author, November 16, 2010. Presently, WVUS uses the five divisions employed by the ecumenical organization Christian Churches Together (Protestant, Roman Catholic, evangelical, Orthodox, and Pentecostal).

55. "Commission of the Church Report," 13; Tim Dearborn, interview by author, June 1, 2010.

56. Kliewer interview, June 27, 2007.

57. "Christian Witness Commission Report," 38.

58. Burgett interview, June 15, 2007.

59. "Christian Witness Commission Report," 19, 31–32, 64.

60. Ibid., 38.

61. "World Vision's Ministry in Resistant Areas," WVI Evangelism and Research Division, March 16, 1980, WVI Central Records.

62. "Christian Witness Commission Report," 51–53.

63. Ibid., 54–55. In such settings, it also trained Christian staff to appreciate and be aware of cultural and religious differences in the field. Sanjay Sojwal, longtime World Vision staffer in Asia, shared one story of World Vision's Christian staff making space within their own worship setting for Muslims to pray in Indonesia. He also retold a story of the respect Muslim staff and aid recipients exhibited while World Vision Christian staff prayed before distributing food. Sanjay Sojwal, director of marketing for Christian Witness, interview by author, November 19, 2010.

64. In 2010, Tim Dearborn estimated that among its current staff, World Vision employed around 2,800 Muslims and 1,000 Buddhists and Hindus (Dearborn interview, June

1, 2010); around the same time, Tom Getman ("Away from Evangelicalism") estimated that between 18 and 20 percent of World Vision's staff (about four thousand) were Muslim.

65. D. Michael Lindsay, *Faith in the Halls of Power: How Evangelicals Joined the American Elite* (New York: Oxford University Press, 2007), 46. World Vision has answered a number of inquiries about its hiring position. See an exchange between Bryant Myers and Thomas H. McCallie III, executive director of the evangelical Maclellan Foundation, inquiring about World Vision's efforts in Mali and North Africa. Thomas H. McCallie III to Bryant Myers, February 17, 1994; Bryant Myers to Thomas H. McCallie III, March 1, 1994, WVI Central Records. In the last decade, WVUS pulled funds from WVI's work in Afghanistan because it felt it could not sell the country's Muslim staff to its American evangelical constituency (Myers interview, June 20, 2007).

66. Dave Robinson, "Historical Timeline of World Vision Ministry in the Muslim World," November 10, 2009, WVI Central Records.

67. Don M. McCurry, *The Gospel and Islam: A Compendium* (Monrovia, CA: MARC, 1979).

68. James Greenelsh and Gospel Light Video, *Islam: Unlocking the Door* (Ventura, CA: World Vision International, 1981).

69. In some contexts, World Vision partnered with local Christian churches, but it was also aware that partnership might draw undue and unwelcome attention to Christians who may have faced religious persecution. One past country director noted partnerships with the evangelical agencies Youth with a Mission (YWAM) and Child Evangelism Fellowship that assisted in mobilizing the church for spiritual and social transformation. See "Christian Witness Commission Report," 54; Torrey Olsen, director of Christian Commitments, WVUS (former country director for Senegal, Mali, and Mauritania), interview by author, November 19, 2010.

70. Ismail Khan, "U.S. Charity Is Attacked In Pakistan; 6 Are Killed," *New York Times*, March 10, 2010, https://www.nytimes.com/2010/03/11/world/asia/11pstan.html.

71. "Christian Witness Commission Report," 16.

72. World Vision's proselytism statement figures prominently in its public communications and on its website, www.worldvision.org. While the distinction is lost on many, World Vision makes the clear separation between evangelism and proselytism. As a humanitarian organization, World Vision refuses to proselytize as required by all signatories to the Red Cross Code of Conduct. See Graeme Irvine, "World Vision and Evangelism: Paper in Process"; Dean Owen, World Vision director of executive communications, interview by author, November 18, 2010, Federal Way, WA.

73. "Policy on Witness to Jesus Christ," in "Christian Witness Commission Report," 34–35, 45–49.

74. "The Will to Make It So," 2007, WVI Central Records. By 2010, Christian Commitments (CC) had over 200 employees throughout the partnership, 190 of whom were designated as CC staff in specific countries; eighteen CC staff members support international programming and overall planning. Claire Okeke, Christian Commitments, interview by author, June 9, 2010.

75. One World Vision U.S. staff member estimated that while all support offices initially committed to raise support for Christian Commitments, World Vision U.S. currently provides 95 percent of partnership funding. See "Strategic Working Group Minutes," August 19–21, 1996, WVI Central Records.

76. "Global Centre Christian Commitments Strategy Overview, 2010–2012"; "Christian Commitment Do's and Assures: Criteria Used in Annual Christian Commitment Country Assessment and Global National Office Dashboard," February 2010; both in WVI Central Records.

77. "Commission of the Church Report," 14–15.

78. See "Commission of the Church Report." World Vision's training exposed staff to the theological and organizational diversity among Christian traditions. For instance, knowing the differences between episcopal, presbyterian, and congregational systems of church governance helped staff to "understand and relate appropriately to the various church structures they encounter in their work." It also established protocols for how the church functioned in various cultural contexts. It identified countries as "Christian majority," "Christian minority," "post-Christian," "restrictive contexts," or "persecuted contexts." Each setting required distinct sensitivities to Christian witness and partnerships with local church communities.

79. Christian Commitments produced an "Integrating Christian Witness Series" for World Vision staff to reflect on Christian witness in its various operations.

80. Dearborn interview, June 1, 2010.

81. "Interfaith Relations Policy Statement," April 2, 2009, WVI Central Records; Chawkat Moucarry, *The Prophet and the Messiah: An Arab Christian's Perspective on Islam and Christianity* (Downers Grove, IL: InterVarsity Press, 2001); Chawkat Moucarry, *Faith to Faith: Christianity and Islam in Dialogue* (Leicester: InterVarsity Press, 2001).

82. Renee Tawa, "World Vision Charity to Leave L.A. for Seattle," *Los Angeles Times*, March 16, 1994; "World Vision Pulling Up Stakes," *Christianity Today*, April 25, 1994, 45.

83. Richard Stearns, WVUS president, interview by author, July 1, 2010.

84. Pew Forum, "Religion and International Development: A Conversation with Andrew Natsios," March 1, 2006, http://pewforum.org/Government/Religion-and-International-Development-A-Conversation-with-Andrew-Natsios.aspx.

85. Lindsay, *Faith in the Halls of Power*, 221–22.

86. World Vision reported Stearns's total compensation as $439,155 in 2010. When he left Lenox, his salary was $800,000. Stearns interview, July 1, 2010.

87. Bob Smietana, "Leaps of Faith," *Christianity Today* 51, no. 3 (March 2007): 58–61; Lindsay, *Faith in the Halls of Power*, 190–94.

88. "Influential & Effective: These Fundraisers Know How to Bring in the Cash and Further the Profession," *Nonprofit Times*, January 15, 2009. Tandon often used his own biography as evidence of the need for World Vision's work. Reared in rural India on less than one dollar a day, Tandon appealed to the sacrifices of his mother to give him access to the education that allowed his success. Kristi Heim, "The Business of Giving: World Vision's 'Slumdog' Vice-President," *Seattle Times*, February 20, 2009.

89. Bartlett and Curran, "World Vision International's AIDS Initiative"; Mussa interview, November 19, 2010.

90. Bob Buford introduced "success to significance" with a series of books and motivational speeches. Buford was the founder of the Peter F. Drucker Foundation for Nonprofit Management as well as the Leadership Network, which coaches everyone from megachurch pastors to corporate executives. See Bob Buford, *Halftime: Changing Your Game Plan from Success to Significance* (Grand Rapids, MI: Zondervan, 1994); Smietana, "Leaps of Faith," 58.

91. Quoted in VanderPol, "The Least of These," 223.

92. Mussa interview, November 19, 2010; Jensen interview, December 7, 2010.

93. Mussa interview, November 19, 2010; Lonsdale interview, November 16, 2010.

94. In its 2006 survey, 91 percent of English-speaking sponsors identified as born-again Christians, while 64 percent of World Vision's donors identified as evangelicals based on the more rigorous Barna definition that described only 9 percent of the general U.S. adult population. In its past 1999 study, born-again Christians were 86 percent of World Vision's English speaking donors while only 43 percent of the U.S. population. And under the Barna definition, evangelicals made up 42 percemt of sponsors and 7 percemt of the U.S. adult population. World Vision also discovered that 80 percent of all donors contributed financially to their local church, and 50 percent contributed to other Christian "electronic ministries." Of all donors, 60 percent identified as politically and socially conservative, 30 percent middle of the road, and 10 percent as liberal. "World Vision: 2006 Comprehensive Donor Survey," July 5, 2006; "World Vision, 1999 Comprehensive Donor Survey," August 1999, WVUS Archives.

95. World Vision's unaided awareness remains surprisingly low (hovering around 4 percent of the general population and around 7 to 10 percent of conservative Christians). Aided awareness is much higher (40 percent of the general population, 76 percent of evangelicals, and 54 percent of born-again Christians). "Americans' Awareness and Perceptions of World Vision," conducted by Barna research for World Vision U.S., August 2001; "World Vision Reputation Research," February–March 2008, WVUS Archives.

96. In recent years, World Vision became concerned that while its name recognition is higher among evangelicals than its peer evangelical humanitarian agencies (such as Compassion or Samaritan's Purse), these organizations are receiving a greater percentage of evangelical support. Nonevangelical agencies like CARE, Christian Children's Fund, and others have also made inroads to gain evangelical support. Lisa Pang, "World Vision U.S. Branding Research Study," June 2004, WVUS Archives; Lisa Pang, director of Strategic Research and Analysis, interview by author, November 18, 2010.

97. Stearns interview, July 1, 2010.

98. World Vision found that only one-quarter of donors to nonprofits gave to international agencies. The focus on poverty remained domestic. Evangelicals were actually twice as likely to give to international causes than the average population (50 percent to 25 percent). "Perceptions of Poverty: Baseline," July 1999, study conducted by Barna Research and commissioned by World Vision, WVUS Archives.

99. Lindsay, *Faith in the Halls of Power*, 28; Christian Smith, *Christian America? What Evangelicals Really Want* (Berkeley: University of California Press, 2000); Marvin N. Olasky, *Compassionate Conservatism: What It Is, What It Does, and How It Can Transform America* (New York: Free Press, 2000).

100. Wuthnow, *Boundless Faith*, 20–21.

101. Ibid., 3.

102. Bob Smietana, "The Southern Baptist S(p)ending Church," *Christianity Today*, October 26, 2015, https://www.christianitytoday.com/ct/2015/november/southern-baptist-spending-crunch-imb-david-platt.html. Independent agencies make up 72 percent of all revenue for overseas missions and 61 percent of U.S. foreign missionaries. Wuthnow, *Boundless Faith*, 128–30, 149.

103. Wuthnow, *Boundless Faith*, 171.

104. Robert J. Priest et al., "Researching the Short-Term Mission Movement," *Missiology* 34, no. 4 (2006): 431–50; Priest also quoted in Brian Howell, "The Global Evangelical," *The*

Immanent Frame (blog), July 28, 2008, http://blogs.ssrc.org/tif/2008/07/28/the-global-evan gelical/.

105. Janel Kragt Bakker, *Sister Churches: American Congregations and Their Partners Abroad* (New York: Oxford University Press, 2013).

106. A growing academic field of world Christianity has pointed to the influence of demographic shifts to explain global Christian growth. Philip Jenkins has popularized this argument through such books as *The Next Christendom: The Coming of Global Christianity* (Oxford: Oxford University Press, 2002). David Barrett bolsters the case through demographic research; see Barrett, Kurian, and Johnson, *World Christian Encyclopedia*. Wuthnow argues that their approaches essentialize global Christianity as distinct from the West and occludes the ongoing, dynamic interactions between West and global South; see Wuthnow, *Boundless Faith*, 32–61.

107. Melani McAlister, "What Is Your Heart For? Affect and Internationalism in the Evangelical Public Sphere," *American Literary History* 20, no. 4 (2008): 870–95.

108. Brian M. Howell, "Mission to Nowhere: Putting Short-Term Missions into Context," *International Bulletin of Missionary Research* 33, no. 4 (October 2009): 206–11; Robert Wuthnow and Stephen Offutt, "Transnational Religious Connections," *Sociology of Religion* 69, no. 2 (June 20, 2008): 209–32.

109. Ronald J. Sider, *Just Generosity: A New Vision for Overcoming Poverty in America* (Grand Rapids, MI: Baker Books, 1999), 217.

110. Myers provided an exhaustive list of evangelical agencies engaged in social ministries. He also noted that over half of new masters students enrolling in Fuller Theological Seminary's School of Intercultural Studies were drawn to international development, children at risk, or urban ministry over church growth and evangelism. Myers, *Walking with the Poor*, 48–49.

111. Campus Crusade established Global Aid Network, and Pat Robertson established Operation Blessing.

112. Cizik resigned under pressure from the NAE in 2008 over his efforts for creation care as well as his refusal to dismiss his potential support of same-sex civil unions. In 2010, he cofounded the New Evangelical Partnership for the Common Good to pursue similar lobbying work. Kristof, "Following God Abroad."

113. See Noll, *The New Shape of World Christianity*, 127–50; in his study of representative evangelical periodicals over the twentieth century, Noll cataloged the rise in coverage of the persecuted church as the most common entrée for American Christians into the growth of global Christianity.

114. The biography of the Voices of the Martyrs founder Richard Wurmbrand is a cult classic among American evangelicals. Published in 1963, it is still in print and often given away free by a number of evangelical organizations. See Richard Wurmbrand, *Tortured for Christ* (London: Lakeland, 1967); Melani McAlister, "The Politics of Persecution," Middle East Research and Information Project, http://www.merip.org/mer/mer249/politics-persecution; Allen Hertzke, *Freeing God's Children: The Unlikely Alliance for Global Human Rights* (Lanham, MD: Rowman & Littlefield, 2004), 107–31.

115. Evangelical voices included World Vision and Sojourners as well as Franklin Graham, the NAE, and the Southern Baptist Convention. Leading congressional voices included Republicans Sam Brownback, Michael Horowitz, and Frank Wolf, as well as Democratic voices Tony Hall and Nancy Pelosi. See Hertzke, *Freeing God's Children*, 237–39.

116. After the passage of the International Religious Freedom Act, evangelicals returned to demonstrate their internal differences. Many evangelicals attacked Seiple for his patient, bureaucratic approach. Tying him to his World Vision background, many claimed he was a Washington insider who was not using his office as evangelicals intended to bring immediate policy changes to countries like Saudi Arabia and China. Seiple dismissed these critiques as grumblings from those who did not grasp the complexities of international relations. Seiple interview, November 8, 2007; Seiple, "De-Seiple-ing World Vision"; Michael Horowitz, "Cry Freedom: Forget 'Quiet Diplomacy'—It Doesn't Work," *Christianity Today* 47, no. 3 (March 2003): 48–51.

117. Accounts of evangelical efforts to pass the International Religious Freedom Act offer a somewhat different analysis. Wuthnow sees the alliance for government-backed religious freedom and human rights language as an issue of an elite strand of evangelicals and not a concern of the people in the pews. Hertzke disagreed. While noting that 70 percent of evangelical elites affirmed that "stopping religious persecution should be given top priority in American foreign policy," the evangelical population registered a higher concern for these issues than the general public. If anything, broad support demonstrated evangelicals' expertise in popularizing and disseminating a message to motivate its constituency. Wuthnow, *Boundless Faith*, 158–60; Hertzke, *Freeing God's Children*, 35.

118. Lindsay, *Faith in the Halls of Power*, 45.

119. "International Justice Mission, Core Commitments," accessed April 22, 2012, https://www.ijm.org/frequently-asked-questions/.

120. Gary Haugen on *The Oprah Winfrey Show*, November 2, 2005; Nicholas D. Kristof, "Raiding a Brothel in India," *New York Times*, May 25, 2011, http://www.nytimes.com/2011/05/26/opinion/26kristof.html; Nicholas D. Kristof, "Sex Slaves? Lock Up the Pimps," *New York Times*, January 29, 2005, http://www.nytimes.com/2005/01/29/opinion/29kristof.html.

121. Lindsay, *Faith in the Halls of Power*, 45.

122. Hertzke, *Freeing God's Children*, 319; Gary A. Haugen, *Good News About Injustice* (Downers Grove, IL: InterVarsity Press, 1999); David P. Gushee, *The Future of Faith in American Politics: The Public Witness of the Evangelical Center* (Waco, TX: Baylor University Press, 2008), 104–5.

123. Micah Challenge takes its name from the biblical passage Micah 6:8, "He has shown you, O Mortal, what is good. And what does the Lord require of you? To *act justly* and to *love mercy* and to *walk humbly* with your God." See http://www.micahchallengeusa.org/.

124. Shapiro, "The AIDS Evangelists." The quote is attributed to Steve Haas, former staff member at evangelical megachurch Willow Creek. Haas now works for WVUS as vice president/chief catalyst to engage churches on the AIDS issue.

125. Vivian S. Park, "Interview: World Vision President Richard Stearns," *Christian Post*, April 19, 2004, http://www.christianpost.com/news/20126/; Shapiro, "The AIDS Evangelists."

126. Bartlett and Curran, "World Vision International's AIDS Initiative," 11–13.

127. Richard Stearns, *The Hole in Our Gospel* (Nashville, TN: Thomas Nelson, 2009), 194; Shapiro, "The AIDS Evangelists"; Haas interview, November 16, 2010.

128. Stearns, *The Hole in Our Gospel*, 195; Bartlett and Curran, " World Vision International's AIDS Initiative," 11.

129. "World Vision: Orphan and Vulnerable Children (OVC) and HIV/AIDS Research," Barna Research Group, January 2001, WVUS Archives; Shapiro, "The AIDS Evangelists."

130. Mark Moring, "Songs of Justice, Missions of Mercy: Why Christian Musicians Are Embarking on a Different Kind of World Tour," *Christianity Today* 53, no. 11 (November 2009): 30–37; Haas interview, November 16, 2010.

131. Today, over 50 percent of the children that World Vision donors sponsor are Hope children. See Shapiro, "The AIDS Evangelists"; Janet I. Tu, "Bringing Message on AIDS Home—via Africa," *Seattle Times*, May 9, 2008.

132. "World Vision: Orphan and Vulnerable Children (OVC) and HIV/AIDS Update Research," Barna Research Group, November 2004, WVUS Archives; "World Vision: 2006 Comprehensive Donor Survey."

133. Shapiro, "The AIDS Evangelists."

134. Ibid.

135. Alan Cooperman, "Evangelical Christians Lobby for AIDS Funds; Groups Endorse Bush's $15 Billion Program," *Washington Post*, June 13, 2003. Despite broad support, PEPFAR has remained controversial. Many have celebrated it as one of the greatest bipartisan successes of the Bush administration. Others critiqued it because of stipulations for the percentages of funds to be spent on abstinence-only programs. While this requirement was lifted in 1998, some continued to worry that those receiving PEPFAR funds (World Vision and other Christian agencies) might privilege abstinence education at the expense of other efforts.

136. Stearns interview, July 1, 2010; Janet I. Tu, "A Journey Of Conscience: With Faith and Funding, Richard Stearns Is Out to Save the World," *Seattle Times*, August 23, 2009; Rebecca Barnes, "The Church Awakens: Christians Make AIDS Fight a High Priority," *Christianity Today*, January 2005, 22–23.

137. Haas interview, November 16, 2010.

138. Timothy C. Morgan and Tony Carnes, "Purpose Driven in Rwanda: Rick Warren's Sweeping Plan to Defeat Poverty," *Christianity Today* 49, no. 10 (October 2005): 32–36; Marc Gunther, "Will Success Spoil Rick Warren?," *Fortune*, October 31, 2005, http://money.cnn.com/magazines/fortune/fortune_archive/2005/10/31/8359189/index.htm; Holly Lebowitz Rossi, "Rick Warren Publicly Pursuing Programs Against World Poverty," *Christian Century* 122, no. 14 (July 12, 2005): 15–16.

139. "The PEACE Plan," accessed September 20, 2018, https://saddleback.com/connect/ministry/the-peace-plan. The plan has gone through several iterations since originally proposed in 2005. After much criticism, Warren changed his first initiative ("planting churches") to "promoting reconciliation." Today it has merged to become "planting churches that promote reconciliation."

140. Gunther, "Will Success Spoil Rick Warren?"; Morgan and Carnes, "Purpose Driven in Rwanda"; Cynthia McFadden and Ted Gerstein, "Rick Warren's 'Long-Term Relationship' with Rwanda," *ABC News Nightline*, July 31, 2008, http://abcnews.go.com/Nightline/story?id=5479972&page=1#.T5hKKdnYGCc.

141. Alan Wolfe, "A Purpose-Driven Nation?," *Wall Street Journal*, August 26, 2005. Warren has also faced criticism from fellow evangelicals for his naïveté and "amateur" approach to humanitarian work. The PEACE Plan evolved as Warren responded to criticisms and learned from his own international experience. See Andrew Paquin, "Politically Driven Injustice: Fixing Global Poverty Requires More Than Rick Warren's Peace Plan," *Christianity Today* 50, no. 2 (February 2006): 22; Timothy C. Morgan, "Rebooting Peace: Rick Warren Adds Reconciliation to an Already Ambitious Missions Strategy," *Christianity Today* 52, no. 7

(July 2008): 17–18; Timothy C. Morgan and Richard Warren, "After the Aloha Shirts: Retooling Saddleback's International Work and Hosting a Presidential Forum Serve a Common Purpose, Says Rick Warren," *Christianity Today* 52, no. 10 (October 2008): 42–45.

142. Jennifer Riley, "Major Contest to Bolster Church's AIDS Fight," *Christian Post*, March 20, 2008, http://www.christianpost.com/news/31604/.

143. Manya Brachear Pashman and Jeff Coen, "After Years of Inquiries, Willow Creek Pastor Denies Misconduct Allegations," *Chicago Tribune*, March 23, 2018, http://www.chicagotribune.com/news/local/breaking/ct-met-willow-creek-pastor-20171220-story.html; Pashman and Coen, "Hybels Steps Down from Willow Creek Following Allegations of Misconduct," *Chicago Tribune*, April 11, 2018, http://www.chicagotribune.com/news/local/breaking/ct-met-hybels-willow-creek-resigns-20180410-story.html; Pashman and Coen, "Willow Creek's Journey from Defending Pastor to Accepting Accusations Unfolds Slowly, Ends in Mass Resignations," *Chicago Tribune*, August 10, 2018, http://www.chicagotribune.com/news/local/breaking/ct-met-willow-creek-resignations-20180810-story.html.

144. One example would be Steve Haas. One of the leading associate pastors at Willow Creek Community Church, Haas came to World Vision in 2001 as chief catalyst. Haas often speaks at chapel services on college campuses. The day I interviewed him at WVUS's offices (November 16, 2010), he had been on the phone earlier with Charles E. Blake, presiding bishop of the Church of God in Christ as well as Rick Warren.

145. K. Connie Kang, "Answering the Call in the Global Fight Against AIDS," *Los Angeles Times*, June 12, 2004.

146. Lonsdale interview, November 16, 2010.

147. James Pedrick Sr., advocacy associate, Acting on AIDS, interview by author, November 17, 2010, Federal Way, WA; Mussa interview, November 19, 2010.

148. David Gushee has popularized the term "evangelical center" in contrast to an evangelical political right and left. See Gushee, *The Future of Faith in American Politics*, 87.

149. Owen interview, November 18, 2010.

150. Stearns interview, July 1, 2010; Mussa interview, November 19, 2010.

151. Owen interview, November 18, 2010.

152. Stearns, *The Hole in Our Gospel*, 2.

153. Ibid., 21–22.

154. Ibid., 190.

155. Myers interview, June 20, 2007; Seiple interview, November 8, 2007.

156. Shapiro, "The AIDS Evangelists"; Daniel Burke, "AIDS Fight Moves to Religious Arena," *Chicago Tribune*, June 2, 2006.

157. Mark Galli, "We Are Not Commanded to Be a Docent in the Art Museum," *Christianity Today*, June 12, 2009, https://www.christianitytoday.com/ct/2009/juneweb-only/richard-stearns-on-americans-biggest-gospel-compromise.html.

158. "Q and A with Richard Stearns," *Christianity Today*, October 2006, 27.

159. Chris Keller, "Interview with Bruce Wilkinson—R.A.P.I.D.S., Zambia," *Other Journal*, August 8, 2005, http://theotherjournal.com/2005/08/08/interview-with-bruce-wilkinson-r-a-p-i-d-s-zambia/.

160. "Q and A with Richard Stearns."

161. J. David Goodman and Jennifer Preston, "How the Kony Video Went Viral," *New York Times*, March 9, 2012, http://thelede.blogs.nytimes.com/2012/03/09/how-the-kony-video-went-viral/.

162. Mareike Schomerus, Tim Allen, and Koen Vlassenroot, "KONY 2012 and the Prospects for Change," *Foreign Affairs*, March 13, 2012.

163. Jesse Eaves and Nathaniel Hurd, "Seizing the 'Kony' Moment," March 20, 2012, https://live-wvblog.d2.worldvision.org/advocacy/seizing-the-kony-moment.

164. World Vision had developed a response distancing itself from Invisible Children since 2005. See "Relationship with 'Invisible Children,'" World Vision U.S. Messaging Guidelines, December 2005, WVUS Archives.

165. A similar dismissal of staff by NAE's World Relief also led to widespread publicity. See Manya A. Brachear, "Help Wanted, but Only Christians Need Apply," *Chicago Tribune*, March 29, 2010, http://articles.chicagotribune.com/2010-03-29/news/ct-met-world-relief-20100531_1_refugee-resettlement-policy-hiring; Lornet Turnball, "World Relief Rejects Job Applicant over His Faith," *Seattle Times*, March 9, 2010, http://seattletimes.nwsource.com/html/localnews/2011301098_worldrelief10m.html.

166. World Vision, "Statement by World Vision U.S. President Richard Stearns on Today's Decision by U.S. Supreme Court," October 3, 2011, http://www.worldvision.org/content.nsf/about/20111003-religious-hiring-rights?OpenDocument.

167. Owen interview, November 18, 2010; Dearborn interview, June 1, 2010; "World Vision's Christian Identity and Hiring Practices," accessed April 23, 2012, http://www.worldvision.org/content.nsf/learn/christian-identity-hiring-practices?Open#hiring.

168. Owen interview, November 18, 2010; Bobby Ross, "Faith-Based Fracas: From the White House to the Courthouse, the Battle Escalates over Whether Christian Groups Have the Right to Employ Only Christians," *Christianity Today* 54, no. 6 (June 2010): 17–20.

169. Ross, "Faith-Based Fracas," 20.

Epilogue

1. Stearns acknowledged that there were more than 60,000 first-time U.S. donors over the first few weeks following the tsunami. This was more than at any previous time in the organization's history and may have only been topped by the Haiti earthquake. See Mark Cutshall, "We've Got an Emergency," *Christian Management Report*, August 2005, 1–3.

2. For examples of this debate among American historians, see Ian Tyrrell, "American Exceptionalism in an Age of International History," *American Historical Review* 96, no. 4 (October 1991): 1031–55; Michael McGerr, "The Price of the 'New Transnational History,'" *American Historical Review* 96, no. 4 (October 1991): 1056–67; David Thelen, "The Nation and Beyond: Transnational Perspectives on United States History," *Journal of American History* 86, no. 3 (December 1999): 965–75; C. A. Bayly et al., "*AHR* Conversation: On Transnational History," *American Historical Review* 111, no. 5 (December 2006): 1441–64.

3. Inboden, *Religion and American Foreign Policy, 1945–1960*; Jason W. Stevens, *God-Fearing and Free: A Spiritual History of America's Cold War* (Cambridge, MA: Harvard University Press, 2010); Andrew Preston, *Sword of the Spirit, Shield of Faith: Religion in American War and Diplomacy* (New York: Knopf, 2012).

4. Johnston, *Faith-Based Diplomacy*; Madeleine Albright, *The Mighty and the Almighty: Reflections on America, God, and World Affairs* (New York: Harper Perennial, 2007); Jonathan Chaplin and Robert Joustra, eds., *God and Global Order: The Power of Religion in American Foreign Policy* (Waco, TX: Baylor University Press, 2010).

5. McAlister, *The Kingdom of God Has No Borders*; Curtis, *Holy Humanitarians*; Kirkpatrick, *A Gospel for the Poor*.

6. William Svelmoe, *A New Vision for Missions: William Cameron Townsend, the Wycliffe Bible Translators, and the Culture of Early Evangelical Faith Missions, 1896–1945* (Tuscaloosa: University of Alabama Press, 2008); Svelmoe claims that, "operating on the frontiers of religious and cultural interaction, missionaries were placed in ideal positions to reanalyze, reinterpret, and perhaps even discard facets of their worldview in favor of startling new paradigms" (380).

7. Scott Harrison, *Thirst: A Story of Redemption, Compassion, and a Mission to Bring Clean Water to the World* (New York: Currency, 2018).

8. Gregory A. Smith and Jessica Martínez, "How the Faithful Voted: A Preliminary 2016 Analysis," *Pew Research Center*, November 9, 2016, http://www.pewresearch.org/fact-tank/2016/11/09/how-the-faithful-voted-a-preliminary-2016-analysis/.

9. One example chosen among many demonstrating recent identity debates within American evangelicalism is Mark Labberton, ed., *Still Evangelical? Insiders Reconsider Political, Social, and Theological Meaning* (Downers Grove, IL: IVP Books, 2018).

10. Hatch, "Response to Carl Henry," 97.

11. Miller, *The Age of Evangelicalism*.

12. The main divide has centered on conservative versus liberal, whether theological, social, or political. The dualisms could also be orthodox/heretical; elite/populist. See Douglas G. Jacobsen and William Vance Trollinger, *Re-Forming the Center: American Protestantism, 1900 to the Present* (Grand Rapids, MI: Eerdmans, 1998); Douglas Jacobsen and William Vance Trollinger, "Historiography of American Protestantism: The Two-Party Paradigm, and Beyond," *Fides et Historia* 25 (1993): 4–15.

13. Martin E. Marty, *Righteous Empire: The Protestant Experience in America* (New York: Dial Press, 1970); and Jean Miller Schmidt, *Souls or the Social Order: The Two-Party System in American Protestantism* (New York: Carlson Publishing, 1991).

14. Robert Wuthnow, *The Restructuring of American Religion: Society and Faith Since World War II* (Princeton, NJ: Princeton University Press, 1988). In contrast to Marty, who dates the two-party system to the fundamentalist-modernist controversy, Wuthnow claimed religious Americans maintained a united civil religion through the 1950s.

15. James Davison Hunter, *Culture Wars: The Struggle to Define America* (New York: Basic Books, 1991).

16. Martin Marty, "World Vision Foreign Aid," *Sightings*, November 14, 2011; Richard E. Stearns, "Evangelicals and the Case for Foreign Aid," *Wall Street Journal*, November 11, 2011, http://online.wsj.com/article/SB10001424052970204190704577026391811161000.html?mod=googlenews wsj.

17. Nicholas Kristof, "Learning from the Sin of Sodom," *New York Times*, February 28, 2010, http://www.nytimes.com/2010/02/28/opinion/28kristof.html.

18. *Burwell v. Hobby Lobby* (U.S. Supreme Court, 2014).

19. Celeste Gracey and Jeremy Weber, "World Vision: Why We're Hiring Gay Christians in Same-Sex Marriages," *Christianity Today*, March 24, 2014, https://www.christianitytoday.com/ct/2014/march-web-only/world-vision-why-hiring-gay-christians-same-sex-marriage.html.

20. Melissa Barnhart, "Assemblies of God Calls on Members to 'Shift Support Away' from World Vision After Policy Change on Same-Sex Marriage," *Christian Post*, March 26, 2014, https://www.christianpost.com/news/assemblies-of-god-calls-on-members-to-shift

-support-away-from-world-vision-after-policy-change-on-same-sex-marriage-116850/; Alex Murashko, "Christian Leaders Shocked, Grieved by World Vision's Decision to Hire Employees in Same-Sex Marriages," *Christian Post*, March 25, 2014, http://www.christianpost.com/news/christian-leaders-shocked-grieved-by-world-visions-decision-to-hire-employees-in-same-sex-marriages-116730/.

21. Celeste Gracey and Jeremy Weber, "World Vision Reverses Decision to Hire Christians in Same-Sex Marriages," *Christianity Today*, March 26, 2014, https://www.christianitytoday.com/ct/2014/march-web-only/world-vision-reverses-decision-gay-same-sex-marriage.html.

22. Sarah Pulliam Bailey, "World Vision Is Getting More Evangelical Leadership in Wake of Gay Employee Debacle," *Huffington Post*, June 26, 2004, https://www.huffingtonpost.com/2014/06/26/world-vision-evangelical-gay_n_5534368.html.

23. Chris Gehrz, "World Vision and Evangelicalism: An Interview with David King," *Pietist Schoolman* (blog), April 3, 2014, http://pietistschoolman.com/2014/04/03/world-vision-and-evangelicalism-an-interview-with-david-king/.

24. Ellen Barry and Suhasini Raj, "Major Christian Charity Is Closing India Operations amid a Crackdown," *New York Times*, March 7, 2017, https://www.nytimes.com/2017/03/07/world/asia/compassion-international-christian-charity-closing-india.html.

25. Jonathan Merritt, "Franklin Graham's Turn Toward Intolerance," *Atlantic*, July 19, 2015, https://www.theatlantic.com/politics/archive/2015/07/franklin-grahams-turn-toward-intolerance/398924/; Lindsey Bever, "Franklin Graham: The Media Didn't Understand the 'God-Factor' in Trump's Win," *Washington Post*, November 10, 2016, https://www.washingtonpost.com/news/acts-of-faith/wp/2016/11/10/franklin-graham-the-media-didnt-understand-the-god-factor/.

26. "Samaritan's Purse Collects Record Number of Operation Christmas Child Shoebox Gifts," February 24, 2017, https://www.samaritanspurse.org/operation-christmas-child/samaritans-purse-collects-record-number-of-operation-christmas-child-shoebox-gifts/.

27. "Forbes: The 100 Largest U.S. Charities; 2017 Ranking," accessed May 10, 2018, https://www.forbes.com/top-charities/list/#tab:rank.

28. Adam Clymer, "Helms Reverses Opposition to Help on AIDS," *New York Times*, March 26, 2002, https://www.nytimes.com/2002/03/26/us/helms-reverses-opposition-to-help-on-aids.html.

29. David von Drehle and Aryn Baker, "Person of the Year: The Ebola Fighters," *Time*, December 10, 2014, http://time.com/time-person-of-the-year-ebola-fighters/.

30. Kate Shellnutt, "Refugee Ban Forces World Relief to Lay Off 140 Staff," *Christianity Today*, February 15, 2017, https://www.christianitytoday.com/news/2017/february/refugee-ban-forces-world-relief-to-lay-off-staff.html; Kate Shellnutt, "Max Lucado, Beth Moore, and Hundreds of Evangelicals Call for Immigration Reform . . . Again," *Christianity Today*, February 7, 2018, https://www.christianitytoday.com/news/2018/february/max-lucado-beth-moore-evangelicals-immigration-dreamers-ref.html.

31. Miller, *The Age of Evangelicalism*, 8.

32. David A. Hollinger, "After Cloven Tongues of Fire: Ecumenical Protestantism and the Modern American Encounter with Diversity," *Journal of American History* 98, no. 1 (June 2011): 21–48, https://doi.org/10.1093/jahist/jar155; Hollinger, *Protestants Abroad*.

INDEX

ACKNOWLEDGMENTS

DESPITE THE COUNTLESS HOURS writing alone, a book is far from a solitary endeavor. I am grateful for an opportunity to express my thanks to the many people who made this work possible.

First, the book would not have been possible without World Vision's openness to my project. One of my first contacts at World Vision, Manfred Grellert, is known to say, "A point of view is a view from a point." I soon found that World Vision recognized the diversity of points of view within its own organization, and I am grateful that World Vision's leaders gave me an opportunity to add mine to the mix. I want to thank the dozens of staff that made time for my questions and proved willing to share their stories and perspectives with me.

I owe a special thanks to a few within the organization. In the World Vision U.S. office, Rich Stearns supported my project and his chief of staff Brian Sytsma and senior communications officer Sheryl Watkins coordinated my visit to Federal Way, Washington. Along with Sheryl, the wisdom of Marilee Pierce Dunker, Torrey Olsen, Bill Kliewer, Bryant Myers, and many others saved me multiple errors in presenting a history. Within World Vision International, Steve Gray, World Vision's original corporate archivist, was a godsend. His knowledge of the materials, his willingness to rearrange his schedule and even stay late to accommodate my time at the WVI offices in Monrovia, California, proved invaluable to my research.

I must also thank the staff at the Billy Graham Center Archives. Bob Schuster, Wayne Weber, and Paul Ericksen went above and beyond in providing access to their collection. I also want to thank Robert Krapohl, university librarian of Trinity International University, for giving me access to Carl Henry's underexplored papers. A special thanks to Andy Tooley for taking a day to drive me from Wheaton to Deerfield and nurturing a new friendship in the process.

A number of groups provided financial support for this project. Thanks to the Institute for the Study of American Evangelicals at Wheaton College, NABPR (National Association of Baptist Professors of Religion), as well as a yearlong fellowship from the Louisville Institute that provided valuable resources as well as even more valuable feedback on early versions of the project.

I am grateful to a host of mentors, colleagues, and friends who helped shaped my work and made the project even more enjoyable. Grant Wacker was an excellent mentor, and he initially encouraged me to explore the topic of World Vision years ago. His interest in my project and my development as a scholar has served as a constant gift to me. I found countless champions and wise counselors at Emory University to engage these topics. Liz Bounds and Jonathan Strom provided insightful feedback and great questions. I could not have asked for a better model for the scholarly vocation than Brooks Holifield. His clarity of thought, attention to detail, and interest in the bigger question profoundly shaped my work. His questions, corrections, and careful reads of multiple drafts of the manuscript made it an infinitely better project.

Samira Mehta, Brian Campbell, and Lerone Martin, as well as other colleagues engaged in questions of international development like Letitia Campbell, read countless drafts and provided great feedback and support. I must also say that within the field of American religious history, we are blessed with tremendous and supportive colleagues. I am grateful to friends like Seth Dowland, Brantley Gasaway, David Swartz, and others for shared hotel rooms and shared reflection on research, our field, and vocation during academic conferences around the country and around the world. During my time as a Young Scholar at the Center for the Study of Religion and American Culture at IUPUI, I found even more colleagues eager to help encourage this project, expand its argument, and sharpen its focus. I want to thank our guides, Bob Orsi and Courtney Bender, my entire cohort, and Philip Goff's wonderful facilitation of the program. I am also grateful to other colleagues at IUPUI and beyond, Ray Haberski, Brian Steensland, and Heath Carter, who offered insightful feedback on my initial proposal. I am indebted to Heather Curtis and David Kirkpatrick for multiple conversations that shaped my thinking as well as mutual support through a shared interest in making sense of global evangelicalism and humanitarianism.

I am grateful for opportunities to publish aspects of this story in earlier forms in several journals and edited collections and want to acknowledge

Oxford University Press, Indiana University Press, Taylor and Francis, and *Religions* respectively for their permission to incorporate a few of the ideas developed therein in this book: "The New Internationalists: World Vision and the Revival of American Evangelical Humanitarianism, 1950–2010," *Religions* 3 (2012): 922–49; "World Vision: Religious Identity in the Discourse and Practice of Global Relief and Development," *Review of Faith & International Affairs* 9, no. 3 (2001): 21–28, copyright © Institute for Global Engagement, reprinted by permission of Taylor & Francis Ltd., www.tandfonline.com on behalf of Institute for Global Engagement. Also chapters within the collections *Religion in Philanthropic Organizations: Family, Friend, Foe?*, edited by Thomas J. Davis (Indiana University Press, 2013), and *The Business Turn in American Religious History*, edited by Amanda Porterfield, Darren E. Grem, and John Corrigan (Oxford University Press, 2017).

From the beginning of this project, I benefited from the continual support and the careful editorial eye of Bob Lockhart. I am grateful for his patient support and for the help of so many at the University of Pennsylvania Press. The book is definitely much better as a result of the careful read of my anonymous reviewers, and I am grateful for their attention to my work.

For the past five years, I have served as the Karen Lake Buttrey Director of Lake Institute on Faith and Giving at the Indiana University Lilly Family School of Philanthropy. Tom Davis first invited me to speak on World Vision at IUPUI years before, and it was there that I first encountered Lake Institute. The next year, a generous fellowship from Lake Institute allowed me the ability to finish the research for this book. Three years later, I was invited to join Lake Institute as its director. Far beyond the financial support, I am grateful to my predecessor Bill Enright for his support and wise counsel. I must thank our entire staff team, who remained patient with me as I worked tirelessly on this book. Particularly, I want to thank Curtis Kester and Anne Brock for their assistance in editing text and images as well as Melissa Spas for her skill in managing our ever growing portfolio of work. Alongside my role directing Lake Institute, I am honored to work with a tremendous faculty, administration, and cohorts of graduate students at the School of Philanthropy. Dwight Burlingame has particularly provided continued support to bring this book to completion. My work teaching philanthropy, leadership, and ethics to students as well as clergy, nonprofit executives, and fund-raisers around the country has helped me see new avenues of application for my research that I hope has made this a better book.

Above all, I owe a debt to my family for their support. My sister and brother-in-law, Jennifer and Michael McCormack, and my in-laws, Glenn and Kathy Stribling, were constant cheerleaders. My parents, Kaye and Douglas King, provided continual support by always asking for updates on this book. Far beyond progress reports on research and writing, however, their continual encouragement has always inspired me to follow my dreams and pursue a unique vocation.

My three children, Audrey, Kathryn, and Andrew, did their best to keep me grounded during these many years of writing and rewriting. What began as diaper changes and bottles at the start of this project has now become school field trips, board games, and choir concerts. They have brought me so much joy over the decade this project was in process, and they always offered a dose of much-needed perspective on which task remains most important.

To my wife, Lauren, simple thanks fall far too short. Without her encouragement, patience, sacrifice, enduring belief in my vocation, and love for me, this project would not have been possible. I can only hope that it reflects something of the daily grace she brings to me and everyone she encounters. I dedicate this work to her.